SLAVES, WOMEN & HOMOSEXUALS

Exploring the Hermeneutics of Cultural Analysis

William J. Webb

InterVarsity Press
Downers Grove, Illinois

InterVarsity Press
P.O. Box 1400, Downers Grove, IL 60515-1426
World Wide Web: www.ivpress.com
E-mail: mail@ivpress.com

InterVarsity Press® is the book-publishing division of InterVarsity Christian Fellowship/USA®, a student movement active on campus at hundreds of universities, colleges and schools of nursing in the United States of America, and a member movement of the International Fellowship of Evangelical Students. For information about local and regional activities, write Public Relations Dept., InterVarsity Christian Fellowship/USA, 6400 Schroeder Rd., P.O. Box 7895, Madison, WI 53707-7895.

Cover illustration: Michael Goss

ISBN 0-8308-1561-9

Printed in the United States of America ∞

Library of Congress Cataloging-in-Publication Data

Webb, William J.
  Slaves, women & homosexuals: exploring the hermeneutics of cultural analysis/
  William J. Webb.
    p. cm.
  Includes bibliographical references and index.
  ISBN 0-8308-1561-9 (pbk.: alk. paper)
  1. Bible—Hermeneutics. 2. Slavery in the Bible. 3. Women in the Bible. 4.
  Homosexuality in the Bible. 5. Christianity and culture. I. Title: Slaves, women, and
  homosexuals. II. Title.
BS476. W38 2001
220.6'01—dc21   *2001016772*

20	19	18	17	16	15	14	13	12	11	10	9	8	7	6	5	4	3	2	1
17	16	15	14	13	12	11	10	09	08	07	06	05	04	03	02	01			

Dedicated to F. F. Bruce and Craig L. Blomberg

Together they typify egalitarians and hierarchalists
who share a redemptive-movement hermeneutic.
What they have in common far outweighs any differences.

Foreword

What do slaves, women and homosexuals have in common? Most would say their humanity—and not much else. But think about the question again. Here are three groups that in one way or another, at one time or another, have been regarded as less than human. In addition, each of these groups has been at the center of theological reflection and debate in the last two centuries.

Many regard these three groups as hermeneutically equal. What we have learned about interpreting slavery texts in Scripture should be applied to our reading of biblical texts about women and homosexuals. But how do we do this? How does one approach the discussion of each group both biblically and culturally? Is the theological hermeneutics surrounding each group really the same?

Slaves, Women & Homosexuals successfully walks the reader through these hermeneutical mazes. The goal is not only to discuss how these groups are to be seen in light of Scripture but to make a case for a specific hermeneutical approach to reading relevant scriptural texts. Such an approach may enable us to think through the application of Scripture on an even broader array of topics.

This book comes with many strengths. Its case study format helps readers appreciate all the dimensions of each discussion. Juxtaposing the three topics allows one to see their similarities and differences. What I like most about this work is its balance and fairness, its truly irenic treatment of these historically contentious areas of debate. *Slaves, Women & Homosexuals* not only advances the discussion beyond current literature, it takes a markedly new direction toward establishing common ground where possible, potentially breaking down certain walls of hostility within the evangelical community. At the very least it lays the groundwork for a much healthier dialogue on these matters.

If, however, you want simply to have your views confirmed, then do not read this book. It is designed to make you consider why you apply Scripture the way that you do—no matter what position you take. Its thoroughness is one of its major strengths, as is its proposed solution. This is serious fare for those willing to examine their beliefs, both theological and cultural, in these controversial areas.

This is precisely how the book should be read and assessed: Does this book help me think through these debated areas more clearly? I think you will conclude with me that it does. I wholeheartedly commend the book to you on that basis and thank Dr. Webb for writing it.

Read *Slaves, Women & Homosexuals*. Chew over its examples. Discuss them with your friends. Here is a full-course hermeneutical meal.

Darrell L. Bock
Research Professor of New Testament Studies
Dallas Theological Seminary

Acknowledgments

I consider myself most fortunate to teach in the beautiful setting of Cambridge, Ontario, in an educational environment such as Heritage Theological Seminary. This book reflects a journey of five years with fellow faculty members. In their critical interaction with my material, these faithful colleagues have been cordial and caring even when expressing points of significant disagreement. I wish to thank the entire faculty for their input—they have enriched my life as a community of reflective academics and as a gathering of friends.

I must also express appreciation to our board, president and administrators for encouraging me as I brought this work to publication. Their leadership, expressed in practical and ideological ways, has made my theological reflection possible. My views, of course, do not represent any official seminary position; a variety of perspectives are represented at Heritage in an atmosphere of gracious deference and mutual respect.

Along the way, my students (both current and former) have made a marked contribution to my thinking and development. Their relentless and idealized pursuit of the truth always spurs me on. Special thanks to Cyril Guerette and Neal Wilson, who researched extensive portions of the appendixes. Also I am indebted to Tim Bahula for his "ninth inning" interaction, which led to a much-improved manuscript.

Without my supportive family this volume would never have taken shape. My wife, Marilyn, has sacrificed generously over the years for our home and ministry. She is truly my closest friend and my beloved soul mate. My brother, Robert, and my father, Bud, both scholars and teachers in their own fields, made this volume far more readable and useful to the classroom. Our broader church family, Community Fellowship in Waterloo, also helped shape this work, especially the last chapter, in a way that makes the entire work more ecclesiastically friendly.

A number of well-respected biblical scholars read through the manuscript in its emerging stages and offered valuable suggestions. I wish to thank Darrell Bock, Steve Spencer, Craig Keener, Dan Block and Craig Evans; their insights have significantly improved the final product. Of course, any remaining short-comings are of my own making.

My thanks to InterVarsity Press for accepting the manuscript for publication. Special thanks to Andy Le Peau and Gary Deddo for successfully guiding it through the editorial process. The sage prompting of Gary Deddo led to a completely new arrangement and flow for the book and a far clearer articulation of the criteria. His substantive critiques strengthened the work well beyond its original state.

The dedication of this volume to F. F. Bruce (in his memory) and to Craig Blomberg may appear somewhat strange, for it celebrates on one page and in one volume the contributions of an egalitarian advocate and a patriarchal proponent. Yet their shared hermeneutic, along with other overlapping considerations (see chapter eight), creates the possibility for a spirit of harmony between two groups who have often related in hostile and polarized ways. Blomberg's use of a re-demptive-spirit hermeneutic permits considerable movement toward an egalitarian position. This "conceptual awakening" is beginning to emerge in a number of evangelical seminaries around the world—including my own seminary. My prayer is that the awakening will eventually change the face of the church by producing a more unified community of Christ's followers.

Introduction

WELCOME TO THE WORLD OF APPLICATION

I welcome my reader to the fascinating world of applying Scripture. Here we encounter the complexities and challenges of moving from words on a page to actually living out the text within our lives. Our mandate is to figure out which statements from the Bible in their "on the page" wording you and I should continue to follow in our contemporary setting. In order to do this we must determine whether we should apply a particular biblical statement in the exact form articulated on the page or whether we should apply only some expression of its underlying principle(s). In this respect, the objective of this book is not to uncover the meaning of the words of the text in their dictionary sense. Commentaries spend much of their time doing this. Rather, our task is one of applying the ancient text in our modern context. So, assuming that a plausible or reasonable understanding of the text's original meaning can be attained, we will put our efforts into grappling with its application.

A quick and fun exercise will immediately engage you in the process of applying Scripture. For each of the biblical commands or statements below I ask my reader to answer one question: *Which of these instructions from Scripture are still in force for us today exactly as they are articulated "on the page"?* If you think an instruction is still in force for us *completely* as stated, please place a check mark (√) before those words. If you think an instruction is still in force only *in part* or *in a modified fashion* through its underlying principle, kindly place an x mark (X) in the blank. Have fun. Consider your answer to be a preliminary guess, not something set in stone. Simply go with your best hunch.

_____ "God . . . said to them [Adam and Eve], 'Be fruitful and increase in number'" (Gen 1:28).

_____ "Love the LORD your God with all your heart and with all your soul and with all your strength" (Deut 6:5).

_____ "When you have finished setting aside a tenth of all your produce . . . you shall give it to the Levite, the alien, the fatherless and the widow" (Deut 26:12).

_____ "Greet one another with a holy kiss" (1 Cor 16:20).

_____ "Women should remain silent in the churches" (1 Cor 14:34).

_____ "Stop drinking only water, and use a little wine because of your stomach and your frequent illnesses" (1 Tim 5:23).

_____ "Set apart for the LORD . . . every firstborn male of your herds and flocks" (Deut 15:19).

_____ "If a man happens to meet a virgin who is not pledged to be married and rapes her and they are discovered, he shall pay the girl's father fifty shekels of silver. He must marry the girl, for he has violated her. He can never divorce her as long as he lives" (Deut 22:28-29).

_____ "Do not approach a woman to have sexual relations during the uncleanness of her monthly period" (Lev 18:19).

_____ "Do not lie with a man as one lies with a woman" (Lev 18:22).

_____ "Do not have sexual relations with an animal and defile yourself with it" (Lev 18:23).

_____ "Go and make disciples of all nations" (Mt 28:19).

_____ "Devote yourself to the public reading of Scripture" (1 Tim 4:13).

_____ "Do not wear clothing woven of two kinds of material" (Lev 19:19).

_____ "Be all the more eager to make your calling and election sure" (2 Pet 1:10).

_____ "Whoever sheds the blood of man, by man shall his blood be shed; for in the image of God has God made man" (Gen 9:6).

_____ "Now that I, your Lord and Teacher, have washed your feet, you also should wash one another's feet" (Jn 13:14).

_____ "Do not go among the Gentiles or enter any town of the Samaritans. Go rather to the lost sheep of Israel" (Mt 10:5-6).

_____ "Heal the sick, raise the dead, . . . drive out demons" (Mt 10:8).

_____ "Sell your possessions and give to the poor" (Lk 12:33).

_____ "Six days you shall labor and do all your work, but the seventh day is a Sabbath to the Lord your God. On it you shall not do any work" (Ex 20:9-10).

_____ "A woman . . . should cover her head. A man ought not to cover his head" (1 Cor 11:6-7).

_____ "If a man has long hair, it is a disgrace to him" (1 Cor 11:14).

_____ "Are you unmarried? Do not look for a wife" (1 Cor 7:27).

_____ "Every male among you shall be circumcised" (Gen 17:10).

_____ "Punish him [your child] with the rod and save his soul from death" (Prov 23:14).

_____ "Do not turn away from the one who wants to borrow from you" (Mt 5:42).

_____ "Bless those who persecute you. . . . If your enemy is hungry, feed him" (Rom 12:14, 20).

_____ "Give beer to those who are perishing, wine to those who are in anguish; let them drink and forget their poverty and remember their misery no more" (Prov 31:6-7).

_____ "Do not . . . put tattoo marks on yourselves" (Lev 19:28).

_____ "Praise God with tambourine and dancing . . . praise him with the clash of cymbals" (Ps 150:4-5).

_____ "Rise in the presence of the aged, show respect for the elderly" (Lev 19:32).

_____ "You are to abstain from food sacrificed to idols, from blood, from the meat of strangled animals and from sexual immorality" (Acts 15:29).

_____ "Slaves, submit yourselves to your masters with all respect, not only to those who are good and considerate, but also to those who are harsh" (1 Pet 2:18).

_____ "A woman must not wear men's clothing, nor a man wear women's clothing" (Deut 22:5).

_____ "If a man's wife goes astray and is unfaithful to him . . . the priest shall take some holy water in a clay jar and put some dust from the tabernacle floor into the water. . . . He is to have the woman drink the water" (Num 5:12, 17, 26).

_____ "I want men everywhere to lift up holy hands in prayer. . . . I also want women to dress modestly . . . not with braided hair or gold or pearls or expensive clothes" (1 Tim 2:8-9).

_____ "Do not take interest of any kind from your countryman" (Lev 25:36).

_____ "Is any one of you sick? He should call the elders of the church to pray over him and anoint him with oil in the name of the Lord" (Jas 5:14).

This exercise should convince almost every modern Christian about the complexity of applying the biblical text. Moving from the ancient text into our modern world is not a simple matter. If you score the above list with a friend or a group, it may be interesting to poll the results from a select number of these examples and to begin talking about the question, *Why?*

Each of us must ask the probing question, *Why?* Why do some biblical instructions have ongoing significance and force in their entirety, while the continued application of others is limited in some manner? How do I determine which components of the biblical text should apply today and which should not? To cite an old rabbinical response, "That would be like trying to explain the entire Torah while standing on one foot!" The journey is not an easy one. Neither is it a short one. There are many twists and turns along the way, and one will have to encounter portions of Scripture that are not entirely pleasant to gaze upon. But the journey is worth it. Those who take that journey will often come to grips with a wondrous and resilient dimension of Scripture of which they had been completely unaware.

So permit me to give a brief overview of the journey. You will find that the book is laid out in three parts. As I outline these major parts below, I will also introduce the individual chapters within each part.

Part I: Toward a Hermeneutic of Cultural Analysis

In part one, I lay out a proper framework for asking the question, *Why?* Why do we continue to apply certain biblical texts in their entirety but not others? Or, why do we apply some things from some texts and not all things? The first chapter, "The Christian & Culture," discusses the role that culture plays in coming to grips with that all-important question. Culture and the phenomenon of "cultural relativity"[1] contribute in a significant way to shaping what it is that we continue to apply in any given text. This first chapter will also orient the reader to the three major case studies in this book: slaves, women and homosexuals. The second chapter, "A Redemptive-Movement Hermeneutic," investigates the big picture or meta-framework through which we look at Scripture. In this chapter I argue that a redemptive-movement framework is much better than a static one, if we are going to develop a credible and enduring answer to our question about contemporary application. Before moving into the details of cultural assessment, the third chapter, "Cultural/Transcultural Analysis: A Road Map," provides a brief overview of where we are headed. To make the process a little easier and to keep from getting lost among the trees, I provide a few instructions and some navigational tools. With these tools in hand, you can read the next two parts with greater understanding and with the potential of tailoring your reading to meet your individual goals.

Part II: Intrascriptural Criteria

Having laid the foundation within the first part, we now focus directly and in-

---

[1]For definitions of *culturally relative* and *transcultural* see chapter one.

tently upon our question of applying Scripture. At this point, we set out to do
some serious work on cultural assessment. Chapters four through seven (this includes the first chapter of part three) contain eighteen criteria for helping us determine what components within the biblical text have ongoing applicational
significance and what components are limited in their application to the original
audience only. The first sixteen of the eighteen criteria are grouped together under this part's heading, "Intrascriptural Criteria." For the most part, these criteria
rely upon elements within Scripture itself for assessing what is cultural and what
is transcultural within the text. The titles of the chapters—"Persuasive Criteria"
(chapter four), "Moderately Persuasive Criteria" (chapter five) and "Inconclusive
Criteria" (chapter six)—should rightly yield the impression that the criteria are
moving from a grouping of extremely strong ones, to moderately strong ones, to
weak ones. This organizational placement of each criterion relates to argument
outcomes alone, not to the credibility of the criterion itself. In other words, the
criteria are laid out according to the how much they contribute to my final conclusions, and in particular, the conclusions on the women's issue. I will leave further introductory details to chapter three, which immediately precedes the criteria
material. For now, however, one might note that these intrascriptural criteria at
times fall into clusters. For example, criteria 1, 2 and 3 (Preliminary Movement,
Seed Ideas and Breakouts) are closely related to each other on the matter of assessing redemptive movement. In a similar manner, criteria 6, 7 and 8 (Basis in
Original Creation, Section 1, Basis in Original Creation, Section 2, and Basis in
New Creation) form a related cluster around the biblical theme of creation.

Part III: Extrascriptural Criteria
The third part of the book, "Extrascriptural Criteria," contains the last two criteria: criterion 17 (Pragmatic Basis Between Two Cultures) and criterion 18 (Scientific and Social-Scientific Evidence). These two criteria are similar to the
preceding sixteen criteria inasmuch as they assist the Christian community in
sorting out which components of the text are cultural and which are transcultural.
For the most part, however, their basis of assessment is derived from data beyond
Scripture instead of material that is directly found within the biblical text. While I
grant a certain measure of methodological deference to the first group of criteria
over this latter group, the criteria within part three are no less weighty. They rely
upon input from truth as it can be determined from God's general revelation. We
need to discover truth in his Word and in his created world. Within this latter part,
then, the strength of the last two criteria appropriately merits the classification of
"Persuasive Criteria." They contribute significantly to the ultimate conclusions of
this book.

Chapter eight, "What If I Am Wrong?" is a curious chapter indeed. Such a chapter is an anomaly within egalitarian and patriarchal publications alike. Here I pause and do some reflective pondering about the degree of certainty in my findings. I ask myself, "What would I do if I were wrong at my point of least strength (greatest weakness)?" In a rather vulnerable move I tip my hand concerning the weakest link in my argument, namely, my assessment of 1 Timothy 2:13. After that, I talk about what I would do if I were to change my mind and accept a completely transcultural understanding of this verse. A number of considerations would, nevertheless, still lead me to apply the Timothy text today in quite a different way than would most patriarchal proponents. Based on these reflective musings, I close the chapter by unveiling what I consider to be two redemptive-movement models, "complementary egalitarianism" and "ultra-soft patriarchy."

The "Conclusion" naturally draws together all of the contributing tributaries within the book into one final, summary articulation. Here is where the journey ends. But, in some respects, it should serve as only a beginning! The redemptive-movement hermeneutic and the cultural/transcultural criteria developed within this work are general enough to be applied to many other crucial questions of application far beyond the three subject areas that I focus upon. Though this book is hardly perfect in form or substance, I hope that it will provide a catalyst and pliable model for future opportunities in which you explore the fascinating world of applying Scripture.

Part One

___

Toward a Hermeneutic of Cultural Analysis

1

THE CHRISTIAN & CULTURE

Most of us are oblivious to the culture around us. Like the air that we breathe, it is invisible and we simply take it for granted. It has been said that human culture is much like the relationship between a fish and water. One could ask the question of a fish, "Is your nose wet?" You and I, of course, know that the fish's nose is wet. Yet, we do not know what a fish actually thinks about the water around itself.[1] If fish were scientists, probably the last thing they would discover is water! So it is with us. We live and move about in the culture with which we are closely and invisibly enmeshed.

What awakens us to culture is contrast. In our global village, the media readily project images of different cultures around the world—from the tribal groups living in the African rain forests to the elite business community who reside in New York's gleaming towers. The contrast becomes even more vivid through travel. Travel allows someone to see, taste and touch different cultures. Yet, the people who are most aware of culture are those who have lived in different parts of the world. This level of contrast leaves a more lasting impression. Those who have *lived* in different settings begin to actually feel the impact of alternative cultures.

---

[1] Alvin J. Schmidt, *Veiled and Silenced* (Macon, Ga.: Mercer University Press, 1989), p. 1.

During my own life, the years spent in Alberta on an Indian reserve, in cosmopolitan Toronto, in the politically charged city of Ottawa, in a remote village of the Northwest Territories, in Baltimore during the racial riots, in the deep south of Texas, etc., have all left their mark. My own awakening to culture has come about quite by accident—through living in these dramatically different cultures.

However, one does not have to leave home to discover culture. There is another way to see culture right where one lives. Mind you, contrast is still the key. But this time we look for differences within one particular location—differences that often occur over time. This awakening to culture comes from viewing changes in our society so that we see an "old" culture and a "new" culture side by side. We can discover culture simply by looking at the changing attitudes, laws, rituals and behavior around us. For example, the electronic highway of the Internet is radically changing the way that people relate to other people within our country and around the world. The youth of today will form quite a different impression of political, intellectual and community boundaries than those of former days. Along similar lines, think about what the last generation was taught in school about the environment. Compare that to what this new generation is learning. The contrast is overwhelming. The changing values and attitudes of our culture provide yet another way to access what is otherwise invisible, or so heavily camouflaged that we never really see it.

The Christian Challenge

As the winds of culture blow, Christians are often faced with incredible challenges. We inevitably encounter difficult choices. Should we endorse the changes in our culture or should we challenge our culture? The question of cultural/transcultural assessment is essentially a very practical one: as I stick my finger into the air and feel the winds of culture blowing, how should I respond? Should I act *counterculturally* or *paraculturally* in my life? Should I go *against* my culture or move *with* my culture? That is the crucial question with which we all wrestle.

So how does a Christian respond to cultural change? Our initial answer is quite simple: *It is necessary for Christians to challenge their culture where it departs from kingdom values; it is equally necessary for them to identify with their culture on all other matters.* This axiom reflects the thinking of the apostle Paul, who often acted very pragmatically when it came to cultural issues. For example, Paul's response to the Corinthians eating meat offered to idols is insightful. The apostle challenges his culture by not eating at public ceremonies held in pagan temples, where such an action would violate the participant's covenant with God (1 Cor 8:10) and potentially destroy the faith of others (1 Cor 10:14-22). However, he sides with his culture whenever he is eating at a non-Christian's house, outside of a cultic context. In that setting Paul would eat meat offered to idols, whether it had been sacrificed by the host or simply purchased at the market as a post-temple special (1 Cor 10:27). The apostle's *Magna Carta* of cultural sensitivity might be found in his words, "I have become *all* things to *all* people, that I might by *all* means save some" (1 Cor 9:22 NRSV, emphasis added). Paul viewed culture as a mixed bag. If something is worth making an issue out of, then challenge culture on the issue. Yet, if something is not terribly important and does not violate one's faith, then utilize it for the sake of the gospel!

Most of the time it is easy to determine where our culture departs from kingdom values. On negative issues such as pornography, abortion, murder, theft and rape, the Christian community generally has very little doubt about its response. We want to challenge any ambivalence within society on these matters and initiate counteraction. Likewise, on positive issues such as care for the elderly, environmental concerns, compassionate health care, community spirit in helping the poor, political freedom, and fair and equitable justice, our response should be clear. We want to applaud our community, speak an encouraging word and lend a hand.

However, sometimes the hardest part is trying to determine what our kingdom values are. Fortunately, these cases are the exception, not the norm. On certain occasions the biblical text is not entirely clear. In part, the lack of clarity may be due to the fact that Scripture itself adopts what we might call "kingdom values" (those which transcend any culture and time) as well as "cultural values" (those which are locked into a particular place and time). Within the text of Scripture we find portions that are transcultural (e.g., love for one's neighbor) and portions that are cultural, or more accurately, portions that contain significant cultural components (e.g., slavery texts). For the original readers these two entities—cultural and transcultural—were not necessarily antithetical. In all likelihood, the distinction between the two would have gone unnoticed for the original readers. Only in the context of a different culture would the distinction be readily seen, due to the principle of contrast mentioned above.

As part of our interpretive task, then, we must distinguish between kingdom values and cultural values within the biblical text. With every change in our culture we have to reevaluate our interpretation of Scripture to determine what our perspective should be. At first glance, one might think that this would be an easy task. But it is not. When we arrive at the doorstep of Scripture, we encounter a text which *itself* was written within a particular cultural grid. It was not written in a vacuum, nor created for some theoretical and utopian society. Not only were the authors influenced by their own cultures, but the text itself was transmitted through various cultural forms, known as genres. Also, the people who first received the text read it within their assumed cultural grid.

If we are to speak to our world today, we must first evaluate the role of culture in the biblical text. It would be a travesty to proclaim to our world a theological position without exploring its cultural/transcultural status. In this venture, we want a balanced approach. We do not want to make something that is transcultural into something that is culturally bound. On the other hand, we do not want to make that which is a cultural non-absolute into an absolute for every culture.

Definition: What Is a "Cultural-Component" Text?

Before moving along too far, we must start by defining our terms. In one sense all of Scripture is cultural. Inasmuch as the biblical text reflects various cultural forms in its making (genres) and addresses different sociological structures in its message (for example, marriage, society, religion, work, politics) it is inextricably bound to culture. In this respect, even the transcultural elements in Scripture have a cultural component. However, this is *not* what is usually meant in biblical studies by the term *cultural* (or *cultural-component*) when it is used in contrast to *transcultural*. This contrastive usage of the term cultural is much more limited in its meaning and is generally a shortened form for various equivalent expressions such as *cultural confinement* or *cultural relativity* or *culturally bound*. When we talk about a text that has a "cultural component" within it, this designation highlights the issue of application between cultures. For our purposes the expression *cultural component* and its various equivalents may be defined as "those aspects of the biblical text that 'we leave behind' as opposed to 'take with us' due to cultural differences between the text's world and the interpreters' world as we apply the text to subsequent generations." In a sense, cultural confinement/relativity is the gap between the world of the text and that of the interpreter, which requires a reapplication of the text.

More helpful than a definition might be a sketch of what is meant by *cultural* and *transcultural* through a series of graphic contrasts. For the Christian who is interested in applying the text today, we must search out and discover what components of a text are cultural as opposed to ones that are transcultural:

cultural component		transcultural component
cultural values	vs.	kingdom values
culturally confined	vs.	beyond cultural limits
time-bound truth	vs.	timeless truth
culturally relative application	vs.	transcultural principle
temporal	vs.	supratemporal
nontransferable form	vs.	transferable function
local	vs.	universal

momentary husk	vs.	enduring kernel
peripheral meaning	vs.	core meaning
wineskins	vs.	wine

If a reader does not like one or more of these distinctions, that is fine. Just delete them from the list. I have provided a sufficient sampling of alternative ways of expressing much the same distinction in order that readers will find at least one or two comparative couplets with which they will feel comfortable. I will generally use the expressions *transcultural* to describe components of a text on one end of the continuum and *cultural* for those components on the other end. When I use the word *cultural* in this applicational or hermeneutical sense, it functions as a short-form for various other equivalent expressions: *culturally confined, culturally relative, culturally bound* and *culturally locked*. But I do not wish to quibble over terminology, so one should find and use whatever words one thinks are suitable. These are simply the various ways that Christian authors describe the phenomenon when applying the text across different worlds.

It is beyond my objective to pursue the finer nuances and philosophical differences in the definition and theology of cultural/transcultural assessment. While such discussion is interesting to the field of hermeneutics, it makes little persuasive difference in the final outcome of evaluating actual cases, such as the ones we will look at. My own objective is much more practical. I will focus primarily on the criteria by which Christians can determine what is cultural and what is transcultural within Scripture.

Contemporary Issues Facing the Church: Women and Homosexuals

The winds of culture are blowing today on two significant issues: the women's issue and the homosexual issue. Social change is taking place in both of these areas. As a result, Christians have to reevaluate their beliefs due to changing attitudes toward women and toward homosexuals. In North America the changes related to women have been developing for more than a century. The changing attitudes and legislation toward homosexuals is comparatively recent (within the last quarter century or so). The impact of these cultural changes upon the Christian community has been felt in somewhat of a delayed response.

Before introducing a hermeneutical model and exploring the various criteria for assessing the cultural and transcultural components of a text, it might be helpful to walk through a broad introduction to these two pertinent issues. I will sketch the range of options and label them. For those readers who have an extensive background and exposure to these issues, this overview will simply introduce the labels and category names I will use in the pages to follow. Such readers may simply want to skim what follows or move ahead to the next chapter. However, for those who are just beginning to wade into these matters, it is important to establish the larger picture of interpretive options before entering into the next chapters. The descriptions below will provide some working handles and set boundaries for interacting with the central issues.

The women's issue

With the women's issue, there are roughly four positions that cross the spectrum of thought today. While these categories have some fluidity and other intermediate positions could be introduced, the four positions below will provide a sufficient framework for our discussions. Each view will be briefly described, then more fully developed in the major three spheres in which men and women relate: home, church and society.

Hard/strong patriarchy (hierarchy)

Overview: Unilateral submission of women with an extensive power differential.

Home: Women focus most of their energies in the home; they are to "submit to" and "obey" their husbands in all things; the husband's word is the final authority.

Church: A woman should not function in any capacity that places her in a position of greater power than a man; women are not permitted to teach in any setting where men are present. Depending upon the ecclesiastical structure, women may or may not be permitted to vote on selecting male leaders and on congregational issues; women should not be ordained to ministry in any capacity.

Society: If a woman works outside of the home, she should not hold positions of authority in any sphere of society (e.g., politics, education, business); men, not women, should provide for the home financially. Women should not be in leadership roles where they can exercise authority over a man; however, women are generally permitted to vote.

Soft patriarchy (hierarchy)

Overview: Unilateral submission of women with a moderate power differential.

Home: Women are free to work outside of the home; within the marriage they function in a cooperative manner with their husbands; ultimately the husband has the *theoretical* right to exercise authority in decision making over his wife, yet this should only be used on rare occasions, if at all. Words with a strong power-differential connotation, such as *obey* and *submission*, are still used but they often fade into the background.

Church: Women may teach men in any setting other than from the pulpit, as the senior pastor would on a weekly basis; they can work on a pastoral staff in a paid position; they can be deacons, but generally they are not permitted to function in an official capacity as elders. Often women function in an extended leadership role through participation on boards or councils with names other than the biblical categories; they are encouraged to vote on leadership selection and on church issues. Women may be ordained to serve in ministry roles other than the senior/preaching pastor.

Society: Women may function in an unrestricted way in society; they may hold positions of power over men; they may teach men; they may pursue any leadership position and are encouraged to vote in political elections.

Evangelical egalitarianism

Overview: Mutual submission with equality of power between male and female. Some argue for no role distinctions; others hold to minimal role distinctions based on biological differences.

Home: Women are free to work outside of the home; husbands and wives relate to each other in a model of mutual (not unilateral) submission; decisions are made based upon mutual consent and consensus. Wives generally play a greater role in nurturing infants and young children, otherwise roles are determined by mutual agreement through an evaluation of individual strengths.

Church: Women function within the church based upon character qualifications, gifts and theological education, not on the basis of gender restrictions; a woman may function as an elder or in pulpit ministry. Women can be ordained to any sphere of church ministry; in a large church the ideal would be to have a shared pulpit ministry utilizing qualified men and women.

Society: Women may function in an unrestricted way in society: they may hold positions of power over men; they may teach men; they may pursue any leadership position and are encouraged to vote in political elections.

Secular egalitarianism

Overview: Equal rights and no gender-defined roles.

Home: Women are often encouraged to work outside the home as a greater
               priority than the family and as a necessity for personal fulfillment.
               The husband-wife relationship is based upon the equal rights of the
               individual, rather than mutual deference; the relationship frequently
               evidences an extreme in personal autonomy, rather than interdepen-
               dence.

Church: Secular egalitarianism generally does not have much of a place for
               religion.

Society: Women may function in an unrestricted way in society: they may
               hold positions of power over men; they may teach men; they may
               pursue any leadership position and are encouraged to vote in politi-
               cal elections.

The homosexual issue

As with the women's issue, our culture and some parts of the Christian subculture
are changing in their perspective toward gays and lesbians. There are several positions that represent the spectrum of thinking on the homosexual issue; each
view is briefly developed here.

Marital heterosexuality only

Homosexuality is not an acceptable lifestyle for Christians, whether between
consenting adults on a casual basis or within monogamous, equal-partner relationships. The only acceptable means of heterosexual expression is within a covenant relationship of marriage between two adults.

Covenant and equal-partner homosexuality

Homosexuality is an acceptable lifestyle for Christians provided the partners
are equal-status, consenting adults and the relationship is one of a monogamous, covenant and lasting kind. The assumption is that the Bible's condemnation of homosexuality is due to the lack of these elements in the ancient
world.

Casual adult homosexuality

Homosexuality is an appropriate lifestyle for any member of society provided it
involves consenting adults. Participation in same-sex eroticism may be in any
form, not simply within covenant relationships or between equal-status partners.

As with the women's issue, we could develop some of the finer variations within each of these views.[2] However, further nuances will become evident below.

At this stage, these three options for homosexuality and four options for women are the primary categories being discussed in theological circles today.

The Ultimate Culture Question

A growing number of Christian voices have begun to argue for removing hierarchy in gender relationships and for doing away with any stigma attached to covenant homosexual relationships. This move away from a straightforward reading of the biblical text clearly reflects the broader move in our society toward a less restrictive viewpoint on these two areas. Our quest, then, is to determine whether the church should move *with* our culture or *against* our culture on these two issues. We need to ask the question, Which components within Scripture are cultural and which are transcultural? Our investigation will focus directly on this question in parts one and two. Before we get there, however, we need to establish a big-picture framework for our thinking. In the next chapter, then, I will address the question of what kind of hermeneutic will best enable us to travel down this road of cultural/transcultural assessment.

---

[2]For a more detailed survey of various perspectives, see Larry R. Holben, *What Christians Think about Homosexuality: Six Representative Viewpoints* (Richland Hills, Tex.: D & F Scott, 1999).

2

A REDEMPTIVE-MOVEMENT
HERMENEUTIC

The term "redemptive-movement hermeneutic" captures the most crucial component of the application process as it relates to cultural analysis, namely, the need to engage the redemptive spirit of the text in a way that moves the contemporary appropriation of the text beyond its original-application framing. A sense of the biblical or redemptive spirit can be obtained by listening to how texts compare to the broader cultural milieu and how they sound within the development of the canon. When taking the ancient text into our modern world, the redemptive spirit of Scripture is the most significant dimension with which a Christian can wrestle. Sometimes, by simply "doing" the words of the text we automatically fulfill its spirit today, particularly where the horizons of the ancient and modern worlds continue to overlap and where the biblical text has already moved the ancient-world standards in a particular direction as far as one could possibly go. At other times, however, living out the Bible's literal words in our modern context fails to fulfill its redemptive spirit.

A crucial distinction drives this chapter and the entire hermeneutic proposed within this book—the distinction between (1) a *redemptive-spirit* appropriation of Scripture, which encourages movement beyond the original application of the text in the ancient world, and (2) a *static* appropriation of Scripture, which understands the words of the text aside from or with minimal emphasis upon their underlying spirit and thus restricts any modern application of Scripture to where the isolated words of the text fell in their original setting. In the process of bridging two worlds, I will argue that a redemptive-movement hermeneutic champions that which is of foremost importance for actualizing the sacred text today. Nothing surpasses the need to live out the redemptive spirit of Scripture. Therein lies its heart. Therein one discovers the essence of good application.

I do not wish to engage in terminology debates. I have coined my approach a "redemptive-movement" hermeneutic because it captures the redemptive spirit *within* Scripture. It looks at a component of meaning *within* the biblical text and canon—a component of meaning easily missed in our application process. Some may prefer calling this interpretive/applicational approach a "progressive" or "developmental" or "trajectory" hermeneutic. That is fine. The label "redemptive movement" or "redemptive spirit" reflects my concern that the derived meaning is internal, not external, to the biblical text.

A Model

Before submerging ourselves in the details of a redemptive-movement hermeneutic, a broad picture or model provides a practical platform from which to work. For the sake of simplicity, I like to refer to the model as "The $X \Rightarrow Y \Rightarrow Z$ Principle." Any letters of the alphabet would do, as long as they indicate progression. The point of the model is to show how perspective and a redemptive spirit work together in the application of Scripture. Within the model below, the *central position* (Y) stands for where the isolated words of the Bible are in their development of a subject. Then, on either side of the biblical text, one must ask the question of perspective: What is my understanding of the biblical text, if I am looking from the perspective of the *original culture* (X)? Also, what does the biblical text look like from our contemporary culture, where it happens to reflect a better social ethic—one closer to an *ultimate ethic* (Z) than to the ethic revealed in the isolated words of the biblical text?

From one direction the Bible looks redemptive (and is); from the other direction it appears regressive (and is). In the model below, the smile on one face and the bewilderment on the other represent the two responses that happen inside the *same* reader as he or she looks at Scripture from these different perspectives. We might sketch the phenomenon as depicted on page 32.

The $X \Rightarrow Y \Rightarrow Z$ principle illustrates how numerous aspects of the biblical text were *not* written to establish a utopian society with complete justice and equity. They were written within a cultural framework with limited moves toward an ultimate ethic. Many of the women and slavery texts discussed in this book exhibit the $X \Rightarrow Y \Rightarrow Z$ principle. Numerous examples have been catalogued in later chap-

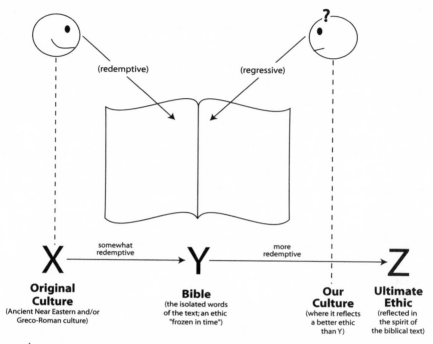

X	somewhat redemptive →	Y	more redemptive →	Z
Original Culture (Ancient Near Eastern and/or Greco-Roman culture)		**Bible** (the isolated words of the text; an ethic "frozen in time")		**Our Culture** (where it reflects a better ethic than Y) / **Ultimate Ethic** (reflected in the spirit of the biblical text)

ters.[1] In order to show how the model works, I will explore two introductory examples, one from the women texts and one from the slavery texts.

The first example comes from those Scriptural passages that speak of taking female virgins as spoils of war. Within the biblical parameters of patriarchy, the capture and claim of virgin women during military conquest is openly permitted. One finds this treatment of women as spoils of battle documented in the legislative texts and illustrated in the narrative stories of Israel's wars (see criterion 11.C). In defense of the biblical text, we should note that Deuteronomy 21:10-14 is at least somewhat redemptive relative to the original culture (X). After all, the Israelite male had to wait one month, marry the girl, and in the case of divorce he could not sell her or treat her as a slave (cf. Num 31:32-35; Judg 5:30; 21:11-12, 15-23). Compared to the horrible rape scenes that often accompanied ancient warfare (not unlike the rape camps of modern Bosnia) these biblical texts are clearly redemptive. Even in "ugly texts" like these, a redemptive spirit surfaces within the Bible, especially when it is read against the backdrop of the ancient culture. One might expect such a redemptive movement, since the core of a biblical ethic is to love God and to love one's neighbor. When compared to the ancient treatment of women in war, the biblical text represents a measure of, or a greater

---

[1]See especially criteria 11.B–C and 18.C.

movement toward, love and compassion.

What we should live out in our modern culture, however, is not the isolated words of the text but the *redemptive spirit* that the text reflects as read against its original culture. In applying the text to our era, we do not want to stay static with the text (Y). Rather, we need to move on, beyond the text, and take the redemptive dimension of those words further to a more redemptive level (toward an ultimate ethic, Z). Surely there is a more humane and just treatment of women POWs than what is reflected in the biblical text. We would not dare take the isolated words of these texts to our modern legislators and ask them to draft a policy from these words on the treatment of women captives in war. We would likely find that a more redemptive policy is already in place in our own contemporary culture, at least in Canada, the United States, Europe, and so on. Yet, even this contemporary form may be open to further refinement. As Christians we should be very careful not to become gridlocked with the isolated words of the text so that we miss reapplying the redemptive spirit that produced the text in the first place. Applications of the Bible in successive generations and different cultures must permit the redemptive spirit of the text to carry forward the unrealized or frozen-in-time aspects of a biblical ethic. Otherwise, we fail to properly apply the text within our own generation.

A second introductory illustration may be drawn from the slavery texts. The Israelites were instructed to provide safety and refuge to slaves fleeing harsh treatment from a foreign country (Deut 23:15-16). Upon crossing Israel's borders, a fleeing slave was to be given shelter, was permitted to live in any of Israel's cities and was not to be handed over to his or her master. The redemptive dimension of this slavery legislation, relative to the surrounding nations, sparkles even brighter than the redemptive component of the previous illustration. In some respects, the entire nation of Israel was to function as a land of refuge for runaway slaves, much like certain designated cities within Israel were to function as a refuge for Israelites in distress.

A static hermeneutic[2] would apply this slavery-refuge text by permitting the ownership of slaves today, provided that the church offers similar kinds of refuge for runaway slaves. The refuge would extend to runaway slaves from harsh, unbelieving masters. Perhaps the covenant community would become the channel to freedom as an underground railway for the twenty-first century. Or, maybe the physical church property would act as the place of refuge. Either way, Christians would dare not speak out against slavery. They would support the institution of slavery, but seek to give refuge to slaves in abusive relationships. Such an ap-

---

[2]We will develop this alternative hermeneutic below.

proach to applying the Bible stays very close to the words of the text—at least the words of the text when understood without their crucial component of spirit-movement meaning.

A brief aside on terminology is important. Hereafter, when speaking of a static approach to the words of Scripture, I will generally insert a qualifying adjective and talk about the *isolated* words of the text. By the qualification *isolated* I mean "a reading of Scripture in cultural and canonical isolation"—that is, a reading of its words in isolation from the spirit-movement component of meaning which significantly transforms the application of texts for subsequent generations. It would make my job a lot easier to speak of the "spirit" versus the "words" of the text when I am contrasting a redemptive-movement hermeneutic with a static approach. But that amounts to oversimplified rhetoric. It creates wrong impressions and a false dichotomy. These two components are *not* antithetical; the words and spirit are fused together in the original text. Rather, what is antithetical are *two different approaches* by Christians to Scripture: one that reads the words of the text with a spirit-movement component of meaning (and sees it as prominent for contemporary application) versus one that either overlooks the spirit component completely or does not grant it sufficient value to move application further (thus minimizing spirit-movement for contemporary application).

While a static approach carefully measures the isolated words of the text in order to find suitable equivalents in the new setting, it fails to breathe into the new setting a measure of the empowering life force that made the text redemptive in its own day. Even more tragic is that, in arguing for or in permitting biblical slavery today, a static hermeneutic takes our current standard of human rights and working conditions *backwards* by quantum leaps. We would shame a gospel that proclaims freedom to the captive, a gospel with both spiritual and social implications. Christians should find it utterly repugnant to think that we can fulfill these biblical slavery texts today by permitting slavery in our modern world, provided we build some kind of equivalent freedom centers for runaway slaves. Such an application is faithful to the isolated words of the text. It fulfills the letters on the page. But it fails miserably in the attempt to fulfill the radically redemptive spirit that lies within the text, as it is read against the broader social environment of the biblical world. This is the core of good biblical application—application that seeks to understand the isolated words of the text but places a far greater interest in discovering and applying its spirit.

Characteristics

A redemptive-movement hermeneutic is characterized by several key components. At the heart of such an approach to the application of Scripture is its focus on (1) redemptive movement, (2) a multilevel ethic, (3) a balanced perspective, (4) cultural/transcultural assessment and (5) the underlying spirit within a text. While my development of a redemptive-movement hermeneutic will be framed in positive terms, I will also argue against a competing alternative, which in functional terms might be called a "static" or a "stationary" hermeneutic.

Some who hold to a static hermeneutic want to portray their position as the "historic" or "traditional" hermeneutic.[3] This, of course, has the benefit of sounding as if it embraces the way hermeneutics has always been done throughout church history. But such is not the case. A redemptive-movement hermeneutic has always been a major part of the historic church, apostolic and beyond.[4] I do not deny that a static hermeneutic has played a significant role throughout the last two millennia of the church's existence, or that it has influenced the application process within Judaism for thousands of years before Christendom. My point is that both approaches to Scripture have been evident throughout Jewish and Christian history. The issues being addressed have changed, but a hermeneutic emphasizing the redemptive spirit of the text is hardly a new idea. Thus a static hermeneutic, as I will call it, should not be presented as the historic hermeneutic of the church. Such a presentation is misleading at best. Both approaches may claim their respective predecessors within the covenant community for whom the Bible has been a cherished and sacred book.

---

[3]Robert W. Yarbrough, "The Hermeneutics of 1 Timothy 2:9-15," in *Women in the Church: A Fresh Analysis of 1 Timothy 2:9-15*, ed. Andreas J. Köstenberger, Thomas R. Schreiner and H. Scott Baldwin (Grand Rapids, Mich.: Baker, 1995), pp. 155-96. While my criticism of Yarbrough's chapter is quite strong, I must commend the book for its exegesis in a number of the other chapters, written by other authors. See my positive commendation in criterion 18.C.3.

[4]A redemptive-movement hermeneutic (chapter two) and the cultural/transcultural analysis to follow (chapters four through seven) are hardly completely new concepts. Aspects of a redemptive-movement hermeneutic are found in other standard approaches to Scripture. For instance, an "analogy of faith" approach considers that all biblical texts must be used in a dialogue of sorts in order to formulate a synthetic understanding of truth; one must never read a text in isolation from the rest of Scripture. A "canonical" approach, a "progress of revelation" approach, a "progressive dispensational" approach and a moderate "covenant" approach—all of these approaches see revelatory movement and development between epochs in salvation history. Various "christological" and "eschatological/telos" approaches see these two centers in theology as foundational for rooting our application of the biblical text in a forward-looking manner. Also, a "grammatical historical" approach tries to understand a biblical text in the greater context of its socio-historical setting; this is not unlike a redemptive-movement approach (cf. "foreign movement" discussion below), which attempts to discover the underlying spirit of the text by hearing it within its broader social context. Aside from these standard approaches to Scripture, the roots of a redemptive-movement understanding of Scripture can historically be seen in every issue throughout church history (and Judaism) that is comparable to slavery. Whether the labels for the approach are the same or different, debates about slavery, polygamy, monarchy, etc. have always had one side of the church appealing to a redemptive-movement hermeneutic (call it what you like) and the other side appealing to a static hermeneutic.

Enough said about history. While of considerable interest, a historical development of church hermeneutics lies outside the bounds of this work. So, we will
move on to examine the characteristics of a redemptive-movement hermeneutic.

Redemptive movement

As one might suspect from its name, a key component of a redemptive-movement hermeneutic is the idea of movement. The Christian seeking to apply
Scripture today should examine the movement between the biblical text and its
surrounding social context. Once that movement has been discovered, there
needs to be an assessment of whether the movement is preliminary or absolute
(see criterion 1). If it is preliminary and further movement in the direction set
by the text would produce a more fully realized ethic, then that is the course of
action one must pursue. The interpreter extrapolates the biblical movement toward a more just, more equitable and more loving form. If a better ethic than
the one expressed in the isolated words of the text is possible, and the biblical
and canonical spirit is headed that direction, then that is where one ultimately
wants to end up.

The alternative, of course, is to work with an understanding of Scripture that is
static. A static hermeneutic does not interest itself in discovering movement. It is
primarily interested in exegeting the text as an isolated entity and finding comparable or equivalent expressions (alternative forms) of how that text may be lived
out in another culture. In the case of slavery, a static hermeneutic would not condemn biblical-type slavery, if that social order were to reappear in society today.
Proponents of a static hermeneutic are generally willing to condemn American
slavery, which was often worse than the biblical form, but they will not speak in a
negative manner about the kind of slavery presented in the Bible. In the meantime, the household codes concerning masters and slaves are transferred to the
modern context of employer/employee relationships. Equivalent admonitions of
"obey" and "submit" are popped in like sure-fit items. This type of application
process amounts to a rather wooden swapping of ancient-world and modern-
world equivalents.

When a static hermeneutic is pressed with the actual words of the slavery
texts, however, it produces grotesque, mutation-like applications. Imagine taking
the words of Peter and advising modern employees to accept physical beatings by
their employers for the sake of the gospel (1 Pet 2:18-25). Or, think about in-
structing contemporary employers from the Pentateuch that, should they limit
beating employees to within a hairbreadth of their life, they would not be guilty
of legal reprisal (Ex 21:20-21). Or, maybe our modern world should consider
handing out lesser penalties for sexual violation against an employee (= slave)

than in the case of sexual violation against an employer or self-employed person (= free) (Deut 22:25-27; cf. Lev 19:20-22). These examples, of course, show the utterly ridiculous nature of a static hermeneutic. Even a static application utilizes a redemptive-movement hermeneutic of sorts, on a lesser scale, by its selective choice of that which can and cannot be carried over to our context. One might be able to persuade a modern congregation into believing that employees should "obey" and "submit to" their employers based upon the slavery texts. This happens all the time. But the outcome reflects a tragic misunderstanding of Scripture. The rest of the slavery material, beyond the obey/submit instructions, is often left at arm's length and simply not applied.

This kind of static approach to the slavery texts is not persuasive. In fact, the wooden nature of a static hermeneutic becomes a liability to any Christian seeking to live out their commitment to God's will, as revealed through Scripture. Having discovered the movement of the biblical texts on slavery relative to the original social context, an extrapolation of that movement today leads to the abolition of slavery altogether. On this issue our culture is much closer to an ultimate ethic than it is to the unrealized ethic reflected in the isolated words of the Bible. In other words, a rough development of the X⇒Y⇒Z model for slavery might be broadly sketched like this:

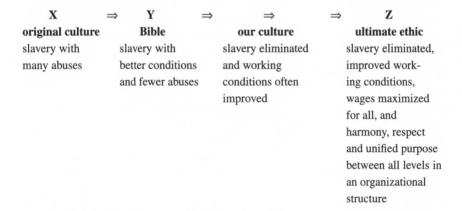

X	⇒	Y	⇒	⇒	⇒	Z
original culture		**Bible**		**our culture**		**ultimate ethic**
slavery with many abuses		slavery with better conditions and fewer abuses		slavery eliminated and working conditions often improved		slavery eliminated, improved working conditions, wages maximized for all, and harmony, respect and unified purpose between all levels in an organizational structure

In addition to the complete removal of slavery, a redemptive-movement hermeneutic proposes quite a different way of applying the household codes in our modern context. A redemptive-movement hermeneutic does not argue that modern Christians apply the household codes through submitting to and obeying their employers. Such an application not only neglects the element of movement to a more fully realized ethic but overlooks fundamental differences between slavery and modern employee-employer relations. The most crucial

difference is that of ownership compared to a contractual basis for working relationships. In the modern contractual setting we should not preach obedience
and submission, but that Christian employees should fulfill the terms of their
contract to the best of their ability in order to bring glory to God and enhance
their gospel witness. In addition, a redemptive-movement hermeneutic seeks to
reapply the spirit or movement component of the slavery texts relative to the
surrounding cultures. Scripture sides heavily with the plight of the slave, the
poor and the oppressed. This life-breathing spirit, which bettered the conditions
for slaves in the ancient world, should also influence the application process today. Contemporary Christian employers, then, should not abuse their power in
pursuit of bottom-line production but advance their businesses in ways that
value their employees as people and encourage their productive contribution in
humane and just ways. Working conditions, levels of income, and disparity between the rich and poor are all issues that the redemptive spirit, evidenced in
scriptural movement, ought to impact as we bring these texts to bear on our
modern world.

Movement within the women texts is equally profound when the biblical account is read against its surrounding culture. The overbearing strength of patriarchy and its abuses were often horrific in the ancient world. The Bible, though by
no means eliminating all patriarchal abuses and injustices (see criteria 11.C and
18.C), certainly moves in a moderating direction. Its patriarchy is of an improved
sort. While retaining some restrictions, Scripture grants considerable freedom to
women and moves in a less-restrictive direction. In terms of a broad scheme, the
$X \Rightarrow Y \Rightarrow Z$ model for the women's texts might be presented as follows:

X	⇒	Y	⇒	⇒	⇒	Z
original culture		**Bible**		**our culture**		**ultimate ethic**
strong patriarchy		moderated patriarchy		secular		ultra-soft
with many		with fewer		egalitarianism		patriarchy or
abuses		abuses		with significantly		complementary
				improved status		egalitarianism[5]
				of women and		and interdepen-
				and emphasis on		dence, mutuality
				individual rights,		and servant-like
				autonomy and self-		attitude in relation-
				fulfillment		ships

Between the Y and Z components above there are a number of intermediate

---

[5]These two models will be developed in chapter eight.

stages that are not sketched. For instance, the patriarchy developed by Piper and Grudem[6] clearly improves upon the biblical scene. To be sure, they present their position as if it were the patriarchy of Scripture. But significant improvements have inadvertently crept into their view. Nevertheless, if one adopts a redemptive-movement hermeneutic, the softening of patriarchy (which Scripture itself initiates) can be taken a considerable distance further. Carrying the redemptive movement within Scripture to a more improved expression for gender relationships, as I will argue, ends in either ultra-soft patriarchy or complementary egalitarianism,[7] depending upon whether one sees primogeniture (firstborn or creative-order prominence) as a transcultural or as a cultural-component value. The implication of a redemptive-spirit hermeneutic cries out for this kind of movement in the appropriation of Scripture.

If we talk about the homosexuality texts within an X⇒Y⇒Z model, we discover a different kind of movement, namely, an absolute movement from X to Y. Scripture evidences a redemptive spirit when it moves the people of God to a complete ban on same-sex activity. Homosexuality was widely accepted within the broader culture, so the movement within the Bible is clearly in one direction and complete—at least complete in terms of its broad-sweeping, negative assessment of the behavior. In this respect, the kind of movement from X to Y is absolute by its very nature. Thus for the most part, other than some minor alterations, the redemptive movement ends at Y. On the issue of acceptability and assessment, our modern culture could either be placed along the continuum at X (equivalent to where the original culture was) or perhaps even to the left of X in what might been viewed as a "W" position. In order to capture the same redemptive spirit today, the Christian community must continue its negative assessment of homosexual behavior and restrict such activity within the church, even if society at large does not.

If a Christian wants to reflect the spirit and direction of the biblical text, a negative assessment of homosexuality needs to be retained. Only a negative-assessment application captures the essence of the movement between the ancient-world setting and the biblical text. Nevertheless, there are differences between the ancient and modern world, which should add a nuanced dimension to our negative response. For instance, our sexual ethic should articulate a variance within a negative assessment of same-sex activity, depending upon the type of homosexuality being addressed. Covenant homosexuality differs considerably from pederasty or homosexual rape. Furthermore, the death penalty within Is-

---

[6]John Piper and Wayne Grudem, eds., *Recovering Biblical Manhood and Womanhood: A Response to Evangelical Feminism* (Wheaton, Ill.: Crossway, 1991).
[7]See chapter eight for a description of these two models. Chapters four through seven provide the rationale.

rael's documents should be transposed to excommunication within the church (e.g., 1 Cor 5:1-13). Within a pluralistic society, such as we experience today, Christians should actually defend the rights and freedoms of homosexuals to live out their beliefs. We should not legally impose our sexual ethic on others. Furthermore, the emerging biological and environmental research suggests that for some individuals the degree of non-volitional disposition toward homoerotic behavior is quite strong. For others it is simply a matter of personal choice, not clouded by volitional issues (see criterion 18.D). Even within a negative assessment we must recognize a sliding scale of culpability, as a Christian ethic does in other areas where non-volitional factors influence a particular behavior. These secondary or minor components of movement toward an ultimate ethic will be developed in detail in the chapters to follow. Nevertheless, only a negative assessment of homosexuality retains the redemptive spirit within the biblical text.

[W] ⇒	X ⇒	Y ⇒	Z
our culture	**original culture**	**Bible**	**ultimate ethic**
almost complete acceptance and no restrictions of homosexual activity	mixed acceptance and no restrictions of homosexual activity	negative assessment and complete restriction of homosexual activity	negative assessment and complete restriction of homosexual activity and greater understanding and compassion, utilization of a sliding scale of culpability, and variation in the degree of negative assessment based on the type of same-sex activity

Of equal importance, however, is the need to live redemptively in our relationships with gay men and lesbian women. Creating a redemptive focus to our lives means that we love homosexual people as ourselves. It means that we treat them with the same kind of grace, respect, care and compassion with which we want to be treated. It means that we fight along side of them against hateful action aimed at their community. It means all of the above, even if we do not agree with their sexual ethic. In the final analysis, they will determine whatever course of action they deem best for their lives. However, a difference of perspective does not mean that the Christian community should be silent about its sexual ethic. Caring for people includes seeking their very best, whatever that may entail. The Christian community needs to lovingly persuade all people toward a sexual ethic that is in their best interests, even if those with whom we dialogue never come to our conclusions. Of course, such dialogue is of little or no value unless it takes place in the context of genuine friendships, where the matter of love and respect is not in question.

A multilevel ethic

A redemptive-movement hermeneutic understands Scripture to embody a multi-level ethic. By a multilevel ethic, I mean that not everything within Scripture reflects the same level of ethical development. As stated above, the X⇒Y⇒Z principle illustrates that many aspects of the biblical text were *not* written to establish a utopian society with complete justice and equity. On the other hand, a static hermeneutic tends to look at Scripture as if it were composed of a mono-lithic, single-level ethic. To speak of improving upon some portion of Scripture is foreign to many Christians, myself included, since we often take a defensive stand against the onslaught of false accusations aimed at undermining the trust-worthiness of Scripture. If the accusations are false, of course, then we need to battle on. However, the Christian community must be careful in its dialogue with unbelieving opponents not to minimize their concerns. As a result of overly reactive posturing toward an unbelieving world we sometimes breed our own worst understandings of the Bible.

A virtual plethora of reasons explains why God orchestrated the composition of Scripture with a multilevel ethic. I will discuss some of these at length below. One example should suffice at this point: In Matthew19:1-12 Jesus interacts with the Pharisees, or at least with one very antagonistic group within the broader Pharisaic movement, on matters of divorce and marriage. Jesus speaks of the hardness of the human heart as one reason for a multilevel ethic, and potential for kingdom service as yet another reason. Moses' instructions about divorce were redemptive in their social context (Deut 24:1-4). They were an attempt to mini-mize the damage of living in a fallen world. A certificate of divorce was a protective measure for the well-being of the wife, who would frequently need to remarry or come under the shelter of another male. In at least a small way it rep-resented a positive action on the part of the husband toward his wife, even during the unpleasant circumstances of divorce.[8] The redemptive component of this di-vorce legislation becomes even more apparent as one reads the biblical text

---

[8]Cf. the divorce legislation in Deut 21:10-14 concerning wives acquired through military conquest. In the case of divorce, the Israelite male was not permitted to sell his wife as a slave. The text encour-ages a measure of respect and love, even in the midst of severely strained relationships.

against the callous and often capricious patriarchy of the broader culture.

If one ponders the underlying spirit of the Deuteronomy divorce legislation, it ultimately points to the restoration of human relationships. I am not suggesting that the writ of divorce was designed to fix the marriage. Obviously it was not. Nor was the act of giving the wife divorce papers necessarily, if ever, inspired by romantic or loving affection on the part of the husband. Yet, whether he liked it or not, Deuteronomy 24:1-4 moved the husband to act positively toward his wife. The text required one final act by which the husband, at least in the context of the ancient culture, treated his wife with a certain measure of decency, consideration and well-being. Whether or not the audience living out the text actually entered into its spirit, the author(s) of the text intended for the prescription to limit the damage that one human could inflict upon another. By limiting the damage a secondary byproduct was that it limited the extent of alienation in the relationship. It kept even further distance from entering into an already strained relationship.

If one carries the spirit of limiting damages and reducing alienation within human relationships to its logical conclusion, one ends up with the ideal of restored, loving relationships. One positive act, however so small, if multiplied many times over, carries with it tremendous restorative potential. I speak of the author's intended spirit here, not of the begrudging spirit that may have accompanied the life players who were acting out the text. One must listen for the redemptive spirit of the text within the author's empowering act of framing its words, not from the deaf ears of those who simply fulfill its words out of respect for custom or out of pressure to conform. Along these lines, a redemptive-spirit journey obviously arrives at harmonious, restored human relationships.[9] It is not surprising, then, that Jesus invokes the Eden portrait of relational harmony as the ideal or goal. It embodies the redemptive better (a fuller realization of the text's redemptive spirit) of marriage without alienation.

Interestingly, within the text of Matthew 19:1-12 Jesus points to a higher possible alternative (or redemptive better) that exceeds even the norms of an Eden-inspired world. Jesus suggests that some may choose the option of not marrying at all in order to devote themselves fully to kingdom service. The Matthew passage nicely illustrates a multilevel ethic within Scripture, since it introduces what we might describe as three redemptive betters: (1) following divorce procedures that minimize the damages, (2) resolving conflicts and striving for marital harmony, and (3) not entering into the good of marriage for the greater good of serv-

---

[9]The redemptive spirit of the divorce text takes us there even if the participants in the Deuteronomy legislation never became restored in their relationship.

ing more fully in the kingdom. One could squeeze in many other levels within these three parameters; these are merely representative.[10]

Nevertheless, these three levels tell us that God recognizes the social factor of fallen humanity and even natural human processes, along with a host of other social-context factors, in the composition of Scripture. Hardened hearts, creative ideals, and kingdom ideals are only three factors that shape a multilevel ethic. In some respects, a fallen world and kingdom ideals represent two extremes. Most of the other factors which influence a multilevel ethic in Scripture, as we will see later, lie somewhere in between that which is strikingly pristine and that which is somewhat tainted. Most of the other factors involve psychological, cultural, environmental, collective or mission issues without necessarily introducing any clear saint-or-sinner connotations. At this point, however, it is reasonable to conclude that a flat-line approach to the ethics of Scripture does not adequately account for what one finds in the text.

In Matthew 19 the gospel writer portrays the Pharisees as having a wrong understanding of Scripture due to their expectation of a uniform ethic. Their approach to the Torah was to read everything on the sacred page as if it were written with the same ethical force. They understood the words of Moses to reflect God's idealized will in every respect. Many of the Pharisees, in a devout effort to orient their lives around the sacred text, felt that they were living out God's best provided they stuck to the isolated words of Scripture. Their wooden hermeneutic made it difficult to see that Moses' words did not represent an absolute ethic; their approach to Scripture made it virtually impossible for them to see further, as Jesus points out, that there was an even greater good of sacrificially serving in the kingdom instead of enjoying the benefits of marriage. As we will discover in subsequent chapters on cultural/transcultural assessment, a multilevel ethic not only surfaces in Jesus' approach to Scripture, it reflects the very nature of the biblical material itself. Through a detailed examination of the slavery and women texts, Christians should be able to confidently say that there is much within Scripture that needs an infusion of greater justice, greater compassion and greater equity in the treatment of human beings.

Admittedly, proponents of a static hermeneutic do distinguish between levels in a social ethic related to slavery. For instance, Yarbrough differentiates between better and worse types of slavery and between better and worse forms of employ-

---

[10]For example, between the first and second level one could initiate a series of improvements in the biblical legislation on divorce (see criterion 11.C.6). Also, one could propose several intermediate levels between the second and third levels in the Matthew 19 text. For example, many married missionaries have significantly limited the size of their families, or chosen not to have children, for the sake of advancing the gospel.

ment.[11] Yarbrough readily acknowledges a difference between American slavery and biblical slavery, with biblical slavery evidencing a better treatment of human beings. I would agree with his assessment. Yet, the Bible does not directly address American slavery. So one might ask, how does Yarbrough know that biblical slavery was a better form of slavery than American slavery? The Bible did not give him the answer, at least not in any explicit fashion. Rather, Yarbrough must have reasoned his way through a comparison of the two forms of slavery and evaluated the details within the two systems of slavery on logical and sociological grounds in order to arrive at his conclusion.

So while those endorsing a static hermeneutic are prepared to evaluate the ethics of social forms *inferior* to Scripture, they are reluctant to apply the same kind of reasoning in determining social forms clearly *superior* to the (unrealized) ethics of the Bible.[12] Without even moving to an abolitionist perspective, Yarbrough and others neglect to develop alternative forms of slavery that improve on biblical slavery.

Slaves

Already Some Movement (relative to original/broader culture)	Needing Further Movement (even aside from the abolition of slavery)[13]
seventh-day rest for all slaves (Ex 23:12)	slaves as property (Ex 21:21)
seventh-year release for Hebrew slaves (Lev 25:39-43; cf. Jer 34:8-22)	no seventh-year release of foreign slaves (Lev 25:39-43)
provisions for slaves upon release (Deut 15:12-18)	use of slaves for reproductive purposes (Gen 16:1-4; 30:3-4, 9-10; cf. Gen 35:22)
admonitions against harshness (Col 4:1; Eph 6:9)	sexual violation of a slave versus a free woman (Lev 19:20-22; cf. Deut 22:25-27)
some limitation on physical beatings (Ex 21:20-21, 26-27)	physical beating of slaves still permitted (Ex 21:20-21)
refuge and safety for foreign runaway slaves (Deut 23:15; cf. Ex 21:26-27)	no similar refuge for runaway Israelite slaves (cf. Deut 23:15)
denouncement of slave traders (Deut 24:7; Ex 21:16; cf. 1 Tim 1:10)	lesser value of a slave's life in capital cases (Ex 21:28-32)

---

[11]Yarbrough, "Hermeneutics of 1 Timothy 2:9-15," pp. 185-90; cf. Guenther Haas, "The Kingdom and Slavery: A Test Case for Social Ethics," *Calvin Theological Journal* 28 (1993): 78, 86.

[12]As with every "superior to the ethics of the Bible" statement within this chapter, I mean the ethics of the Bible *as measured by its isolated words alone*.

[13]Even if someone were to stay within a slavery framework, these elements of the biblical version of slavery could stand a little improvement.

The strengths are on the left side; the liabilities are on the right side. Without even arguing for the abolition of slavery, one can easily develop a social ethic for slavery that exceeds the one found in a letters-on-the-page reading of the Bible. It does not take much imagination nor skilled reasoning to formulate a kind of slavery that would be much improved beyond the slavery ethic of Scripture as seen in its isolated words.

Now, it is understandable why certain Christians and evangelical scholars do not want to propose a social ethic, nor any other ethic, that exceeds (in realized form) the ethics of Scripture. It is likely that they think such a view impugns the testimony of the biblical witness. Furthermore, it creates a dilemma of how to interact with unbelievers who propose some kind of advanced social ethic. Typically, those who advocate a static hermeneutic overlook the potential for improving biblical slavery, even if they were to stay within a slavery framework and not move to abolition. Also, when faced with the competing option of abolition and bettering employment conditions, they frequently downplay the benefits of abolition and confuse the issue by talking about slavery as a metaphor.[14] While their motives may be honorable, the outcome of their view is extremely damaging to the very Scriptures they are attempting to protect. By not accepting a multilevel ethic within Scripture, they inadvertently muzzle the Bible's redemptive spirit. Preferring to stay with the safety of the text's isolated words, their application process sweeps aside the most important component imaginable.

A similar kind of multilevel ethic within Scripture can be observed as one examines the women texts. The chart on pages 46-47 illustrates the lack of any ultimate social ethic within the women texts as well as the culture-entrenched nature of such passages.

By initiating some basic improvements to the right-hand column, it would not be difficult to forge a social ethic that far exceeds Scripture (at least "Scripture" in the sense of its isolated words alone).[15] The extremely ragged edges of biblical patriarchy make it very simple to propose a better social ethic without even departing from a patriarchal framework. The same is true of the soft patriarchy advanced today by various Biblical Manhood and Womanhood publications.[16] Their brand of patriarchy, though better than that of Scripture, has potential for significant advancement to either an ultra-soft patriarchy or a complementary egalitarian position (see chapter eight). Choosing between these last two options is not

---

[14]Yarbrough, "Hermeneutics of 1 Timothy 2:9-15," pp. 185-90.

[15]Of course, a social ethic based upon the spirit of Scripture takes on a completely different configuration.

[16]For a complete listing of publications, write Council on Biblical Manhood and Womanhood, P.O. Box 7337, Libertyville, IL 60048 <www.info@cbmw.org>.

Women

Already Some Movement	Needing Further Movement
(relative to original/broader culture)	(even aside from the removal of patriarchy)
softening husband's side of hierarchy (Eph 5:25-32)	women as property (e.g., Ex 20:17; cf. Deut 5:21; Judg 5:30)
women given equal say in sexual domain (1 Cor 7:2-5)	husband as "new father"; wife as "child" (Num 30:1-16)
husband contributes to the home in significant ways, not shirking responsibility (1 Tim 5:8)	husband as sole/primary provider (Ex 21:10-11; cf. Is 4:1)
wife contributes to the home in productive ways, not becoming a busybody or gossip (1 Tim 5:13-14; Tit 2:5)	wife to be primarily in the home (1 Tim 5:13-14; Tit 2:5)
permitted to inherit property if no males (Num 27:5-8; 31:1-9)	no property inheritance in general (Deut 21:16-17; cf. Num 27:5-8; 31:1-9)
at least theoretical equality between male and female (Gal 3:28; 1 Cor 11:11-12; cf. 1 Cor 12:13; Eph 2:15; Col 3:11)	rape laws require the father to be paid damages and the female victim to marry the rapist (Deut 22:28-29)
some great women on certain occasions permitted in leadership (Eg., Deborah, Huldah, Priscilla, Junias)	virginity expectations focus almost exclusively on the female (Gen 24:16; Num 31:35; Esther 2:2, 17-19; Ps 45:14-15; Mt 25:1-13; Lk 1:27; cf. Gen 19:8; Judg 19:24; 21:11-12; 2 Sam 13:2, 18; 1 Kings 1:2; Song 6:8; Deut 22:13-14; Ezek 22:10-21; 23:42-45; Mt 1:18-19)
adultery viewed as destructive to the home (Num 5:11-31; Lev 20:10; Deut 22:22-24; Ex 22:16-17; cf. Deut 22:28-29)	adultery laws scrutinize the woman involved, not the man, and penalize women more severely (Num 5:11-31; Lev 20:10; Deut 22:22-24; Ex 22:16-17; cf. Deut 22:28-29)
women initiate divorce in one Jesus saying (Mk 10:12) and in one Pauline text (1 Cor 7:10-16)	divorce legislation disadvantages women in initiation process and especially in settlements (Deut 20:10-14; 22:1-4, 19, 29; 24:1-4)
polygamy legislation protects wives somewhat (makes basic provisions [Ex 21:10], minimizes rivalry [Lev 18:18], and maintains first-born rights [Deut 21:15-17])	polygamy favors men and creates extreme vulnerability for women (relationally and in the case of divorce) (see criterion 11.C.7)
	females valued less in vow redemption (Lev 27:1-8)

females not abandoned at birth (broader culture
  kills more female than male infants)
  (See Tal Ilan, *Jewish Women in Greco-Roman
  Palestine* [Peabody, Mass.: Hendrickson, 1996],
  p. 46.)

lesser value of female offspring (see criterion
  11.C.7) and greater impurity assessment of
  female offspring   (Lev 12:2-4; cf. 12:6-7)

women as gardens in reproductive models
  Gen 38:9; Lev 15:16-18, 32; Ps 78:51; 105:36;
  Deut 7:13: 28:4, 11, 18, 53; Mic 6:7; Ps 128:3)

infertility as primarily a female problem
  (In Scripture only women are viewed as "barren"
  or infertile)

Jesus and Paul (contra Old Testament and rabbinical
  emphasis) have female disciples

daughters of secondary importance in the
  passing on of Torah tradition
  (Deut 4:9-10; 6:2, 7, 20; 11:19, 21; 32:46;
  cf. Ex 10:2; 12:26; 13:8, 14)

women/virgins as trophies to be won
  (Josh 15:16; cf. 1 Sam 17:25; 18:12-27; 2 Sam
  3:14; 6)

protective measures for women captured
  in battle (e.g., mourning period and unable
  to sell as a slave) (Deut 21:10-14; cf. 20:14)

women/virgins as spoils of war
  (Num 31:32-35; Deut 20:14; 21:10-14; cf. Judg.
  5:30; 21:11-12, 15-23)

husband's implied authority to physically
  discipline his wife
  (Hos 2:1-3, 10; Jer 13:20-27; Ezek 16:32-42;
  23:22-30; cf. Is 47:3; Nahum 3:5-6)

women as wimpy warriors (Is 19:16; Jer 50:37;
  51:30; Nahum 3:13)

women as poor leaders (Is 3:12)

women as more easily deceived than men
  (the traditional interpretation of 1 Tim 2:14;
  see criterion 18 and appendix B)

entirely easy. The line between them becomes exceedingly fine. And, the decision
about staying on one side of the line or the other is informed by much less data
than is the case here in selecting one's broader hermeneutic. Nevertheless, both
egalitarians and patriarchalists need to work from a redemptive-movement
framework; that much should be certain.

If the women's debate is to make any progress in the years that lie ahead, evangelical leaders on the patriarchy side will need to emerge with one clear message: *as with slavery, the patriarchy found within the Bible does not offer us an ultimate social ethic*. Regardless of whether one ever becomes an egalitarian, patriarchal proponents need to wrestle with, and even celebrate, the implications of this affirmation for their view.[17] On the other hand, egalitarian leaders must likewise confess their inappropriate casting of the issue into the polarized extremes of moral right and moral wrong. When egalitarians talk about biblical slavery or biblical patriarchy under the category of "a hideous evil," they have fallen into an anachronistic fallacy and forgotten the redemptive component within Scripture.[18] It is not surprising that neither side is listening to the other. Both patriarchalists and egalitarians must agree upon a hermeneutical framework that is grounded in an understanding of redemptive betters. Both sides must agree upon making the redemptive spirit in Scripture and its multilevel ethic a central, not peripheral, component in the dialogue.

At this point, you may be asking how does one determine that something is better? What does a redemptive better look like? On what basis can we talk about inferior versus superior? These are good questions. Should you be asking these kinds of questions, I would commend your critical and inquisitive thinking. Yet, I ask that you would kindly carry them with you into chapters four through seven, where the bulk of this book is headed. There I answer these questions in detail. A broad answer will have to suffice here. The basis for judging redemptive betters hinges on what we might eclectically call "the *-als*" of Christian theology. Each of these assessment words shares an *-al* ending: for example, biblical, theological, logical, sociological, ethical, canonical, empirical, even practical. Chapters four through seven collectively establish this basis.

Before leaving this section, let me caution against overly simplistic argumentation once common hermeneutical ground is agreed upon. Imagine a fictitious conversation between two individuals who are committed to a redemptive-movement hermeneutic; one is a complementary egalitarian and the other an ultra-soft patriarchalist. After surveying the charts above on slavery and women, the egalitarian might be inclined to say that the conclusion is obvious: "Not only should

---

[17]A redemptive-movement approach to patriarchy should at least move its application for today to an ultra-soft form, if not to an egalitarian form (see chapter eight).

[18]This polarized framework breeds miscommunication in the dialogue. Patriarchal authors often think that they simply need to write arguments against an egalitarian understanding of biblical slavery and/or patriarchy as "grave social evils." For an example of this reactive posturing, see Haas, "Kingdom and Slavery," pp. 74-89; Haas, "Patriarchy as an Evil That God Tolerated: Analysis and Implications for the Authority of Scripture," *Journal of the Evangelical Theological Society* 38 (1995): 321-36.

the church community move redemptively toward ultra-soft slavery and ultra-soft patriarchy, but it also should accept the inevitability of an egalitarian position as it historically has accepted abolition." The drawback with such reasoning, however, is a major difference between the two cases. There is a marked difference between "the last thing to go" when moving from ultra-soft slavery to abolitionism and "the last thing to go" when moving from ultra-soft patriarchy to egalitarianism. With ultra-soft slavery the crux is *ownership*; with ultra-soft patriarchy the last vestige of that position before moving to egalitarianism is some kind of minimalist *hierarchy*. It is much easier to argue that no human being should ever own another human being than to argue that no human being should ever exist in a hierarchal relationship to another human being. In fact, I cannot argue the latter. There are numerous social relationships where hierarchy makes good sense.[19]

The ultra-soft patriarchalists might be inclined to think that their argument is won. Having established the acceptability of hierarchy in *some* human relationships (and in divine relationships as well), they might be lulled into a false sense of confidence. However, any confidence at this stage of the dialogue is short-lived. The only thing that an ultra-soft position has really established to this point is that hierarchy in human relationships is not inherently evil. This should silence some egalitarian rhetoric. It certainly places the discussions about moving beyond ultra-soft patriarchy into an entirely different realm than talks about moving beyond ultra-soft slavery. Yet, it does not advance a positive argument for staying with ultra-soft patriarchy instead of moving to complementary egalitarianism. All it does is shut down one particular egalitarian argument for movement. Having agreed upon a redemptive-movement approach, both sides still need to talk in terms of redemptive betters. Both sides must reflect upon whether mutual deference (complementary egalitarianism) is any better than minimalist hierarchy[20] (ultra-soft patriarchy) for the particular case of adult male/female relationships.

A balanced perspective

A third way of describing the X⟹Y⟹Z model is to talk about its balanced perspective. Before doing so, it might be helpful to flip back and look at the model in order to have a fresh picture in mind. We can talk about the model in terms of its "left side" and its "right side." The model has a left-side perspective relative to the original culture. This viewpoint captures the X⟹Y part of the diagram, but leaves out Y⟹Z. Also, the model has a right-side perspective relative to our modern culture, where it happens to reflect a better (more realized) ethic somewhere

---

[19] For starters, one can look at criterion 17.B.

[20] Or, one might propose some kind of symbolic male prominence (see chapter eight).

on a continuum toward an ultimate ethic. This captures the Y⟹Z part of the diagram, but leaves out X⟹Y.

A static hermeneutic is unbalanced inasmuch as it omits the Y⟹Z component. It incorporates only a left-side understanding of the Bible. Proponents of a static hermeneutic generally overlook the relevance of Y⟹Z in shaping the application of Scripture for today. Attempts at application by a static approach inevitably skew the process toward the ancient world. They often lack the building materials to construct a strong hermeneutical bridge to the modern world. The proponents of a static hermeneutic are satisfied with the understanding that biblical slavery was better than American slavery. They are satisfied knowing that biblical slavery was better than ancient-world slavery. On that note, they fold their hands in contentment. According to their view, as long as we bring a person's individual life and our collective social ethic up to the level of the Bible's isolated words, our job is done.

On the other hand, a secular hermeneutic is unbalanced inasmuch as it omits the X⟹Y part of the equation. Secularists and radical feminists, along with most radical reader-oriented approaches, will come at Scripture from only a right-side perspective. They too live in denial, for they disregard the redemptive power of X⟹Y. They often build a bridge to the modern world and then burn it. Or, maybe it would be more accurate to suggest that they leap to a modern approach and burn the ancient text. They speak of Scripture as "sexist" or "repressive." Once they have sufficiently deconstructed the ancient text, based on their modern perspective, they too are satisfied. They begin to devise a social portrait that is often not tied to the text at all.

A redemptive-movement hermeneutic argues for a balanced perspective—one that wrestles with left-side implications as well as right-side implications. It is *not*, as some critics have said, that Scripture is repressive or sexist regarding slaves and women. That is to talk about Scripture in a vacuum, devoid of its original setting or cultural backdrop. Such is an anachronistic reading of the text! Relative to when and where the words of Scripture were first read, they spoke redemptively to their given communities. Yet, to stay with the isolated words of the text instead of their spirit leads to an equally tragic misreading. To neglect reapplying the redemptive spirit of the text adds a debilitating impotence to a life-transforming gospel that should be unleashed within our modern world. Such an approach truncates the application process; it severely dwarfs the positive potential of Scripture.

A solid bridge between the ancient and modern world can only be constructed with a redemptive-movement hermeneutic. A static approach attempts to construct a bridge out of the isolated words of the text and so transposes ancient referents with modern ones in order to do the job. As long as the words fit, even in a loose or sloppy fashion, they think they have conquered new territory. But often their bridge does not reach the modern world when set upon many texts, and when it does reach the modern world, it is frequently rickety and weak, for they have had to be extremely selective in terms of which word-materials they have used. Alas, a secular or radical approach is no better at bridge building. They often seek to show why a bridge should not be built in the first place, for their world is much better anyway. They are so busy building their modern structures, without any bridge, that they lose biblical influence on their architecture altogether. In some sense, they have the potential for transforming a modern world, but they have no definitive direction for guiding advancements beyond the text.

A static hermeneutic lacks power and relevance, while a secular or radical hermeneutic lacks direction. Only a view that utilizes the redemptive spirit within Scripture as its core can construct an enduring connection between the ancient and modern worlds. A redemptive-spirit approach honors the words of Scripture by not forcing them into modern molds that do not fit. The words of Scripture, as read against the ancient world, provide the Christian with an understanding of its spirit and direction. The redemptive spirit generates the power to invade a new generation; the words of Scripture as read within their broader social context provide the much-needed direction for guiding the invasion of that power within today's world. Once upon modern soil, a redemptive-movement hermeneutic channels its renewing spirit into the modern world with power to change social structures and direction to guide the renewal process.

Cultural/transcultural assessment

As mentioned earlier, everything within Scripture is cultural in the sense that the Bible represents God's communication to human society through cultural forms. All communication takes on a cultural dimension. In this book, however, I am not simply interested in that broad sense of culture as human behavior expressed in social forms, customs, patterns, values, rituals, taboos, and so on. Rather, this work develops culture as an aspect of the hermeneutical process. In this sense, then, cultural analysis distinguishes between two features within the text: that which is "culturally bound" and that which is "transcultural." Here we are talking about the *application process* in hermeneutics and asking the question of what aspects of the text should we continue to practice and what aspects should we discontinue or change due to differences between cultures.

The chapters to follow should convince the reader that a redemptive-movement hermeneutic distinguishes between cultural and transcultural components within Scripture. A redemptive-movement hermeneutic is committed to the rigorous and methodical pursuit of assessing what elements within Scripture fall into the one category or the other. A redemptive-spirit approach does not want to make that which is truly transcultural in Scripture into something cultural; nor does it want to grant that which is truly cultural a transcultural status. Good application of the ancient text demands that the Christian community wrestle with this kind of assessment.

I am not suggesting that the alternative approaches do not distinguish between cultural and transcultural components within Scripture. One finds proponents of a static hermeneutic and a radical feminist or radical reader-oriented hermeneutic making assessments of a cultural/transcultural nature. What I would like to point out here are simply tendencies or dispositions in their approach. Those with a radical agenda often point to several cultural items within Scripture, as if by the very existence of these examples the reader should accept anything else they deem as cultural to be an accurate assessment.[21] Their methodology for cultural analysis is ad hoc at best and their logic is often strained. Just because *some* things in Scripture are cultural, that does not mean that *everything* in Scripture is cultural.

Proponents of a static hermeneutic are not vulnerable to the debilitating tendencies of a radical hermeneutic. However, in their attempts to preserve that which is transcultural in Scripture, they are often victimized by extremes in the opposite direction. They frequently assume that just because *some* things in the Bible are transcultural, that *everything* in the Bible is transcultural. While they do not invoke this fallacy on the Bible as a whole, they often apply it to portions of the biblical text. A classic case surfaces in their treatment of the original creation material. Invariably they quote Jesus' statement about the creation perspective on marriage as having more weight than Moses' divorce legislation.[22] I agree with their assessment to this point.[23] However, they go on from there to suggest that the garden therefore provides us with a paradigm of that which is ongoing and transcultural. Here is where their reasoning is no better than that of a radical hermeneutic, only it betrays a weakness in the opposite direction. They falla-

---

[21]E.g., Letha D. Scanzoni and Virginia R. Mollenkott, *Is the Homosexual My Neighbor? A Positive Christian Response* (San Francisco: HarperCollins, 1994), p. 65; Richard Cleaver, *Know My Name: A Gay Liberation Theology* (Louisville: Westminster John Knox, 1995), pp. 29-34; Keith Hartman, *Congregations in Conflict: The Battle over Homosexuality* (New Brunswick, N.J.: Rutgers University Press, 1996), p. 43. Finding something cultural in Scripture does not automatically demonstrate that other matters are cultural. One cannot simply jump from ceremonial purity texts, food laws, etc. to the homosexuality texts in order to establish their cultural status. A clearly articulated logic must be used in moving between examples.

[22]E.g., Terrance Tiessen, "Toward a Hermeneutic for Discerning Universal Moral Absolutes," *JETS* 36 (1993): 194-97; William W. Klein, Craig L. Blomberg and Robert L. Hubbard, Jr. *Introduction to Biblical Interpretation* (Vancouver: Word, 1993), p. 417; Daniel G. Lundy, "A Hermeneutical Framework for the Role of Women," *Baptist Review of Theology* 2 (1992): 63; Bruce K. Waltke, "The Role of Women in the Bible," *Crux* 31 (1995): 29-30.

[23]Even a static hermeneutic is forced to accept a multilevel ethic as long as subsequent Scripture explicitly points out the levels!

ciously assume that everything within the creation material is transcultural just because some things within the creation material are transcultural. As will be explained below, however, this assumption is fraught with problems. There are numerous items within the creation material that should be understood as cultural (see criterion 6.B.1-10).

There is a greater potential for faulty thinking on either extreme of the hermeneutical spectrum in the process of cultural/transcultural assessment. I am not suggesting that a redemptive-movement hermeneutic is somehow impervious to faulty logic. Nor am I saying that my own assessment of that which is cultural or transcultural is perfect. I have written a final chapter titled "What If I Am Wrong?" in order to reflect upon the possibility of error. What I am saying, however, is that those who embrace a redemptive hermeneutic, whether egalitarian or patriarchal, are less likely to fall into a "one sample proves all" kind of thinking that often plagues both a static and a radical hermeneutic.

The spirit of a text

The final and most important characteristic of a redemptive-movement hermeneutic is its focus on the spirit of a text. As mentioned earlier, the coinage "redemptive-movement hermeneutic" is derived from a concern that Christians apply the *redemptive spirit* within Scripture, not merely, or even primarily, its isolated words. Finding the underlying spirit of a text is a delicate matter. It is not as direct or explicit as reading the words on the page. In order to grasp the spirit of a text, the interpreter must listen for how the text sounds within its various social contexts. Two life settings are crucial: the broader, foreign ancient Near Eastern and Greco-Roman (ANE/GR) social context and the immediate, domestic Israelite/church setting. One must ask, what change/improvement is the text making in the lives of people in the covenant community? And, how does the text influence the larger ANE/GR world? Through reflecting upon these social-setting questions the modern reader will begin to sense the redemptive spirit of the text. Also, a third setting permits one another way of discovering the redemptive spirit, namely, the canonical movement across various biblical epochs. The movement between the Old and New Testaments is perhaps the most familiar epochal shift. All three ways of measuring movement—foreign, domestic and canonical—will be developed below (see criterion 1).

The *redemptive spirit* underlying a text should be distinguished from what is commonly known as the *principle* underlying a text. Permit me a quick preamble comment before making the point of distinction. The principle underlying a text relates to the degree of abstraction needed to cross between two worlds in the application process. When discovering the underlying principle, some refer to the helpful concept of a "ladder of abstraction":[24] along a continuum highly abstracted ideas are found at the top of the ladder, while more concrete expressions are found at the bottom. One could "principle-ize" *any* text with the highest level of abstraction, "Glorify God." Yet, how high one climbs on the ladder of abstraction to form a principle depends upon the *similarities* and the *differences* between the ancient and modern worlds. Differences push one up the ladder; similarities push one down.

Having introduced the ladder of abstraction, now we may distinguish between *redemptive spirit* and *principle*. Using an analogy, one might compare the principle to the sails on a boat, which can be raised or lowered on the mast (the mast being the ladder of abstraction). The redemptive spirit, however, is another matter—it is more like the wind that catches the sail to move the boat forward. When applying the slavery texts to modern employment, a static hermeneutic will generally move up the ladder of abstraction to the principle "submit to/obey those in authority within the workplace," thinking that this sufficiently covers both worlds. The liability with this approach lies both at the level of principle and redemptive spirit. With respect to principle, the static approach fails to push high enough on the ladder of abstraction to account for the difference between ownership (their world) and contractual relationships (our world). The submit/obey language should be dropped in our application. The principle should be one of honoring God in the way one relates to authority/management in the workplace and the contemporary application in the modern world should construct an imperative along the following lines: Fulfill the terms of your contract to the best of your ability, that is, in a manner that glorifies God and brings unbelievers closer to the kingdom.

With respect to redemptive spirit, the static approach often fails to let the winds of Scripture advance its slavery portrait. Such an approach stifles an absolutely crucial component of meaning from the slavery texts for our generation. Christians ought to welcome the biblical spirit "blowing on the sails" of our contemporary setting with movement-type ideas. The underlying spirit/movement of the slavery texts holds multifaceted implications for our modern work world. It certainly includes an employee at times choosing to go beyond what the contract calls for. It also takes into consideration the incredible movement of Scripture, compared to the ancient world, in that it betters the working conditions and treatment of slaves. This aspect of redemptive spirit eventually leads to the abolition

---

[24]For a visual illustration and explanation of the ladder of abstraction, see criterion 17.A. I am not entirely sure from where I got the "ladder of abstraction" idea. I thought it came from Haddon W. Robinson, *Biblical Preaching* (Grand Rapids, Mich: Baker, 1980), but I could only find a discussion of "principle" in his book. For a similar development of "principle" in the application process, see William W. Klein, Craig L. Blomberg and Robert L. Hubbard Jr., *Introduction to Biblical Interpretation* (Dallas: Word, 1993), 401-26.

of slavery altogether. Yet, when reapplied in our modern context, the same biblical spirit voices a concern for improving the plight of the modern worker. It
quickly qualifies any unreasonable fulfillment of managerially "stretched" contractual obligations, unsafe working conditions, abusive treatment of employees,
and so on. On the other hand, it passionately, not reluctantly, pursues the positive
well-being of all within the organization, whether management, laborer or owner.
It speaks to issues such as benefits, a family-supportive environment, people-first
values and meaningful motivation, as well as to bottom-line issues.

On the surface a static hermeneutic appears to be more faithful to the words of
Scripture—due to a focus on its *isolated* words—than a redemptive-movement
hermeneutic. Proponents of a static hermeneutic can point to the actual words on
the page and say that, based upon those words, a modern employee needs to submit and obey. They can easily charge a redemptive-movement hermeneutic with
overlooking these words of Scripture. However, what should be obvious from the
grotesque applications that would flow from a consistent use of a static hermeneutic (see examples cited in the "redemptive movement" section above [see pp.
36-37) is that such an approach must pick and choose which words it seeks to apply. Also, if all of the slavery and women examples cited below (criteria 11 and
18) are any indication of hermeneutical process, then a static hermeneutic also
overlooks entire passages of Scripture. A number of passages never enter into the
discourse of those developing patriarchy through a static model. Those authors
who relentlessly cling to a static hermeneutic simply do not publish scholarly discussion on these painful passages. These troublesome texts are left completely
untouched by biblical-slavery advocates and by most patriarchy proponents. In
this respect, a static hermeneutic not only steers clear of certain words found in
Scripture, it also selectively disregards entire passages of the text.[25] One must
ask, then, which hermeneutic is actually more faithful to the words of Scripture.
Surface perceptions are not always an accurate reflection of reality.

A Theological Rationale

We now turn our attention to a theological rationale for a redemptive-movement
hermeneutic. In some respects, the characteristics of a redemptive-movement
hermeneutic, outlined above, provide a philosophical rationale for the approach
to Scripture found in this book. A static hermeneutic does not furnish an adequate

---

[25]For a typical example, see Haas, "Kingdom and Slavery," 74-89. Haas develops a slavery ethic without any reference to Old Testament texts (a significant part of God's unfolding kingdom) and without any integration of the most difficult aspects within the New Testament texts. On these grounds
alone, his social-ethic understanding of slavery is untenable. For a similar treatment of biblical patriarchy, see Haas, "Patriarchy as an Evil That God Tolerated," pp. 321-36.

model for applying Scripture. Only a redemptive-movement hermeneutic places sufficient emphasis on the spirit of a text, as that text is read against its broader cultural milieu. However, aside from the philosophical issues, a theological framework should motivate Christians to adopt a redemptive-movement hermeneutic. The theological basis for a redemptive-movement hermeneutic is rooted in two crucial considerations: the authority of Scripture and the wisdom of God.

The authority of Scripture

Church creeds have long declared that Scripture provides the authoritative basis for Christian life and faith. To this sacred authority I am deeply committed. Nevertheless, I must confess that, as I have grown in my understanding of what is actually contained within the pages of Scripture, I have had to rethink my hermeneutic. I have had to rethink my hermeneutic in order to retain my commitment to the authority of Scripture! You might say that this is something of a backwards process. I would not disagree; I am simply sketching the journey in my own life, as it happened to unfold.

Without a redemptive-movement hermeneutic the authority of Scripture is diminished. Let me describe how the damage takes place in very tangible terms. As Christians and non-Christians alike read the pages of Scripture, they encounter troublesome texts that record horrific acts blessed by God and legislation that is anything but perfect. For a sampling I invite my readers to visit the examples given in criteria 11 and 18. The scope of these examples is limited to the slavery and women texts in the Bible. But they are sufficient enough to make my case.

These troublesome texts often cause a journey of faith. For some Christians these texts lead to a complete crisis of faith. They abandon the God of the Bible altogether. For secularists, these texts provide clear proof that a God of transcendent justice did not write the Bible.[26] In order to retain one's faith in the inspiration and authority of Scripture, we ultimately must come to grips with certain "repugnant monuments" in the museum of patriarchy and "unpleasant pictures" in the halls of slavery. Without placing certain components within these texts into a kind of culture-component classification, many of us would struggle immensely in our Judeo-Christian faith. Many people find these texts a hindrance in coming to faith at all; while others, who have not encountered a redemptive-movement hermeneutic, struggle with retaining their faith.

A static hermeneutic tends to sweep many of these ugly texts under the carpet.[27]

---

[26]E.g., Paul Kurtz, *Forbidden Fruit: The Ethics of Humanism* (Buffalo, N.Y.: Prometheus, 1988), pp. 27-44.

[27]For a classic example of developing a social ethic related to slavery from a highly selective number of passages, see Haas, "Kingdom and Slavery," pp. 74-89. In a similar fashion, typical static-hermeneutic assessments of the women's issue selectively work with five or six biblical texts.

It simply cannot provide credible answers for the inquisitive seeker, the critical secularist or the troubled Christian. I am not suggesting that we swing to a radical feminist or a radical reader-oriented approach. Such approaches often deal with these texts by sweeping them away completely. Only a redemptive-movement hermeneutic deals adequately with these texts. It seeks to highlight their underlying spirit within the ancient social context and to harness that same spirit in the contemporary application process, while not minimizing the question of where a Christian ethic really ought to be; it often ought to reflect an ethic well beyond that which is depicted in an isolated understanding of the Bible's words.[28] This approach permits the Christian to answer the tough questions with integrity and in a way that preserves sacred tradition. In fact, a redemptive-movement hermeneutic highlights a wonderful blend of realism and idealism within Scripture. The Christian who embraces a redemptive-spirit approach cannot help but be profoundly influenced by the resilient character of the ancient text as it continues to speak to our modern world.

The wisdom of God

Along with the authority of Scripture, the wisdom of God is probably the most significant theological category for understanding how a redemptive-movement hermeneutic represents the best possible approach to Scripture. The Bible frequently proclaims that the God we worship is an all-wise, all-knowing God (e.g., Ps 111:10; Jer 10:12; Rom 11:33; 1 Cor 1:18-25). As Christians we often take this truth about God for granted and appreciate God's wisdom only at an abstract level. However, as we begin to probe Scripture from the vantage point of a redemptive-movement hermeneutic, we discover inductively the validity of its deductive statements about God's wisdom. Through a redemptive-movement reading of the Bible, we encounter a God of profound wisdom.

When faced with the evidence in support of a redemptive-movement hermeneutic within Scripture, my students will sometimes ask me why God would choose to communicate his will to humanity in this fashion. The question is an excellent one. Why does God convey his message in a way that reflects a less-than-ultimate ethic, that gathers together cultural and transcultural components, that evidences an underlying redemptive spirit and some movement in a positive direction, yet often permits its words to stop short of completely fulfilling such a spirit? Why did God not simply give us a clearly laid out blueprint for an ultimate-ethic, utopia-like society? How could a God of absolute justice not give us a revelation containing absolute justice on every page? How could a God of infinite

---

[28]By "isolated words" I mean an understanding of the words of the Bible that fails to draw upon the foreign, domestic and canonical contexts in order to discover the "spirit" component of meaning.

love decide to limit the degree of love shown in aspects of his communication to humanity for shaping their behavior? The biblical answer to all of these questions is basically the same. The answer lies in understanding divine wisdom. God demonstrates profound insight into who we are, into the world in which we live and into what would work best for moving our lives toward a redemptive goal.

The collective answer lies in the wisdom of God. However, the magnificence of God's wisdom may be illustrated from many different perspectives. While I will discuss a variety of reasons for why God communicated through Scripture in this redemptive-spirit approach, they all converge as various multifaceted dimensions of his wisdom. The God who calls us to skillful and productive lives demonstrates in his own course of action an amazing capacity for the complex task of formulating an ethic for human relationships. In each rationale developed below, we see a God whose transcendent nature does not keep him from intimately touching his beloved creation.

Pastoral component. As God joins with the human author in the formation of Scripture, his wisdom is magnificently demonstrated within the pastoral dimension of the text. Both the divine and human authors function together in a gentle, pastoral relationship to the covenant community. Biblical texts often represent pastoral letters, written with the tenderness of a pastor's heart. Their words are designed to "stretch" the covenant people as far as they could go, like an elastic band, but not to cause them to "snap." Change is always difficult. People do not alter their social patterns easily. God brings his people along in ways that were feasible adaptations and in ways that recognize the nature of humanity.

A good example of this pastoral feature is found in 1 Corinthians 7, a chapter that might be entitled, "Sex Counseling for Ascetics." In the previous chapter, Paul formulated a sexual ethic for those in his congregation who thought sex was as morally neutral as eating food. Their slogan was roughly, "If you are hungry, fix yourself a sandwich!"[29] They endorsed a libertine view of sex. Now, in chapter seven Paul addresses the other extreme within the church, those who thought that sex was inherently evil. Their slogan concerning sex even for married couples was, "Never touch the stuff!"[30] Therefore, 1 Corinthians 7 does not represent a sexual ethic for happy, balanced couples. Healthy, balanced couples do not need the kind of argumentation Paul develops in 1 Corinthians in order to engage in sexual intercourse. The Song of Solomon represents a much better motivational framework than 1 Corinthians 7 for those with a healthy perspective on sex. The

---

[29]1 Cor 6:13 contains the slogan used by the sexual-freedom group at Corinth, "Food is for the stomach and the stomach is for food."

[30]1 Cor 7:1 literally reads, "It is good for a man not to touch [have sexual intercourse with] a woman." This statement embodies the ascetic slogan, which Paul then addresses in the rest of the chapter.

Song of Solomon portrays a positive and passionate celebration of sex within marriage; 1 Corinthians 7 provides a tightly reasoned argumentation for continuing intercourse in marriage for couples who have a negative view of sex.

It is important to recognize the pastoral approach within 1 Corinthians 7. In no way does Paul completely rip his ascetic readers out of their moorings and drag them all the way to a balanced sexual ethic. Such an action on the part of Paul could well have created an overreaction within this segment of the community. Rather than bringing them to a completely central, healthy sexual ethic, he simply coaxes them back from the edge of this danger. As a good pastor, he gently tugs at his audience in order to draw them away from the most destructive components of an ascetic philosophy. He tells those who are married to keep having sexual intercourse, because it is their marital duty and because of the dangers of prolonged abstinence. His words for motivating sex within marriage are hardly appropriate for couples that enjoy having sex as a celebration of God's creative goodness and their covenant partnership! But they are words that help Christians with strong ascetic leanings to moderate their extremes. In the rest of the chapter, the same kind of pastoral moderation shapes the apostle's instructions to those contemplating divorce and to virgins. Paul gently moves them away from the most harmful implications of an ascetic view of sex. However, he does not come close to sketching an ultimate ethic on sexuality. Unfortunately, many modern Christians read Scripture without understanding that its words are often shaped by the heartfelt tensions of pastoral ministry. The Spirit of God and the human authors provide pastoral instruction for their flock, which gently moves them along in a good direction.

Pastors should especially recognize this pastoral component within Scripture. In moving people toward a particular goal, wise pastors will gently and lovingly shepherd their people along at a pace that they can handle. A well-seasoned pastor understands that one cannot change another person's worldview overnight. One cannot change entrenched social patterns on the spot. Only in matters where the flock is wandering perilously close to the edge or where in some cases they have actually gone over the edge do the instructions of Scripture become firm or sharp or sound alarmist. Notice the distinct change in Paul's tone of voice between chapters six and seven of 1 Corinthians.[31] Only in chapter six, where the is-

---

[31]Paul curbs the extremes of both the sexual-license group (1 Corinthians 6) and the sexual-ascetic group (1 Corinthians 7). However, the extreme and immediate dangers for the license group necessitate a far more harsh and direct interaction. His counsel of the ascetics could be much softer. Even if the Corinthian ascetics never accepted a positive sexual ethic like that conveyed in the Song of Solomon (which Paul clearly does not attempt to articulate here), the apostle's slight modification of their thinking at least guards them from the most immediate dangers. It gently leads a confused wing of the Corinthian church in the right direction, but does not take them as far as a fully developed sexual ethic would go.

sue is urgent, does Paul get emotionally heated in his instructions; in chapter seven the apostle returns to his pastoral calm. Generally, pastors lead their people in soothing, quiet ways along a path toward where they ought to be. Many portions of Scripture might be classified as gentle nudges from God, the all-wise, transcendent pastor, as he quietly urges us along a redemptive path. But, it is a path, not a period. At times we discover that a fair bit of trail lies ahead of us. Scripture provides the direction toward the divine destination, but its literal, isolated words are not always the destination itself. Sometimes God's instructions are simply designed to get his flock moving. Rather than laying out the entire journey, some texts simply outline the first major steps along with way.

Pedagogical component. Beyond its pastoral brilliance, the wisdom of God shines through the pedagogical dimension of Scripture. God is not only an excellent pastor; he is the best of teachers. A good teacher is aware of the way to move students ahead in the learning process. As one of my mentors used to say to me, "You don't back the truck up and dump it all at once!" A good professor takes his class through progressive stages of learning, starting with the basic building blocks and then moving on to more refinement. The nature of teaching and communication is such that it is often unwise to reveal the whole picture at once. It simply will not be seen or understood, until the more fundamental components are securely in place. Scripture, as with a good teaching methodology, is designed to take people from where they are (the known) and help them move to a foreseeable future (the unknown) that has enough continuity with the present so that they can actually find their way into the preferred future. The basic building blocks are laid within Scripture, especially as its words give witness to the underlying redemptive spirit. But Scripture does not provide complete ideological refinement for every detail within the teaching manual.

With each generation, in a sense God has had to start over in moving a new group of people toward his redemptive goals. The author of Hebrews laments that many in his congregation are still struggling with the basics of their Christian faith and are slow to learn (Heb 5:11—6:3). From an educational perspective, communication takes on a rather complex configuration. The level at which a teacher chooses to teach is directly related to the level of his or her audience. In turn, the receptive level of an audience depends on a host of considerations: age, maturity, character, motivation, aptitude, previous formal education, resources to accomplish learning, and so on.

As the divine teacher instructs his people, God surely reflects upon the needs of his students. Many of the audience considerations mentioned above would have set the subject development at a basic level. The Bible may be cherished and diligently studied by theologians, but it was written for the community of faith as a whole. Its authors intend for their literature to be read orally before an eclectic gathering of the covenant people. Consequently, the educational receptivity of the audience affected the level at which the human and divine instructors could teach. This pedagogical shaping of sacred tradition, while not directly addressed by the writers of Scripture, is at least suggested in several ways. For one thing, the biblical authors are often distressed over the learning stage or level of their audience. The author of Hebrews is not alone in this lament (1 Cor 3:1-2; cf. Mt 13:11-17). Another clue that pedagogical levels impacted the formation of the biblical message is found in the higher expectations God has for those who teach Scripture within the community. Both the Old and New Testaments contain something of a heightened expectation for priests, high priests, prophets, elders, deacons, and so on (e.g., 1 Tim 3:1-13; Tit 1:6-9). Their level of learning and their position place them in a special category. Teachers within the covenant community are seen as bearing a greater responsibility for their actions (Jas 3:1; Lk 20:45-47).

Good teachers, then, set the level of the instructional material at the level of their students. A lower level of delivery might encompass the basics, but it will often not have the advantage of development or refinement that one might like. In one respect, the Bible represents a message and ethic designed to speak to the majority of people in the covenant community. Due to the nature of this wider audience, it often reflects entry-level discussions about its subject material. In this respect, the pedagogical component within Scripture underscores the sensitive teaching abilities of God and of the human authors as they seek to instruct the covenant people.

Fallen humanity, creation and kingdom components. Jesus' development of a multilevel ethic in Matthew 19 provides helpful insight into at least three factors that influence the formulation of the biblical message: the hardness of people's hearts, creative expectations and kingdom service. Each of these components makes it possible to find a wide variety of theological reflection upon marital, divorce and single lifestyles within Scripture. Through the interface of these divergent vantage points or horizons, as well as other factors discussed in this section, one will discover quite a range of redemptive betters within the biblical text. It is also possible to create an even wider range of redemptive possibilities through logical and theological reflection. Since we have already examined Matthew 19 along these lines, a further example might be more helpful to ponder.

The use of a redemptive-movement hermeneutic may also be seen in Jesus' approach to Scripture in Matthew 5. Here Jesus interacts with a cluster of Old Testament texts concerning murder, adultery, divorce, oaths, eye-for-an-eye retaliation and loving one's neighbor. In each case he quotes the biblical tradition, "It has been said . . ." and then moves to what he understands as a redemptive better, "But I tell you . . ." The contrast is not between Jesus' teaching and the Jewish

Scriptures, as if to imply that Jesus wants to abandon sacred tradition. Only a moment earlier within the same sermon, Jesus had established the unshakable validity of the Old Testament law (Mt 5:17-20). Some of the disjunction may well be due to the new era ushering in a different type of law. As a new Moses, Jesus leads his community to a heightened ethic beyond their old law code.[32] Even so, the text at least affirms a multilevel ethic in Scripture, which advances one dimension of my thesis. However, much of the contrast also seems to be rooted in a different approach to Scripture, a different way of applying the Old Testament text, a strikingly different hermeneutic. The Pharisees, with whom Jesus often interacts (cf. Mt 23:1-39) are more interested in an externalistic understanding of the Hebrew Bible, one which gravitates toward fulfilling only the isolated words of the text. On the other hand, Jesus' approach to Scripture goes beyond focusing on its isolated words to meditate deeply upon its underlying spirit. With great ease, Jesus captures the spirit of the Old Testament text and so engages his audience in specific ways of "improving upon" the words of their sacred tradition.[33] Along with an emphasis on internal application, he teaches them a redemptive-spirit approach to reading the Bible.

Together, Matthew 5 and 19 highlight a variety of factors that shaped the original composition of Scripture. Within the Matthew 19 text alone, we discover the complexity of thinking about marriage from the diverse perspectives of a fallen world, a creation ideal, and a kingdom ideal. If these factors influenced the encoding of biblical words, then surely they should influence our decoding of what the text should mean for our lives. It should unlock an application-type decoding of its message that causes us to ponder a text far beyond a surface reading. As with Jesus, modern Christians should pursue an understanding of God's revelation that courageously applies its spirit beyond the confines of its isolated words. In so doing, we acknowledge a magnificent component of God's wisdom—a revelation of his will in a manner that reflects the complexity of the different world(s) we live in.

Using examples from Matthew 5 and 19 may be unfairly charged, since Jesus pits his approach to the Old Testament against that of the Pharisees. I am reluc-

---

[32]See Robert A. Guelich, *The Sermon on the Mount: A Foundation for Understanding* (Waco, Tex.: Word, 1982), pp. 175-271.

[33]On the discussion of the oaths, Carson notes, "It must be frankly admitted that here Jesus formally contravenes Old Testament law: what it permits or commands (Deut 6:13), he forbids. But if his interpretation of the direction in which the law points is authoritative, then his teaching fulfills it." See D. A. Carson, "Matthew," in *The Expositor's Bible Commentary*, ed. Frank E. Gaebelein (Grand Rapids, Mich.: Zondervan, 1984), 8:154. While one might want to qualify or soften Carson's comment about Jesus "forbidding" oaths (we must acknowledge the hyperbolic nature of the oath prohibition and of numerous other rhetorically driven statements within the sermon), his assessment about direction and fulfillment of the Old Testament law through Jesus' new law is quite appropriate.

tant to use these examples, as within Christian tradition the Pharisees are generally portrayed in a negative way. I am not trying to transfer everything that was true about the Pharisees and paint modern proponents of a static hermeneutic in that light. The one and only point of comparison is their approach to applying Scripture in contrast to Jesus' approach: Jesus emphasized the underlying spirit, while the Pharisees became mired in the isolated words of the text.

Evangelistic component. At least from God's perspective, Christians live within a world that is dominated by an evangelistic mission. God has a tremendous passion for a ministry of reconciliation to pervade the lives of his people as they interact with the people of this world. Quite often the instructions of Scripture do not reflect an ultimate ethic simply because they are absorbed with the greater good of facilitating the mission (see criterion 4). The accomplishment of Christian mission frequently calls upon believers to sacrifice their personal best for the sake of winning others. Or, it assumes the status quo in many areas of life, with only modest improvements, in order to place its central focus on the mission. Understanding these mission-oriented texts to present "what ought to be" in sociological structures overlooks the purpose of the biblical text and the people it addresses. It is a text with a mission, addressing a people with a mission.

Of all people, missionaries should be able to appreciate the shaping of Scripture by its orientation toward missions. An experienced missionary can quickly size up what aspects of social reform in a given culture require immediate attention, as opposed to ones that have to wait. There is a similar sense of mission priority within the Bible. Along these lines, the household codes in the New Testament instruct Christians to make their lifestyle evangelistically winsome to unbelievers. The reform within these codes was enough to better existing sociological structures, but not so radical that it would jeopardize other aspects of Christian mission or overtly threaten governmental structures. Anyone who has spent time on the mission field knows these kinds of social tensions all too well. With the passion and discernment of a veteran missionary, God instructs his people toward a ministry of reconciliation which threads its way through a labyrinth of mission-related issues. At times the question of social reform is met head-on in Scripture, especially when reform is needed in order to advance the gospel (e.g., helping the poor or removing Jew/Gentile inequality). At other times, however, social reform is only addressed in quiet ways through the tacit and subtle undercurrents of the biblical message, so that the core mission remains intact.

Embedded-values component. At the heart of a redemptive-movement hermeneutic lies the conviction that engaging in social ethics is a complex process. Life is not simple. Many times the aspects of a less redemptive framework have sustained within them other good values. For example, slavery functioned as something of a social welfare net in ancient cultures. Particularly the one form of debt slavery in Israel provided a way of assisting those who were in great financial need. It served a good and noble purpose. Also, the assumption within the biblical texts that the male owned the female(s) helped support the good value of gender differentiation. Gender differentiation and helping the poor are good things. However, a redemptive-movement hermeneutic argues that, if at all possible, these good values need to be sustained through a non-embedded framework. In other words, because the biblical framework of male ownership of the female upheld a good value of gender distinction and differentiation, it was done at the sacrifice of other values. A celebration of gender differences today needs to be supported through more suitable means.

Ancient world components. Under the broad heading of ancient world components I will gather together a variety of social-context factors that influenced the way God and the human authors shaped the text. The ancient world in its agricultural focus, monarchical structures, extended families, survival issues, and so on, contributes significantly to the formation of Scripture within a redemptive grid. Many things true of the ancient world are simply not a part of our modern world. One would be hard pressed to place the majority of these social-context components into either a strictly positive or a strictly negative category. For instance, our study of primogeniture (firstborn customs) in a later chapter will demonstrate just how dominant this social pattern was in the ancient world and within Scripture. Yet, we will discover something of even greater significance. The reason we do not practice primogeniture today is because our modern world no longer has the same physical/social components that produced that kind of thinking in the ancient world (see criterion 7.B–C.2). In other words, primogeniture is a highly culture-bound type of custom. Due to the nature of the ancient world, the practice of primogeniture was actually a good practice. It was built around issues of survival, agriculture, land, inheritance, lineage, large families, and so on. In such a milieu, primogeniture had certain strengths. It made a valuable contribution. In our modern context, however, such thinking and practices represent a liability because the social-context factors that drove primogeniture in the ancient culture are no longer present today. We must change our inheritance and sibling-dominance patterns in order to function redemptively in a culture where the mitigating factors have changed. The ancient-world rationale no longer exists in our modern world (see criterion 7.C.2 and criterion 17). A new set of social-context factors endorses sibling equality.

Social-science component. An all-wise God sometimes conveys his revelation with an element of accommodation. His communication does not unveil the crucial distinction between relative and absolute social-scientific data.[34] A statement within Scripture could be made from an absolute social-science perspective just as easily as it could from a relative social-science perspective. We do not find footnotes in the text explaining which one is the case in any particular verse. As a wise father, God sometimes talks to his children in language, perception and reality that correspond with the world they actually see and experience. Many statements within Scripture reflect this type of cultural-component social perspective.

For example, as people developed an understanding of gender in the ancient world, their social environment profoundly shaped their concept of women. God works within that framework of a cultural-component social reality without informing people of Copernicus-type discoveries way ahead of their time. Only in years to come do we discover that some women, as do some men, make good warriors. Only centuries later do we find out that men can be infertile as well as women and that the seed-garden paradigm for human conception, while reflecting delightful creative imagery, is probably not the best way of depicting the process.[35] Only many generations after the text do we discover that what made women more easily deceived than men were cultural, not transcultural, factors. Having made this discovery and with the assistance of time eroding away these cultural factors, we are now able to apply the concerns of texts like 1 Timothy 2:14 to both genders, not simply to one; those who lead and teach in the community of faith, whether men or women, should be individuals who are not easily deceived.

Idealism-versus-realism component. The last component brings into focus perhaps the broadest factor that appears to have played a formative role in the shaping of Scripture, namely, the tension between idealism and realism. Most of our lives echo something of the tension between these two components. So the idealism/realism tension within Scripture should at least be a readily understandable concept. I would argue that a redemptive-movement reading and application of Scripture sheds helpful light on these two components within the text, and subsequently on the extraordinary abilities of the author(s) behind the text.

With incredible wisdom God shaped the product of Scripture so that its final composition held these two aspects, idealism and realism, in a delicate balance. At times our lives can swing from one extreme to the other. We all know certain people who are characterized by one extreme or the other. A vision of extreme idealism, apart from any realism, often leads to disillusionment and discouragement. It tends to produce cynicism. On the other hand, realism without idealism

---

[34]See criterion 18.A for definitions.

[35]The woman contributes far more to the emerging infant than what people had initially thought; the ancient view of reproduction and fertility fed into a culture-based rationale for patriarchy.

becomes mired in the present, or worse yet, it enshrines the past and has no future. It tends to breed complacency. Realism is safe, but it does not go anywhere. It fails to make our world into a better place to live. Through a redemptive-movement hermeneutic one discovers a wonderful blend of realism and idealism within sacred Scripture. The underlying spirit of the text reflects its idealism, whereas the isolated words of the text often express its realism.

Summary. After considering the thoughtful blending together of all of the above components in the composition of Scripture, one cannot help but stand in awe of the God who orchestrated such a process. He is the all-wise God. A redemptive-movement reading of the Bible brings us face to face with the profound wisdom of our God. In the formation of the sacred text, God's wisdom is evident from a variety of perspectives. The complexity of the biblical tradition becomes apparent as we ponder the way in which God communicates his will to us. Alongside the human authors, God functions as a seasoned pastor who gently shepherds his flock, as a skilled teacher who instructs his pupils in ways that they can learn the best, as the immanent-transcendent One who speaks within a fallen world and yet draws us to other worlds beyond this one, as an experienced missionary who infuses our lives with passion for the lost, as an informed sociologist who knows completely the makeup our social worlds, as a father who lovingly talks to his children in ways that they can understand and as a leader who wrestles to find the delicate balance between realism and idealism.

A Closing Thought

The essence of a redemptive-movement hermeneutic will unfold further in the cultural/transcultural analysis that lies ahead. I hope that this chapter on hermeneutics, along with the analysis to follow, will make a convincing case for understanding the Bible from a redemptive-spirit framework. If this is so, then it is my earnest desire that this approach will instill a new or renewed sense of the beauty of the text. Understanding the Bible from a redemptive-movement viewpoint should add a wondrous and resilient component to the way in which its pages, our daily bread, continue to shape our lives. Only a redemptive-movement reading engages the application process with sufficient power and direction. Along these lines, my ultimate hope and prayer is that the God of the text will loom much larger in our thinking after we traverse these paths. Approaching the text from a redemptive-movement viewpoint ultimately leads us to a God who is incredible and majestic in wisdom. Such a God is worthy of our trust and adoration.

3

CULTURAL/TRANSCULTURAL ANALYSIS

A Road Map

Doing cultural analysis is not easy. At the very outset, I will openly admit that there are no clearly established rules. Compared to other areas of hermeneutics, this is a severely underdeveloped discipline. So I would caution my reader not to expect a single, simple, rule-of-thumb approach to discovering what is cultural and what is not. The criteria discussed herein have been used by Christians for centuries, but in a haphazard way so that the Christian community has often been oblivious to the fact that they were actually doing cultural analysis. For most individuals who have received formal theological education today, the training they received in *exegesis* is often long and extensive, especially for those entering the pastoral field. By comparison, however, training in *application* is given little or no rigorous focus. This creates an unhealthy imbalance and unwittingly leaves the impression that exegesis itself yields application. Hopefully this work contributes in some small measure to restoring a greater emphasis on application. What I have attempted to do in this book is to catalogue various criteria for assessing cultural and transcultural aspects within Scripture. These are systematically applied in an illustrative manner to two debated issues in the Christian community. Yet, since most of the criteria are generic, they should enhance the application process for many other issues.

While cultural/transcultural analysis will never yield 100 percent certainty, it does produce something of a cumulative effect by coming at the question from as

many different angles as possible. Also, the process itself is not without a logical
and commonsense foundation. As for the broadest methodology, it seems reasonable to include three steps in our quest:

1. Develop various rationale that *appear* to indicate that a component of a text/
teaching is culturally relative.

2. Develop various rationale that *appear* to indicate that a component of a text/
teaching is transculturally binding.

3. Weigh the relative strengths of these two streams of data.

Within each criterion the process is fairly straightforward. Whenever possible,
each criterion will be derived from neutral examples before dealing with the
more sensitive issues of women and homosexuals. The book's title *Slaves,
Women & Homosexuals* reflects the idea that in cultural/transcultural analysis the
Christian community needs to move from neutral examples, like slavery, to the
debated issues. By "neutral" examples, I do not mean that absolutely no one debates these examples. Rather, they are examples that have already been more
widely accepted by the church to this point. Also, within each criterion some reflective evaluation of the criterion will be provided. An overview of the procedure
within each criterion is as follows:

1. State the criterion.

2. Establish the criterion from "neutral"[1] examples.

3. Apply the criterion to the women's issue.

4. Apply the criterion to the homosexual issue.

5. Evaluate the criterion.

6. Summarize.

The next four chapters develop eighteen cultural/transcultural criteria along
the lines of this methodology. The eighteen criteria are categorized most broadly
according to ones that utilize evidence within Scripture (intrascriptural [1-16])
and those that draw upon evidence that is beyond the realm of Scripture (extra-
scriptural [17-18]). Aside from this broad grouping, the various criteria are di-
vided further into three subcategories: "persuasive," "moderately persuasive" and
"inconclusive." These three subcategories do not rate the *quality* of the criterion
itself—an "inconclusive" criterion may be an excellent criterion for cultural/tran-
scultural analysis. Rather, they tell the story in terms of the *outcome* of each criterion as it contributes to the issue being investigated.

While the book investigates two debated issues (gender roles and homosexual-

---

[1]By "neutral" examples I mean examples that are not a part of our two central issues. Also, these
examples have a generally accepted status as either cultural or transcultural by the Christian community.

ity), a grouping of the eighteen criteria according to "outcome" or "findings" could logically reflect only *one* of these issues at a time. Or, perhaps I should say that all of my attempts to organize the criteria according to outcomes on *both* issues sank into an organizational quagmire. It became overly complex. For the sake of simplicity, then, the subdivisions within the book have been organized around the women's issue. In the layout below (and the one reflected in the chapters to follow) the left column reflects the degree to which each criterion contributes to the women's issue. The right column reflects the degree to which each criterion contributes to the homosexuality issue—a hypothetical ordering of the criteria according to outcomes regarding that issue. The numbering below (1-18) reflects the present or actual order of the cultural/transcultural criteria.

Outcomes Women's Issue	Outcomes Homosexual Issue

INTRASCRIPTURAL CRITERIA

PERSUASIVE	PERSUASIVE
#1: Preliminary Movement	#1: Preliminary Movement
#2: Seed Ideas	#2: Seed Ideas
#3: Breakouts	#3: Breakouts
#4: Purpose/Intent Statements	#4: Purpose/Intent Statements
#5: Basis in Fall and/or Curse	#12: Penal Code
	#15: Contextual Comparisons

MODERATELY PERSUASIVE	MODERATELY PERSUASIVE
#6: Original Creation, I: Patterns	#6: Original Creation, I: Patterns
#7: Original Creation, II: Primogeniture	#8: New Creation
#8: New Creation	#9: Competing Options
#9: Competing Options	#10: Opposition to Original Culture
#10: Opposition to Original Culture	#11: Closely Related Issues
#11: Closely Related Issues	#13: Specific Versus General
#12: Penal Code	
#13: Specific Versus General	

INCONCLUSIVE	INCONCLUSIVE
#14: Basis in Theological Analogy	#5: Basis in Fall or Curse
#15: Contextual Comparisons	#7: Original Creation, II: Primogeniture
#16: Appeal to Old Testament	#14: Basis in Theological Analogy
	#16: Appeal to Old Testament

EXTRA-SCRIPTURAL CRITERIA

PERSUASIVE   PERSUASIVE
#17: Pragmatics Between Two Cultures   #17: Pragmatics Between Two Cultures
#18: Scientific Evidence   #18: Scientific Evidence

You will notice by examining the two lists that different criteria support the two issues with differing degrees of contribution. A number of the criteria play an equally determinative role in both issues. However, as the next four chapters will reveal, a select number of criteria produce substantive evidence for only one issue or the other.

Should you have a significantly greater interest in one of the two issues, it is possible to read the criteria section (chapters four through seven) in a way that reflects your particular interest. For instance, if you are reading with a primary interest in the women's issue, it would be better to follow the left-hand order. However, if you are reading with a primary interest in the homosexual issue, the right-hand order might facilitate that goal better. I still encourage you to read the material on both issues within each criterion in order to maximize your understanding of how each criterion functions. Nevertheless, a reading that follows one column or the other may correspond better with your personal reading objectives.

Part Two

INTRASCRIPTURAL CRITERIA

4

PERSUASIVE CRITERIA

CRITERION 1: Preliminary Movement

A. Statement

A component of a text may be culturally bound if Scripture modifies the *original* cultural norms in such a way that suggests further movement is possible and even advantageous in a *subsequent* culture. Two questions bring this criterion into focus: (1) Has Scripture modified the original cultural norms? (2) If so, is the movement an "absolute movement" or a "preliminary movement"?

By "absolute" and "preliminary" movement I mean the following:

☐ *Absolute movement:* the biblical author has pushed society so far and that is as far as it is supposed to go; further movement is not desired.

☐ *Preliminary movement:* the biblical author pushed society as far as it could go at that time without creating more damage than good; however, it can and should ultimately go further.

We might illustrate these two concepts with a sports analogy—moving the line of scrimmage and scrimmage markers in a football game. In the household codes, for example, Paul clearly does move the scrimmage marker in terms of his own culture. The question is, did he move them in an *absolute sense* (all the way to the goal line) or only in a *preliminary way* (from midfield to the thirty-yard line)?

When investigating biblical movement, one must always have a point of reference in mind. Much of my discussion will focus on assessing movement relative to foreign, ancient Near Eastern and Greco-Roman (ANE/GR) cultures. But this foreign-type movement is only one kind of movement or, more accurately, one kind of measure for movement. As will be discussed under the evaluation section below,

movement relative to foreign cultures must always be integrated with one's understanding of movement as discovered within the covenant community itself and
movement as found within the canon. Thus three measures for movement give us
an understanding of the underlying spirit of the text: (1) "foreign movement"—
change relative to ANE/GR cultures, (2) "domestic movement"—change compared
to what was currently happening within the covenant community itself and (3) "canonical movement"—change across broad redemptive epochs, such as from the
Old Testament to the New Testament. The issue of biblical trajectory and its implications for contemporary application need to be forged on these three anvils.

B. Neutral example: Slavery

Both the Old and New Testaments make significant modifications to the institution of slavery relative to their broader cultures. In biblical legislation some of the
redemptive components relative to the surrounding cultures are listed below. The
biblical treatment of slaves moves in a direction away from much of its surrounding world:

  1. Generous number of days off work. Many ANE/GR cultures gave slaves
time off for festival holidays.[1] By comparison, however, the extent of holidays for
festivals (Deut 16:10-11; 31:10-13) and for the weekly Sabbath rest (Ex 23:12) in
Israel was very generous.

  2. Elevated status in worship setting. Some ancient cultures restricted slaves
from involvement in the sacred rituals. The Roman Empire, for example, barred
slaves from the ceremonial aspects of the religious festivals because they were
thought to have a defiling or polluting influence.[2] On the other hand, the Israelite
and church community encouraged full participation of slaves in worship and religious activities (Ex 12:44; Lev 22:11; Deut 12:12, 18).

  3. Release of Hebrew slaves after six years. Most ANE cultures had no legal
requirement for the release of slaves. Since the duration of ownership was completely in the hands of the master, many slaves served for life or at least until they
could purchase their freedom. The latter was often a practical impossibly. Both
the biblical text (Lev 25:39-43; cf. Jer 34:8-22) and the laws of Hammurabi established a clear limit on the duration of the debt-type slavery. But this kind of
prescribed release of debt slaves after a certain number of years was a unique and
highly redemptive legislative feature compared to most other ANE cultures.[3]

  4. Provisions given to slaves upon release. Material assistance for released

---

[1]For example, see K. R. Bradley, *Slaves and Masters in the Roman Empire* (New York: Oxford University Press, 1987), p. 40.

[2]Ibid., p. 40; cf. Milton Meltzer, *Slavery: From the Rise of Western Civilization to the Renaissance*
(New York: Cowles, 1971), p. 23.

slaves stands out as a generous act of biblical law (Deut 15:12-18); other law codes do not appear to include this act of compensation and stabilization.

5. Limitations on physical beatings; freedom for damaged slaves. Biblical slavery limited the severity of beatings that masters could inflict upon their slaves (Ex 21:20-21). Also, any slaves who were physically damaged by their master automatically gained their freedom (Ex 21:26-27; cf. 27:3-4). Most other cultures were only constrained in the physical abuse of slaves through the logic that they would be damaging their own property. But this logic often gave way to the torturous treatment of select slaves as an object lesson for other slaves. Most foreign laws were extremely lax in restraining the abusive hand of the master. The mutilation of slaves in the ANE[4] as well as in the GR[5] context generally held little or no consequences for the owner. The physical and sexual abuse of slaves was generally seen as an owner's prerogative. In the Roman context there was even legislation that prescribed the torture of slaves in certain legal cases.[6]

6. Admonitions toward genuine care. The flip side of the limitations against abusing slaves is found in the positive injunctions in the Bible toward masters. These texts were intended to turn masters away from harshness and to foster genuine care for slaves (Col 4:1; Eph 6:9). One senses the underlying force of such instructions when hearing them in the context of a world that often did not care for their slaves. For instance, the ancient writers Suetonius and Dio Cassius both described the circumstances of many sick slaves who were left to die without treatment.[7]

7. Condemnation of trading stolen slaves/people. Scripture explicitly points to foreign practices in its denunciation of slave trading by means of stealing people. For example, Gaza and Tyre are condemned along these lines.[8]

---

[3]Gregory C. Chirichigno, *Debt-Slavery in Israel and the Ancient Near East* (Sheffield: JSOT Press, 1993), pp. 193-94; cf. Bradley, *Slaves and Masters*, p. 96.

[4]Israelite laws on physical abuse, unlike certain cultures that simply protected debt slaves, covered both chattel slaves and debt slaves. In this respect, the biblical laws concerning physical assault are quite radical. Cf. Chirichigno, *Debt-Slavery*, pp. 146, 177; Ronald de Vaux, *Ancient Israel. Social Institutions* (New York: McGraw-Hill, 1965), 1:85.

[5]Bradley, *Slaves and Masters*, pp. 114-37; cf. Thomas Wiedemann, *Greek and Roman Slavery* (London: Croom Helm, 1981), pp. 167-80; Milton Meltzer, *Slavery: A World History* (New York: DaCapo, 1993), p. 50.

[6]Yvon Garlan, *Slavery in Ancient Greece,* trans. Janet Lloyd (London: Cornell University Press, 1988), pp. 42-44.

[7]See citations in Wiedemann, *Greek and Roman Slavery*, p. 184.

[8]Ex 21:16; Deut 24:7; 1 Tim 1:10 (NIV, "slave traders"). Paul's reference to people-theft or "kidnapping" would certainly include slave traders who frequently used that means to procure slaves (cf. Amos 1:6, 9). Abolitionists have wrongly used Ezek 27:13 to make a negative evaluation of slave trading. Ezekiel's primary point in surfacing slavery in the condemnation of Tyre seems to be as an illustration of their wealth. Cf. Ronald de Vaux, *Ancient Israel*, 1:81.

8. Refuge and safety for runaway slaves. In the ancient world runaway slaves were often sought for bounty. Captured slaves were at times executed along with their families or accomplices.[9] For instance, the code of Hammurabi prescribed the death penalty for aiding and abetting a runaway slave. Most nations held extradition treaties with other countries in order to facilitate the return of runaways. In a radical departure from prevalent views, the entire land of Israel was considered a safety zone, a place of refuge for runaway slaves (Deut 23:15-16; cf. Is 16:3-4). Runaway slaves were not to be returned to their masters.

When these biblical texts are read against the ancient Near Eastern and Greco-Roman context, the issue of movement becomes increasingly clear. These biblical alterations brought greater protection and dignity for the slave compared to the treatment of slaves in surrounding environments. Cyrus Gordon summarizes biblical slavery in this manner: "The general picture emerges . . . that the lot of a slave in ancient Israel was far better than that of a slave elsewhere."[10]

This improvement in the conditions of slaves relative to the original culture was a redemptive action by the biblical authors. However, it was not redemptive in any absolute sense. Scripture only moved the cultural "scrimmage markers" so far. Yet, that movement was sufficient enough to signal a positive direction in terms of where further improvements were possible for later generations. In reapplying the text to later generations, we can easily stumble over the isolated words on the page if we do only what the text says and fail to let its underlying spirit carry the application further. It is the *redemptive spirit* of the text in its original context that we once again want to reapply in our modern context.

C. Women

As one compares the biblical texts about women to their surrounding foreign context and correlates that comparative picture with domestic and canonical movement, a certain impression emerges. On the whole, the biblical material is headed toward an elevation of women in status and rights. At times foreign movement sends mixed signals, depending upon the specific area and which particular country is examined. However, domestic and canonical inputs generally clarify how to read this ambiguity. A sampling of illustrations will show the interactive relationship between foreign, domestic and canonical movement. An overall sense of redemptive movement can be seen in each of these examples.

1. Improved rights for female slaves and concubines. The ANE world permit-

---

[9]Ronald de Vaux, *Ancient Israel*, 1:87; Bradley, *Slaves and Masters*, p. 32.
[10]Cyrus H. Gordon and Gary A. Rendsburg, *The Bible and the Ancient Near East* (New York: W. W. Norton, 1997), p. 156.

ted the sale of girls to *any* male, whether domestic or foreign. These young women or concubines fulfilled whatever sexual purposes the owner deemed fit. They held virtually no rights of their own. While the Old Testament permitted the sale of daughters as chattel slaves and concubines, it made a significant redemptive move against this blatantly unchecked expression of patriarchy (Ex 21:7-11). Unlike foreign law codes, the biblical text limited the sale of concubines to within the Israelite nation and granted to these women "rights that were normally afforded to daughters who were married in the customary manner."[11]

2. *No bodily punishment of a wife.* Ancient women were extremely vulnerable to physical punishment by their husbands. Sometimes a husband's punishment was mediated through the community, but often it was administered directly within the household. As an example of the former, Babylonian codes stipulated drowning for women who, in opposition to their husbands, neglected their home.[12] Assyrian law granted husbands stronger and more direct disciplinary rights over their wives. As part of daily living, the males were permitted to scourge their wives, pluck out their hair, and bruise or pierce their ears. For more severe acts of insubordination, the husband had the right to mutilate or cut off certain parts of his wife's body and in a few cases was even permitted to kill her.[13] While physical punishment of wives may have occurred within Israel, such harsh measures were fortunately not enshrined as a husband's right in biblical legislation. For the most part, the spirit of biblical law seems to have taken husband-wife relationships in quite a different direction.

Add to this foreign comparison the later canonical emphasis on sacrificial, servant-type love for one's wife, and there emerges within Scripture a striking sense of elevated respect for the female marriage partner.

3. *Women's gain of (limited) inheritance rights.* The daughters of Zelophehad courageously asked to inherit their family land in view of their father dying without any sons to whom he could pass on the land inheritance (Num 27:1-11; 36:1-13). In essence they pushed the boundaries of patriarchy as it related to land inheritance. Ultimately, these rights were granted to them. The movement is minor and might be assessed today as trivial, for it hardly grants equal inheritance to sons and daughters. But, it is an indication of movement in a particular direction.

Canonical movement further augments this domestic movement in the Zelo-

---

[11]Chirichigno, *Debt-Slavery,* p. 251.

[12]Elizabeth Mary MacDonald, *The Position of Women as Reflected in Semitic Codes of Law* (Toronto: University of Toronto Press, 1931), p. 30.

[13]G. R. Driver and John C. Miles, *The Assyrian Laws* (New York: Oxford University Press, 1935), pp. 23-27, 44-47, 81-82, 286, 290-92, 351-52. Cf. MacDonald, *Position of Women,* p. 40.

phehad case. With the emergence of the early church, any gender-based land/ inheritance restrictions appear to fade away completely.[14] Taken in conjunction with the inheritance breakout found in Job (see criterion 3.D.5), Scripture's domestic and canonical portrait provides a sense of where the text is moving the boundaries—toward a considerably more liberal or equality-based interaction with women.

4. The right of women to initiate divorce. In something of an assumed fashion, the Old Testament limits the initiation of divorce proceedings to men (e.g., Deut 20:10-14; 22:19, 29; 24:1-4). The New Testament, however, extends the right of initiating divorce to women.[15] This kind of canonical movement sets a clear direction about the emerging status of women in the Judeo-Christian context.

5. Greater rights in divorce cases. As with Hebrew women, Babylonian and Assyrian women enjoyed very little voice in matters of divorce. Most ANE countries assumed male initiative and rarely, if ever, restricted the male's power by limiting the grounds for divorce.[16] In fact, legislation in this area frequently penalized women in terms of monetary support, if the grounds for the divorce were due to her shortcomings. Divorced women could be sent away empty-handed. In some situations they forfeited their dowry and their children, and were even subject to drowning if they falsely accused their husbands in the divorce proceedings. Since trivial grounds could be invoked as the basis for divorce, wives were extremely vulnerable to the tyranny of their husbands.

Compared to other countries, Israelite males had at least some minimal "red tape" to work through in divorcing their wives—a bill of divorce had to be written (Deut 24:1-4; cf. Is 50:1), in at least one case a charge had to be brought to the court (Deut 22:13-19), no divorce was ever permitted in either the case of a falsely-charged wife (Deut 22:15) or in the case of violating a virgin (Deut 22:19), and the strict limitations on remarriage to a former wife would have made the husband think twice about the rationale for the divorce (Deut 24:1-4). While from an ultimate-ethic perspective this legislation hardly goes far enough, within

---

[14]Early Christians did not feel the constraints of Jewish law regarding its inheritance/property restrictions on women. Even within Judaism there was considerable modification of inheritance laws during in the second temple period and beyond. For a fascinating look at the expanding borders of inheritance laws, see Tal Ilan, *Jewish Women in Greco-Roman Palestine* (Peabody, Mass.: Hendrickson, 1996), pp. 167-72.

[15]Mk 10:12; 1 Cor 7:10-16. For a helpful explanation of Matthew's husband-only statements compared to Mark's more egalitarian perspective, see Craig S. Keener, *And Marries Another: Divorce and Remarriage in the Teaching of the New Testament* (Peabody, Mass.: Hendrickson, 1991), p. 47. It would appear that the Palestinian vs. Roman social context may have played a role in the apostolic shaping of these respective traditions.

[16]MacDonald, *Position of Women*, pp. 18-20, 40-41.

its own day it granted Israelite women a greater dimension of dignity.

Once a canonical perspective augments this foreign assessment, the radical nature of the biblical divorce laws becomes evident. In the hearing of a Jewish audience, Jesus raises the stakes further by limiting the grounds for divorce to adultery. He may have simply been clarifying how Jewish law should have been understood, or as typical of his emerging new Torah, Jesus may have been taking the old law one step further toward an improved, more fully realized ethic. Either way, Jesus' words put a substantial dent in the powers of patriarchy.

6. *Fairer treatment of women suspected of adultery.* Should an ANE husband suspect his wife of adultery, he would take her to the temple and have her pronounce a curse upon herself. If, however, the activity of a suspected adulteress had become a community affair with widespread gossip, then the wife was subjected to a "trial by water" with guilt attached either to sinking or floating.[17] Fortunately, Scripture only takes the seemingly saner of these two routes (cf. Numbers 5). Yet, neither in Israel nor in other ANE countries was there a reciprocal ordeal for the wife to impose upon the husband suspected of adultery. Thus a clear gender inequality existed in Israel and its broader environment. However, the fact that Israel had the more civil and less-easily-abused approach to the matter yields a sense of quiet reduction in patriarchal powers compared to its foreign context. The suspected adulteress is simply turned over to Yahweh in an oath and temple ritual.

Furthermore, canonical development demonstrates that the lopsided, one-gender-only treatment of the issue falls away. The early church no longer continued Israel's practice of scrutinizing suspected adulteresses. Taking our lead from the divorce laws (see above), it would appear that the apostolic church moved toward much greater gender equality in dealing with divorce as well as with some of its precipitating factors, such as adultery. In this example, foreign and canonical movements combine to set a particular direction for patriarchy.

7. *Elevation of female sexuality.* Women often functioned as prostitutes in the ANE and GR world.[18] Prostitution was readily available as a part of pagan worship in various temples and as a component of everyday commerce in the marketplace. While it may have provided a service of sorts (similar to concubines and polygamy), it often did so at a terrible cost to women and their dignity as human beings. Compared to the ancient world context, biblical values clearly elevate fe-

---

[17]For a helpful comparison of Numbers 5 with other ANE texts, see Michael Fishbane, "Accusations of Adultery. A Study of Law and Scribal Practice in Numbers 5:11-31," in *Women in the Hebrew Bible: A Reader*, ed. Alice Bach (New York: Routledge, 1999), pp. 487-502; cf. MacDonald, *Position of Women*, p. 19.

[18]For ANE examples, see MacDonald, *Position of Women*, pp. 26, 47.

male sexuality (Lev 19:29; 21:9; Deut 23:17-18; cf. 1 Cor 6:10, 15). Women, as well as men, were to be treated as persons and not as sexual objects. While not going as far as one might like (see criterion 11.C.4-7), the covenant community took significant steps against the sexual exploitation of women. Within its own setting and time, these developments were nothing short of amazing.

8. *Improved rape laws.* Assyrian rape laws punished the female victim whether she was forced or seduced and at times held her alone as guilty while the man went free.[19] The unmarried male perpetrator merely paid a monetary fine; whereas, if the perpetrator was a married male, this man's own wife was subsequently taken out by others and sexually ravished for his crime.[20] While justice may have been achieved in the eyes of men, it often created a double atrocity for women. Biblical rape laws have their own inherent difficulties.[21] But they are much improved over the patriarchy found in certain law codes of the ancient world.

9. *Softening the husband side of the household codes.* In our modern culture it is the wife side of the New Testament household codes that is so striking and "out of step." But this was not the case in their original setting. For the first-century audience it was not the wife material that was radical or strange; it was the husband material.[22] As with slavery, Paul modifies the "top end" of the hierarchical structure. He pushes the cultural expectations primarily on the husband side of the hierarchy. His words to husbands soften the hierarchy compared to the broader sociological setting. Aside from reading Ephesians 5:22-33 against the backdrop of its original setting, one evidence for softening the top end of the hierarchy is seen in the imbalance between the actual imperatives found in the passage. Paul commands wives to "submit." Correspondingly, he does not command husbands to "rule" or "lead" (the reciprocal imperative to submit) but to "love." The husband's rule or authority is assumed in the discussion, but softened considerably through Paul's altered focus and the use of sacrificial imagery. In this way, Paul assumes the status quo for women; however, he pushes the boundaries for men with the direction of his command.

Let us summarize the broad picture of redemptive movement related to women. Bringing together the three streams—foreign, domestic and canonical— one immediately senses where Scripture is moving on the issue of patriarchal

---

[19]MacDonald, *Position of Women,* p. 43.

[20]Ibid, pp. 38-39.

[21]Cf. criterion 11.C. If a man raped a Hebrew virgin, he paid the girl's father a fine and had to marry her without possibility of divorce (Deut 22:28-29).

[22]Cf. William Klein, Craig L. Blomberg and Robert L. Hubbard Jr., *Introduction to Biblical Interpretation* (Vancouver: Word, 1993), p. 418.

power. An overall assessment is expressed well through the words of Eckart Otto who, in his study of family law in Deuteronomy, captures the redemptive spirit that I have sought to illustrate in Scripture as a whole:[23]

> The family laws in the book of Deuteronomy had a progressive and protective attitude to the legal status of women. They were deeply concerned with the restriction of male predominance. This did by no means imply that these provisions really overcame the patrilineal and patriarchal pattern of Judean society, but they were intended to install women even in matters of family law as legal subjects vested with rights and titles of their own that were not derived from rights and decisions of men. In modern eyes this may be too little and be no means enough—but in antiquity and for women at that time it meant very much.

D. Homosexuality

The homosexual texts also move the yardage markers relative to the original culture. Homosexuality was openly practiced in the surrounding cultures. However, the Israelite and Christian communities did not accept these sexual practices in their theology, in their temple worship or in their everyday community living. Scripture, then, interacts with the foreign scene of homoerotic behavior on at least three levels:

1. Challenging the portrait of the ancient gods. The ancient gods were not particularly restrained in their sexual practices. Canaanite deities, for instance, were involved in incest and bestiality, as no doubt some of the Canaanite people were themselves engaged in these acts.[24] Ancient gods were often involved in homosexual acts ranging in nature from casual encounters to extended homoerotic relationships between two gods.[25] On the principle of *imitatio dei* one can only surmise that the people in some ways imitated their gods. Read against this background, Judeo-Christian sources alter the face of ancient religion because they choose *not* to depict Yahweh in sexual acts of bestiality, incest or homosexuality.

2. Removing homosexual practices from the temple cult. Homosexual acts were most likely performed as a part of ancient temple worship. In Ugarit, for instance, there was a group of male temple prostitutes known as *qedeshim* (who had their female counterparts, the *qedeshot*). It would appear that these prostitutes engaged in sexual acts for their temple clientele. Although we do not know

---

[23]Eckart Otto, "False Weights in the Scales of Biblical Justice? Different Views of Women from Patriarchal Hierarchy to Religious Equality in the Book of Deuteronomy," in *Gender and Law in the Hebrew Bible and the Ancient Near East*, ed. Victor H. Matthews, Bernard M. Levinson and Tikva Frymer-Kensky, JSOT Supplement Series 262 (Sheffield: Sheffield Academic Press, 1998), p. 140.

[24]Gordon and Rendsburg, *Bible and Ancient Near East*, p. 159.

[25]Martti Nissinen, *Homoeroticism in the Biblical World: A Historical Perspective* (Minneapolis: Fortress, 1998), pp. 19-24.

exactly the range of sexual activity, given that their gods were involved in hetero-sexual and homosexual acts, it is entirely probable that these sacred prostitutes serviced their people in more than heterosexual activities. The biblical texts ex-plicitly ban these kinds of male and female prostitutes within the Israelite cult (Deut 23:18).

3. Legislating against homosexual practices within community life. As with the gods and the temple activities, homosexuality was practiced with varying de-grees of affirmation within foreign nations. Scripture moves in a particular direc-tion relative to these cultures by its broad-sweeping ban of homosexuality within the covenant community. The Israelite people were prohibited from engaging in any kind of sexual act that replicated heterosexual intercourse yet was performed outside of the male-female categories (Lev 18:22; 20:22).

So biblical tradition moved the cultural norms on homosexuality from a sig-nificant amount of tolerance and acceptance to non-tolerance and non-acceptance within the covenant community. Scripture thus sets a clear direction in terms of foreign movement on the homosexual issue. A domestic and canonical investiga-tion simply reinforces these findings within the foreign realm. When one comes to the New Testament, there is no softening of Scripture's negative assessment of homosexuality found in the Old Testament.

E. Evaluation of the criterion

Assessing redemptive movement has its complications. Without going into an elaborate explanation, I will simply suggest a number of guidelines: (1) the ANE/GR *real* world must be examined along with its *legal* world, (2) the bibli-cal subject on the *whole* must be examined along with its *parts*, (3) the biblical text must be compared to a number of other ANE/GR cultures which them-selves must be compared with each other and (4) any portrait of movement must be composed of broad input from all three streams of assessment—for-eign, domestic and canonical.

Provided the interpreter uses these sorts of commonsense considerations, the movement criterion provides a wonderful vehicle through which to understand the text more fully. Observing the movement of any biblical text relative to the surrounding cultures is an important aspect to uncovering a component of mean-ing. This meaning is lost with a static approach, which looks at the words of the text in isolation and, even if aware of movement, fails to let that underlying spirit impact the application process. Somehow we must package into our hermeneutic a component of listening to a text within its *literary* context as well as hearing that same text within its immediate and broader *cultural/social* context. I must not only look up and down the page to the preceding and following paragraphs within Scripture (the literary context); I must also reflect upon how the words sounded to the ears of the ancient covenant community as it interfaced with the world around them (the social context). A well-developed hermeneutic will not only reflect upon where the words fell on the page; it will ponder where they land in relation to what else was being said and practiced in the ancient Near Eastern or Greco-Roman culture.

The movement criterion adds a new dimension to the reading of Scripture—a third depth dimension as opposed to what might be called a flat, two-dimensional reading of the text. Many Christians, particularly at a popular level, read the Bible simply as a flat-surfaced, two-dimensional kind of text. They seek to understand what the words of the text say as if they were spoken in a vacuum. Unfortunately, this approach overlooks what the words of the text said relative to the social context in which they were spoken (foreign and domestic) and in relation to developments in later biblical tradition (canonical).

F. Summary

Scriptural movement relative to the original culture does not *answer* the question of whether the movement should be viewed as preliminary or absolute, but it does *raise* that intriguing question. More important, however, scriptural movement provides a crucial factor for setting the *direction of movement* should further movement be appropriate. In this respect, the women texts, like the slavery texts, are generally "less restrictive" or "softening" relative to the broader culture, while the homosexuality texts are "more restrictive" or "hardening" relative to the surrounding environment. A domestic and canonical investigation of movement further reinforces these foreign-movement findings.

CRITERION 2: Seed Ideas

A. Statement

A component of a text may be cultural if "seed ideas" are present within the rest of Scripture to suggest and encourage further movement on a particular subject. As the imagery implies, the seed is not fully grown. So too, the seed idea describes something at an early stage. It is in seedling form, not fully developed. In some respects, it is merely suggestive of what could be. Texts with seed ideas would probably have moved the original audience only in a limited fashion. Nonetheless, within what they affirm these texts imply that the scrimmage marker could be pushed further. If later readers in another place and time draw out the implications of the seedling idea from one text, this can lead to taking other texts beyond their original-audience application and form to a more realized expression of the spirit within.

B. Neutral example: slavery

On the surface, certain texts within the Bible appear to support slavery.[26] These texts were used by the pro-slavery position to prove that slavery was a biblical norm. Yet, relative to the original culture these very slavery texts often incorporated a redemptive dimension, as we have discussed in the last criterion.

In addition to the redemptive element within the texts themselves (relative to their environment), we have certain other scriptural passages that provide a "seedbed" in which the redemptive element could grow. In the case of slavery, a variety of texts quietly reinforce further movement:

1 Corinthians 7:21	"If you [as a slave] can gain your freedom, do so."
1 Corinthians 12:13	"We were all baptized by one Spirit into one body—whether Jews or Greeks, slave or free . . ."
Galatians 3:28	" . . . neither Jew nor Greek, neither slave nor free . . . in Christ Jesus."
Colossians 3:11	Within the new humanity/society, "There is no longer Greek or Jew . . . slave or free, but Christ is all, and is in all."
Philemon 15-16	"Have him [Onesimus] back for good—no longer as a slave, but better than a slave, as a dear brother."

These texts are quietly suggestive. They foster the idea that the legislative texts could be adapted or modified by later generations to take the redemptive dimension of Scripture to a higher level. Regarding the impact of Paul's letter to Philemon on slavery, F. F. Bruce writes, "What this letter does is to bring us into an atmosphere in which the institution [of slavery] could only wilt and die."[27] Similarly, a patriarchalist such as Craig Blomberg comments on 1 Corinthians 7:21 that "Paul sowed the seeds for a revolutionary alternative in Christ which in time could only but threaten social institutions of oppression [such as slavery]."[28]

C. Women

1. Galatians 3:28 (cf. Acts 2:17-18; Joel 2:28-29). Galatians 3:28 states, "There is neither Jew nor Greek, slave nor free, male nor female . . . in Christ Jesus." Pa-

---

[26]For a sampling, see Ex 21:20-21, 32; Lev 22:11; Eph 6:5-8; Col 3:22-25; Tit 2:9-10; 1 Pet 2:18-25.
[27]F. F. Bruce, *Paul: Apostle of the Heart Set Free* (Grand Rapids, Mich.: Eerdmans, 1977), p. 401.
[28]Craig Blomberg, *1 Corinthians*, NIVAC (Grand Rapids, Mich.: Zondervan, 1994), p. 148.

triarchalists argue that this verse is simply talking about our salvation in Christ, without any social implications.[29] The point of the verse is simply to say that all believers have the same status in Christ. In Christ believers are redeemed equals. In other spheres such as the household, however, there remains a submission hierarchy within the measure of equality that all share in Christ.

Egalitarians agree that Galatians 3:28 is speaking about salvation. The real issue, however, is whether the salvation equality in Christ held any sociological implications for Paul and/or should hold sociological implications for us. Along these lines, there is much within Pauline theology to commend the idea that this verse has social implications.[30] Aside from Galatians 3:28, on three other occasions Paul develops a similar "in Christ" formula:

☐ "For we were all baptized by one Spirit into one body—whether Jews or Greeks, slave or free—and we were all given the one Spirit to drink" (1 Cor 12:13).

☐ "His [Christ's] purpose was to create in himself one new man [i.e., one new humanity or society] out of the two [Jew and Gentile] . . ." (Eph 2:15).

☐ "Here [in the new humanity/society in Christ] there is no Greek or Jew, circumcised or uncircumcised, barbarian, Scythian, slave or free, but Christ is all, and in all" (Col 3:11).

These "in Christ" lists are simply representative. In other words, the elements within them are roughly interchangeable between the four lists. Each of the "in Christ" lists could equally well have included the "neither male nor female" statement of Galatians 3:28.[31] Paul simply rehearses areas of social inequality and (by way of contrast) says that the Jew and Gentile, the slave and free, the male and female (and any other sociological grouping where there is pronounced inequality) share an equal status "in Christ."

Once Galatians 3:28 is set within the broader corpus of Pauline theology, there is no question that the "in Christ" formula had social implications. This is immediately evident in the relationship between Jews and Gentiles. In this area the "in Christ" formula carried significant sociology-of-cult implications. Formerly, the

---

[29]E.g., S. Lewis Johnson, "Role Distinctions in the Church: Galatians 3:28," in *Recovering Biblical Manhood and Womanhood*, ed. John Piper and Wayne Grudem (Wheaton, Ill.: Crossway, 1991), pp. 154-64; John J. Davis, "Some Reflections on Galatians 3:28, Sexual Roles, and Biblical Hermeneutics," *JETS* 19 (1976): 201-8.

[30]For an extensive development see Richard N. Longenecker, *New Testament Social Ethics for Today* (Grand Rapids, Mich.: Eerdmans, 1984).

[31]The tradition history behind Gal 3:28 may be Joel 2:28-32 (cf. Acts 2:17-21; Rom 10:12-13). Women are included as equal recipients of the Spirit's eschatological activity . . . during the "new creation" age. See Klyne R. Snodgrass, "Galatians 3:28: Conundrum or Solution," in *Women, Authority, and the Bible*, ed. A. Mickelsen (Downers Grove, Ill.: InterVarsity Press, 1986), pp. 161-88.

Gentiles were physically partitioned off from the rest of the Jewish cult[32] and eth-nically restricted from any involvement in the priesthood.[33] They were outside of the covenants of promise (Eph 2:12; cf. 3:6). Also, purity boundaries played havoc during social gatherings between the two groups (Gal 2:11-14). However, "in Christ" the inequality was eliminated; the two became equal partners. In the worship setting, believing Gentiles became equals with believing Jews. They en-joyed an equally shared possession of the covenants, which had formerly been granted to the Jewish nation. Furthermore, the new relationship between Jew and Gentile "in Christ" brought about changed attitudes regarding the eating of meals together in various social settings.

Paul worked out Jew-Gentile equality in his generation. Much of his ministry was given over to seeing Jew-Gentile equality fleshed out in concrete and tangi-ble terms—terms that embraced sociological implications. Why did Paul place such an emphasis on the Jew-Gentile component of the "in Christ" list? From a pragmatic standpoint, ethnic equality meant success for the gospel. Without it, there would probably be no universal gospel today. If Christianity was to expand beyond the boarders of Palestine, if it was to become a worldwide religion with a message of salvation for all peoples, it needed to embrace equality between Jew and Gentile. What was redemptively true needed to become a practical reality. The ontological or salvation equality needed to transform the functional level. Otherwise, the roots of Judaism would strangle its own offspring.

Conversely, for Paul to press for social implications in the slave and the fe-male categories might have been detrimental. It would likely have done more damage than good. Clearly the Jew-Gentile issue was the greatest stumbling block for the gospel in Paul's day. While Paul granted slaves and females equality "in Christ," there was not the same kind of urgency in terms of working out the social dynamics. If one compares the inertia within the early church for Gentile equality to the pressure for equality in the cases of slaves and females, it would be like placing Niagara Falls next to a dripping tap. Beyond this comparative lack of urgency, carrying out sociological implications for slaves and females may have actually impeded the gospel. Nevertheless, once the church caught sight of the social ramifications of the Jew-Gentile equality, it eventually began to trans-

---

[32]The temple courts during the time of Christ included the court of priests, the court of Israelites (male), the court of women, and the court of Gentiles. The Gentiles had the most external of courts within the temple (Josephus *War* 5.5.2; *Middoth* 2; cf. Eph 2:14). Interestingly, at one point in American history, black slaves similarly had to sit in a segregated part of the church congregation (see Alvin J. Schmidt, *Veiled and Silenced* [Macon, Ga.: Mercer University Press, 1989], p. 32).

[33]Ex 28:1; 29:9; 45:12-15; Lev 1:7. The priests were to be from the sons of Aaron (obviously Israelites and not Gentiles).

form redemptive equality for slaves into a social reality. With time and with greater social readiness the church ultimately worked out the implications of Galatians 3:28 (and of the other "in Christ" texts) for slaves.

One must now ask if the "in Christ" formula should carry social implications for the equality of women. It certainly did in Paul's day for Gentiles. And, it did over the course of church history for slaves. Why should it not today for females? In this manner Paul's sociological outworking of the Galatians 3:28 text becomes a paradigm of equality for these other categories of social inequality.

2. *1 Corinthians 11:11-12*. The text of 1 Corinthians 11:11-12 reads, "In the Lord, however, woman is not independent of man, nor is man independent of woman. For as woman came from man, so also man is born of woman. But everything comes from God." These two verses provide an interesting interjection into the flow of 1 Corinthians 11:2-16. Soft hierarchalists agree that these verses qualify the preceding verses about headship and head coverings to a certain extent.[34] Correspondingly, egalitarians should probably concede that Paul is not intending to overturn completely all of his previous discussion, at least not in this particular situation within the setting of Corinth and within his generation.

Nonetheless, the equality and the mutual dependence of verses 11-12 call into question what Paul is attempting to argue in the surrounding material. These two verses clearly form a tension on a theoretical level with his previous arguments. Furthermore, the phrase "in the Lord" (much like "in Christ") suggests that Paul may have had in mind not simply the Christian community as a redeemed people,[35] but as a redeemed people *quite apart from the social realities of the old world* that they still lived in and that in some measure they still reflected in their midst. If so, 1 Corinthians 11:11-12 provides another seed idea whose potential could only be realized as the larger social climate permits.

D. Homosexuality

There are no homosexuality texts that provide a seedbed to suggest further movement. As noted above, by "further movement" I mean movement in the *same direction set by Scripture itself* that other texts go relative to the original culture. For example, the bulk of the biblical texts concerning slaves and women move in a less restrictive or freeing direction relative to their original culture. They may not go as far as we might like, but they clearly move in a liberalizing direction relative to the setting in which they were given. On the other hand, the homosex-

---

[34]E.g., Blomberg, *1 Corinthians*, p. 216.
[35]Contra Blomberg, *1 Corinthians*, p. 216. For further discussion of 1 Corinthians 11, see appendix D.

ual texts move in a conservative or restrictive direction relative to the original culture. That is why criterion 1 is crucial for setting direction in movement. A
seedbed text, then, would be one that took this conservative direction further.
Since the movement in the homosexual texts was absolute in its restrictive positioning, further movement is not feasible. It would be unlikely to find seedbed
texts that are suggestive of movement in a direction opposite to the direction set
by other, say legislative texts, as they are read in relation to their original culture.
In fact, we do not find any such antithetical-movement texts.[36]

Having just said that no homosexuality texts provide a seedbed for further
movement, it should be noted that Galatians 3:28 *could be* and *is* used by homosexual advocates to make their point. But, they use it in quite another way than I
am using the seedbed criterion. As the argument goes, perhaps "neither male nor
female" in Christ should lead to freedom in sexual orientation for the Christian
community.[37] Why is this text not a seedbed for less-restrictive or liberalizing
movement as in the case of women or slaves (above)? The important qualifier is
that the movement in a seedbed text must be in the *same direction of movement
set by Scripture* as evidenced in the movement of other same-topic texts relative
to the broader social context. That is why, as stated above, it is unlikely in the homosexual issue to have further movement. If one were to posit Galatians 3:28 as a
seedbed text, it would provide movement not in the same direction, but in an opposite direction to the movement of other texts relative to the original audience.
The scriptural movement in the homosexual texts goes from open or mixed acceptance in the surrounding nations (broader culture) to no acceptance within Israel and the church (biblical material). The direction of the movement is fairly
clear.

Furthermore, an examination of Galatians 3:28 shows that the verse has
nothing to do with the breaking down of social stigma concerning homosexu-

---

[36]For example, we have no biblical texts that suggest that "there is neither homosexual nor heterosexual in Christ." Nor do we find any biblical text that suggests that homosexuality might be acceptable
in some form or another.

[37]A number of homosexual proponents cite or allude to Galatians 3:28 as if it supports their case, e.g.,
Kathy Rudy, *Sex and the Church: Gender, Homosexuality, and the Transformation of Christian Ethics* (Boston: Beacon, 1997), p. 85; Letha D. Scanzoni and Virginia R. Mollenkott, *Is the Homosexual My Neighbor? A Positive Christian Response*, 2d ed. (San Francisco: HarperCollins, 1994), p.
16; Richard Cleaver, *Know My Name: A Gay Liberation Theology* (Louisville: Westminster John
Knox, 1995), p. 27. Cf. the discussion about Gentile inclusion as a model for including gay and lesbian Christians by Jeffrey S. Siker, "Gentile Wheat and Homosexual Christians: New Testament
Directions for the Heterosexual Church," in *Biblical Ethics and Homosexuality*, ed. Robert L. Brawley (Louisville: Westminster John Knox, 1996), pp. 145-46; "Homosexual Christians, the Bible, and
Gentile Inclusion," in *Homosexuality in the Church: Both Sides of the Debate*, ed. Jeffrey S. Siker
(Louisville: Westminster John Knox, 1994), pp. 178-94.

als, on either an exegetical level or in terms of extrapolated implications for subsequent generations. Using this text in support of homosexuality incorrectly interprets the referents of "male" and "female." In this verse the referent is to two groups of people: biological males (who are generally heterosexual) versus biological females (who also are generally heterosexual). It is not the heterosexual element that is removed "in Christ." For two reasons this is not the crucial distinction being made. First, Paul slices the population of his entire world into two broad and general groupings: male and female. This verse classifies all of humanity (in general) into these two groups, as is the case with slave-free and Jew-Gentile. This *broad* grouping would be primarily heterosexual (for both male and female). Therefore, Paul is not talking about "in Christ" equality in terms of sexual orientation. Rather, he is making his point in terms of social inequality between the men and women (who are generally heterosexual). Second, the "neither male nor female" statement is focused upon the existing and predominant social stigma between these two groups due to inequality in power and status. This understanding again coordinates well with the other two categories selected (slave-free and Jew-Gentile). Just as the existing stigma in the slave-free and Jew-Gentile domains relates to well-known socioeconomic and religious inequalities, Paul is looking at the domination of males over females in society within his male-female statement. He is not commenting on sexual orientation, which would then be a completely different grouping (containing males and females on *both* sides of the polar split) and which would not have been the existing and predominant focus of inequality for the original audience.

If one was to add homosexuality as one of Paul's concerns, then it would look something like the following: In Christ there is neither

☐ Jew nor Greek
☐ slave nor free
☐ male nor female
☐ gay nor straight

My point, then, is that exegetically Paul is *not* attempting to remove any social stigma between "gay" and "straight" groups, whereas he *is* pointedly speaking to the issue of social stigma in the other three relationships cited above. Thus one cannot argue the kind of forward projection from the seed idea of Galatians 3:28 using extrapolated implications for subsequent generations based upon what happened in Paul's day in raising the status of Gentiles. That kind of trajectory only works with slaves and women, if one is to extrapolate the original intent of the verse.

Nevertheless, for a moment let us put the original intent of the verse aside. Even if Paul was not talking about social stigma for homosexuals, maybe one could still apply Galatians 3:28 (by secondary deduction) to the breaking down of social stigma between gays and straights. For example, I could apply this verse through secondary deduction to various areas of social stigma. In this respect, a paraphrase might go as follows: In Christ there is neither

☐ rich nor poor

☐ blue collar nor white collar

☐ black nor white

☐ baby boomer nor generation Xer

☐ single nor married

However, what makes these legitimate categories of "secondary deduction" is the fact that elsewhere Scripture directly or indirectly addresses these kinds of categories in order to break down the social barrier between such groups. Also, in no scriptural texts is there a hint of any of these categories being inherently wrong or sinful. On the other hand, suppose that I were to paraphrase the verse in this fashion: In Christ there is neither

☐ erotic lover of animals nor erotic lover of humans

☐ adulterer nor faithfully married

☐ sexually active single nor waiting virgin

☐ incestuous person nor nonincestuous person

Some would want to remove all social and moral stigmas related to a Christian sexual ethic—for example, serial divorce and remarriage, incest, bestiality, adultery, premarital sex and pornography. For instance, Billy Joel's song about a young girl named "Virginia" (an obvious play on "virgin") captures the attitudes of some toward the church for its views on premarital sex: "Catholic girls start much too late!"[38] Any of the areas of a Christian sexual ethic, virginity or otherwise, creates some kind of social stigma. When compared to these four examples above, obviously Galatians 3:28 offers no hope for those who wish to move from that verse by secondary deduction to removing any or all categories of sexual taboo in Scripture. A case would first have to be made from biblical texts outside of this verse that attempt to break down the social stigma of a particular area. Then, and only then, might Galatians 3:28 be invoked in a secondary manner.

E. Evaluation of the criterion

Chapter two developed a redemptive-movement hermeneutic that seeks to understand and reapply the movement component of meaning—the underlying spirit of a text—through foreign, domestic and canonical means. Seed ideas and break-

---

[38]Billy Joel, "Only the Good Die Young," *Greatest Hits Volume 1: 1973-1977,* Columbia Records.

outs simply augment that picture, for they capture the component of movement in other ways. Back in chapter two, I critiqued the alternative of a static hermeneutic and suggested that it reads the letter well—the isolated words on the page—but neglects the spirit of the text.

F. Summary

During Paul's day the seed ideas of various texts helped shape not only a theoretical equality between Jew and Gentile, but also an equality that had profound implications for Christian society and worship gatherings. Seed texts also played a significant role for abolitionists in seeing that the preliminary movement within the slavery texts could and should be taken further. This same kind of social-equality implication appears to be extremely pertinent to the women's issue today. Egalitarians often overstate the power of these seed texts, while patriarchalists fail to see the clear social implication that existed even for Paul (beyond the realm of salvation). The homosexual texts do not contain any seed ideas for further movement. Whether through exegesis, exegetical trajectory or secondary application, Galatians 3:28 does not persuasively support removal of social/sexual boundaries between gays and straights.

CRITERION 3: Breakouts

A. Statement

A component of a text may be culturally confined if the social norms reflected in that text are completely "broken out of" in other biblical texts. Scripture sometimes reveals variance in the treatment of a subject, so that at times the cultural norms are followed, at other times cultural norms are dramatically overturned. This criterion takes the last two criteria one step further. We move from "slight modifications" of existing cultural norms to "seedbed" ideas and now to "breakouts" that prepare the way for further movement. While a seedbed idea is subtle and quiet due to its unrealized form, a breakout is a much more pronounced deviation by Scripture from the cultural norms. Here the text completely overturns the expected norms. Also, the seedbed is theoretical/potential, whereas the breakout is real or actualized relative to the original audience. It challenges the standard sociological patterns in the present reality.

Once again, it is important to note that the direction of the further movement in the breakout is the *same direction* as the preliminary movement in other texts relative to the broader culture. Both the preliminary movement and the breakout must be assessed relative to the surrounding culture. While a breakout may appear markedly different than or even at odds with a piece of biblical legislation that upholds an expected social norm,[39] at the same time it may well be an extension of the direction that the legislation is/was headed relative to the larger environment. A breakout, then, extends the direction of the movement relative to the original audience (criterion 1) and functions at a more pronounced reality level than a seedbed idea (criterion 2).

	Preliminary Movement	Seed Ideas	Breakouts
Degree of change	moderate	radical	radical
Nature of change	actual/real	theoretical/potential	actual/real

Degree and nature of change relative to existing social conventions

B. Neutral examples

1. Left-handedness. In the ancient Near East being left-handed was considered a liability, while right-handedness was celebrated as a strength. This status and value judgment can be seen in a number of texts. For instance, one of the tribes of Israel was named "Benjamin," which means "son of (my) right hand." The right hand was used to confer a blessing (Gen 48:18). When a person served at the right hand of another, it conveyed integral strength and extension of duties and power (1 Chron 6:39). In this way, the idiom is similar to our expression, "my right-hand man/person."

Right-handed superiority (in contrast to left-handed inferiority) also gets theologized extensively in the Old and New Testaments. For example, Yahweh shows his great strength by redeeming his people with his right hand (Ex 15:6, 12). As in a co-regency relationship, Jesus Christ sits at the right hand of God, enthroned as his son (Ps 110:1; cf. Mt 22:44). Despite cultural adaptation and extensive theologizing of right-handed superiority, it would be ridiculous to consider left-handedness a liability today. In part, our culture has consciously chosen to change the way it designs products to accommodate either-handedness. Also, we have chosen to change the way we think about people who are left-handed. It is simply no longer viewed as a handicap or a weakness. In fact, most are aware of the tremendous earning potential for good left-handed pitchers in the major leagues!

---

[39]From our standpoint the difference *appears* as if the texts are contradictory, unless of course the breakout extends further the preliminary movement (relative to the original culture) of a broad-based selection of texts on the subject.

What helps us assess the biblical material as cultural on this matter is the fact that we find some unusual breakouts. For example, it is the left-handed Ehud (ironically a Benjamite) whom God uses to slay Eglon, the oppressive king of Moab (Judg 3:12-30; cf. 20:16). God used someone whom society viewed as weak to perform his mission and task. When God breaks out of the societal norms and its viewpoint on left-handedness, this breakout text gives us a hint that Scriptural affirmation of right-handed superiority and left-handed inferiority is culturally relative. It is not an absolute, transcendent value with God. Despite the frequent affirmations of right-handed superiority in Scripture, it would hardly be a sin to move against the grain on this issue in our own society. Why? Well, Scripture itself breaks out of the standard framework now and then.

2. *Long hair.* At one point, Paul speaks of long hair on men as a shame and a disgrace (1 Cor 11:14). One might get the impression that this is a transcultural teaching by the apostle. However, there are other biblical texts that provide breakouts in this area. For example, the Nazarite actually honored God by not cutting his hair for the duration of his service (Num 6:1-21; cf. Acts 18:18). In this fashion, Samuel the priest remained longhaired all of his life (1 Sam 1:11; cf. Lk 1:15). Furthermore, long hair on men at other times in the Bible was viewed as an appealing and attractive physical trait.[40] Therefore, it is difficult to assess anything inherently evil about long hair for men. In all likelihood, the hair length evaluations in Scripture are culturally based and should not be understood in an absolute manner. In one culture long hair on men could be a shameful sight, in another it was a thing of honor. A similar analysis could be made about beards[41] and the length of beard hair.[42]

3. *Meat sacrificed to idols.* Acts 15:20, 29 provides what appears to be a universal prohibition against eating meat sacrificed to idols. This apostolic decree calls for Gentile believers "to abstain from food polluted by idols" and "to abstain from food sacrificed to idols." However, in 1 Corinthians 10:23-30 Paul, the apostle to the Gentiles, recommends that in certain circumstances believers can

---

[40]2 Sam 14:25-26. The editorial comments on the perfection of Absalom's physical appearance, with one of the main features being long hair, would indicate an acceptance of that particular physical trait.

[41]In the Israelite culture a beard was often a sign of wisdom, knowledge and maturity. The Hebrew expression "the bearded ones" (e.g., Exod 3:16) was used as a Hebrew idiom for the elders of Israel. Our English translations will often simply put the word *elders* in the text to clarify the idiom. One might contrast this perception with certain Christian subcultures where a beard is viewed negatively because one is not clean-shaven or because it covers the face and hides the real person.

[42]This same cultural assessment would appear to apply to the Old Testament injunction not to cut the hair at the sides of one's head or at the edges of one's beard (Lev 19:27). While this prohibition is still followed by certain conservative Jews, most would recognize the cultural basis of the injunction relative to practices in foreign cults.

eat meat offered to idols. What becomes clear is that the original apostolic decree is culturally relative—relative to achieving cultural harmony between the Jews and Gentiles (i.e., the Acts context). In a similar manner, Paul's own prohibition against eating idol meat in 1 Corinthians 8:1-10 is also relative—relative to the presence of weak believers for whom the practice would be to their spiritual detriment. Neither the apostolic decree in Acts 15, nor Paul's prohibitions in 1 Corinthians 8 are absolute, even though they get stated in absolute and emphatic terms. The breakout of 1 Corinthians 10:23-30 helps us assess the relative nature of those texts.

4. Firstborn (primogeniture) customs. Scripture adopts and utilizes various customs about the rights and privileges of firstborns. There is legislation related to the practice (Deut 21:15-17). And, firstborn privileges are frequently theologized in both Testaments. The custom plays a heavy role in Old Testament redemptive patterns (e.g., Ex 13:1-10; Num 3:11-13, 45) and enters into the New Testament especially in the area of Christology (e.g., Rom 8:29; Col 1:15; Heb 1:6). The firstborn usually was given a double inheritance (the birthright) and enjoyed a special dominance over the other siblings that would extend beyond childhood into adulthood, and sometimes into successive generations.

In view of the biblical legislation and theologizing of firstborn predominance and power, one might be persuaded to think that this is a transcultural value to be retained in every Christian home and in every culture. However, certain texts related to birth order suggest that firstborn prominence is simply a cultural-bound custom. We might describe these texts as breakouts. They have consciously abandoned the norm that is upheld in other texts:

☐ "The Lord said to her [Rebekah], 'Two nations are in your womb . . . and the older will serve the younger' " (Genesis 25:23; cf. Mal 1:2-3).

☐ The blessing in the Ephraim and Manasseh scene is reversed between the elder and the younger (Genesis 48:12-20).

☐ The tribe of Judah is chosen over that of Reuben, the eldest (Genesis 49:8).

☐ Samuel thought he should anoint Jesse's firstborn son (Eliab) as king of Israel, but to Samuel's surprise God selected the youngest son, David, as the nation's leader (1 Samuel 16:6, 11; 17:13-14).

This overturning of firstborn practices would appear to indicate that from a divine perspective, primogeniture practices were little more than a cultural custom, not a transcultural absolute. So today, Christians should not feel under any compulsion to leave a "double inheritance" to their firstborn or to give the firstborn any special dominance over the children born later.

5. Slavery. As we have seen already, in Scripture we find legislation concerning the institution of slavery. Furthermore, slavery is often theologized in various ways. However, we also encounter significant breakouts in this domain. The exodus event itself qualifies as one of the greatest breakouts within the slavery texts. The exodus from Egypt emerges as a paradigm of release from slavery both on a physical and a spiritual level. For example, Yahweh states, "I am the Lord your God, who brought you out of Egypt so that you would no longer be slaves to the Egyptians; I broke the bars of your yoke and enabled you to walk with heads held high" (Lev 26:13). Surely if this "heads held high" status is the best for God's people, then it might well be an ultimate good for all peoples to be set free from slavery. Also, the gospel itself is couched in a "setting the captives free" terminology, reflecting either first- or second-exodus language (e.g., Is 42:7; 49:9; 61:1).

In sum, the breakouts related to left-handedness, long hair, idol meat, primogeniture practices and slavery help the interpreter appraise the cultural-component status of other biblical texts.

C. Women

Most of the time the authors of Scripture proclaim oracles (e.g., Is 3:12; 19:16), narrate (e.g., Num 31:32; Josh 15:16; Judg 11:30-31) and legislate (e.g., Ex 20:17; Num 30:3-15) within a patriarchal, male-authority framework. On many occasions they show a softening movement and modification of patriarchy relative to the original culture. At other times they plant seed ideas, which are suggestive of further movement. However, there are certain occasions where they totally break out of patriarchal forms. The following examples not only move to a softer or less restrictive positioning relative the original culture, they amazingly take the preliminary movement to its extreme and flip the standard status and role expectations for women. They actualize the potential within the seed ideas.

1. Deborah. Within biblical traditions Deborah stands out as a significant reversal of leadership norms. Her life breaks away from the standard patterns of male leadership and authority as she functions in various roles of leadership within the Israelite community. As an elder/judge, she holds court under the "Palm of Deborah" and Israelites come to her to have their disputes decided (Judg 4:4-5). As a prophetess, she communicates the will of God to her people (Judg 4:6-7), predicts the outcome of the battle (Judg 5:9) and creatively leads the people in celebration through singing a hymn (Judg 5:1-31). As a military leader, she courageously musters the forces of Israel against Sisera and his Canaanite army (Judg 5:8-16).

There is some evidence that might suggest that God viewed Deborah's role with disapproval. First, the military role of Deborah openly mocks the social expectations of men fighting in the army—a point later "driven home" by Jael's tent peg (Judg 4:9, 17-22; 5:24-27). In armies dependent upon physical strength, women were considered the weaklings. Men were supposed to fight the battles; women stayed at home with the children. Perhaps, some might argue, God only in a reluctant fashion allowed Deborah to function in a leadership role, since there were no men around to do the job. Second, the upheaval during the time of the Judges as a whole might reflect negatively on the Deborah incident. For instance, the book characterizes the period of the judges as a time when "everyone did what was right in their own eyes" (Judg 17:6; 21:25; cf. 18:1; 19:1). Perhaps the role of Deborah as female leader was simply indicative of this upheaval and instability within the nation. Maybe male leadership was seen as something that would restore stability. Third, the book of Judges is full of mixed examples. Samson is a good case in point. God did use Samson, but only in spite of his moral failures, not because of them. Similarly, maybe God used a woman such as Deborah in leadership, something that is morally wrong, but he chose to act through her despite her disobedience to his divine standards.

In response to the above portrayal, it might be helpful to look first at the matter of the male polemic. The argument that Deborah was permitted to take the leadership role because there were no good men around falters under examination. On the one hand, she *is* married. The text names her husband as Lappidoth (Judg 4:4). If there was anything ethically inappropriate to Deborah's role, she could have taken a soft hierarchical approach and ruled Israel together with her husband. Then, Lappidoth could have stated the final verdicts in the various cases they judged together, with the male issuing the decision as a "final say" between them. On the other hand, there was another judge and military leader named Shamgar. Shamgar lived and ministered at the same time as Deborah,[43] although she seemed to have the larger and more lasting influence upon Israel. Shamgar did not lack for courage. Surely he could have taken over Barak's role upon his default and assumed Deborah's role as elder/judge. In this regard, the text's mocking of male leadership appears to be directed against Barak, not against all Israelite males of that era. The point is to draw out Barak's unfaithfulness and timidity, particularly in contrast to his daring name, which meant "thunderbolt." His name suggests that he was summoned to be the Lord's "flashing sword" (Judg 4:8, 16; 5:12; cf. Deut 32:41). Yet, he fails to live up to his name, so God uses a woman to accomplish the initial summons and final blow.

There can be little doubt that the Deborah story mocks a male (Barak) for his lack of leadership and courage, and any other males who lacked the courage that he lacked. However, the real question for our cultural analysis is whether Deborah's involvement in leadership should be viewed negatively in and of itself, re-

---

[43]Judg 5:6; cf. "after Ehud" in 3:31 and 4:1.

gardless of what Barak or other men did. In other words, did God view what Deborah did as wrong and only with reluctance allow her to act in leadership? Or, did God choose to break out of the cultural standards, which themselves carried social stigmas, and show his approval and blessing upon Deborah?

While breaking the conventions of a patriarchal society, a number of considerations suggest that Deborah does not violate any moral boundaries or absolute values. First, we find no words of rebuke for the actions taken by Deborah. This may be an argument from silence. But one needs to compare this silence to the Pentateuch story, of which Judges is a canonical extension (e.g., Judg 3:9), where the narrator openly criticizes the overstepping of power and role boundaries within the community (e.g., Num 12:1-16; 16:1—18:32; cf. Num 21:4-9). Second, the author of Judges mocks the lack of male leadership through Deborah's military role, not through her judicial role. The military mock is present in Deborah's words to Barak and the concluding triumph of Jael (Judg 4:9, 22). However, Deborah also functioned within Israel as the leading elder or supreme judge, adjudicating for people from different cities all over Israel, which would have had their own community elders sitting at the city gates (cf. Judg 9:35, 40, 44; 16:2-3; 18:16-17). The text does tell us that she held court between Ramah and Bethel at a well-known location and that Israelites, presumably from every region, "came to her to have their disputes decided." Deborah's judicial/elder role was equally a breakout within the biblical text, as was her military role. However, no shadows are cast over this role due to a literary mock on males. She appears to function in her judicial capacity with God's blessing and approval, regardless of gender expectations for that role within her society.[44] Third, the expression "everyone did what was right in their own eyes" is not a blanket statement from which to evaluate everything as evil within the book. Rather, that phrase is directly connected to the polemic for a (Davidic) king to rule the nation (Judg 16:6; 18:1; 19:1; 21:25). Ironically, when the nation finally gets a king, he (the king) does whatever is right is his own eyes! Thus the thematic statement should not be viewed as a polemic against female leaders. Fourth, the moral and spiritual portrait of Deborah is one of a person who loved and served God with all of her strength and being. If it were morally wrong for her to function in the leadership capacity that she did, one would expect that she would have simply refused to do so, as she refused to worship and serve foreign gods.[45] Fifth, there is an underlying theme within Judges that God can use individuals who society deems as weak.[46] The writer

---

[44]Both the opening narration of Deborah's judicial role (Judg 4:4-5) and the concluding comment of peace for forty years (Judg 5:31) portray a sense of God's blessing upon her life and ministry.

[45]Judg 4:1; 5:8. Cf. the theme of spiritual adultery: Judg 2:11, 13, 19; 3:7; 8:33-34; 9:27, 46; 17:5-6.

[46]The theme is very similar to the words of Paul in 1 Cor 1:26-31.

uses this theology of cultural overturn to stress God's power. Thus we see that God used individuals like Ehud, who is viewed as weak within his culture because he is left-handed; or Shamgar, who fights with only an oxgoad (not the latest nor greatest military weapon); or Deborah and Jael, who display the power of God in a mighty way because they are viewed by society as weak. It would appear that God flaunts an open dismissal of common societal evaluations of strength and conventional power models in order to demonstrate his power.

In this fashion, Deborah should probably be aligned with an Ehud, not a Samson. A comparison and contrast with Ehud and Samson supports such an alignment:

Deborah and Ehud	Samson
Both are given their "weakness" at birth (not by choice).	Samson becomes spiritually and physically weak as a result of his own poor choices.
Both are spiritually gifted leaders of noble character.	Samson is a proud and rash person.
Both have Israel's interests at heart.	Samson primarily indulges his own interests.
Both are morally pure.	Samson is immoral.

In sum, the Deborah breakout has interpretive difficulties. However, it would seem that God blesses Deborah for her leadership role in Israel regardless of her gender, not in spite of her gender. He does so purposefully in order to demonstrate his power in a way that mocks standard social conventions. By overturning these conventions, the divine perspective would seem to categorize the standard norms as culturally bound.

2. Huldah. While a lesser-known figure, Huldah plays an important role during the reign of Josiah. Hilkiah the priest and an expedition sent from the king seek her out to hear from the Lord and to give them understanding about what was written in the book of the covenant (2 Kings 22:14-20; 2 Chron 34:22-28). The cultural breakout here is to have a woman, such as Huldah, being consulted by the king, priest, delegation of male leaders (elders)[47] and broader community about the Hebrew Scriptures.[48] She provides an authoritative understanding of the text for the delegation.

So why did the delegation seek out Huldah? After all, Jeremiah and Zephaniah

---

[47]The elders, or a representative from them, may have made up at least part of the group that went to consult Huldah (2 Chron 34:29; cf. 34:19).

[48]This may have been the Pentateuch or a portion of Deuteronomy (cf. Deut 31:24, 26; 2 Chron 34:14).

were well-known prophets during this time. Perhaps it was because of Huldah's accessibility, since she lived in Jerusalem (2 Kings 22:14). This pragmatic factor may have influenced their thinking. However, one still has to wonder about Huldah's response. There is no inhibition about the way she handles the situation. She does not defer to her husband (who is named in the text [2 Kings 22:14]) or to Jeremiah or Zephaniah or another male prophet. If gender roles were an ethical issue, then this kind of deference would be expected. However, she does not withhold her proclamation based on gender. She speaks with authority about the nature and essence of God's covenant Scriptures. Upon receiving her word, the king and elders act in response to the text. By assuming such an authoritative role in relationship to Scripture, Huldah overturns the sociological expectations of a patriarchal society and of other texts that are reflective of that hierarchal norm (e.g., 1 Tim 2:11-12).

3. Priscilla. Priscilla and her husband Aquila ministered with Paul in founding the church at Corinth (Acts 18:1-4). Afterwards they left with Paul for Asia and established a house church in Ephesus (Acts 18:18-19; 1 Cor 16:19). What provides a breakout from patriarchy is Priscilla's dominant ministry role in relationship to her husband. This is suggested by her name being placed first within the text before her husband Aquila.[49] She is at least a co-leader, and probably a primary leader, in the process of church planting and evangelism. This kind of dominance or hierarchy of leadership through the ordering of names is seen elsewhere in Acts in the Paul-Barnabas relationship.[50] Furthermore, Priscilla is likely the major participant, as indicated by name order, in the correction and instruction of the male preacher, Apollos. Apollos was an educated man with a thorough knowledge of the Scriptures and had already been instructed in the way of the Lord. Nevertheless, Priscilla along with her husband instructs him further in the way of God (Acts 18:24-26). It would appear that Priscilla herself was well trained in Scripture and in early church theology, that is, in the teachings of Jesus and apostolic tradition. Out of her knowledge she provides instruction for a male leader.

4. Junia. Linguistic evidence indicates that the name Junia(s) in Romans 16:7 is probably feminine, not masculine, as it has often been understood.[51] If so, then Junia is an apostle along with Andronicus: "They [Andronicus and Junia] are outstanding among the apostles and they were in Christ before I [Paul] was." As an apostle, Junia would have been included among a group of apostles broader than the original twelve. In this role, the church would likely have recognized her in some official capacity as a preacher of the gospel (cf. Acts 14:4, 14; 1 Thess 2:7).

---

[49]Acts 18:18, 19, 26; Rom 16:3; 2 Tim 4:19; cf. Acts 18:2; 1 Cor 16:19.

[50]Acts 11:26, 30; 12:25; 13:1-2, 7; contrast: Acts 13:42-43, 46, 50; 14:1, 23; 15:2, 12, 22, 35.

[51]For a detailed argumentation see Richard S. Cervin, "A Note Regarding the Name 'Junia(s)' in Romans 16:7," *NTS* 40 (1994): 464-70.

The lack of female apostles is understandable within a patriarchal society. However, it is interesting that we have at least one breakout in this otherwise male-dominated field.

5. Job's daughters and inheritance. In the book of Job we find a significant departure from the typical treatment of women when it comes to inheritance. Women in Israel generally received no part of the inheritance. Yet, it would appear that Job gives his daughters an equal share in the inheritance: "Nowhere in all the land were there found women as beautiful as Job's daughters, and their father granted them inheritance along with their brothers" (Job 42:15). This inheritance breakout is especially intriguing since it fits within the idealized ending of the book. We have already noted under criterion 1 that the daughters of Zelophehad push the boundaries of the inheritance laws. Now in the Job story, we discover a complete breakout from the norm. This would suggest that the inheritance restrictions on women assumed elsewhere in Scripture are simply cultural aspects of the text. An idealized world might contain a different portrait.

6. Sexual realm in marriage. We find another breakout from the hierarchal norm in the area of sexual relations between husbands and wives. To the Corinthian community Paul gives instructions about how marital partners should make decisions concerning having and not having sexual intercourse within their relationship. What is so striking is that he grants equal power to each partner. According to Paul, a Christian couple should make sexual-fulfillment decisions on the basis of mutual deference, while sexual-abstinence decisions are to be based upon mutual consent (1 Cor 7:3-5).

But this kind of model with "equality in power," "mutual consent" and "mutual deference" is nothing other than an egalitarian model, only with limited application to one realm. In an attempt to synthesize Paul's teaching as a whole we might picture his model for decision making within marriage in the following way:

Marriage

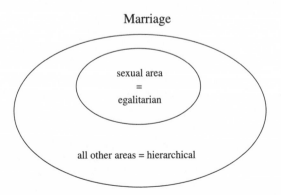

Those holding to the soft patriarchal position handle 1 Corinthians 7:3-5 in a rather peculiar manner. After acknowledging that the text teaches mutuality and equality of power, they go on to use it as a basis to show how the marriage relationship as a whole ought to function. This is an ironic twist indeed. Piper and Grudem state, "This text [1 Cor 7:3-5] is one of the main reasons we prefer the term *leadership* for the man's special responsibility rather than *authority*. . . . Texts like this transform the concept of authority so deeply as to make the word, with its authoritarian connotations, easily misunderstood."[52] Rather than admitting that this text is an exception to the rule (i.e., an exception to patriarchy), they insist that this passage is the model for all decision making within marriage.

However, Piper and Grudem's synthetic proposal is not very persuasive. On the one hand, their approach ultimately abandons their own position when it comes to maintaining the distinctiveness crucial to soft patriarchy. Once one has eliminated any power differential and set up mutual deference and mutual consent as the basis for *all* decision making in a marriage (such as Piper and Grudem have done) there is nothing that makes the view substantially different from egalitarianism. Their attempt to establish a distinction by talking about leadership amounts to little more than rhetoric. If a husband must lead his household without any power differential (i.e., both have equal power) and he must always gain agreement on every decision, then to suggest some special leadership role for the husband is nothing more than a hollow gesture. In reality this view amounts to shared leadership between the husband and wife. Both partners have equal power in shaping the direction of the home, but only the husband retains the label of leader.

Furthermore (and more importantly), Piper and Grudem's view does not fit well with the rest of Scripture. Paul's call for equal power and mutual deference in the sexual realm *does* constitute a radical departure from many other texts. For starters, we might look at the household codes and submission lists. Are we to assume that there is no power differential (and instead a model of mutual agreement and mutual deference) between the first-century government and its subjects, between parents and children, between masters and slaves, between elders and the church community? Not likely.

Paul's call for power equality in the sexual realm is an intriguing breakout in view of the profound dominance of males over females in every area of life and especially in the sexual domain. After all, wives were to submit to (and obey) their husbands in "all things," presumably with the only exceptions being areas of ethical conflict. Sex within marriage would not fit into an ethical exception clause. Also, decision-making about service to the Lord (e.g., vows) clearly gives

---

[52]Piper and Grudem, *Biblical Manhood and Womanhood*, p. 88, emphasis in original.

the male greater authority over his wife (Num 30:1-16). If this were applied to
service that would require sexual abstinence for a certain time period, then the
husband would unquestionably hold decisive authority. Along these lines, Scripture's treatment of women in the sexual and procreative domain repeatedly gives
the male greater power and at times includes a dimension of conquest.[53] This subject will be developed in detail below (see criterion 11.C).

In sum, Paul's breakout in 1 Corinthians 7 establishes an egalitarian pattern
within *one* area of the marital relationship. This equality of power (mutual agreement and mutual deference) model of decision making in the sexual realm breaks
with the standard biblical model. As such, it calls into question whether the hierarchal model for marriage as a whole is a culture-bound phenomenon.

D. Homosexuality

Some see the David and Jonathan story and the Ruth and Naomi story as positive
examples of homosexual love within Scripture.[54]

1. David and Jonathan. Some of the incidents in the David and Jonathan narrative might lead one to believe that the two were homosexual lovers. For instance, David and Jonathan embrace, weep together and kiss each other (1 Sam
20:41-42), they make a covenant of friendship (1 Sam 18:1; 20:8, 16-17, 42;
23:18) and express their love for each other in strong terms (1 Sam 18:3; 19:1;
20:17). At Jonathan's death, David writes a passionate lament for Saul and
Jonathan in which he articulates his love for Jonathan: "I grieve for you, Jonathan
my brother; you were very dear to me. Your love for me was wonderful, more
wonderful than that of women" (2 Sam 1:26).

While the relationship between David and Jonathan could be construed to be homosexual, there are factors that suggest otherwise. Embracing, weeping together
and kissing were (and still are) standard customs among heterosexual males in the
Near Eastern world. Rather than establishing a sexual union, "the covenant" between David and Jonathan was a covenant of loyalty and regal recognition set in the
context of transferring throne rights to David and symbolized by Jonathan giving
David his cloak and armor. Also, the description of their love as "more wonderful
than that of women," while intriguing data, is part of a poetic lament full of passionate hyperbole. In the same poem David speaks of Jonathan and Saul as "swifter
than eagles . . . stronger than lions" (2 Sam 1:23). Thus the poetic nature of the pas-

---

[53]The clearest example would be taking virgins as spoils of war (Deut 21:10-14; cf. Num 31:32; Judg
5:30) for sexual and procreative fulfillment. Cf. giving women as prizes for battle efforts (Josh
15:16).

[54]Tom Horner, *Jonathan Loved David: Homosexuality in Biblical Times* (Philadelphia: Westminster
Press, 1978), pp. 26-46; cf. Cleaver, *Know My Name*, p. 102.

sage argues against a homoerotic reading of the lament.

2. *Ruth and Naomi.* Certain features of the Ruth and Naomi story might similarly suggest a lesbian love relationship. There are scenes of physical intimacy (e.g., kissing and weeping together [Ruth 1:10]). Also, Ruth expresses in covenant terms (not unlike marriage covenants) her relationship to Naomi: "Where you go I will go, and where you stay I will stay. Your people will be my people and your God my God. Where you die I will die, and there I will be buried" (Ruth 1:16-17).

Despite these intimate features, the possibility of lesbian love being presented in the Ruth story is highly improbable. The language of covenant develops the broader theme within the book of Ruth—crossing between people-group boundaries, not necessarily voicing the idea of marriage; this language is used elsewhere to express loyalty between people without sexual connotation (e.g., 2 Sam 15:21). Also, the proposal of lesbian love seems farfetched when one considers that Naomi did not really want Ruth to come with her. Naomi functions as something of a matchmaker for Ruth and Boaz, and Ruth's marriage to Boaz at the end of book "fills up" the empty and bitter Naomi. The intimacy between the two women seems fully accounted for in the "mother and daughter" model that the story presents.

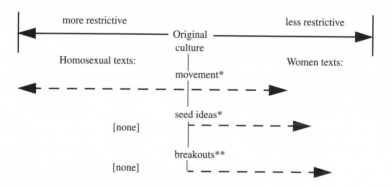

*movement relative to the original culture
**breakouts and seed ideas extend the "movement" of other texts relative to the original culture (in the *same* direction)

Movement of women texts versus movement of homosexuals texts

In sum, there are no viable breakouts in the homosexuality texts. Few recent authors advocating a homosexual position use these biblical examples to support their case for homosexuality; most scholars arguing for same-sex relationships do not find such texts persuasive. Therefore, one may conclude that there are no breakouts in this area within Scripture.[55] Granted, this is an argument from silence. However,

---

[55]We might add that we do not find breakouts in *any* of the sexual-perversion texts.

it is quite understandable or predictable that we do not have any breakouts. If breakouts are generally an extension of and in the same direction as seed ideas (criterion 2) and preliminary movement found across a broad-based selection of texts (criterion 1), then the likelihood of a breakout from the homosexual texts is incredibly small. The movement in the homosexual texts relative to the original culture has already "hit the wall" so to speak. The homosexual texts have already achieved maximum movement relative to the original culture.

Since the movement in all of the homosexual texts relative to the original culture is a complete banning, it is understandable why there is no further movement in that same direction. It is not possible to have other texts take this movement further in what would then be a breakout relative to the soft movement texts.

E. Evaluation of the criterion

One who is opposed to seed ideas and breakouts might argue that these cases are simply exceptions to the general rule. Rather than dismiss the rule, they merely reinforce the rule, since these exceptional texts are relatively infrequent. On the surface this objection appears convincing. Yet, several considerations make it suspect. First, these breakout texts can only be taken as mere exceptions if one reads Scripture in a flat two-dimensional manner. Within such a perspective, I would have to agree. They are simply exceptions and should serve to show the preponderance of the general situation. Yet, from a three-dimensional reading of the text—one that listens to the underlying spirit—seed ideas and breakouts converge with the preliminary movement of the broad spectrum of texts elsewhere. Preliminary movement tells us that the ethic of Scripture is moving the covenant people in a particular direction of which seed ideas and breakouts are an extension. Thus what might look like contradictions or exceptions to the rule are better seen as extensions of the movement of within so-called "rule texts" themselves. Second, the history of interpretation cautions us against dismissing these breakout texts as "mere exceptions" within Scripture. This is exactly how slavery advocates argued regarding the seed ideas and breakouts within the slavery texts.

F. Summary

The breakouts within the women texts, like those of the slavery texts, argue strongly for egalitarian conclusions. In themselves, they may appear as mere exceptions to the general rule of patriarchy. However, when viewed in conjunction with broad scriptural movement relative to the original setting (the softening of patriarchy found in preliminary movement) and with theoretical presentations of equality within social orders (found in seed ideas) these break-outs function as an extension of what has already been happening. The homo-sexual texts do not have any breakouts, as might be expected in view of what was discovered under the assessment of the movement criterion. Breakouts would be unlikely, since the movement of those texts was already realized to its fullest potential.

CRITERION 4: Purpose/Intent Statements

A. Statement

A component of a text may be culturally bound, if by practicing the text one no longer fulfills the text's original intent or purpose.[56] The other side of this crite-rion is that a text is more likely to be transcultural to the degree that its original purpose is fulfilled when practiced in a subsequent culture and time. With this criterion we enter into the whole issue of explicitly stated and/or implied pur-poses for instructions within the biblical text.

B. Neutral examples

1. Holy kiss. Five times within the New Testament, Christians are instructed to "greet one another with a holy kiss."[57] In the Hellenistic-Roman culture the origi-nal purpose of the holy kiss was to encourage closeness and community among Christians. For many people today in our culture, however, such a greeting would be distasteful. Most North Americans, with the exception of several ethnic sub-cultures, are not comfortable with kissing among males. The act of kissing (espe-cially on the lips) is usually reserved for more intimate male-female rela-tionships. Also, the practice of kissing as a broad greeting ritual has diminished today due to increased awareness about how cold viruses and other organisms are transmitted. A hug, a smile or a handshake is often more appreciated.

What should clue us into the cultural component within this New Testament imperative is the fact that we are no longer fulfilling the original purpose of the text. If we obey the text, we may violate the purpose of making people within the Christian community feel a warm welcome and a special bond. In many situa-tions today, continuing the greeting would probably do more harm than good. So, by literally "doing the text" in our contemporary setting we would no longer be doing the intent of the text—we would fail to fulfill its original purpose. In fact,

---

[56]William M. Swartley, *Slavery, Sabbath, War & Women: Case Issues in Biblical Interpretation* (Waterloo, Ontario: Herald, 1983), p. 202; Mary Hayter, *The New Eve in Christ* (Grand Rapids, Mich.: Eerdmans, 1987), pp. 149-50.

[57]Rom 16:16; 1 Cor 16:20; 2 Cor 13:12; 1 Thess 5:26; 1 Pet 5:14.

we may be undermining that purpose. The underlying principle of Christian community and friendship remains transcultural, while the holy kiss itself is a culture-bound expression of these values.

2. New Testament submission lists. Within the New Testament submission lists one finds such explicit purpose statements as "to make the gospel attractive" and "to win unbelievers." The following examples relate to slaves, government and women:

☐ Slaves are instructed "to be subject to their masters in everything, to try to please them, and not to talk back to them . . . *[purpose]* so that in every way they will make the teaching about God our Savior attractive" (Tit 2:9-10).

☐ Slaves are to submit to their masters *[purpose]* "so that God's name and our teaching may not be slandered" (1 Tim 6:1).

☐ Christians are to "submit . . . to the king . . . *[purpose]* for it is God's will that by doing good you should silence the ignorant talk of foolish men" (1 Pet 2:13-15).

☐ Wives are instructed "to be busy at home . . . and to be subject to their husbands, *[purpose]* so that no one will malign the word of God" (Tit 2:4-5).

☐ Wives must "be submissive to your husbands . . . *[purpose]* so that, if any of them are disobedient to the word, they may be won over without words by the behavior of their wives" (1 Pet 3:1; cf. 1 Pet 2:12).

The one clear purpose statement within the submission lists is that of evangelism and Christian mission. We will now look at this purpose statement within the various categories of slaves, government and women.

3. Slavery. Today, unbelievers would be offended if Christians would argue for a literal slavery-form submission based on the submission lists, although Christians clearly did so in the past.[58] In our context the continued practice of slavery-type submission no longer achieves the stated purpose of winning others to Christ. At this point we need to stop and ponder the text's purpose statement. When we jeopardize Christian mission by continuing to perform a text, which was originally designed to enhance Christian mission, we may well have stumbled upon a text with a significant cultural component.

Clearly the underlying principle of showing deference/respect in order to win people (employers) continues to have transcultural relevance. However, only in this more abstracted form are we able once again to fulfill the evangelistic purpose statement within the biblical text. The aspect of literal slavery-type submission should be classified as a cultural component within the command. Thus,

---

[58]See Swartley, *Slavery*, pp. 31-66 for an excellent review of how Christians argued from Scripture to support slavery.

when a text's explicit purpose statement is no longer being met, it provides an interpretive clue that maybe we should move up the ladder of abstraction[59] to a more abstracted form of applying the text.

4. Civil government. In the past, the submission texts cited above were used by Christians to support monarchy as the only appropriate, God-honoring form of government. However, to keep living out a monarchy-type submission/obedience in a democratic society no longer fulfills the text's stated purpose of making the gospel message winsome to unbelievers. In a democratic society a Christian admonition to "submit to" and "obey" the president or prime minister is strikingly foolish. Instead of commending the gospel to the unbelieving community in which we live, it would discredit the gospel. We certainly should pray for our leaders within a democracy, but we do not obey them. In a democratic society all citizens are equal under the law. Therefore, Christians in this kind of modern setting should not be instructed to obey their politicians, but to obey the law as it governs the whole of society (politicians included).

The underlying principle of honor and respect (toward our political leaders) and submission (to the law) continues to provide a transcultural expression of the text for our day. When we act in this manner, we once again fulfill the text's stated purpose or intent. However, the aspect of monarchy-type submission itself must be classified as a culture-bound component of the text. Only by moving to a more abstracted level of application are we able in our culture to fulfill the Christian mission purpose within the text.

C. Women

The submission lists instruct Christian wives to submit to and obey their husbands. In fact, wives are told to model their obedience after Sarah, who addressed her husband as "master/lord" (1 Pet 3:6). For this criterion, it is important to note that a wife's submission is explicitly linked to purpose statements about evangelism and Christian mission. For instance, Paul instructs wives to submit to their husbands "so that no one will malign the word of God" (Tit 2:5). Likewise, Peter tells wives to obey their husbands so that unbelieving husbands "may be won over without words" (1 Pet 3:1).

Today, unilateral-type submission and obedience of a wife toward her unbelieving husband, adorned by her addressing him as "master/lord," generally fails to fulfill the mission statements within the biblical text. For today's unbelieving husband who values his wife as a completely equal partner and who happily functions within a mutual-deference and mutual-honor framework, this kind of

---

[59]For a detailed development of the "ladder of abstraction," see criterion 17.

unilateral, patriarchy-type submission may actually repulse him and prevent him from being won to Christ. In other words, the stated evangelistic purpose of the text is not likely to be fulfilled in our contemporary setting. By *actually* doing the text (the literal imperative), we no longer be doing the *intent* of the text (the purpose statement).

Certainly the underlying principle of showing deference/respect in order to win people (whether employers or husbands) continues to have transcultural application. But, we must recognize that only in this more abstracted sense are we able once again to fulfill the evangelistic purpose statement within the biblical text. As with slavery and government above, the lack of fulfilling the text's explicit purpose statement provides a hint that maybe we should move up the ladder of abstraction in our application of the text today in order to recapture that aspect of the biblical text. Only deference and respect in a mutual-submission framework allows for the evangelistic or winsome gospel purpose statements to be realized in our social context.

Granted, there may be more than one purpose involved in giving a biblical command. Perhaps unilateral, patriarchy-type submission should be viewed as transcultural based on other purposes. Such a possibility clearly exists. In this situation one would be left with fulfilling certain purposes but failing to fulfill others. Such an outcome would call for evaluating the weight and gravity of each purpose. In the final analysis, there may be a modified application of the text anyway in order to maximize all of the multiple purposes as far as that is possible.

Nevertheless, the explicit purpose statement repeatedly tied to a wife's (unilateral, patriarchy-type) submission is its evangelistic benefit. While we could posit other purposes, this is the one that comes across loud and clear. Ultimately, we have to modify something in our application today in order to fulfill this purpose statement. If we are to fulfill the Christian mission statement in our setting, we must take the underlying transcultural principle—showing deference and respect tends to win people to a cause—and utilize an alternative form of that principle in our setting. A wife today can still achieve the evangelistic purpose statements within the biblical text by showing her husband deference and respect within a mutual-submission, rather than a unilateral-submission, framework.

D. Homosexuality

We might start off our discussion of homosexuality with a similar line of reasoning to that used with the women's issue. Perhaps granting covenant homosexuals an equal and accepted status within the church would make the church and the gospel message more attractive to society. Also, one might argue that to maintain a prohibitive stance against covenant homosexuality is to place unnecessary barriers in the way of unbelievers.

Should the church, therefore, accept a homosexual lifestyle within its own community because to do otherwise would make the gospel less attractive to the unbelieving community? This might sound like a good idea in light of the direction of our discussion about women. However, such reasoning is fallacious. This purpose-statement criterion does *not* suggest that what is attractive to society should become the basis for all that the church does. Rather, the criterion asks the interpreter to evaluate the degree to which *the stated purpose of text* is being fulfilled.

Here lies the crucial difference. In contrast to the submission lists (and their explicit purpose statements), we do not have any biblical texts where the purpose for prohibiting homosexual activity is linked to making the Jewish or Christian movement more attractive to its surrounding culture. None of the homosexuality texts instruct the believing community to "do this" or "don't do this" in order that their behavior will facilitate the gospel. We simply do not find any admonitions that Christians practice only heterosexual activity (and abstain from homosexual acts) for the purpose of making their lives and gospel message more appealing to the surrounding cultures.

In fact, what we find is quite the opposite. For example, the prohibitions against homosexuality are related to purposes such as the appropriateness of sexual intercourse within the male-female physical relationship, in contrast to same-sex intercourse (Lev 18:22; 20:13; cf. Rom 1:27). The implied purpose within the Leviticus and Romans texts is that sexual intercourse was intended for a male-female relationship, not a male-male relationship. By "doing the text" within our modern context we still fulfill the original purpose through affirming the distinctiveness of the male-and-female sexual union, in contrast to other possibilities for intercourse. It is not that the doing of the text in our society no longer fulfills the (original) purpose of the text, as with the texts regarding women.

Furthermore, the prohibitions against homosexuality within Scripture often carry a countercultural purpose in relationship to society. The kingdom of God is marked by different sexual behavior than what is permitted in the kingdom of this world (1 Cor 6:9-10). The homosexual prohibitions, like other sexual prohibitions, often challenge behavior within the larger society. The holiness code of Leviticus, for instance, provides a clear purpose (related to the external society) for the sexual prohibitions: "You must not do as they do in Egypt, where you used to live, and you must not do as they do in the land of Canaan, where I am bringing you" (Lev 18:3; cf. Lev 18:24-30; 20:22-24). The purpose is so that Israel's practices, in contrast to the practices of the surrounding cultures, would be acceptable to Yahweh. These very acts of sexual perversion had led Yahweh to drive the nations out of the land that the Israelites were to inherit.[60]

Therefore, the purpose of the New Testament submission lists and the purpose of the sexual-behavior codes are directly antithetical. The one was established in order for God's people to attract society to the gospel and not impede their witness; the other was given in order to be distinct from society. Unlike the submission lists, the homosexuality prohibitions do not concern themselves with an attempt to gain society's approval.

E. Evaluation of the criterion

The application of this criterion makes its greatest contribution whenever the purpose statements are explicit and consistent in the biblical text. A clear liability to this criterion is that a biblical instruction may have more than one purpose. If several purposes can be determined, then obviously each purpose should be given a hearing by the interpreter. Explicit purpose statements should be given greater priority over any implicit or inferred intentionality. Also, if there are multiple purposes, one might still "reculturalize" the application of a text depending upon the weight of each purpose and what alternate form would best encompass a fulfillment of the collective purposes.

F. Summary

While multiple purposes may complicate the picture, the "purpose statement" criterion is an excellent tool for determining whether or not a component of a text is cultural. The stated purpose in the submission lists provides a substantial argument in favor of an egalitarian position. Only by moving up the ladder of abstraction and working with an alternative form (mutual submission) of the transcultural principle (showing deference and respect tends to win people to a cause) can we continue to obey the purpose statements of those texts. On the other hand, the purpose statements within the homosexual texts can continue to be upheld in our modern culture only by keeping the prohibition as originally given. The homosexuality texts evidence the transcultural flip side of the purpose-statement criterion, namely, that a text is more likely to be transcultural to the degree that its original purpose is fulfilled even when practiced in a subsequent culture and time.

CRITERION 5: Basis in Fall or Curse

A. Statement

A component of a text may be transcultural if its basis is rooted in the Fall of hu-

---

[60]Cf. a related discussion in criterion 9.

manity or the curse. Since the curse has an ongoing effect (it is still painful to have babies, the ground still produces weeds and people still die), then it might appear that something rooted in the curse should be classified as transcultural. The effects of the curse have been evident in a wide variety of cultural settings around the world. While the degree or proportion of curse-related pain may vary, all cultures suffer from its downward pull.

B. Neutral examples

1. Childbirth pain. A part of the curse oracle brought pain into the birthing process: "I [God] will greatly increase your [the woman's] pains in childbearing" (Gen 3:16). This theme continues in Scripture and is evident today on a transcultural basis.

2. Weeds. Similarly, the curse brought pain and struggle into the task of producing food: "through painful toil you will eat of it [the ground] . . . it will produce thorns and thistles" (Gen 3:17). Once again, this is obviously a transcultural phenomenon.

3. Death. After the Fall, God's curse upon humankind resulted in their death: "Dust you are and to dust you will return" (Gen 3:19; cf. 2:17; 3:3-4; 5:5). The theme of curse-death continues throughout biblical revelation and is realized today on a global basis as a universal certainty.

In sum, the effects of the Fall are transcultural in the sense that they extend to all of humanity regardless of culture, particularly in the broadest terms of sin and death.

C. Women

As one relates the Fall/curse to the women's issue, at least four facets of this picture must be examined: the perpetuation of the curse, the order of the Fall, the nature of the Fall and the possible origin of hierarchy in the curse.

1. Perpetuation of the curse (imperative or indicative). The subordination of women is obviously related in some way to the curse after the Fall, "He [your husband] will rule over you" (Gen 3:16; cf. 1 Tim 2:14-15). In view of this connection, one might argue that women should continue in subordinate roles based on the ongoing nature of the curse. As noted above, it is still painful to have babies, the ground still produces weeds and people still die. Therefore, maybe women should still submit as a part of the curse.

However, such an argument assumes a faulty, and extremely dangerous, premise about the perpetuation of the curse. It wrongly assumes the curse should be perpetuated. Nothing could be further from the truth. It is not a part of Christian mission to perpetuate the curse; it is our mission to *fight* the curse. We would not lobby today for the elimination of modern technology in agriculture to fight weeds, or in medicine to fight illness, pain or death. In the past the church has not handled the curse material very well. The story of Eufame MacLayne, who was burned at the stake by the church for using pain medication during pregnancy, illustrates all too well the confusion in this area.[61] So the curse is something the redemptive community should "swim upstream against."

While the curse carries forward indicative implications (what is), it should not carry any imperative implications (what ought to be) especially within the redeemed community. Fortunately, most hierarchalists today are well informed about the pitfalls of arguing for mandatory ongoing implications from the Fall/curse material.

2. Order of the Fall (woman first; man second). Some Christians argue for the ongoing application of hierarchy in view of the fact that "woman was created second, yet first to fall."[62] Here we will focus on the first-to-fall argument, since several subsequent criteria discuss the first-to-be-created argument. While it makes for a nice oratory slogan, the first-to-fall argument is not persuasive. For one thing, if those who hold this position are attempting to derive it from Paul, they are quite mistaken. Paul focuses on the nature of the Fall (woman's deception), not the order of the Fall. Second, both Adam and Eve are present when the snake makes his crafty appeal[63] and eventually both Adam and Eve sin. The fact that Eve ate the fruit first may have been due to her gullibility, so that the snake more easily swayed her than Adam. This would support our first point, that the issue is one of Eve's deception. The order of Fall may reflect the deception difference between Adam and Eve. However, this is only speculation. Neither the Genesis text nor the Pauline text tells us why Eve sinned first. To base a transcultural hierarchy on interpretive speculation is hardly responsible. Third, the Fall and curse are not a valid basis for the perpetuation of anything on an imperatival level due to implications of redemption in Christ (see above).

3. Nature of the Fall (woman deceived; man not deceived). In 1 Timothy 2:14-15 Paul relates the subordination of women to two key aspects of the Fall/curse:

---

[61]This fascinating story can be found in several sources: Mickelsen, *Women, Authority, and the Bible*, pp. 12-13; Bernard Seeman, *Man Against Pain* (Philadelphia: Chilton, 1962), p. 96; A. D. White, *A History of the Warfare of Science with Theology in Christendom*, vol. 2 (New York: Dover, 1960), p. 62.

[62]This first-to-fall rationale influenced the Southern Baptist Convention in June 1984 to exclude women from ordination to senior pastor: "Man was first in creation and woman was first in the Edenic fall." See Richard Groves, "Conservatives Dominate Southern Baptist Meeting," *The Christian Century* (July 18-25, 1984): 701-3.

[63]The statement in Gen 3:6, "who was with her," appears to place Adam with his wife during the time of the temptation.

Eve's deception (2:14; cf. Gen 3:13) and childbirth (1 Timothy 2:15; cf. Gen 3:16). It is obvious that there is some connection in Paul's mind; it is not so obvious what that connection is, nor exactly how he makes it. It is difficult to know how Eve's deception carries an ongoing application for today.

Throughout church history the traditional interpretation of 1 Timothy 2:14 has been that women are more easily deceived than men. This fits well within the context because it explains why women were to have subordinate teaching roles to men—they were more vulnerable to deception than men. From the traditional perspective this makes perfect sense. According to this view, men should have the authoritative teaching positions in the church. (For a survey of this teaching by early church fathers and subsequent church leaders, see appendix B.)

The only problem with the traditional interpretation is that most Western Christians today, patriarchalists included, recognize that this perspective is factually incorrect. Women are not inherently (by virtue of their gender alone) more easily deceived than men. It is not only politically incorrect to say so today, it simply does not square with the hard data. Such a perspective can be dismissed on the basis of social-scientific testing (see criterion 18 and appendix C). The degree to which one is deceivable or gullible is primarily related to factors such as age, experience, intelligence, education and personality. In our culture, gender is simply not a viable explanation for this phenomenon.

As a result, many contemporary patriarchalists have abandoned the church's traditional teaching about women. Only a handful would still hold that women are more easily deceived than men, although in recent years the view has seen resurgence.[64] Nevertheless, many soft patriarchalists have sought out an alternative explanation. They hold that verse 14 alludes to Adam and Eve's "role reversal" in the temptation by Satan.[65] Adam was not deceived by Satan; Adam sinned with full knowledge of what he was doing. He listened to his wife and ate the fruit. Eve, however, was deceived by the cunning of the serpent. Thus Paul is contrasting the ways in which they sinned. The woman should have gone to her husband instead of listening to the snake. The man should not have listened to his wife

---

[64]Although modified from the historic position, a revival of this view is found in Köstenberger, Schreiner, and Baldwin, eds. *Women in the Church: A Fresh Analysis of 1 Timothy 2:9-15*. For a critique of their revised-historic view, see criterion 18.C.4. Note also Robert D. Culver, "A Traditional View," in *Women in Ministry: Four Views*, ed. B. Clouse and R. G. Clouse (Downers Grove, Ill.: InterVarsity Press, 1989), p. 41.

[65]E.g., see David Dockery, "The Role of Women in Worship and Ministry: Some Hermeneutical Questions," *Criswell Theological Review* 1 (1987): 373; Homer Kent Jr., *The Pastoral Epistles* (Chicago: Moody, 1958), pp. 114-15; Douglas Moo, "The Interpretation of 1 Timothy 2:11-15. A Rejoinder," *Trinity Journal* 2 (1981): 204; George W. Knight III, "The Family and the Church," in *Biblical Manhood and Womanhood*, p. 529.

(since he was/is the head), but presumably should have gone to God for counsel. Thus the way in which they sinned broke the proper patterns of hierarchy. In verse 14, then, Paul advances a second reason why men should have authority in the church—due to the disastrous consequences of the first act of role reversal by Adam and Eve. According to this view Eve sinned by taking the initiative over the man, and thus Paul calls her/women into submission.[66]

However, the greatest difficulty with the role-reversal interpretation is that it must be *inferred* from Paul's words. The words in the text do not say anything about a role reversal, rather they focus on the issue of who was deceived and who was not deceived: "And Adam was not the one deceived; it was the woman who was deceived and became a sinner" (1 Tim 2:14). Compared to the traditional interpretation, the role-reversal interpretation is convoluted; it requires the reader to bring unnecessary and unwarranted information to the text.

Alternatively, two egalitarian interpretations are worth consideration. The first might be labeled as the "illustrative" interpretation. Rather than understanding Paul to be making a statement about all women, he may have been using the Eve material in an illustrative manner. The problems that Paul faced with heretical teaching at Ephesus often involved women. Women appear to have been the vulnerable victims of the false teachers.[67] As a result, Paul instructs women to learn in submission and not to teach. Eve fits well as an analogy or illustration of this problem at Ephesus. In this case, Paul is providing pastoral solutions to a particular problem; he is not making statements that should apply in all instances. Assuming that the problem was to be resolved through adequate instruction and teaching, the prohibition would no longer carry any force.

A second egalitarian approach might be coined, the "cultural" interpretation. Here we return to the traditional interpretation of the church, that women are more easily deceived than men. Perhaps Paul *was* saying that women (in general) are more easily deceived than men. This traditional interpretation is too easily dismissed simply because our modern experience has taught us otherwise. So, we read our contemporary understanding of women into what Paul is saying and assume that he could not possibly be saying that women are more gullible than men. However, as I have argued from many neutral examples in this book, with

---

[66]A few soft patriarchalists attempt to distance 1 Tim 2:14 from the earlier prohibitions in 2:11-12. In this case, 2:14 does not provide a second reason for women submitting to men. Paul simply relates additional thoughts that were triggered as he discusses the creation account. This "disconnected" interpretation has not met with much of a following among patriarchalists. For two proponents, see Paul Barnett, "Wives and Women's Ministry: 1 Timothy 2:11-15," *Evangelical Quarterly* 61 (1989): 234; Craig Blomberg, "Not Beyond What is Written. A Review of Aída Spencer's *Beyond the Curse: Women Called to Ministry*," *Criswell Theological Review* 2 (1988): 413-14.
[67]2 Tim 3:6-9; cf. 1 Tim 1:3; 3:11; 4:7; 5:13-15; 2 Tim 3:13; Tit 1:10.

cultural analysis we can affirm what Paul was saying to his original culture without denying that something might have changed in the meantime. With this solution we return to our traditional-interpretive roots, while recognizing the input and validity of our modern social context. What Paul was saying to the original audience could have been validated in that particular culture. Women probably were, in general, more easily deceived than men because of gender differences in education, marital age, social exposure, financial vulnerability, etc. From this perspective, Paul's statement contains a significant cultural component (aside from underlying transcultural principles). Much of the women's material in the Bible has been shown to function on these two levels.[68] So the potential of the same thing happening here in 1 Timothy 2:14 is entirely likely. (For a fuller development of this verse see criterion 18.)

4. Origin of hierarchy (creation or curse). Finding explicit statements of hierarchy in the Genesis text before the Fall is an elusive task. There are no clear or explicit statements formulating a hierarchal relationship between man and woman until after the Fall. It is the curse dialogue that explicitly introduces hierarchy. When describing the plight of the wife, the text reads, "he [your husband] will rule over you" (Gen 3:16).

Patriarchalists maintain that the curse introduced only a distortion of the husband's rule over his wife (rule over his wife had been given to him from the very beginning). Perhaps we should read the Genesis text this way. Clearly aspects of the curse distorted existing relationships. Just as pain entered the natural process of childbirth (Gen 3:16; cf. 1:28) and working the land (Gen 3:17-19; cf. 2:15-18), so also it is possible that pain enters into the hierarchal relationship between man and woman. If so, man ruling over his wife was a natural part of the existing relationship as much as bearing children and working the land were a part of the original creation pattern.

However, such a reading assumes its conclusion from the start. It is just as easy to work from the assumption that hierarchy and submission were a part of the pain that entered into a previous relationship of mutuality and equality. Adam and Eve obviously functioned with complementary roles based on their gender differences (Adam would not have given birth to children; during times of child-bearing Eve would not have participated as directly in provisional tasks that fulfilled their joint mandate to "subdue creation"). Even from an egalitarian perspective, mutuality and equality do not have to obliterate complementary roles. I will develop below a position called "complementary egalitarianism"—a type of egalitarianism that functions on the basis of equality but continues to cel-

---

[68]See the biblical texts discussed under criteria 11 and 18.

ebrate gender distinctiveness and the complementary interdependence that gender differences bring (see chapter eight). The crux of the question within this current criterion is whether *hierarchy* needs to be part of the celebration of gender differences in our application of Scripture for today.

An answer to our application question comes in part through looking at when hierarchy entered into human relationships—pre-Fall or post-Fall. A post-Fall introduction of hierarchy is suggested by three factors. First, an explicit statement of hierarchy between humans and animals is provided pre-Fall, whereas no similar statement is mentioned at that time regarding hierarchy between male and female. As a culmination of creating the animals, an explicit formulation of hierarchy is given: humans were to rule over them (Gen 1:26-28; cf. 2:5, 15). This provides a very important purpose statement related to the relationship between humanity and the animal/plant kingdoms. Yet, no submission statement occurs following the creation of woman. The specification that man rules over woman comes after the Fall. If man's mandate were to rule over woman, one would have expected its statement in the pre-Fall material (as is the case with the animals).

Second, while naming the animals expresses Adam's rule over them, the way he names the woman suggests something quite different. Within the creation narrative God instructs humankind (both man and woman) to rule over the animals (Gen 1:26, 28; cf. Gen 9:2; Ps 8:6-8; 115:16). It is likely, then, that we should understand Adam's naming the animals as a quiet expression of the mandate for humanity to rule over them. God brings the animals to Adam and he gives each of them a name. However, when God brings the woman to him, the name that Adam suggests is extremely significant. What he calls the woman is *'ishshah* (Gen 2:2). That is like saying, "Wow, this one is like me!" Through the sound play between his name (*'ish*) and her name (*'ishshah*), Adam pronounces an affinity between the woman and himself. This act of naming places man and woman as partners in the dominion over the animal/plant kingdom, much more so than placing them in some hierarchal relationship to each other.

In this respect, the narrative reflects something of divine humor. After parading the animals in front of Adam, which is followed by Adam's brief "nap time," God "sneaks another one into the line-up" to see what Adam would say. She is "brought to him"[69] just like one of the animals. It was the ultimate surprise package from God. Adam calls her *'ishshah* not to subordinate her below himself like the animals, but to raise her to his level in contrast to the animals. In calling her *'ishshah* Adam is saying, "You're not one of those animals I named as part of

---

[69]Cf. the similar wording in Gen 2:19 and 2:22.

God's mandate to rule over creation . . . you're one of me!" To suggest that this act of naming in Genesis 2:23 infers subordination (but not to the level of the animals) becomes overly complex, forgets that as a narrative/story there has been no preparatory statement about man's mandate to rule over woman (like that which purposefully sets up the animal-naming scene [Gen 1:26]) and overlooks the content of the name he gives the woman as it plays off of his own name.

On the other hand, the point at which Adam actually takes a marked initiative to name his wife in a new and original way is immediately after the Fall. In the second naming of woman, Adam departs from their closely related names, perhaps initiating a post-Fall dominion over woman, and calls her "Eve." Interestingly, with the animals an explicit statement of hierarchy followed by naming is pre-Fall; with woman the explicit statement of hierarchy and personal naming are ultimately post-Fall. It is a rather curious feature of the text that the man's name (Gen 1:26, 27; 2:7) does not change after the Fall (he retains his original name), whereas the woman is given a new name. In fact, the names by which we most commonly remember and retell the Eden story today are "Adam and Eve." Yet, one is pre-Fall and one is post-Fall.

Third, the blessing/cursing formulas often involved the initiation of a higher or lower status. For example, in the original Edenic curse the snake experiences a loss of his former status (Gen 3:14-15). This lower-status phenomenon in one part of the original curse (for the snake) at least raises the possibility of it happening in another part. It presents a plausible scenario for understanding what happened with the woman. Both the snake and the woman receive as part of their involvement in the Fall a similar reduction in status: the snake is "made low" (lower than the other animals) and the woman is "made low" (lower than other humans, i.e., man). The snake is cast down among his peers; the woman is cast down among her equals. This pattern of assigning status as a part of blessing/cursing is a prominent aspect of the theology of Genesis. The poetic blessing/cursing of offspring often raises or lowers the status of the children and subsequent generations coming from these children. Several blessing/cursing texts may be quoted to illustrate assignment of a status:

Noah: Cursed be Canaan!
The lowest of slaves will he be to his brothers.
Blessed be the Lord, the God of Shem!
May Canaan be the slave of Shem.
May God extend the territory of Japheth;
may Japheth live in the tents of Shem,
and may Canaan be his slave. (Gen 9:25-27)

Isaac: May nations serve you [Jacob]
              and peoples bow down to you.
              Be lord over your brothers,
              and may the sons of your mother bow down to you.
              May those who curse you be cursed
              and those who bless you be blessed.
              You [Esau] will live by the sword
              and you will serve your brother.
              But when you grow restless,
              you will throw his yoke from off your neck. (Gen 27:29, 40)

Jacob: Reuben, you are my firstborn,
              my might, the first sign of my strength,
              excelling in honor, excelling in power.
              Turbulent as the waters, you will no longer excel,
              for you went up onto your father's bed,
              onto my couch and defiled it.

              Judah, your brothers will praise you;
              your hand will be on the neck of your enemies;
              your father's sons will bow down to you. . . .
              The scepter will not depart from Judah,
              nor the ruler's staff from between his feet. . . .

              Issachar is a rawboned donkey
              lying down between two saddlebags.
              When he sees how good is his resting place
              and how pleasant is his land,
              he will bend his shoulder to the burden
              and submit to forced labor.

              Let all these [blessings] rest on the head of Joseph,
              on the brow of the prince among his brothers.
              (Gen 49:3-4, 8, 10, 14-15, 26)

These blessing/cursing texts make a valuable contribution to understanding the curse formulas of Genesis 3:14-19. When the curse pronouncement falls upon the woman, it includes an assignment of status relative to those around her. She is given a lower status than the man: "Your desire will be for your husband, and he will rule over you" (Gen 3:16). Having examined other bless-ing/cursing oracles in Genesis[70] and the rest of the Pentateuch,[71] several ob-servations may be made about the assignment of status. First, when the blessing/cursing formulas assign status, they generally initiate a change in status different from what the person formerly held. Applying this finding to Gen 3:16 would suggest that the woman's former status was *not* one of the man ruling over the woman. Before the Fall, they were equals; after the Fall, he rules over her. Second, from the blessing/cursing oracles we discover that subordination under another individual usually does not involve any particular abuse or distortion of hierarchy. It merely involves a formation of hierarchy. While the hierarchy relationship is not always pleasant and often includes an element of struggle, it does not necessarily imply an abusive or harmful rule by the person on top. The only exception would be where the context is one of military conquest (e.g., Num 24:17-19) and then only for the initial period of takeover. This suggests that the "rule" of man over woman in Genesis 3:16 is not intended to portray the introduction of an abusive or distorted domination/rule into an already-existing (perfect) hierarchy.[72] The hierarchy introduced in the case of man and woman is a typical status-and-power hierarchy (one rules, the other serves), not necessarily an abusive hierarchy. Third, the curse ora-cles frequently introduce two elements into human relationships: rule and conflict. The word "desire" in 3:16 may indicate an element of conflict or struggle in the husband-wife hierarchy.[73] The woman will struggle for power in the relationship. Both egalitarians and hierarchalists are open to the conflict element. However, hierarchalists like to see *only* conflict introduced in this verse, since they argue that rule (if understood in a good sense) must have simply been a continuation of something earlier. However, the curse oracles suggest that *both* a change in status (one person now rules; the other is subor-dinate) and a conflict (struggle within the hierarchy) are initiated with the curse.

These features within the Genesis text present a reasonable case for a post-Fall hierarchy. If hierarchy was introduced into human relationships post-Fall as a part of the curse, then there is no need to sustain hierarchy as part of gender rela-tionships today. A redemptive approach to the curse would be to restore equality, not to perpetuate hierarchy.

---

[70]In addition to the Genesis texts quoted above, see Gen 1:28; 17:16, 20-21; 22:17-18; 24:60; 25:23.
[71]Cf. Num 22:5-6; 24:17-19, 20-24; Deut 15:6; 28:7, 12-13, 25, 43-44; 33:16, 20, 27-29.
[72]Contra most hierarchalists.
[73]See Susan Foh, "Male Leadership," in *Women in Ministry*, pp. 74-75. The word for "desire" is used in this sense in Gen 4:7.

	Pre-Fall (creation)	**Post-Fall (curse)**
rule statement:	humanity rules *(radah, kabash, mashal)* over the animals[74]	male rules *(mashal)* over female (Gen 3:16)
naming:	the animals (Gen 2:19-20)	[no second naming]
	man as *'ish* (Gen 2:23)	[no second naming]
	woman as *'ishshah* (Gen 2:23)	woman as Eve (Gen 3:20)
snake's status:	equal to other animals	lower than other animals (Gen 3:14)
woman's status:	??	lower than man (Gen 3:16)

Putting aside what I have just said, however, let us assume that hierarchy was not a result of the curse. Suppose that hierarchy was a part of the original creation pattern and the Fall/curse simply distorted that relationship. Patriarchalists generally end their argumentation here, as if the case was closed. However, it still does not follow that hierarchy should be an ongoing dimension of male-female relationships today. As the next criterion—on original creation—will show, creation patterns contain cultural components within them (see criterion 6). Finding something within the original creation does not automatically guarantee its transcultural status.

D. Homosexuality

Since homosexuality is not stated as part of the original curse, this criterion does not apply to it.

E. Evaluation of the criterion

One might wonder how nakedness and clothing fit within this Fall/curse criterion. Adam and Eve were originally naked in the garden only to be clothed after the Fall (Gen 2:25; 3:7, 21). If we are to "fight against the curse" (rather than perpetuate it) as this criterion recommends, does this mean we should lobby for a nudist style of living? The question is understandable given our subject matter. However, an argument for nudity based on this criterion is wrongly conceived. Such an argument reveals a lack of understanding about how nakedness and clothing function in the opening chapters of Genesis. Clothing within the Fall story is not a part of the curse oracles (like the other examples cited

---

[74]Gen 1:26 *(radah* and *kabash);* cf. Gen 9:2; Ps 8:6-8 *(mashal);* 115:16. A variety of Hebrew words are used to describe humans "ruling" over the animal kingdom as a part of the creation mandate, one of which is *mashal* (Ps 8:6). The word *mashal* is the same word found in the Genesis curse oracle, which describes the male ruling over the female. All three terms are in a close semantic range, especially *radah* and *mashal.*

above). If we look at the various curse proclamations in Genesis 3:14-19, we will find nothing stated about clothing. In fact, clothing is part of God's redemptive action in order to "swim upstream" against the Fall/curse—it is an action taken to counteract the Fall. The two opposite directions of flow within the story may be illustrated as follows:

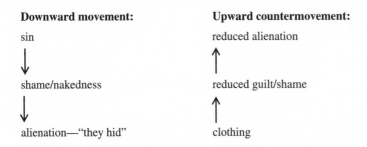

Downward movement: **Upward countermovement:**

sin   reduced alienation

shame/nakedness   reduced guilt/shame

alienation—"they hid"   clothing

God's provision of animal skin garments was a practical solution to reduce/counteract the effects of the Fall—it was a gracious way of reducing Adam and Eve's guilt and shame (Gen 3:7, 21). It sought to bridge alienation by making contact with God feasible even in a broken world. Furthermore, the garden's clothing (and God's act of slaying animals for clothing) prefigures an ultimate, greater act of God, which would reduce human alienation further by dealing with sin itself. So, in a criterion that champions our fighting the curse, the answer is not to throw away our clothing. Only in a very limited sense is clothing an "effect" of the curse—only with several intervening cause-and-effect components and, most importantly, with a dramatic reversal in the flow of redemptive movement. Fighting the Fall/curse does not mean becoming nudists. It means that we fight sin (as first causative act), acknowledge guilt/shame (rather than living in denial) and accept clothing from God as a practical (and ultimately theological) way of reducing shame/guilt and relational alienation. Clothing practically and symbolically counteracts the effects of the Fall; it is not a perpetuation of either the Fall or the curse.

F. Summary

There is one sense in which the curse is transcultural (as an indicative, "what is") and another sense in which it is not transcultural (as an imperative, "what we should do"). From the perspective of Christian mission, we need to fight the effects of the curse, especially within the redeemed community. It is not our task to perpetuate the curse. Pertaining to the women's issue, the curse should never be used to argue for required hierarchy implications, as it was by earlier patriarchalists. Fortunately, such arguments are rarely seen today. What is not as clear, however, is how hierarchy relates to the curse. If the curse brought a *distortion* of hierarchy, this would allow for but not necessarily preclude an ongoing requirement of patriarchy. We will look at creation patterns next (criterion 6) in order to address this question. If, however, hierarchy *itself* was a part of the curse, not just a distortion of it, then an egalitarian position is favored. The curse criterion does not apply to the homosexual issue.

5

MODERATELY PERSUASIVE CRITERIA

CRITERION 6: Basis in Original Creation, Section 1: Patterns

A. Statement

A component of a text may be transcultural if its basis is rooted in the original-creation material. Gen 1:1—2:25 provides us with an account of the creation of humanity. Since God designed everything within creation to function in a good and harmonious manner, one might expect that the creation material would yield an ongoing pattern and purpose.[1]

Our discussion of the original creation material will be subdivided into two areas:

Section 1: Patterns

Section 2: Primogeniture

Under Section 1 ("Patterns") we will explore the degree to which Eden functions as a pattern or model for subsequent generations. In Section 2 ("Primogeniture") we will investigate the degree to which the "Adam first" argument carries transcultural force.

B. Neutral examples

The following examples demonstrate that the application of "creation pattern" in

---

[1] Due to a dependency upon a far too narrow sampling, Edenic patterns often get portrayed as something of an *automatic* universal. For instance, see Terrance Tiessen, "Towards a Hermeneutic for Discerning Universal Moral Absolutes," *JETS* 36 (1993): 194-97. Other than this oversight, there is much that is helpful in Tiessen's article on universal absolutes. Cf. William W. Klein, Craig L. Blomberg and Robert L. Hubbard Jr., *Introduction to Biblical Interpretation* (Vancouver: Word, 1993), p. 417.

the lives of ancient Israelites and modern Christians is not always a simple matter. One cannot automatically assign a transcultural status to all that is found
within the garden—some things will be transcultural while others will be cultural. The nine examples below present a range of variation within creation pattern, from strong continuance of pattern (divorce), to partial modification of
pattern (Sabbath), to a significant component of pattern discontinuance (procreation commands, length of work week, etc.). I will not attempt to prove the cultural or transcultural status of the examples below; I must entrust this task to my
reader. Using the other criteria within this book, a case could be made in each instance. Though not without some controversy and diversification of approach, the
following sample cases enjoy a considerable measure of Christian consensus.

1. *Divorce.* In order to establish the permanence of marriage Jesus appeals to
the Genesis creation text (Mt 19:4-6; cf. Gen 1:27; 2:4) and places its binding
force on a higher level than subsequent legislation by Moses which allowed for
divorce: "Moses permitted you to divorce your wives because your hearts were
hard. But it was not this way from the beginning" (Mt 19:8; cf. Mal 2:16; Mt
5:31-32). The social structure of lifelong marriage takes precedence over divorce
regulations, since it reflects a higher moral ideal. In this instance, the creation
pattern carries a strong transcultural force.

2. *Polygamy.* While polygamy breaks with the original creation pattern in
some aspects of marital form, the original audience within Scripture certainly
does not pick up on its implications for their lives (cf. criterion 11.C.7). The un-
easy juxtaposition between the creation account and the polygamous patriarchs
(only a few chapters later in the narrative) seems to have been missed by the original audience. In this instance, the creation pattern carries a mild transcultural
force that has its realization in redemptive-movement application only within
later Jewish and Christian generations.

3. *Singleness.* Eden portrays man and woman in a marriage or covenant relationship (Gen 2:24). If the creation material provides a tightly ordered paradigm
for all of humanity to follow, one might get the impression that singleness was
outside the will of God. Every Christian woman or man ought to find his or her
corresponding "soul mate" and get married.[2] In this instance, most Christians
would view departure from creation pattern as an acceptable option.

4. *Farming as an occupation.* In the garden man was instructed to till the
ground and eat of its produce (Gen 2:5, 15-17). Today, however, very few urban
people continue to make a living off the land. In our culture only a small percent-

---

[2]Other portions of Scripture teach that singleness is an honorable and, under certain circumstances, a
preferable choice for some human beings. See Mt 19:11; 1 Cor 7:7-9, 25-35.

age of the population is involved with farming. Even within the agricultural industry, new technologies, such as hydroponics, permit farmers to grow many items without soil and without tilling the ground. In this example, the creation pattern seems to carry no binding implications for today other than at a principle or abstracted level of working to obtain food.

5. *Ground transportation.* Presumably the mode of transportation within the garden was walking.[3] Perhaps one could extend the walking idea within an agricultural setting to talk about transportation by horse and other animals. Of course, a few Christian communities today restrict their transportation to horse and buggy. The creation patterns square nicely with their lifestyle. On the other hand, most Christians would see this as a nonbinding pattern within the creation texts.

6. *Procreation command.* In the garden, God instructs Adam and Eve: "Be fruitful and increase in number; fill the earth and subdue it" (Gen 1:28). While part of the original-creation pattern, this procreation command hardly carries the same weight today as it did in the original setting. Both Protestant and Catholic communities, while gravitating toward different means of birth control, commend responsible family planning. Even though birth control breaks with creation pattern, it may be a wise action in terms of personal resources and our collective environmental resources. Procreation remains a good value, but it must now be set within limits. Our world differs significantly from the garden. In this instance, the creation pattern must be heavily modified.

7. *Vegetarian diet.* Within the creation story Adam and Eve eat from seed-bearing plants and fruit-bearing trees (Gen 1:29; 2:16). Seemingly, humans did not eat animals in the pre-Fall garden. At the very least, a vegetarian lifestyle reflects creation design as depicted in the Genesis text. However, application for today is another matter. Practicing a vegetarian lifestyle today for food chain concerns or for perceived health benefits is one thing, but doing it in order to comply with the creation pattern is quite another. For a variety of reasons (not developed here), it is unlikely that this component of the creation pattern should carry any strict binding force today.

8. *Sabbath.* The Israelites were instructed to keep the Sabbath, since it replicated the creation story: "Remember the Sabbath day by keeping it holy. Six days you shall labor and do all your work, but the seventh day is a Sabbath to the Lord your God. . . . For in six days the Lord made the heavens and the earth . . . but he rested on the seventh day" (Ex 20:8-11; cf. Gen 1:3—2:1; 2:2). While affirming transcultural components to Sabbath (worship of the Creator God, a work-and-

---

[3]Gen 3:8. Adam and Eve heard God "walking" through the garden in the cool of the day.

rest rhythm, etc.), most Christians today depart from the sabbath pattern in significant ways.[4] For example, most have changed the sabbath day from Saturday to
Sunday and many have softened the work prohibitions and penalties. Further,
many Christians, while accepting various underlying Sabbath principles, do not
prescribe any specific day of the week for its fulfillment. Although I will not attempt to prove the case here,[5] Sabbath offers a good example of a creation pattern
with a significant cultural component. Though the approaches differ, there is general Christian consensus that this aspect of creation pattern should be modified to
some extent.

9. *Length of a workweek.* Along with the Sabbath issue comes the question
about how long a workweek should be. God certainly models a six-day workweek within the creation text (Gen 1:3-31). Based upon God's example, the biblical text advocates a six-workday pattern followed by one day of rest for humans
(Ex 20:9; cf. Ex 16:23-26; 31:15-17; 34:21; 35:2). Interestingly, this same work/
rest ratio from creation also gets applied to working the land and letting it rest—
six years of working the land followed by one year of rest (Ex 23:10-12; cf. Lev
25:1-8; 26:34-35). The tie to original creation is fairly obvious. While affirming
the transcultural principle and value of work (for people) and of appropriate soil
usage (for the land), most modern Christians would see a cultural component to
the ratio aspect of the text. We live in an industrial, technological and informa-
tional society. The six-day work schedule was probably related to the agrarian
setting of the original audience. In all likelihood, Christians can still honor God
with their lives without living out the workweek of the creation pattern in a strict
"letter for letter" correspondence. Likewise, modern Christian farmers can probably still honor God with their land through crop rotation and fertilization that
clearly departs from original-creation patterns. We need to embrace the garden's
underlying principles, while distinguishing these from its culture-bound components.

10. *Summary.* In sum, original creation patterns do not provide an automatic
guide for assessing what is transcultural within Scripture. Each of the nine examples has an underlying principle that endures, but the point of this criterion is to
distinguish these continuing abstracted components from the cultural components within the creation patterns. The applicational force of the garden varies

---

[4]Seventh-day Adventists, of course, view the Sabbath as transcultural and on the same level as the
other nine commandments of the Decalogue.

[5]Developments in salvation history (along with a movement away from an agrarian culture) have
helped bring about a relinquishing or reworking of the Sabbath pattern. Cf. Gal 4:10; Col 2:16. For a
helpful survey of positions, see Willard M. Swartley, *Slavery, Sabbath, War & Women: Case Issues
in Biblical Interpretation* (Waterloo, Ontario: Herald, 1983), pp. 67-96.

considerably: at times the garden carries strong ongoing implications (divorce); at times it holds comparatively weak continuing implications (polygamy); sometimes its non-abstracted form carries no continuing force (length of workweek, singleness, vegetarian diet); other times we modify the material to make it more effective in our culture (Sabbath regulations); several times the contemporary setting has changed so dramatically that the original-creation pattern provides abstracted principles but holds no binding implications in its most concrete level of expression (procreation commands, farming as occupation, length of workweek). One cannot help but get the impression that some aspects of Eden are simply a part of the story and nothing more, while other aspects are extremely significant. Even if later writers invoke the Edenic pattern (Sabbath, workweek, land rest), that does not mean it is automatically transcultural. The particular pattern may well be tied to salvation historical factors and/or agricultural concerns that are time-bound and cultural.

C. Women
Various features of the creation narrative describe the relationship between man and woman in one fashion or another. Some of the background components of the creation story reflect an egalitarian spirit, while other features convey subtle overtones of patriarchy.

1. God's image. One of the earliest statements in the Bible about man and woman is that they both are recipients of God's image and likeness: "Then God said, 'Let us make man [humankind] in our image, according to our likeness'" (Gen 1:26). This text appears to affirm the equality of male and female as joint recipients of the image and likeness of God.

2. Creation mandate: ruling together. Immediately after the image affirmation, God gives to both man and woman the creation mandate: "and let them [man and woman] rule over the fish of the sea and the birds of the air, over all the livestock, over all the earth, and over all the creatures that move along the ground" (Gen 1:26). This text, like the previous one, appears to give both man and woman an equal share in the mandate to rule over creation. This suggests a shared and balanced power-and-responsibility model in the relationship. Eve did not come along in order to help Adam achieve a mandate given singularly to him. Both man and woman share equally in the mandate to rule creation. Such a text suggests equality.

The next six examples, however, provide possible hints of patriarchy within the garden.

3. Helpmate. Gen 2:18-20 reads, "The Lord God said, 'It is not good for man to be alone. I will make a helper suitable for him.' Now the Lord God had formed out of the ground all the beasts of the field. . . . But for Adam no suitable helper was found." Our English word "helper" often conveys a lower, servant-like status, particularly when used in the context of modern-day roles and job classifications. So a reader today might get the impression that "helpmate" (KJV) or "suitable helper" (NIV) implies a lower status for the woman.[6] Egalitarians are quick to point out, however, that the Hebrew term *ezer* is frequently used of persons with a superior status, or of God himself, helping those of lower status and power. Egalitarians often use this lexical data to bolster their position.[7]

Yet, a survey of the Hebrew word for "helper" (*ezer*) should caution against using the word itself to support either position. When including both the noun and verb forms, there are about 128 occurrences in the Old Testament. The large majority of uses (72%) are of superior-status individuals helping those of a lesser status. Yet, there are a number of examples where the "helper" is either of equal status (18%)[8] or of lower status (10%)[9] than the one being helped. Therefore, the word *ezer* itself tells us nothing about the status of the individual doing the helping. Only contextual factors beyond the word should be used to establish whether the status of the helper is higher, lower or equal to the one being helped.

4. Adam's rib. Some hierarchalists propose that the taking of woman from man's rib (Gen 2:22) places her in a subordinate role to man. One writer juxtaposes Adam's position as head with Eve's lower position as rib: "Does the rib rebel against the head?"[10] On the other hand, egalitarians can just as easily suggest that Eve was made from the rib to imply that she was an equal to Adam. As has commonly been said, "She was created not from his head to be over him, nor from his feet to be under him, but from his rib to stand at his side (as his equal)." Such speculation is not helpful. At the most, the rib imagery depicts the solidarity and unity of man and woman in their one-flesh relationship (cf. Gen 2:23). To go beyond this and argue for either hierarchy or equality amounts to little more than creative folklore.

5. Man names the woman. Man names woman twice, once pre-Fall with a joint-name that corresponds to his own, and once post-Fall with a personal

---

[6]At times patriarchalists wrongly use the English connotation of "helper" to their rhetorical advantage. For example, Susan Foh talks about the man as "head" and woman as "helper" within the same sentence ("Male Leadership," in *Women in Ministry: Four Views*, ed. Bonnidell Clouse and Robert G. Clouse [Downers Grove, Ill.: InterVarsity Press, 1989], p. 73).

[7]E.g., see Aída B. Spencer, *Beyond the Curse: Women Called to Ministry* (Peabody, Mass.: Hendrickson, 1985), pp. 26-29.

[8]E.g., verb form: Josh 10:4, 33; 2 Sam 8:5; 1 Kings 20:16; 1 Chron 18:5; 2 Chron 20:23; Ezra 10:15; Job 9:13; Is 41:6; Jer 47:4; Ezek 30:8 32:21; Dan 11:45; noun form: Job 6:13; Dan 11:34; cf. Judg 5:23.

[9]E.g., verb form: 2 Sam 21:17; 1 Kings 1:7; 1 Chron 12:1, 17, 18, 21, 22; 22:17; 2 Chron 26:13; 32:3; noun form: Ezek 12:14.

[10]Foh, "Male Leadership," p. 73; cf. p. 72.

name that is totally distinct from his (Gen 2:23; 3:20). Patriarchalists generally focus on the first naming, while egalitarians emphasize the second. A discussion of this feature is covered under the previous criterion (criterion 6.C.4). If patriarchal overtones are to be derived from the first naming incident, which is strikingly different than the second naming, it is at best a very subtle dimension of patriarchy.

6. *Man leaves and cleaves, not woman.* The text of Genesis 2:24 reads, "For this reason a man will leave his father and mother and be united to his wife, and they will become one flesh." Some hierarchalists appeal to this passage to show that the man functions as leader and initiator in the marriage union, since he is the one who leaves and cleaves (not the wife).[11]

Aside from the fact that we no longer apply this text in our culture, or at least we modify its application significantly,[12] the leave-and-cleave statement should probably not be used to support an original-creation hierarchy. It is doubtful whether such a statement reflected pre-Fall conditions. It more likely represents an application of the creation material to the existing patriarchal culture in Moses' day, rather than a direct statement about creation reality.[13]

7. *God addresses man first.* After Adam and Eve hid in the trees because of their sin and shame, God called out to the man: "Where are you [Adam]?" (Gen 3:9). Some patriarchalists contend that this act of addressing man first implies a hierarchy.[14] One might be inclined toward this perspective based upon the flow of the narrative. For instance, the story in Gen 3:1-19 moves along an ABC—CBA—ABC pattern as sketched below:

---

[11]E.g., Raymond C. Ortlund Jr., "Male-Female Equality and Male Headship," in *Recovering Biblical Manhood and Womanhood: A Response to Evangelical Feminism*, ed. John Piper and Wayne Grudem (Wheaton, Ill.: Crossway, 1991), p. 103.

[12]In our modern, egalitarian culture we provide premarital counseling that instructs *both* spouses-to-be about the need to leave and cleave. Cf. the similar way in which we apply the female-oriented virginity expectations in Scripture (criterion 11.C.4, pp 165-66) to both genders.

[13]First, the statement is an interjected comment into the flow of the narrative. The verses immediately before and immediately after Genesis 2:24 contain the story line. In 2:24 itself, however, the story is suspended. These are not the words of Adam; they are the words of the narrator relating Adam's words to his own post-exodus generation. Within the Pentateuch this kind of interjection is at times a clue that something is being applied to a later day and time (e.g., Num 12:3). Second, that Genesis 2:24 does not represent pre-Fall conditions is obvious from the fact that there were no "fathers" or "mothers" from whom Adam could leave. So clearly this verse does not provide an original-creation pattern in all aspects of its wording. Only in one aspect of the statement is the writer attempting to connect with the original-creation paradigm: that man and woman were specially made for one another, i.e., in a one-flesh relationship. The word "flesh" *(basar)* provides the primary verbal link between 2:24 and its context. To build a case for patriarchy within pre-Fall material based upon other aspects of this verse is indeed tenuous.

[14]Foh, "Male Leadership," p. 74.

Eating the fruit:	A serpent	(3:1a)
	B woman	(3:1b-6a)
	C man	(3:6b-7)
Inquiry:	C man	(3:8-12)
	B woman	(3:13)
	A serpent	(3:14a)
Curse oracles:	A serpent	(3:14b-15)
	B woman	(3:16)
	C man	(3:17-19)

Egalitarians might look at this pattern and say that the matter of who is addressed first simply relates to stylistic features around which the writer builds his story. There is a natural flow back and forth (three times) through the triad of players in the garden. Since man eats the fruit last, he is the one addressed first in the inquiry. Since the serpent is mentioned last in the inquiry, he is addressed first in the curse oracles. On the other hand, the chiastic structure (ABC C′B′A′ A″B″C″) of the text may place some emphasis on the man and on the serpent, as chiasms sometimes focus on the centered components. Or, perhaps we are reading too much into the text with this observation. At any rate, God does address Adam singularly at first (not both Adam and Eve), and maybe the chiastic flow of the story places a heightened focus on Adam. Without making too much out of it, one might classify this address feature as a quiet whisper of patriarchy within the garden.

8. Creation order (man created first; woman second). In the Genesis narrative, God created man first and woman second (Gen 2:7; cf. 2:22). God formed Adam, and then he made Eve. The text of Genesis itself does not explicitly draw out any implications from this sequencing. However, in 1 Timothy 2:13 Paul relates the creation order to the subordinate role of women. After stating that women should submit to male authority and not teach men, he introduces material from the Genesis text to highlight the relative order of man and woman at creation: "For Adam was formed first, then Eve."

In view of our analysis of the creation story so far, it seems fair to say that this element of creation order supplies one of the strongest pieces of patriarchal data. The reason modern readers do not see its patriarchal significance today relates to a lack of primogeniture practices within our contemporary culture. We simply do not understand the logic. However, if one incorporates primogeniture into one's thinking, then a patriarchal picture emerges with a fair degree of clarity. Primogeniture will be the topic of the next criterion. At this point, it is sufficient to draw attention to this feature of patriarchy within the creation account. Nevertheless, it is a quiet background feature and not a dominant focus within the story, which is primarily intended to present Yahweh as the Creator God over against the pagan gods who are merely components within his creation.

9. *Summary.* We have surveyed eight features within the Genesis text that are appealed to in the gender debate. Two of these affirm equality between man and woman (creation image and mandate). To varying degrees, six other features create a patriarchal portrait within the garden. Some of these elements should probably not be used to argue for patriarchy within the garden (Adam's rib and the leaving-and-cleaving statement). The description of the woman as helper does not in itself support patriarchy; only other contextual factors can create that framework. Certain items may be classified at least in a tentative fashion as quiet hues of patriarchy on Eden's canvas (the naming of Eve and the order of address). The most credible piece of data in support of patriarchy in the creation story, as written and read through a primogeniture framework, seems to be the order in which man and woman were created.

Nevertheless, these quiet overtones of patriarchy in the garden do not confirm the transcultural status of patriarchy. The neutral examples above have illustrated numerous cultural components within Eden's creation patterns. Finding something within the garden, therefore, does not provide solid ground for determining cultural/transcultural status one way or the other. The next criterion, on primogeniture, will take our investigation of patriarchy in the garden one step further.

D. Homosexuality

The original creation story portrays a male (Adam) and female (Eve) as the pattern for sexual relationships (Gen 1:27; 2:21-25). Obviously, this pattern does not sit well with homosexual relationships, whether the covenant or casual type. No biblical passages refer back to the creation material in a direct manner to make a point about homosexuality (although one Pauline text mentions creation within the immediate context and an inference might be drawn[15]). Regardless of whether the biblical texts make the connection, the Christian community is aware of the connection. Some invoke the adage "God made Adam and Eve, not Adam and Steve." So the link between the creation account and homosexuality is clearly made on a popular level.

One must grant that Eden's patterns carry no binding force against sexual ab-

---

[15]E.g., Rom 1:20, 25 explicitly refers to the original creation (cf. the allusions in 1:23). This provides the broader context for Paul's comments about homosexual relationships (1:26-27). In view of these references to creation, it is likely that the original creation setting influenced his discourse on homosexuality. The expressions "natural relations" and "unnatural relations" (1:26-27) may allude to the original creation context as well as speaking about nature in general.

stinence cases. While the garden presents sexuality (monogamous heterosexuality) as normative, no one would use this pattern to condemn sexual abstinence. It is completely acceptable for the physically or mentally impaired, the celibate, the impotent or the single person to depart from the creation paradigm. For one reason or another all of these individuals do not fulfill the creation pattern of heterosexuality. These people abstain from sexual activity within a heterosexual marriage or simply by not entering into marriage.

But to argue for homosexuality from these abstinence cases (as some do)[16] produces a considerable leap in logic. It is one thing to abstain from heterosexual relationships; it is quite another to find sexual fulfillment through means outside of heterosexual relationships. Abstinence cases break from creation pattern, but they do so by *limiting* one's sexual fulfillment. Homosexual cases break from the creation pattern by *broadening* the scope of one's sexual fulfillment (as bestiality would broaden one's sexual fulfillment options beyond the creation pattern). The departure from creation order in abstinence cases does not imply that any and every kind of sexual fulfillment is acceptable. Abstinence from sexual fulfillment makes sense in certain cases, but its departure from creation pattern does not conversely argue for sexual fulfillment through any means. While one might grant that abstinence cases raise the question concerning homosexuality as a possible departure from creation, they do not answer the question. Each departure from the creation pattern of sexuality needs to be handled on its own merits.

Besides abstinence cases, advocates of homosexuality appeal to deviation from creation patterns in the sexual practices of masturbation, oral sex and anal sex within heterosexual marriages.[17] If the church is not willing to openly condemn these practices, then why should homosexuality be condemned? The point is well taken. These practices do depart from creation pattern, at least as we can retrospectively establish it through biological and textual routes. While the church today is unwilling to make a blanket condemnation of these practices, neither is it willing to unquestionably endorse them. These practices depart from creation order, yet not to the degree of homosexuality. Also, they are never censored in the biblical text in the way that homosexuality is censured. At this point my reader may be looking for me to either endorse or dismiss such sexual practices. I am inclined to do neither. Such cases need to be handled on their own

---

[16]E.g., Victor Paul Furnish, "The Bible and Homosexuality: Reading the Texts in Context," in *Homosexuality in the Church: Both Sides of the Issue*, ed. Jeffrey S. Siker (Louisville: Westminster John Knox, 1994), pp. 21-23.

[17]Letha D. Scanzoni and Virginia R. Mollenkott, *Is the Homosexual My Neighbor? A Positive Christian Response*, 2d ed. (San Francisco: HarperCollins, 1994), pp. 130-32.

merits, judging a complex of factors that go much beyond the bounds of this work. Each sexual-variation case needs to be judged on its own merits, just as with abstinence cases and homosexual cases. Creation pattern is only one factor in assessing the legitimacy of sexual actions.

What permits the creation account to make a plausible statement about homosexuality is its correlation with other criteria within this book. By itself, the creation story is not very helpful in assessing what is cultural and what is transcultural. Too much variance was found in the neutral examples above (criterion 6.B.1-9) for any dogmatic assertions. Only as an interpreter establishes a dialogue between the creation story and other criteria can there be any emerging assurance of creation's continuing applicability or its needed discontinuance. With respect to homosexuality, several other criteria correlate with the creation story. For example, the criteria of options (criterion 9) and opposition (criterion 10) suggest that the creation pattern may be more reliable as a transcultural indicator in the homosexuality issue. Alternative options existed in the surrounding cultures, and a negative assessment of the practice by biblical authors sets up dissonance with the acceptance of the practice by many in other cultures. This increases the possibility that the author of Genesis understood the creation story as a statement about normative sexual patterns being heterosexual. The criterion of comparative contextual factors (criterion 10) shows that one of the major concerns in the sexual taboo lists is the issue of crossing structural boundaries. These boundaries match those of the creation story. Also, the scientific criterion (criterion 18) highlights significant physiological patterns that suggest that from the beginning of creation sexual fulfillment was intended for male-female relationships. Once again, these physiological patterns complement the creation story.

E. Summary

One may conclude that everything within the garden was created for the good of humanity. Yet, this is far different than saying that everything within the garden provides a transcultural pattern for today. A considerable number of cultural-bound components were discovered in the Edenic material. The variation in neutral examples surfaced above should cause us to use creation patterns in a cautious fashion. Simply finding something within the garden provides no assurance of its transcultural status. At times Eden's patterns should be strongly affirmed; sometimes they should be completely abandoned; on other occasions they need to be significantly modified for future generations. Consequently, the original-creation material should play a *supplementary* role in the evaluation of what is cultural and transcultural within Scripture.

An interactive discussion must be established between the garden and other criteria if one is to make an accurate cultural assessment. Such a forum of interchange may be applied to our two case studies. While quiet overtones of patriarchy appear within the garden story, this does not automatically mean that Christians should live out that kind of social structure today. A dialogue between the garden and other criteria places the transcultural status of patriarchy in considerable doubt. When taken in isolation, the heterosexual patterns found in the garden provide no simple solution about what should be done today regarding homosexuality. However, an interaction between the garden and other criteria in a secondary fashion confirms male-female sexuality as normative and casts a negative light on homosexual patterns. Only in this supplementary way can one establish the degree to which the garden should speak to a particular issue.

CRITERION 7: Basis in Original Creation, Section 2: Primogeniture

A. Statement

A component of a text may be transcultural, if it is rooted in the original-creation material and, more specifically, its creative order. By "creation order" what is being referred to is the chronological priority in which Adam and Eve were created: "Adam was formed first, then Eve" (as noted by Paul in 1 Tim 2:13). This order seems to carry considerable weight for the apostle Paul as he *applies it* to the issue of teaching within the church. On the grounds of this creative order he grants men, not women, the prominent/authoritative teaching positions in the church. This second area of original-creation exploration will investigate primogeniture customs and the logic of Paul's statement in 1 Timothy 2:13.

B. Primogeniture as the basis for Paul's logic

While we do not know for certain what Paul sees as the logical relationship between creation order (1 Tim 2:13) and the restrictions on women teaching (1 Tim 2:11-12), the most plausible explanation is that it is based upon, or is an extension of, primogeniture customs. Today's leading proponents of patriarchy acknowledge primogeniture as the essence of Paul's logic in 1 Timothy 2:13. Here is a sampling of the prevalent use of firstborn customs to explain the force of Paul's argument:

Piper and Grudem: "The contextual basis for this argument [from 1 Tim 2:13—i.e., male authority based upon the man being created before the woman] in the book of Genesis is *the assumption throughout the book that the 'firstborn' in a human family has the special responsibility of leadership in the family.*"[18]

Blomberg: "People in the ancient world familiar with *the privileges that first-born sons retained (of dynastic succession, inheritance, etc.)* would not have found Paul's argument unusual."[19]

Schreiner: "It seems the unclarity [of logic in 1 Tim 2:13] is in the eye of the beholder, for the thrust of the verse has been deemed quite clear in the history of the church. The creation of Adam first gives the reason why men should be the authoritative teachers in the church. James Hurley notes that the reasoning would not be obscure to people of Paul's time, for *they were quite familiar with primogeniture.*"[20]

If one ventures into the dusty archives of the church's past, there awaits an interesting discovery: by far the clearest explanation throughout church history for the logic of 1 Timothy 2:13 is primogeniture. Much of the time no explanation is given. There is an assumption that readers understand the logic. When an explanation was given, however, primogeniture is the clearest elaboration of the logic. Modern proponents of patriarchy, then, are joined by numerous ancient voices within church history to support the primogeniture thesis. (Appendix A develops a brief historical survey of the interpretation of 1 Timothy 2:13.)

Like the practice of primogeniture in which the firstborn is granted prominence within the "creative order" of a family unit, the first within the "creative order" of humanity (the larger family) is also given prominence. We might state the general idea of primogeniture logic this way: the first within any "creative order" receives prominence or special attention. Primogeniture logic finds expression on five or six levels of application within Scripture, yet under this one overriding theme: The first within any "creative order" receives special prominence over others in that order.

☐ *Society:* Man is the firstborn in the creative order of the human family; woman comes second.

☐ *Home:* The firstborn sibling in the creative order of an individual family is given prominence.

☐ *Kingship:* The firstborn in the creative order of the royal family becomes the

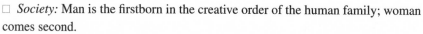

---

[18]John Piper and Wayne Grudem, "An Overview of Central Concerns," in *Recovering Biblical Manhood and Womanhood: A Response to Evangelical Feminism* (Wheaton, Ill.: Crossway, 1991), p. 81. Italics mine in each of the three quotations.

[19]Craig Blomberg, *1 Corinthians*, NIVAC (Grand Rapids, Mich.: Zondervan, 1994), p. 216.

[20]Thomas R. Schreiner, "An Interpretation of 1 Timothy 2:9-15," in *Women in the Church: A Fresh Analysis of 1 Timothy 2:9-15*, ed. Andreas J. Köstenberger, Thomas R. Schreiner and H. Scott Baldwin (Grand Rapids, Mich.: Baker, 1995), p. 136; cf., James B. Hurley, *Man and Women in Biblical Perspective* (Grand Rapids, Mich.: Zondervan, 1981), p. 208.

heir apparent, co-regent, and ultimately the king over the nation/covenant people.

☐ *Church:* Man, as first within the human family, receives firstborn status within the church or covenant family.

☐ *Agriculture:* The firstborn animals and "firstborn" produce (firstfruits) are given special prominence in being offered to God.

☐ *Theology:* Christ as the firstborn has prominence in status over all creation.

In sum, it would appear that in 1 Timothy 2:13 on an *explicit* level Paul parallels society (the human family) with the church (the covenant family) in a way that utilizes primogeniture-like logic. On an *implicit* level, however, the other examples of home, agriculture and theology utilize similar primogeniture-type logic in a manner that, at least in a secondary fashion, informs what is going on in the Timothy passage.

C. Primogeniture as a cultural value and practice

It is entirely likely that Paul uses primogeniture logic in 1 Timothy 2:13 in order to establish his point about the status of men over women. Having made this concession, however, it does not mean that a contemporary Christian should necessarily utilize or endorse this kind of logic and its subsequent practices today. There are good reasons why such logic (and its values/practice) should be viewed as having a significant cultural component.

1. Scripture frequently overturns primogeniture values. The likelihood that primogeniture logic contains a dominant cultural component is suggested by the treatment of the practice within Scripture itself. Even within an ancient-world setting where primogeniture had some merit, its value was often superseded by more important concerns. As a social convention, primogeniture carries considerable force within Scripture. However, the numerous breakouts within biblical texts place primogeniture-type logic into something of a questionable category. At many points throughout Scripture, God (or a human figure) consciously and often conspicuously abandons the norm of granting greater status and honor to those first within the "creative order":[21]

☐ God curses the firstborn Cain, while accepting the younger son's firstborn offering from the flock (Gen 4:1-16).

☐ Shem carries a higher status than his older brother Japheth (Gen 10:1, 21; 11:10).[22]

---

[21]For a detailed analysis, see Ktziah Spanier, "Aspects of Fratriarchy in the Old Testament," (Ph.D. diss., New York University, 1989), pp. 154-207.

[22]Notice the favoring of the younger son Shem in the listings of the brothers "Shem, Ham, and Japheth" (10:1) and more important, in the path of promise being carried through Shem to Abram (11:10-32).

☐ After the flood, God creates a "second humanity"[23] through Abraham, who in his honored role as a "second Adam" does not appear to have come upon that privilege as a firstborn child (Gen 11:31—12: 5).[24]

☐ Isaac is chosen as the recipient of the covenant blessing instead of Abraham's eldest son Ishmael (Gen 16:15; 17:19-22).

☐ The Lord says to Rebekah, "Two nations are in your womb . . . and the older [Esau] will serve the younger [Jacob]" (Gen 25:23; cf. Mal 1:2-3).

☐ Similar to Esau and Jacob, the younger twin Perez takes precedence over the older sibling Zerah[25] (Gen 38:27-30).[26]

☐ The blessing upon Ephraim and Manasseh is reversed between the elder and the younger son, with the greater blessing befalling the younger. (Gen 48:12-20)

☐ Judah is granted rule and Joseph the double inheritance[27] instead of the eldest, Reuben, who should have received both of these honors according to creative order (Gen 49:8, 22-26; cf. Gen 48:6; 1 Chron 5:1-2).

☐ Within the book of Genesis, then, a curious pattern unfolds whereby the firstborn *(bekor)* expects the blessing *(breach)* but does not always receive it.[28]

☐ God chose the younger son Moses, instead of Aaron, to lead the Israelites out of slavery (Ex 6:20; 7:1).

☐ Instead of the older-son tribes, the tribes of younger sons—Judah, Issachar and Zebulun—head up the military procession during the wilderness travels. Most notably, Reuben, the "firstborn," is displaced from the lead position (Num 1:20; 2:3-7).

☐ The elder brother Ahitub seems to be dependent upon his younger brother Ichabod (1 Sam 14:3).[29]

---

[23]That Abraham's offspring become a "second humanity" (with Abraham as a second Adam) seems clear from the seventy nations (cf. the Babel genealogy) patterned within the seventy children who go down into Egypt and the seventy elders within Israel.

[24]As the listing of "Shem, Ham and Japheth" is not a chronological order (Gen 10:1; cf. 9:24-27; 10:21), so it would appear that the listing of "Abram, Nahor and Haran" (11:26) might not be chronological. Haran dies much earlier than his other two brothers (11:28). The order of Abram at the lead in 11:26, as with Shem in 10:1, would focus on the "most blessed" among the offspring.

[25]Zerah is considered the eldest/first since his hand comes out of the womb first.

[26]Perez becomes the head of a leading clan in Judah and the ancestor of David (Ruth 4:18-22; cf. Mt 1:1-6).

[27]This is a good example where some of the primogeniture functions are split up among younger siblings (Judah and Joseph). Joseph receives the double blessing through his two sons being placed in the blessing list; Judah receives the aspect of rule.

[28]On the alliteration that draws attention to this feature, see David F. Pennant, "Alliteration in Some Texts in Genesis," *Biblica* 68:3 (1987): 390-92.

[29]The likely dominance of younger over elder is indicated in the fratronym: "Ahitub brother of Ichabod." Ichabod gets this respectful type of naming, though he was clearly the younger son—his mother delivered Ichabod upon hearing of his father's death (1 Sam 4:19-21).

☐ Saul grooms his firstborn Jonathan as heir apparent, only to discover that the throne will go to another within Jesse's household and not to a firstborn (1 Sam 20:2).

☐ Samuel thought he should anoint Jesse's firstborn son Eliab as king of Israel, but to his surprise God selected the youngest son David as the nation's leader (1 Sam 16:6, 11; cf. 1 Sam 17:13-14).

☐ While Abishai appears to be the firstborn, Joab leads within his family as frat-riarch[30] and within David's army as confidant and chief of staff (2 Sam 2:13-18; cf. 1 Chron 2:16).[31]

☐ David selects Solomon as heir to the throne over Adonijah (1 Kings 1:5-6) and over others (cf. 1 Chron 3:5) who were ahead of him in line of succession (1 Kings 1:17).[32]

☐ Jotham, while probably not his father's firstborn,[33] served as co-regent with his father before succeeding Azariah to the throne of Judah (2 Kings 15:5).

☐ Manasseh seems to have been granted the throne by his father Hezekiah with-out the hereditary right of firstborn (2 Kings 18:2).[34]

☐ Amon, like his father Manasseh, was granted rule, although he probably was not the firstborn (2 Kings 21:1).[35]

☐ Ram seems to have functioned as the fratriarch over his brothers and was blessed with Davidic lineage, instead of the firstborn Jerachmeel (1 Chron 2:9, 25).[36]

☐ Abijah was chosen to succeed his father Rehoboam, despite the fact that he was not the firstborn (1 Chron 11:18-22).

☐ The Chronicler highlights the breaking away from primogeniture patterns: "Shimri was chief [in his family] although not the firstborn, for his father [Hosah]

---

[30]Joab's role as fratriarch may be seen in fratronymic (1 Sam 26:6; 2 Sam 23:18) and matronyic (2 Sam 17:25) descriptions, as well as his lead role in avenging the death of their brother (2 Sam 3:30).

[31]2 Sam 3:24-25, 30; 10:9-10; 13:26-28; 16:9-10; 19:6-8.

[32]Cf. 2 Sam 3:4. Solomon becomes heir because of David's promise to Bathsheba (1 Kings 1:17) and by virtue of his positive attributes (2 Sam 12:24-25; 1 Kings 1—11).

[33]Azariah became king at the age of sixteen and ruled fifty-two years (2 Kings 15:2); Jotham was twenty-five when he ascended the throne (2 Kings 15:33). Due to the significant time lag between Azariah coming to the throne and the birth of Jotham (27 years), it is unlikely that Azariah had no sons prior to the birth of Jotham.

[34]Cf. 2 Kings 21:1. Hezekiah was forty-two years old at the birth of Manasseh, which makes it unlikely that Manasseh was the firstborn. Cf. Spanier, "Aspects of Fratriarchy," p. 178.

[35]Cf. 2 Kings 21:18-19. As with the two cases above, the age of the father in relation to the son makes it likely that Manasseh had other sons before Amon.

[36]Cf. 1 Chron 2:10-12, 18-24. While Jerachmeel was firstborn, Ram appears to function as fratriarch due to the arrangement of the genealogical listings, where his descendants get listed ahead of off-spring born to Hezron through another wife and ahead of Jerachmeel's household, and the Davidic dynasty emerging from his line.

made him chief" (1 Chron 26:10-11).

God's path of promise frequently overturns the "firstborn rules" convention in order to draw attention to character, disposition of the heart toward God and leadership abilities. If this qualified perspective of Scripture was true in an ancient-world culture and setting where primogeniture had sociological merit (see below), how much more in our modern-world setting where its social merit is almost entirely lost. These overturns or breakouts within Scripture are often an internal clue that part of the value conveyed in a practice is shallow rooted (cultural) compared to a broader underlying principle (transcultural). An earlier discussion of breakouts (criterion 3) has surfaced other biblical examples.

2. Primogeniture is tied to the ancient world. Studies of primogeniture within the Bible[37] as well as contemporary sociological research on the practice[38] have shown that primogeniture is fundamentally tied to an assortment of time-locked, culture-bound factors. These factors make primogeniture understandable within certain settings, but not something that should be lauded as a universal norm. For example, at the heart of this creative order custom lie concerns about agriculture, land transference, lineage survival, large/extended families, sufficient provision for animals, and so on. In other words, primogeniture was a good practice in agricultural societies or in societies where property was held throughout several generations in estate forms.

In order to grasp the cultural dimension to primogeniture practices, it may be helpful to highlight various practical considerations that made this social convention flourish in certain cultures but not in others. Studies of primogeniture rights provide us with a range of social-setting rationales for why *one* sibling (unigeniture) is favored over the others:

Survival/success of lineage: Investing a greater portion of family resources in one heir increased the likelihood of at least one line surviving across several gen-

---

[37]For some of the best developments of primogeniture in the Bible, see Ktziah Spanier, "Aspects of Fratriarchy," pp. 1-228; Roger Syren, *The Forsaken First-born: A Study of a Recurrent Motif in the Patriarchal Narratives*, JSOT Supplement Series 133 (Sheffield: JSOT Press, 1993), pp. 1-159; Eryl W. Davies, "The Inheritance of the First-born in Israel and the Ancient Near East," *Journal of Semitic Studies* 38:2 (1993): 175-91; Gershon Brin, *Studies in Biblical Law: From the Hebrew Bible to the Dead Sea Scrolls*, JSOT Supplement Series 176 (Sheffield: JSOT Press, 1994), pp. 166-281.

[38]For the sociological rationale behind primogeniture practices, see Sarah Blaffer Hrdy and Debra S. Judge, "Darwin and the Puzzle of Primogeniture: An Essay on Biases in Parental Investment After Death," *Human Nature* 4:1 (1993): 1-45; Paula Sutter Fichtner, *Protestantism and Primogeniture in Early Modern Germany* (New Haven: Yale University Press, 1989), pp. 1-125; John W. Probyn, ed., *Systems of Land Tenure in Various Countries* (Freeport, N.Y.: Books for Libraries Press, 1971), pp. 1-534; Lee J. Alston and Morton Owen Schapiro, "Inheritance Laws Across Colonies: Causes and Consequences," *The Journal of Economic History* 44:2 (1984): 277-87; Radhabinod Pal, *The History of the Law of Primogeniture* (Calcutta, India: University of Calcutta Press, 1929).

erations.

Agricultural concerns: Equal distribution of land and cattle simply was not a feasible route due to grazing ratios and production possibilities.

Land-based cultures: Often it does not make sense to split up farms (or estates) into smaller packages.

Elderly parents: Creating greater resources for one heir sometimes ensured better care of aging parents.

Large families: Unigeniture practices flourish in cultures with large families; it decreases significantly with smaller families, since equal distribution of wealth and power becomes more feasible.

Within this broader framework of favoring one offspring, the rationale for choosing the *eldest* as the sibling leader is readily understandable:

Age: The firstborn would often have the natural edge over other siblings due to being older and thus having greater physical strength and maturity.

Sibling rivalry: Early identification of the primary heir minimized rivalry among siblings.

Parental death: Premature parental death made the firstborn selection an easy one since younger offspring would require care.

Survival/success of lineage: All of these factors tie either directly or indirectly into the encompassing rationale for primogeniture, for example, the success of lineage in terms of offspring, passing on of wealth, agricultural developments.

As can be seen from the above survey,[39] primogeniture had considerable merit for certain settings. However, primogeniture becomes a counterproductive practice in societies where there are fewer children in the family, where land is not tied to survival, where properties are not parceled in estate-like packages, where monetary wealth has greater liquidity, where higher mobility and nuclear families

---

[39]The favoring of sons over daughters decreases and is ultimately eliminated in cultures with lower numbers of children per family, with land no longer being a critical factor for economic success, with legal systems improving the resource-holding potential of females, with the decline in polygamous societies that favored males in reproduction strategies (i.e., through multiple wives ensuring the greatest number of offspring), with physical strength no longer needed for agricultural and military pursuits, with greater potential earnings for females, etc. Thus in cultures where these factors no longer shape social/family structures (such as our own), women generally get an even distribution of inheritance and play significant leadership roles among their siblings. In our contemporary culture where strength is measured in mental and character capacity (not in physical strength), where laws permit females to retain resources, where polygamy no longer prevails, where family battles are fought in a court of law (not through military excursions), etc., the preference for *a male* leading the other siblings is no longer sustainable. Ability and gifting become the standard for leadership among siblings, not gender and not birth order. For a discussion of these factors, see Spanier, "Aspects of Fratriarchy," pp. 111-53; Hrdy and Judge, "The Puzzle of Primogeniture," pp. 21-27.

exist, etc. In the latter settings, studies have shown that these kind of societies move away from primogeniture generally into more egalitarian-type orders or, in a few cases, ultimogeniture (last-born) orders.[40] These changes away from primogeniture happened in order to sustain the same good values for the family unit as a whole that primogeniture had done earlier. What is ultimately sacred is not the establishment of honor and rule related to being first within a creative family order, but the stability and well being of the family as a whole. If primogeniture no longer accomplishes these goals (as it does not in our Western context today), then alternative distribution of honor and power among those in a creative order must be sought.

One might ask if pragmatic factors like these should influence our cultural/transcultural analysis of Scripture. In short, the answer is yes. The pragmatic factors that drove primogeniture customs were part of the ancient setting but they are no longer part of our world. Pragmatic factors tend to shape the formation of biblical text not so much at the upper abstracted levels of principle, but at the lower concrete expression of principle as it gets fleshed out within a particular cultural context. Later, in criterion 17 ("Pragmatics Between Two Cultures") I will argue that when we move between two cultures, the lack of a sustained pragmatic basis serves as a signal that something might be cultural. The lack of a sustained pragmatic basis generally causes us to move up the ladder of abstraction and work with the underlying transcultural principle. In the case of primogeniture we might express this universal principle as "Grant honor to whom honor is due." Within ancient communities this transcultural principle often took on a cultural expression in the form of primogeniture-based distribution of honor.

3. *Christians no longer apply primogeniture today.* It is important to lay out the encompassing functions of the fratriarch (rule by one sibling) within Scripture in order to see that inheritance is only the tip of the iceberg. Aside from receiving a double portion of the inheritance (Deut 21:16-17), the fratriarch led in military protection for the family (Gen 14:14-16; 1 Sam 17:13-14), avenged wrongs done against family members (2 Sam 2:12-13, 18, 22-23; 3:27), performed religious ceremonies (1 Sam 20:29; 22:3; 1 Kings 1:9), looked after the physical well-being of family members,[41] organized and carried out burial rites (Gen 47:29; 50:1-10, 14), acted as confidant in decisions made by the family patriarch (1 Sam 2:20), and arranged marriages for sisters within the household

---

[40]In certain societies the tax laws on land inheritance caused a move to ultimogeniture (favoring the last-born) in order to maximize the number of years between land transference and thus minimize the amount of tax.

[41]Gen 37:22, 29-30; 42:37 (cf. 37:26-27; 43:8-10; 44:14, 33-34; 46:28); 47:11-12.

(Gen 24:29, 57; 25:20).

In our modern setting, siblings no longer relate to each other along primogeniture lines. Neither do we practice the broad scope of fratriarchy as developed within Scripture. Our families generally chose leadership roles for grown siblings based on ability, not birth order. If one is to invoke the ongoing logic of primogeniture today, then it holds much broader ramifications for family functioning than simply how men and women ought to relate within the family of God. While I grant that nonapplication of primogeniture today is the weakest of my three arguments (perhaps Christian siblings are not doing what they should be doing today), it is interesting that those who appeal to primogeniture in affirming the transcultural status of 1 Timothy 2:13 say very little about the sustained application of other primogeniture texts for our lives.

D. Evaluation of the criterion

Some questions on this criterion may still linger. I will deal with two of them. One question is whether primogeniture logic would have played a role in 1 Timothy 2:13, given that Israel's firstborn customs relate to male offspring, not to female offspring. While this is so, Paul's development of the firstborn ideas has sufficient elasticity to include women within the sibling group. For instance, in Romans Christ's exalted status of firstborn among many brothers uses the term *brothers* in a generic sense to include women believers: "For those God foreknew he also predestined to be conformed to the likeness of his Son, that he might be the firstborn among many brothers" (Rom 8:29). The reference to those foreknown by God obviously includes the entire congregation (both males and females), as would the "many brothers." In a similar manner, the author of the book of Hebrews includes women within firstborn logic. In this example, women are given firstborn status along with men in the congregation: "You have come . . . to the church of the firstborn [literally, "firstborns"] whose names are written in heaven" (Heb 12:22-23). The word translated "firstborn" in the NIV is plural in the Greek text and contextually refers to the entire Christian assembly. Thus, in Romans women are included at the lower sibling level of firstborn logic (the younger siblings), while in Hebrews women are part of the higher sibling level of firstborn logic (the eldest sibling). With this fluidity in firstborn ideas within Scripture it is unlikely that Paul would have hesitated in applying firstborn logic (1 Tim 2:13) to the case of Adam and Eve, simply because Eve was female.

A second question is how cultural features could possibly be found in the garden before the influence of culture. Several explanations exist. First, the whispers of patriarchy in the garden may have been placed there in order to anticipate the curse. For example, literary foreshadowing of the curse is also seen in the portrayal of the snake: "The serpent was *more crafty* than any of the wild animals."[42] In a context such as the Genesis account, with its connection between Satan's deception and the snake, a pejorative sense of "cunning" or "crafty" seems preferable.[43] Such a portrait of a "cunning" or "crafty" snake poses an interesting question. If the garden is completely pristine, how could certain creatures in the just-created animal kingdom reflect craftiness? Obviously, this Edenic material embraces an artistic foreshadowing of events to come.[44] Other portraits in Scripture paint with overlapping hues between two theoretically distinct dispensations or epochs.[45] We may do a disservice to the Genesis text by trying to draw neat lines between pre-Fall and post-Fall material.

Second, Eden's quiet echoes of patriarchy might be a way of describing the past through present categories. The creation story may be using the social categories that Moses' audience would have been familiar with. God sometimes permits such accommodation in order not to confuse the main point[46] of what he wants to communicate with factors that are secondary to that overall theme. In biblical eschatology (as in protology) one finds a similar present-day projection. For example, Ezekiel's eschatological hope includes a temple where Jews still have a prominent priestly position over Gentiles. In broad terms, the picture of hope is accurate. However, certain details (e.g., Gentile exclusion, sacrifice, special days)[47] are more likely projections into the future of then-present realities

---

[42]Gen 3:1 (NIV). Cf. NRSV, NASV and KJV for similar kinds of pejorative translations.

[43]For an example of the term's negative connotation in its verbal form, see Ps 83:3.

[44]The craftiness of the snake is one element that links the creation and Fall section. See Victor P. Hamilton, *The Book of Genesis Chapters 1—17*, NICOT (Grand Rapids, Mich.: Eerdmans, 1990), p. 187.

[45]For example, Isaiah's portrait of the new heavens and earth should not be picked apart for those elements that are "millennial" and those that are "eternal state" (Is 65:17—66:16). Nor should we dissect John's narrative too closely simply because he places "leaves for the healing of the nations" within his portrait of the new heavens and new earth (Rev 22:2; cf. Ezek 47:12). This element cannot be taken as a strictly literal event in the future since people will be already healed and fully redeemed. While the portrait fails to fit within a dissection-like reading of the material (i.e., one that tries to determine what will precisely happen in one epoch as opposed to another), it makes a wonderful point of transition within the book of Revelation.

[46]The main point of the creation narrative is that Yahweh created the heavens and all that is in them and Yahweh created the earth and all that is in it—God made everything. For the original audience of Genesis this main point sets up a tremendous polemic against the worship of the pagan gods who were merely created objects (the moon, stars, rivers, oceans) or plant and animal life (produce or animals). These pagan gods were subservient to the one true Creator God!

[47]The New Moon and Sabbath celebrations of Ezek 46:1-3 are unlikely to be held in the future, except metaphorically through the presence of Christ who is the fullness of what these special days foreshadowed (Col 2:17).

than a literal portrait of what will actually happen.[48] Similarly, the precious stones depicted within the eschatological New Jerusalem probably reflect present reality projected into the future.[49] Another example is seen in the final fall of world powers idealized as a Rome-like or Babylon-like nation. In this apocalyptic portrait the merchants of the world mourn because their source of income has dried up. One of the things they mourn about is the loss of income from their slave trade (Rev 18:13; cf. 19:18). Few would want to press this text to say that in the final days slavery will return as a major component of commerce around the world.[50] Rather, the eschatological portrait utilizes sociological categories of the present in order to convey its broader point. Also, the final eschatological battle is depicted as a gathering together of "the kings of the earth" (Rev 17:2, 18; 18:3, 9; 19:19) against the rider on the white horse. The text does not jump ahead in time and explain that the major world powers are now democracies and not monarchies. The author simply utilizes the forms of the present in talking about the future. This is typical eschatological accommodation. These two examples (slavery and monarchy) are particularly helpful since they illustrate how a biblical author can construct a time-displaced portrait with respect to its sociological components.

Third, given the agrarian base to primogeniture logic, the patriarchy of the garden may reflect God's anticipation of the social context into which Adam and Eve were about to venture. An agrarian lifestyle without the benefits of modern machinery and technology would naturally produce some kind of hierarchy between men and women. The male would spend the bulk of his time raising food; the female would spend most of her time raising children. Classic agrarian roles often produced an automatic hierarchy of sorts, since the women were more dependent upon the men for provisions. The presentation of the male-female relationship in patriarchal forms may simply be a way of anticipating this first (and major) life setting into which humankind would enter.

---

[48]Even for progressive dispensationalists who are open to a millennial temple, too much has gone on in salvation history to make Ezekiel's model a likely casting of the future. Ezekiel's temple is an appropriate expression of hope to an audience from that time frame, but it probably does not provide us with a strictly literal projection of the future. God does not complicate the communication by including parts of the vision that would not be readily understood by the immediate audience.

[49]Rev 21:15-21. The listing of precious metals and stones is culturally rooted. Our generation has never heard of some of the materials used in building the New Jerusalem. On the other hand, it is rather strange from our modern perspective that diamonds are missing. Yet, such a depiction of the eschatological city is entirely understandable; diamonds were not a precious stone in the ancient world.

[50]Also, the entire list of what merchants would mourn over in Rev 18:11-13 would be significantly different in a twenty-first-century world. It would at the very least replace some of agricultural-based list with more "high-tech" items.

In sum, the patriarchy within the original creation narrative can be accounted for as a literary anticipation of the curse, as a backwards projection of patriarchy into protology or as a practical and gracious anticipation of the agrarian setting into which Adam and Eve were headed. The garden's patriarchy can be explained through any one of these possibilities or a combination of them.

E. Summary

Continuing the insights of many ancient commentators, leading patriarchalists today explain the nature of Paul's logic in 1 Timothy 2:13 on the basis of primogeniture practices. That logic, in conjunction with the garden (pre-Fall) setting, gives them sufficient assurance of the transcultural nature of Paul's reasoning. While agreeing with primogeniture being the essence of Paul's point and acknowledging the obvious pre-Fall setting, I am not as confident about drawing a transcultural conclusion as some.

A more convincing assessment of the matter might be to admit a cultural component to creative order logic as applied to people. Not only are firstborn customs frequently overturned within Scripture, but current sociological studies have demonstrated that primogeniture and its resultant social structures are the products of culture-locked, time-bound concerns. Furthermore, as the previous criterion points out, finding something in the Edenic garden does *not* make it transcultural. While the method of honor allotment within primogeniture may well be culturally shaped, one would still apply the text's underlying principle of "granting honor to whom honor is due." Or, we could more pointedly express the transcultural principle within the 1 Timothy 2 context of concern for the teaching leaders. Having discovered the cultural component within the text, we should now apply the underlying principle of the text to both genders: *choose teachers/ leaders who are worthy of high honor within the congregation.*

Nevertheless, the amount of material to work with in assessing the cultural/ transcultural status of 1 Timothy 2:13 is minimal. It calls for both sides to reflect seriously upon a "what if I am wrong" scenario, as I will attempt to do toward the end of this work (see chapter eight).

CRITERION 8: Basis in New Creation

A. Statement

A component of a text may be transcultural if it is rooted in new-creation material. We now turn from considering the original, first creation to looking at the new or ultimate creation. For Paul the redemptive aspects of the eschaton are already being realized in the present "in Christ" community. The old creation is in the process of passing away; a new creation has dawned with the first coming of Christ. The new society "in Christ" is rooted in the eschaton. Even so, its redemptive aspects and social modifications are to be realized as much as possible in the way we live now. Perhaps if anything transcends culture, it should be the theology of ultimate new creation. After all, the new creation as expressed in the Christian community is intended to carry through this epoch until Christ returns.

I have already discussed Galatians 3:28 and its related Pauline cluster (1 Cor 12:13; Eph 2:15; 4:22-24; Col 3:11) at length,[51] so my comments here will be brief. This criterion will simply introduce a new twist to the theme. On the one hand, we need to consider this cluster of texts from the perspective of "new creation." They add a fresh counterpart and balance to our previous discussion of the original creation patterns. I will suggest that the closer the new-creation community moves toward the eschaton, the more likely it will engage transcultural perspectives.

On the other hand, when creation ideas are explored through the broad sweep of Scripture (not simply within the opening chapters of Genesis), they help us appreciate the creation motif as an unfolding set of two or three new creations. Beyond the original creation, there is a formation of a "new humanity" under Abraham and under Jesus—both of which are considered God's "new creation." They respectively move the covenant community toward ultimate redemptive fulfillment. However, it is crucial to recognize that culture-bound components existed in some of these other creation acts. This should curb any artificial expectations toward finding only transcultural components in the original creation material. God's creation of humanity at various stages utilized cultural components, whether with Adam or with the new humanity under Abraham. In both cases, creation patterns contain cultural and transcultural elements.

B. New-creation community—a "new humanity"
The apostle Paul sketches what the new humanity or new-creation community looks like. It often stands in contrast to the old humanity in Adam. Five Pauline texts describe this new "in Christ" society:

☐ "For we were all baptized by one Spirit into one body—whether Jews or Greeks, slave or free—and we were all given the one Spirit to drink" (1 Cor 12:13).

☐ "There is neither Jew nor Greek, slave nor free, male nor female . . . in Christ Jesus" (Gal 3:28).

☐ "His [Christ's] purpose was to create in himself one new man [i.e., one new humanity] out of the two [Jew and Gentile]" (Eph 2:15).

☐ "You were taught, with regard to your former way of life, to put off your old

---

[51]See criterion 2 for an extended discussion of Gal 3:28. Cf. criterion 9.

self [identity in the old humanity/society] which is being corrupted by its desires
. . . and to put on the new self [identity in the new humanity/society], created to
be like God in true righteousness and holiness" (Eph 4:22-24).

☐ "Here [in the new society in Christ] there is no Greek or Jew, circumcised or
uncircumcised, barbarian, Scythian, slave or free" (Col 3:11).

For purposes of this criterion it is important to highlight the new-creation motif found within these Pauline texts:

☐ "in Christ" vs. "in Adam" (Gal 3:28; Col 3:11)

☐ new man/humanity (Eph 2:15; 4:24; Col 3:10)

☐ renewal (Eph 4:23; Col 3:10)

☐ created to be like God (Eph 4:24; cf. 2:15); made in the image of its Creator
(Col 3:10).

☐ new clothing (Gal 3:27; Eph 4:22, 24; Col 3:9-10).

It should be clear from looking at these texts that the new-creation community
in Christ intentionally replaces the old humanity in Adam. In other words, new-
creation patterns should be given prominence over the old-creation patterns.

C. Women

Patriarchalists and egalitarians often confine their discussion of Galatians 3:28 to
the context of Galatians. This isolated perspective is unfortunate, since it misses
Paul's broader development of the new community in connection with the familiar rubric of "neither this, nor that" in Christ. As argued before, these texts should
be taken as a collective grouping. The "neither male, nor female" designation of
the Galatians text could just as well have been placed in any of the other lists. The
categories are simply *representative* of social inequality. Once this larger framework is established, then one can proceed with a development of Paul's new community thinking in relation to men and women.

I have made the case earlier that these texts need to be read with sociological
implications and not salvation concerns alone (see criterion 2.C.1). Taken as a
group, 1 Corinthians 12:13; Galatians 3:28; Ephesians 2:15; 4:22-24 and Colossians 3:11 held clear and profound sociological implications for Jew and Gentile.
Paul emphasized those implications during his lifetime. The church has subsequently seen fit to implement the social ramifications for slavery. For today's generation, it is now a question of how to apply the social implications for women.

The point of resurfacing this cluster of Pauline texts is to add a further component to the "in Christ" perspective, namely, new creation. Implicit within
Paul's development is a priority given to patterns found in the new creation. If
any patterns should be granted ongoing significance, it should be those found
within the new-creation material. The original-creation patterns, as founda-

tional as they are, simply do not have the same potential for reflecting transcultural features as do new-creation patterns. Conversely, original-creation patterns are far more likely to have culture-locked components within them. We have already found a number of cultural components within the original-creation materials (see criterion 6). By comparison, I do not find any cultural components within the "in Christ" new-humanity texts. In fact, the counterculture dimension to these texts (see criterion 10) underscores their predisposition toward a transcultural framework.

Aside from setting a priority of new creation over old, the "creation of a new humanity" theme throughout Scripture also raises a helpful case study for seeing other time-locked or culture-based features found in God's earlier acts of creation. Genesis 1—3 may have been the original creation act of God. But, it was followed by another creation, the creation of a new humanity. After the flood and the tower of Babel, God decided to form a new humanity, a second creation of sorts. The promise of a new people emerges with Abraham. It is Abraham's offspring who part ways with the former world—the seventy nations of the "old world" (Gen 10) are now replaced by an emerging "new world" reflected in the seventy descendents of Jacob that go into Egypt (Gen 46:27; Ex 1:5; cf. Deut 32:8) and the seventy elders of Israel (Ex 24:1, 9; Num 11:16; cf. Ex 15:27). Israel as the new humanity parallels the creation of old humanity begun in the garden. This "seventy" parallel, along with other parallels,[52] provides a literary way of saying that with Abraham and the nation Israel God starts over and creates a new humanity—this is a "second creation" of humanity! This example is important within the creation theme because it helps us recognize once again that cultural and time-locked components are not incompatible with God's creation patterns. A juxtaposition or discontinuity between this "second creation" under Abraham and the new and emerging "ultimate creation" in Christ will be a significant focus of the evaluation section below.

D. Evaluation of the criterion

The "new creation" criterion raises questions about discontinuities between God's first creation and the ultimate, new creation in Christ. Patriarchalists are often willing to see a modification of patriarchy due to redemption or new-creation patterns "in Christ" but not its complete removal, since patriarchy was part of the original garden. Most can readily understand how redemption over-

---

[52]For further parallels between the old humanity from the garden and Israel as the new humanity, see William J. Dumbrell, *The Search for Order: Biblical Eschatology in Focus* (Grand Rapids, Mich.: Baker, 1994), pp. 29-30.

turns dimensions of the curse. But, to propose that redemption "improves upon" the original creation simply does not sound feasible. Terrance Tiessen raises the question of discontinuity with the original creation and expresses the perplexity this way: "The suggestion that redemption goes further [beyond curse removal] and improves on creation . . . leaves us unsure of where it is taking us."[53] Tiessen's comment raises two issues pertinent to the use of new creation patterns to reformulate original-creation patterns: (1) the issue of destination—where are new creation patterns "taking us" and (2) the issue of development—how could one possibly "improve" upon the original creation. These two issues will be addressed in turn.

The destination issue raises a crucial question: Where are these new-creation patterns taking us?[54] The question is a good one. Without a clear answer one is left with the impression that modification of the original creation patterns is open-ended. However, Galatians 3:28 and the other Pauline clusters set definite limits to the modification. An examination of the categories—Jew and Greek, slave and free, male and female, barbarian, Scythian, and so on—demonstrates that Paul had limits in mind. Paul is not denying *differences* in gender and race, nor is he denying the reality of *differences* in socioeconomic positions. A distinction must be made between renewal of human relationships and an alternation of the essence of humanity into some unknown indefinite kind of being. Paul does not intend the eradication of race or gender or employment structures. Renewal does not mean that humanity becomes something other than what it was in its essential essence and its categories of being. It is humanity itself that is renewed, not created *de novo* again. It is not so much that humans change in their created being, as it is that relationships between humans change. Relationships are to be perfected and re-ordered according to Christ's perfecting love. Essential aspects of the original creation such as race and gender are in not obliterated in the new creation community. They remain and are transfigured, sanctified and celebrated. The new humanity must use the differences to bless and raise up instead of destroy and disadvantage.

In sum, Paul limits the modification of original-creation patterns—differences in humanity are to be celebrated and renewed in their relationships, not denied and

---

[53]Tiessen, "Universal Moral Absolutes," p. 206. Cf. the concern regarding a unity of biblical ethic, voiced by Guenther Haas, "Patriarchy as an Evil that God Tolerated: Analysis and Implications fo the Authority of Scripture," *JETS* 38 (1995): 334. Haas's disjunction problems are compounded by his responding to a (faulty) polarization of patriarchy.

[54]The insights of Gary W. Deddo were especially helpful in shaping my response to the destination question. While the book as a whole has been improved by his skillful interaction, I am particularly indebted for his reflection in this area.

obliterated. So the relations between men and women are to be perfected in their intimacy and closeness. New-creation theology does not intend for "male and female" intimacy and complementary relations to degenerate into homosexual relations, that is, no relations between men and women. Where, then, are new-creation patterns "taking us"? Well, one clear answer is toward a newly restored heterosexuality—a strengthening of relationships between male and female. Such reflection answers the destination question at least in terms of negative definition. It explains where new creation is *not* taking human relationships.

Now we can talk about the issue of destination within these parameters. I have already argued that Galatians 3:28 and its Pauline cluster intends for implications of social equality and mutuality (see criterion 2). Given that Paul has in mind social equality and renewal of relations between people in these different groups, then, the question of destination is worth exploring. It might be helpful to start with the more neutral examples of race (Jew, Gentile, Scythian) and economic relationships (slave and master, rich and poor). Race distinctions were to benefit the new-creation community in Christ through diversity. Unlike former days, no longer was race to be the basis for leadership and status within the community. Similarly, economic structures were not to define participation and status within the covenant people. Slaves and masters were to renew their relationships, one aspect being the eventual movement to abolition. Rich and poor were to benefit each other. The latter need material blessing and the former need (just as much so) to relinquish material blessing. A slave, a Scythian, a Greek, a poor person—all of these people obtained a strikingly new status of equality within the "in Christ" society. To ponder these examples, should lead to a fairly clear vision for the destination of women within the new-creation humanity. Even if this vision were not entirely realized by the early church, that does not nullify the vision.

The development issue raises another crucial question: How could one possibly "improve" upon the original creation? The question could be expanded in order to draw out the problem: If the original creation pattern included patriarchy (as quiet hues in the background), and if that creation was viewed by God as "good" (as overtly stated in the text), then how could one possibly "improve" upon the patriarchy of the garden? The question is an excellent one and one that often keeps patriarchalists (even of the redemptive-movement and ultra-soft type) from crossing the line to becoming an egalitarian. The best answer is one that peels away the faulty assumptions involved in the question. I will look at three faulty assumptions. First, the question assumes something about development in its use of "improve" language. Once one talks about "improving" that which God has declared as good, it sets up a scenario that sounds like heresy. When reading and using "improve" language, it is possible to include a moral sense. If so, then the answer is clear: patriarchy needs to stay! No one (not even God himself) can improve morally upon that which is already morally good. But, if one were to limit the improvement idea to utilitarian or functional or cultural categories, then the answer changes. Improvement or change in a time-limited and situation-specific sense is entirely possible.

Second, the question assumes that patriarchy within the original creation scene must be a pristine and permanent social entity. For the proponents of patriarchy, a "good" garden could not possibly be modified because it is perfect. This thinking, however, assumes in an automatic fashion that all things found within the Eden material (patriarchy included) have a transcultural status. The last two criteria on patterns and primogeniture counter this assumption and raise the possibility (if not probability) that patriarchy within the garden should be seen as a cultural component of the portrait.

Third, the question assumes more broadly that one creative order cannot be "improved upon" or significantly modified by another creative order. The biblical labels of "new" and "old" creation assume at least some dimension of disjunction. While not specifically answering our question about patriarchy, they do at least permit disjunction. More importantly, the triple-creation theme in Scripture permits creative disjunction as well. This multi-creation story in Scripture moves from Adam to Abraham to Christ. Within the Abrahamic "new creation" a Jew-Gentile inequality emerges that the next redemptive creation "in Christ" eliminates.

We might pull the contributions of several criteria together now. Proponents of patriarchy often overlook the possibility of God's accommodation and/or anticipation within the garden of what lay ahead. What lay ahead for humanity was not simply the curse, but a type of culture and society in which primogeniture made sense and would have sustainable value. It was a culture in which even patriarchy had certain sustainable merits. In this respect, polarized assessments of patriarchy as either "a terrible evil of the Fall" (by many egalitarians) or as "a pristine good of creation" (by many patriarchalists) are not helpful and ultimately counterproductive.[55] Transcultural assumptions about original creation frequently fail to wrestle with the cultural merits of primogeniture and patriarchy. They do not ac-

---

[55]As an alternative, I am proposing that the original-creation order may reflect protological accommodation (comparable to eschatological accommodation) in its sub-themes in order to make its broadest point that Yahweh created the heavens and earth and that these created entities are not to be worshipped as the pagans do. And/or, the original creation may reflect a gracious and practical anticipation of what would work best within the kind of world into which humanity was headed (see criterion 7.D). For a polarized approach, see Haas, "Patriarchy as an Evil that God Tolerated," pp. 321-36.

count for neutral examples of cultural components within the garden. Yet again, unwarranted transcultural assumptions overlook the case of the Gentiles within God's second creation of humanity. Within this God-created entity known as Israel, we find inequality for Jew and Gentile. That inequality is later removed (theoretically and practically) in the new in-Christ humanity. Just because something is a God-made creation, such as the first creation of Eden or the second creation of Israel, that does not mean that every aspect within it is transcultural.

E. Summary

The in-Christ lists within the New Testament express a theology of new creation. One can hardly talk about old-creation patterns within Scripture without engaging in a discussion about these new-creation texts. In Pauline thinking we encounter a new Eden, a new creation and a new humanity. Since it has already been argued that this grouping of texts carries tacit sociological implications, what becomes important here is to reflect upon their transcultural predominance. While our lives are obviously rooted in the original creation in certain respects, it is ultimately the new understanding of community in Christ that should guide us to the eschaton.

Some things change, while other things do not. New-creation patterns do not change the essential aspects of the original creation—it celebrates rather than obliterates gender and race distinctions. These relations are to be strengthened and perfected. Men and women are to grow together in their intimacy and closeness. In this sense, new-creation theology argues against replacing male-and-female oneness with homosexual relations (the dissolution of relations between men and women). On the other hand, new-creation theology transforms the status of all of its participants—whether slaves, Greeks, Scythians or barbarians—into one of equality. Along these same lines, it calls for equality and relational renewal between men and women and as such heavily favors an egalitarian position. At the very least, the equality of new creation patterns encourages redemptive movement toward a profoundly reconfigured type of patriarchy—an ultra-soft patriarchy that retains only symbolic components of honor differential (see chapter eight). However, for those who find patriarchy and its primogeniture-type logic as culturally bound, the winds of equality carry the application one step further.

CRITERION 9: Competing Options

A. Statement

A component of text is more likely to be transcultural, if presented in a time and setting when other competing options existed in the broader cultures. Conversely, the probability of a component of a text being cultural is greater if alternatives would not have been readily imagined or conceived of by the original writer. Fee and Stuart underscore the issue of competing cultural options in similar terms: "The degree to which . . . a writer agrees with a cultural situation in which there is *only one option* increases the possibility of the cultural relativity of such a position."[56]

B. Neutral examples

1. Slavery versus abolition. It would appear that no cultures in the ancient world were abolitionist in their perspective, unlike much of the modern world. Slavery was an accepted way of life for the people of ancient societies. The biblical treatment of slaves clearly moves in a redemptive direction. However, the absence of a fully developed abolitionist perspective in Scripture may in part be due to the lack of such an alternative within the ancient world—it was not a well-known option in the ancient world. The lack of alternatives increases the likelihood that biblical interaction with slavery addressed this limited (culture-bound) horizon.

2. Geocentric versus heliocentric cosmology. Biblical cosmology utilizes a geocentric perspective of the day when it comes to depicting the relationship between the earth and various luminaries. This is not surprising since there were no heliocentric models available.[57] Again, the lack of alternative options assists us in making an assessment of biblical cosmology as most probably cultural.

3. Monarchy versus democracy. While there were some variations in governments within the ancient world, monarchy was the most dominant form. Democracy, however, was not an option. Therefore, the affirmations of monarchy by the writers of Scripture were likely not intended as a statement against democracy. While such affirmations played into the hands of monarchists within church history, their use of such material to support monarchy as a binding form of government was markedly fallacious.

C. Women

Within the ancient world, patriarchy was almost a monolithic norm. There is an emerging consensus among scholars that no society, ancient or modern, has ever been strictly matriarchal. Social anthropologists now talk about the "myth

---

[56]Gordon D. Fee and Douglas Stuart, *How to Read the Bible for All Its Worth,* 2d ed. (Grand Rapids, Mich.: Zondervan, 1993), p. 73. (The italics are theirs.) Cf. Craig Keener, *Paul, Women, and Wives: Marriage and Women's Ministry in the Letters of Paul* (Peabody, Mass.: Hendrickson, 1992), p. 199.
[57]For an extended discussion of cosmology, see criterion 18.B.1.

of matriarchy."[58] Therefore, when assessing the ancient world, we can, with some confidence, rule out matriarchy as a competing option. The story of egalitarian societies is different, but not by much. All of the *major* agricultural and urban societies in the ancient world functioned with social structures that can be described as patriarchy. One must leave the door open for the possibility of egalitarian societies among *small and remote* nomadic groups that moved extensively and lived a hunter-and-gatherer kind of existence. Even here, it would appear that the majority of these primitive or simple societies would have been patriarchal. However, conjecture about the ancient world must remain open to some ancient nomadic tribes being egalitarian in view of what we find in our modern world. Today, we have discovered some nomadic, hunter-and-gatherer groups (e.g., Navajo Indians, Hottentots, Mbuti pygmies, !Kung San and Inuit) with social systems that anthropologists would classify as egalitarian.[59] On the basis of these modern finds and limited archeological evidence from the prehistory era, there is conjecture that some ancient egalitarian nomadic groups may have existed. In sum, the ancient Near East and Greco-Roman worlds may have had a few remote, small-sized examples of egalitarian social structures among the nomads, but the likelihood of these people groups having any significant influence on the biblical writers is very small. The biblical authors lived within a different social context—a world where patriarchy was the uncontested option.

It is reasonably safe to assume, therefore, that the social reality of the biblical writers was the world of patriarchy. It mattered little that the ancient societies surrounding Israel had female gods within their myriads of polytheistic deities. Patriarchy was still their social reality. Broadly speaking, the law codes and social institutions of the ancient world favored the male. No ancient society of which I am aware founded its legal codification upon stated principles that decried discrimination based upon gender and, conversely, affirmed equal rights for both genders. All of the cultures of the ancient Near East—Sumer, Akkad, Syria, Assyria, Babylon,

---

[58]Joan Bamberger, "The Myth of Matriarchy: Why Men Rule in Primitive Society," in *Women, Culture and Society*, ed. M. Z. Rosaldo and L. Lamphere (Stanford, Calif.: Stanford University Press, 1974), pp. 263-80; Cynthia Eller, *The Myth of Matriarchal Prehistory: Why an Invented Past Won't Give Women a Future* (Boston: Beacon, 2000); cf. Helen Fisher, *The First Sex: The Natural Talents of Women and How They are Changing the World* (New York: Random House, 1999).

[59]Robert L. Kelly, "Egalitarian and Non-Egalitarian Hunter-Gatherers," in *The Foraging Spectrum: Diversity in Hunter-Gatherer Lifeways* (Washington, D.C.: Smithsonian Institution Press, 1995), pp. 293-331; James G. Flanagan, "Hierarchy in Simple 'Egalitarian' Societies," *Annual Review of Anthropology* 18 (1989): 245-66; Gary G. Coupland, "Restricted Access, Resource Control and the Evolution of Status Inequality Among Hunter-Gatherers," in *Status, Structure and Stratification*, ed. T. D. Price and J. A. Brown (Calgary, Alberta: Calgary University Archaeological Association, 1985), pp. 217-26.

Egypt, Phoenicia, etc.—were patriarchal to some degree or another.[60] Similarly, ancient Greece and Rome were in a broad sense patriarchal.[61] Exceptions may have existed. However, the major cultures with which Israel and the early church had contact did not exhibit an egalitarian alternative. Thus it is understandable that the biblical writers spoke to their communities from the perspective of patriarchy. Such was the limited experiential horizon of their world. An egalitarian alternative was hardly a flaming issue (among other competing alternatives) for these ancient cultures. This consideration increases the likelihood of patriarchy being a cultural component within Scripture. It assuredly does not decide the case in any absolute sense; nevertheless, it raises the probability. This is one criterion among many, and its findings must be taken in a cumulative fashion along with the findings of other criteria.

D. Homosexuality

The case of homosexuality should be discussed on two levels, casual homosexuality and covenant homosexuality. When the prohibitions of Scripture are considered in relationship to casual homosexuality, the alternative options criterion argues strongly against same-sex lifestyles. Unlike the women's issue where patriarchy was essentially a given across the ancient world, when the biblical authors spoke on homosexuality, they spoke within a broader foreign context with divergent views on homosexuality. Some ancient writers affirmed homosexuality, while others denounced it. There were at least these two broad options within the culture. Thus when the authors of Scripture speak to the issue, they must wrestle with the cultural interface of their message and consciously choose one side over the other.

At first glance, covenant and/or equal-status homosexuality appears to fare a little better under the options criterion. One of the arguments used to support covenant, equal-status homosexuality is that the biblical type of homosexuality does not match this contemporary type. Proponents of covenant, equal-status homosexuality suggest that the ancient world did not know of an adult homosexual re-

---

[60]The law codes of many of these ANE civilizations have been translated into English (some are listed in my bibliography). While legal codes provide only one cross-sectional way of understanding a society, they do provide an extremely important look at the status of women relative to men. For a brief and accessible overview of women in the ANE, see Ruth B. Edwards, "Women," in *The International Standard Bible Encyclopedia,* rev. ed. (Grand Rapids, Mich.: Eerdmans, 1988), 4:1089-90. For more extensive treatments, see the section of this book's bibliography titled "Women in the Ancient Near East and the Greco-Roman World."

[61]For a brief survey of women in ancient Greece and Rome see Everett Ferguson, *Backgrounds of Early Christianity,* 2d ed. (Grand Rapids, Mich.: Eerdmans, 1993), pp. 70-73. For a more detailed survey see the helpful overview by Linda L. Belleville, *Women Leaders and the Church* (Grand Rapids, Mich.: Baker, 2000), pp. 71-131. Although there is variance within the picture, "patriarchy" is accurate as a summary term to describe gender relationships within these two major ancient cultures that influenced the New Testament world.

lationship that was caring and lasting in nature and granted both partners equal status. In other words, the biblical authors were addressing various expressions of homosexuality, but not covenant, equal-status homosexuality. When the idea is argued along these lines, I am willing to grant an initial openness to it.

However, several considerations dissuade me from affirming covenant homosexuality on the basis of this criterion. First, some covenant, lasting-relationship homosexuality appears to be part of various ancient cultures. I would grant that casual encounters, pederasty, cultic prostitution and, at times, rape were a significant part of homosexuality in the ancient world. Yet, lasting homosexual relationships between adults seems to have been an option as well.[62] Research is still forthcoming in this area, so I do not want to overstate the case. But, if the option was available, then it increases the likelihood of Scripture speaking to such relationships.

Second, the rationale that was used by ancient secular writers as they weighed the competing options would have covered covenant homosexuality. Ancient secular writers utilized arguments from sexual design, reproduction and nurturing capacity. It is unlikely, even if a lasting form of covenant homosexuality was not available, that adding the adjective *covenant* would have altered the ancient debate in any significant measure.

Third, while active/passive and unequal-status issues may well have colored the way the ancient world viewed homosexual relationships, the argument from this difference between the their world and our world does not free us to accept homosexual practices today. In *Homoeroticism in the Biblical World* Martti Nissinen has done a masterful job of demonstrating that two related issues—socially conditioned expectations of active/passive roles and the corresponding unequal status of participants—were part of the ancient picture of homosexuality. Nevertheless, his analysis amounts to a reductionistic view of both the ancient world concerns and the biblical concerns. If these were the only two issues, I would be more persuaded toward his case. However, they were not. His thesis is already strained when applied to lesbian relationships, where it was common for ancient women to use strap-on penises of the single and dual type. Between two women there would be no automatic need to declare that the one female was continually functioning in an active role as "more the male" than the other, especially with equipment where they could engage sexually with each other in quite mutual forms. Of much greater significance, however, is the fact that there was a

---

[62]See Donald J. Wold, *Out of Order: Homosexuality in the Bible and the Ancient Near East* (Grand Rapids, Mich.: Baker, 1998) and Martti Nissinen, *Homoeroticism in the Biblical World: A Historical Perspective* (Philadelphia: Fortress, 1998). These recent studies of the historic data, argued from quite different perspectives, present an important area of research where the evidence is still being sifted.

broader set of issues informing the ancient world and biblical text regarding homosexuality. These broader concerns, which happen to be transcultural in nature,
are developed in other criteria (e.g., see criteria 12, 15 and 17).

E. Evaluation of the criterion

The options criterion is a good one. The strength of such an evaluative framework
is in discerning the clarity of scriptural communication on a particular issue. If
the issue was a debated topic with competing positions in the ancient world, then
it is more likely that when Scripture "speaks" to that subject, it is attempting to
say something within a grouping of options. Also, the criterion benefits from the
rigors of communication when competing options are present. If all options were
on the table in the larger setting of the ancient world, then the ancient debate
would have had a greater degree of overlap with the contemporary. Consequently,
the scriptural interface with the ancient world will have more continuing validity
for our contemporary world. Of course, if the opportunity for interaction with
competing options did not exist in the ancient setting, then it weakens the case
that a scriptural statement has transcultural value.

F. Summary

The competing options criterion has considerable value in cultural/transcultural assessment. When applied to the women's issue, it increases the probability of patriarchy being cultural. When applied to homosexuality in general, it strongly favors an
assessment of the prohibitive statements in Scripture as transcultural. In the particular case of covenant homosexuality, the research is still unfolding. From what has
been done thus far, it would appear that lasting same-sex relationships between
adults was an option, among other forms of homosexual activity. Also, even if cove-
nant-like homosexuality were entirely unheard of, the nature of the ancient debates
over homosexuality would not likely have changed by adding the covenant qualifier.
An argument for equal-status homosexuality today, utilizing this criterion, struggles
with what is known of ancient female relationships (where mutuality was quite possible). Also, a focus on the status of homosexual participants, while surfacing a typically cultural component of the ancient picture, fails in its reductionistic approach.
The biblical concerns cannot be reduced to status and active/passive issues; biblical
concerns go beyond these issues and are more substantive than these.

CRITERION 10: Opposition to Original Culture

A. Statement

A component of a text is more likely to be transcultural if it counters or stands in opposition to the original culture. When Scripture speaks directly against a particular practice within the ancient setting, the dissonance with the original context generally ensures its transcultural status. Walter Kaiser states the opposition principle this way: "When practices are identified as integral parts of pagan culture and yet . . . are forbidden in the Old Testament and NT, they are [should be] forbidden in our culture as well."[63] The same criterion has a natural flip-side expression, which highlights cultural findings. The converse idea might be stated as follows: the probability of a component of a text being cultural increases at points where certain components of a text go along with the cultural norms of the ancient world. One might describe the two sides of this criterion as an investigation of where Scripture is either countercultural or paracultural in relation to the ancient world.

B. Neutral examples

1. Slavery. Much of slavery within Israel reflects the norms of the surrounding cultures. Inasmuch as Scripture does not openly challenge slavery *as a social institution*, it increases the likelihood of the social structure itself being a cultural casting within the text. On the other hand, where Israel markedly departs from the surrounding cultures is in the softening or bettering of conditions within slavery. For instance, the refuge given runaway slaves illustrates a dramatic countercultural component within the slavery material. This carries tremendous potential for conveying transcultural implications, not in terms of the static/isolated words (i.e., designating cities of slave refuge for today) but in terms of the redemptive spirit (i.e., reapplying the spirit of the text toward an even better treatment of human beings and eventually eliminating slavery). The counterculture components within the slavery materials continue to speak louder today than those that simply reflect the cultural norms.

2. Cosmology. Interestingly, Israel's cosmology went against the broader culture by prohibiting the worship of heavenly luminaries; such practices were strictly forbidden in Israel.[64] However, its cosmology clearly adopted the geocentric perspective of the day when it came to depicting the relationship between the earth and various luminaries. As with slavery, the cosmology texts nicely illustrate both sides of the opposition criterion.

---

[63]Walter C. Kaiser, Jr., "Legitimate Hermeneutics," in *Inerrancy*, ed. N. L. Geisler (Grand Rapids, Mich.: Zondervan, 1980), p. 143. For a brief but helpful development by Kaiser on the role of culture in the application process, see Walter C. Kaiser and Moisés Silva, *An Introduction to Biblical Hermeneutics* (Grand Rapids, Mich.: Zondervan, 1994), pp. 173-90. On this opposition criterion, see also Klein, Blomberg and Hubbard Jr., *Introduction to Biblical Interpretation*, p. 418.
[64]Deut 4:19; 17:2-5; 2 Kings 17:15-16, 18; Neh 9:6; cf. Is 47:13-15.

3. Prohibitions against worshiping foreign gods. Scripture directly challenges the pagan cultures in its commands against worshiping foreign gods, against joining in the meals and prostitution rituals of the foreign cults, and against the worship of local pagan deities on the high places. Some specific aspects of these commands may be time-locked in the polemic against a local god that no longer has a following (e.g., Baal or Marduk). Nevertheless, these biblical texts should prohibit the worship of false deities today and enshrine the worship of the one true God as a transcultural value.

On the other hand, some aspects of Israel's cult—animal sacrifice, temple construction and worship on mountains/high places—reflect patterns that also characterized the surrounding cultures. Within these three worship examples one will find certain subcomponents that counter the foreign practices; these subcomponents most likely carry transcultural significance. Also, the biblical triad of sacrifice, temple and mountain contains numerous underlying principles of wonderful application for the modern Christian.[65] Nevertheless, the concretized forms of expression themselves should probably be assessed as cultural. The fact that these worship rituals (in large part) reflected the rituals of other ancient societies increases the probability that certain cultural components may be present within them.

4. Bestiality and transvestite activities. Scripture openly condemns bestiality and transvestite activities. To varying degrees, such practices were a part of the ancient pagan cultures.[66] In view of these prohibitions having a countercultural edge, they are more likely to retain a continuing significance for our contemporary setting. The probability of their transcultural status increases due to the countercultural nature of the texts.

5. Non-retaliation and enemy love. Statements about non-retaliation and enemy love in the Bible stand out in striking contrast to the surrounding cultures (Mt 5:43-44; Lk 6:27; Rom 12:17-21; 1 Pet 2:23-25; 3:9, 15-16). These "strange" words about love were as ill-suited to the original setting as they are for us today. These weighty words continue to challenge our modern setting. In fact, if our modern film industry were to eliminate all of the revenge plots from the market, it would put many people in Hollywood out of a job! Statements in Scripture about deferring justice to God and about loving our enemies are incredibly difficult texts to actually

---

[65]Having written a master's thesis on "Levitical Sacrifice as a Background to the Lord's Supper," I have been overwhelmed with aspects of continuity and sustained applicability between Israel's sacrifices (reparation, purification, burnt, grain, peace) and a theology of approach to God for the modern Christian.

[66]Cyrus H. Gordon and Gary A. Rendsburg, *The Bible and the Ancient Near East*, 4th ed. (New York: W. W. Norton, 1997), pp. 158-61.

practice, but the probability of their being transcultural in status is incredibly high.

C. Women

The passages in Scripture that restrict the activities of women (compared to men) generally reflect the cultural norms of the day (e.g., Num 30:1-15; 1 Cor 14:33b-35; 1 Tim 2:11-15). Women were viewed as less capable than men and thus ill suited for leadership roles. Like the biblical text, the cultural norms expected the submission and obedience of wives to their husbands (mutual submission was not on the horizon). This gender-based hierarchy was an accepted component of daily life in the ancient world. Furthermore, the legislative inequality in the treatment of women within Scripture (compared to men) often reflects the kinds of legislative inequality found in the surrounding cultures (see criterion 11.C). While not making any absolute airtight case, the existence of paracultural components within these texts increases the probability of such components being cultural.

On the other hand, there are a number of countercultural aspects within the women texts. For instance, one might think about the household codes and the way in which Paul softens the hierarchy. His directions toward those on the top of the hierarchy are much more radical within the original culture than what he says to those on the bottom. Or, one might reflect upon the countercultural dimension of Paul's statement in Galatians 3:28, "neither Jew nor Greek, slave nor free, male nor female." These words directly contradict the common benediction said by the Jewish male at the beginning of morning prayers: "Blessed be He who did not make me a Gentile; blessed be He who did not make me a boor [i.e., an ignorant peasant or slave]; blessed be He who did not make me a woman."[67] It is interesting that worship in Second Temple Judaism reinforced the inequality of this prayer through its separate court for the Gentiles and its court for women. The morning prayer and temple courts echoed the kinds of social inequalities that were typical of Judaism and other surrounding cultures. Paul's statement, however, directly counters Judaism and these broader cultures. Whatever implications should come from this verse, its teaching should be classified as transcultural. Elsewhere I have argued that Galatians 3:28 carries equality implications on both a salvation and social-community level (see criterion 2.C.3). If my development of Galatians 3:28 has merit, then this verse should be given a significant weighting within one's configuration of the women texts.

---

[67]This well-known Jewish prayer occurs in several rabbinic sources (*tBer.* 7.18; *yBer.* 9.2; *bMen.* 43b). The second component is the general idea of "boor/ignoramus" in two accounts, but this is replaced with "slave" in *bMen.* 43b. For a discussion of this and the additional categorization of "women, slaves, and minors" in rabbinic sources, see Tal Ilan, *Jewish Women in Greco-Roman Palestine* (Peabody, Mass.: Hendrickson, 1996), pp. 176-77.

D. Homosexuality

The biblical text clearly speaks against homosexuality as a pagan practice in which the people of God are not to engage.[68] The countercultural dimension of these pronouncements serves as a strong indicator that the prohibitions should be viewed as transcultural. The writers of Scripture intentionally pit the heterosexual practices of the redeemed community against the homosexual practices of some in pagan cultures. By its very nature, the biblical statement reflects a crosscultural interface. On the basis of this opposition criterion, Scripture's condemnation of the general practice of homosexuality, as an alternative lifestyle to heterosexuality, should probably be taken as binding for today.

The question of covenant homosexuality must also be considered. If, as pointed out in the previous options criterion, there is some evidence of lasting-and-loving homosexual relationships between mature adults in the original culture, then the broad sweeping prohibitions of Scripture probably include this form. Since there is some evidence of covenant-type or lengthy-commitment adult homosexuality in the ancient world, I am inclined to give a tentative weighting (on the basis of this criterion) toward the biblical texts continuing to speak to today's situation.

E. Evaluation of the criterion

This counter-/paracultural criterion works well in conjunction with the competing options criterion. Grant Osborne captures the concern of both of these criteria when he suggests the following rule of thumb for cultural/transcultural assessment: "Teaching that transcends the cultural biases of the author and his readers will be normative."[69] Both the counterculture and competing-options criteria engage the interpreter in reflection about the degree to which Scripture has simply absorbed its practices in an area and the degree to which it has consciously sought to shape the covenant community in order to be different from society.

The glaring weakness of the counter-/paraculture criterion is the limited nature of its evaluative scope. Obviously, more material should be classified as transcultural within Scripture than simply those practices that oppose the surrounding cultures.[70] So the criterion suffers from a type of myopic vision.

---

[68]Lev 18:22; 20:13 (cf. Lev 18:3, 24-30; 20:22-24); Rom 1:26-27; 1 Cor 6:9-10.

[69]Grant R. Osborne, "Hermeneutics and Women in the Church," *JETS* 20 (1977): 339. For an excellent apologetic by the same author concerning the role of cultural analysis in hermeneutics, see Osborne, *The Hermeneutical Spiral: A Comprehensive Introduction to Biblical Interpretation* (Downers Grove, Ill.: InterVarsity Press, 1991), pp. 326-38.

[70]For example, the hierarchy between parents and children that Scripture endorses should be assessed as transcultural (see criterion 17.B.2). This is a good example of something paracultural relative to the ancient world, which nevertheless should be viewed as transcultural today.

Nevertheless, this liability provides no reason for discarding the criterion. Instead, it needs to be used in conjunction with other criteria. Correspondingly, the cultural-component side of the criterion—that something that aligns with the ancient environment increases its likelihood of being cultural—needs to be stated in terms that are less dogmatic than the transcultural statement of the criterion. The countercultural side to the criterion is almost always accurate in detecting something of transcultural value, whereas the converse expression simply increases the probability of something being cultural.

F. Summary

The opposition criterion provides valuable insight when assessing what is cultural and what is transcultural within Scripture. Due to limitations in scope, transcultural findings based on this criterion need to be given a significantly greater weighting than cultural outcomes. A cultural assessment derived from this criterion merely increases the probability of the item being cultural. It is not as conclusive as transcultural assessments.

When applied to the women's issue, the criterion indicates a high degree of probability that Paul's *softening* of patriarchal structures and the equality implications from Galatians 3:28, which seem to include a sociological component, should be understood as transcultural. The texts of Scripture that restrict the activities of women (compared to men), that create legislative inequalities between men and women (giving men a significant advantage) and that place women in a submission/obedience framework should possibly be viewed from a cultural-component status. This criterion does not make the case in any absolute sense, but it does increase the likelihood of significant cultural components existing within these biblical texts. On the homosexual issue, the criterion strongly supports viewing the general prohibitions against homosexuality as transcultural. The implication for covenant homosexuality may be either negative or moot depending upon considerations from the previous criterion.

CRITERION 11: Closely Related Issues

A. Statement

A component of a text may be cultural if "closely related issues" to that text/issue are also themselves culturally bound. When aspects related to a particular issue are culturally relative, then quite possibly the related issue itself is culturally relative. If we were to draw a comparison from the legal world, this criterion would be similar to what is known as circumstantial evidence. We need to examine related factors that impact a case. These factors are not directly incriminating or vindicating, but as the circumstantial evidence adds up, it can play an important part in the final verdict.

With this related matters criterion we are not simply looking for some other related subject area. The related matter must be *intrinsically linked* or *logically related* to the issue at hand. For example, the New Testament braided hair prohibition (1 Tim 2:9) is in the same subject area as women but is not logically connected to the issue of patriarchy. Most today would take the hairstyle component as culturally relative (with the underlying concern for modesty as the transcultural component). Yet, while the braided hair prohibition falls into the broad subject area of "women," it does not directly feed into patriarchy, nor is it an extension of patriarchy. The issues discussed below must be connected issues. They must either flow into the core issue or flow out of it.

B. Neutral example: slavery

Without taking the time to prove each case, I offer the following as issues closely related to slavery and as issues that themselves appear to have a significant cultural component.

1. Attitude/perspective of ownership/property. In addition to permitting slavery, biblical narrative and legislation explicitly promote the perspective that Israelite masters owned slaves and that their slaves were considered property (e.g., Ex 12:44; 21:20-21, 32; Lev 22:11).

2. Release for Hebrew slaves versus foreign slaves. The seventh year of release was an extremely humane modification in the slavery situation that Israel had for her own people (Lev 25:39-43). The treatment of slaves purchased from the nations around them was unfortunately not as humane, since there was no such release (Lev 25:44-46; cf. 1 Kings 9:20-23).

3. Using slaves for reproductive purposes. The Israelites used their slaves to produce offspring for their infertile owners (Gen 16:1-4; 30:3-4, 9-10; cf. Gen 35:22). Once the children were born, the slave owner's wife, not the birth mother, named the children and they were viewed as hers.

4. Sexual violation of a slave versus a free woman. Sexual violation of a betrothed slave woman led not to death as in the case of a free woman (Deut 22:25-27). Instead of death, the offender only had to make a reparation offering and pay damages (Lev 19:20-22). Ownership carried implications for the sexual domain.

5. Physical beating of a slave. Torah legislation assumes the right of an Israelite master to beat his slave: "If a man beats his male or female slave with a rod and the slave dies as a direct result, he must be punished, but he is not to be punished if the slave gets up after a day or two, since the slave is his property" (Ex 21:20-21). Not only is the owner permitted to physically beat his slave; he may do so in a rather severe manner. The owner could beat the slave as hard as he wanted and receive no punishment whatsoever as long as the slave survived. The reason stated in the text for permitting this kind of treatment is that, after all, the slave was the owner's property. Even if the beating led to the slave's death, it is unlikely that the owner's punishment would have been death. It is more probable that he would have paid a monetary fine to the slave's family.[71]

6. *Value of a slave's life versus a free person's life.* In biblical legislation there is striking inequality in the value placed on a slave's life compared to a free person's life. For example, if a bull has a habit of goring, the owner is warned and must take protective measures to ensure the safety of the community. If the owner fails to pen up the bull and it kills a man or woman, both the bull and the owner must be put to death. However, if the bull kills a slave, only the bull is put to death. The bull owner lives and pays the slave owner 30 shekels (Ex 21:28-32).

In sum, the above examples raise a number of closely related issues to the issue of slavery itself. While all of these texts have a transcultural component within them, I have simply isolated the cultural component for purposes of this criterion. To call the biblical treatment of slaves "abusive" in terms of the original culture would be anachronistic indeed. Relative to the original culture, many of these texts were slightly to moderately redemptive.[72] Nevertheless, these biblical practices are problematic and in need of movement toward an ultimate ethic. A much better treatment of human beings can be legislated and lived out.

The cultural component to these "related issues" within the slavery texts presents a challenge for contemporary application. These related issues are intimately connected to slavery. Maybe one could propose a soft or ultrasoft slavery position, which attempts to clean up these liabilities and permit the redemptive spirit (already within the slavery texts as a whole) to be taken further. However, such an approach may well be a makeshift solution and what is really needed is reworking the framework or sociological structure itself. Perhaps this circumstantial evidence should lead us to abolitionist conclusions. It certainly provides a "significant nudge" in that direction.

C. Women

Once again I will not take the time to prove each case below. However, I offer the following cases as issues closely related to patriarchy and as issues that themselves appear to have a significant cultural component.

---

[71]Cf. Ex 21:28-32. The formula "he will be punished" is quite vague. Apparently, the precise nature of the penalty was left to the discretion of the judge. Cf. Bervard S. Childs, *The Book of Exodus*, OTL (Philadelphia: Westminster Press, 1974), p. 471.

[72]See the discussion of slavery under criterion 1.B.

1. Attitude/perspective of ownership/property. Within the biblical text one discovers an ownership mentality in the treatment of women. Women are frequently listed with the cattle and servants (Ex 20:17; cf. Deut 5:21; Judg 5:30). There is no verb for "to marry" in the Old Testament. Instead, the man "takes" *(ba'al)* a wife for himself, thus transferring her possession from her father's household to his own (e.g., Gen 20:3). The husband pays the bride's father a bride price to obtain the daughter as his wife.[73] If a man's debt was not paid, his wife could be sold into slavery.[74] These property overtones continued into the marital relationship with the woman being referred to as *be'ulat ba'al* (a wife owned by her husband) (e.g., Deut 22:22) and with the ongoing custom of the wife calling her husband *ba'al* (master) or *'adôn* (lord).[75] As Roland de Vaux points out, a woman addressed her husband "as a slave addressed his master, or a subject his king."[76]

2. The father-to-husband transfer. A wife in biblical law transferred from being under the authority of her father to being under the authority of her husband. In terms of power and authority, the husband becomes the "new father." For example, if a man wrongly slandered his wife regarding her virginity, he did not pay the fine to his wife. Rather, he paid a fine to his wife's father (Deut 22:19). Also, if a man raped a virgin, he paid the girl's father (not the girl) fifty shekels of silver (Deut 22:28-29). The wife was transferred from the father to the husband in a way that continued the property and power dynamics and bypassed the girl altogether. Similarly, the father could overturn the vows of his daughter, as could the husband overturn the vows of his wife, once she had left her father's house (Num 30:1-16). The authority of the father is transferred to the new husband. Nothing is said about overturning the vow of the son while he is still within his father's house. One final example should suffice. The son sold into slavery by the father was permitted to go free in seven years, whereas the daughter remained the property of her master and he had the power to determine her sexual and marital destiny.[77]

3. Inheritance/ownership of property. The ownership of property was generally restricted to males. Property inheritance was transferred to the sons, not daughters (Deut 21:16-17). Only in exceptional circumstances could women inherit property in ancient Israel (Num 27:5-8; 31:1-9).

4. Virginity expectations. The biblical texts express considerable concern for

---

[73]Gen 24:53; 34:12; Ex 22:16-17; Deut 22:29; 1 Sam 18:25; cf. Gen 29:18-20, 27-30; 30:26; 31:41; Hos 12:12.
[74]While the practice was more common for children (Ex 21:7; 2 Kings 4:1; Neh 5:3-5), it seems to have been extended to wives as well (Is 50:1).
[75]Gen 18:12; Judg 19:26-27; Amos 4:1; cf. Esther 1:20-22; 1 Pet 3:6.
[76]Ronald de Vaux, *Ancient Israel: Social Institutions* (New York: McGraw-Hill, 1965), 1:39.
[77]Ex 21:7-11. Cf. Deut 15:12-15 where the man or woman sells *himself or herself* into slavery. If a woman sold herself into slavery, she would be released after seven years.

the virginity of females. Comparatively little or no interest is shown toward the male's virginity. For example, when seeking a bride, two elements are most often raised: her beauty and her virginity.[78] The groom, however, is never applauded for his virginity. Also, proof of virginity is required for females, but not for males (Deut 22:13-19; cf. Ezek 23:42-45; Mt 1:18-19). In addition, if a female was not a virgin upon marriage, she was to be stoned (Deut 22:20-21). There is no reciprocal punishment for the nonvirgin male. Similarly, the high priest had to marry a virgin, but no text speaks about the need for his virginity (Lev 21:13). For prostitution the daughter of the high priest was to be burned by fire; no similar expectation is stated for the son.[79]

5. *Adultery and extramarital sex legislation.* The Torah included an elaborate ritual for the wife suspected of adultery (Num 5:11-31) but not for the husband suspected of adultery. In the case of marital infidelity, a wife was always to be stoned (because she belonged to another man), whereas a husband was only stoned if his infidelity involved another man's wife (Lev 20:10; cf. Deut 22:22-24).

6. *Divorce legislation.* While it was never explicitly forbidden for a woman to initiate a divorce, the drafting of the Old Testament legislation assumed that it was the male who initiated the divorce (Deut 21:10-14; 22:19, 29; 24:1-4). The divorced woman would not receive an equal division of all goods and property acquired during the marriage. While the grounds for remarriage appears to be adultery (Mt 19:19) and possibly desertion by an unbeliever (1 Cor 7:15), the grounds for divorce itself would seem to be much broader. A comparison of two Deuteronomy texts (20:10-14 and 22:1-4) suggests that the male could initiate divorce if he simply found something displeasing in his wife.[80] Uneven divorce settlements, along with these broad-based grounds for divorce left women in an extremely vulnerable position.

7. *Other features probably related to patriarchy.* The biblical portrait of patriarchy appears to have included other culture-based components: the practice of polygamy[81] and concubinage,[82] levirate marriages,[83] unequal value of men and

---

[78]Gen 24:16; Num 31:35; Esther 2:2, 17-19; Ps 45:14-15; Mt 25:1-13; Lk 1:27; cf. Gen 19:8; Judg 19:24; 21:11-12; 2 Sam 13:2, 18; 1 Kings 1:2; Song 6:8.

[79]Lev 21:9. Cf. Lev 19:29 where the concern is for daughters in general.

[80]The husband's displeasure is left vague in the Deut 22:1-4 text. It would certainly include adultery, but it is difficult to limit the text to that alone. In the Deut 20:10-14 text the displeasure is almost certainly not limited to adultery because of the circumstances that surround the acquisition of that wife. Here the husband's displeasure could simply mean an attitudinal dislike for the woman, i.e., some aspect of incompatibility.

[81]E.g., Gen 4:19-24; 25:1-4; 26:34 (cf. 28:9); 29:14-30; 35:23-24; 36:1-4; 46:10; Num 12:1(?); 2 Sam 5:13; 12:11; 1 Kings 11:1-4; 2 Chron 11:18-21.

[82]E.g., Gen 16:1-4; 35:25-26; 2 Sam 5:13; 1 Kings 11:1-4; 2 Chron 11:18-21; cf. Gen 20:3; 26:1-11.

[83]Deut 25:5-10; cf. Gen 38:8; Ruth 4:5; Mt 22:24-28.

women in vow redemption,[84] the double impurity for female offspring (compared to male offspring),[85] the passing on of tradition primarily to sons,[86] the treatment of women as trophies of war,[87] the treatment of women as spoils of battle,[88] the husband's implied authority to physically discipline his wife,[89] the lopsided focus in the book of Proverbs on contentious women,[90] the restriction of the sign of the old covenant to males,[91] along with the view of women as wimpy warriors,[92] as poor leaders,[93] and as more easily deceived than men.[94]

In sum, the above examples surface a number of closely related issues to the issue of patriarchy itself. While some of the examples might be debated regarding their close connection with patriarchy and regarding their cultural-component status, many of these examples would clearly meet these two requirements for their inclusion within the "closely related matters" criterion.

To speak of the biblical portrait of women as "sexist" is just as anachronistic as talking about biblical slavery as "abusive." Relative to the original culture, the biblical treatment of women as a whole was redemptive.[95] Yet, the Christian who embraces a redemptive-movement hermeneutic will surely carry the redemptive spirit of the biblical text forward in today's setting.

Perhaps one could propose an ultra-soft patriarchy position, which attempts to clean up these culture-based liabilities and permits the redemptive spirit (already within the women texts) to be taken much further. However, as with slavery such an approach may well be a makeshift solution and what is really needed is re-working the framework or sociological structure itself. At the very least, these related aspects of biblical patriarchy develop a broad base of support for a redemptive-movement hermeneutic. While their impetus may not make it all the way to egalitarian conclusions (egalitarian writers are prone to overstate their contribution), they certainly provide a "substantial nudge" in that direction.

D. Homosexuality

As with the slavery and gender issues, we need to search Scripture for related

---

[84]Lev 27:1-8.
[85]Lev 12:4; cf. 12:6-7.
[86]Deut 4:9-10; 6:2, 7, 20; 11:19, 21; 32:46.
[87]Josh 15:16 (Acsah); cf. 1 Sam 17:25; 18:12-19 (Merab); 1 Sam 18:20-27; 2 Sam 3:14; 6 (Michal).
[88]Num 31:25-32; Deut 21:10-14; cf. 20:14; Judg 5:30; 21:11-12, 15-23.
[89]Hos 2:1-3, 10; Jer 13:20-27; Ezek 16:32-42; 23:22-30; cf. Is 47:3; Nahum 3:5-6.
[90]Prov 21:9; cf. 19:13; 21:19; 25:24 (a twice-repeated proverb).
[91]Gen 17:14; cf. 15:17; Jer 34:18-19.
[92]Is 19:16; Jer 50:37; 51:30; Nahum 3:13; cf. Judg 9:54.
[93]Is 3:12.
[94]This reflects the traditional interpretation of 1 Tim 2:14. Cf. criteria 5 and 18 and appendix B.
[95]See the discussion of women under criterion 1.C.

matters that might influence our understanding of the homosexuality texts. It would be helpful to examine the various sexual taboos in the Bible in order to see how many of them are subject to cultural relativity. Christians who argue for homosexuality today often appeal to such sex-related texts in order to make their case. We will examine only a sampling here, since I have already raised a number of sexuality examples in the above material on women. For a broader collection of examples, however, I encourage reading a section of Walter Wink's essay subtitled "Biblical Sexual Mores."[96] While some of his examples might be disputed, most Christians would concur that the greater portion of the ones he raises possess significant culture-locked components to them. In one respect, his point about sexual mores within the Bible is well taken. There are a number of biblical texts in the subject area of sexuality that the contemporary church community, for the most part, would classify as "cultural"—that is, in addition to transcultural principles embedded within these texts, they exhibit substantial cultural components.

   1. Blood, semen and sexual intercourse. For the contemporary reader, Scripture contains some rather strange laws about blood, semen and sexual intercourse during menstruation. For example, the Israelite female was considered ceremonially unclean for seven days during her monthly period (Lev 15:19). The male was likewise unclean from the emission of semen, whether through nocturnal emissions (Deut 23:10) or as a part of sexual intercourse (Lev 15:16-18). After emitting semen, the male (and the female in the case of intercourse) would wash and be unclean until evening. As a part of these impurity laws, the male was prohibited from approaching a woman for sexual relations "during the uncleanness of her monthly period" (Lev 18:19). If the flow of blood happened accidentally during intercourse, that was permissible (the male was simply ceremonially unclean for seven days, like his wife) (Lev 15:24). However, if the act was intentional, the violation was extremely serious. Both the man and woman were "cut off" from the covenant community (Lev 20:18; cf. Ezek 18:6; 22:10).

   Homosexuality advocates appeal to the menstrual-intercourse law as an example of a sexual taboo that is culturally relative. Commenting on the holiness code of Leviticus 18:1—20:27, Scanzoni and Mollenkott argue that "if Christians insist on invoking the Israelite holiness code against twentieth-century homosexual people, they should likewise invoke it against . . . marital intercourse during a menstrual period."[97] The same-sex position argues that menstrual-intercourse

---

[96]See Walter Wink, "Homosexuality and the Bible," in *Homosexuality and Christian Faith: Questions of Conscience for the Churches* (Minneapolis: Fortress, 1999), pp. 37-42.
[97]Scanzoni and Mollenkott, *Is the Homosexual My Neighbor?* p. 65.

laws are no longer observed today, so perhaps we should abandon sexual taboos about homosexuality.

Certainly menstrual intercourse is a "related matter" to homosexuality inasmuch as they both are part of the sexual taboo domain. Furthermore, one has to admit that we no longer apply the menstrual-intercourse prohibition today. We might generally comply with the text simply out of personal preference and comfort levels.[98] However, if by mutual consent, a husband and wife have intercourse during menstruation, would they be sinning today? Likely not. The New Testament has repealed the cultic impurity laws.

Granting that menstrual laws and sexual intercourse during menstruation are not directly applicable today, should the cultural nature of this sexual taboo persuade contemporary Christians to accept homosexuality? For at least two reasons, the answer is no. First, the homosexual prohibition is not tied to mere ceremonial impurity.[99] The severe penalty of death for homosexual behavior (Lev 20:13) indicates that the level of defilement is not simply an issue that could be rectified through ceremonial washing.[100] Also, the New Testament repealed the ceremonial impurity laws. For Christians all of the impurity laws were abandoned. Yet, the Christian community retained the sexual taboos related to homosexuality. In fact, some of the New Testament prohibitions against homosexuality appear to be directly derived in their wording from the holiness code.[101] Thus the early church did not interpret these Old Testament prohibitions against homosex-

---

[98]This kind of compliance may be considered the same as taking a shower after intercourse and semen emission. While we may still do the text, we would not feel under any covenant obligation to do so.

[99]Contra Scanzoni and Mollenkott, *Is the Homosexual My Neighbor?* pp. 64-65.

[100]The penalty for menstrual intercourse was being "cut off" from the covenant community (probably excommunication). However, this penalty was most likely less than the death penalty within the holiness code (cf. Gordon J. Wenham, *Leviticus*, New International Commentary on the Old Testament [Grand Rapids, Mich.: Eerdmans, 1979], p. 279). Despite its severity, the menstrual-intercourse law should probably be placed into the category of blood taboos and thus be considered ceremonial. However, the severity relates primarily to (1) the more direct contact with the source of the blood flow and therefore a greater taboo than normal contact, (2) the blatant disregard in this case for the ceremonial law (cf. Lev 15:24, which probably implies unintentional contact), and possibly (3) the vulnerability of the woman during this time. Of these three reasons, it is the first one which is mentioned in the text: "He has exposed the source of her flow" (Lev 20:18). While in Western thought this does not account for the severity of the punishment, the gradation of holiness in the Old Testament was extremely sensitive to space and intimacy as applied to contact purity. For an excellent discussion, see Philip Peter Jenson, *Graded Holiness: A Key to the Priestly Conception of the World*, JSOT Supplement Series 106 (Sheffield: JSOT Press, 1992), pp. 56-144.

[101]For example, in 1 Cor 9:6-11 and 1 Tim 1:9-10 the word for homosexual is literally "male bedder," a short-form of "one who lies in bed with a male." The expression is likely derived from the LXX version of the holiness code: "whoever may lie in bed with a male as with a female" (Lev 20:13; cf. 18:22).

ual activity as part of ceremonial law to be left to a previous era.

Second, and of greater significance, no intrinsic or logical connection exists between the menstrual-intercourse prohibition and the homosexual prohibition. The most we can say is that they both fall into the domain of sexual taboos. Yet, as mentioned at the outset of discussing this criterion, that kind of subject area connection is not sufficient enough to establish circumstantial evidence for the case at hand. We must not simply look at other examples in a related subject area, such as sexual taboos. That is an important starting point, but the connection must be more substantial. The related subject area must be *intrinsically linked* or *logically related* to the issue at hand.

In a similar fashion to menstrual intercourse, semen-emission laws are used to support a cultural understanding of the homosexuality laws. In the Old Testament the emission of semen resulted in ceremonial uncleanness. So perhaps homosexuality was prohibited because it was viewed as a double uncleanness: two males would be involved in semen emission.[102] As one might anticipate, homosexual advocates argue that sexual laws related to semen emission are no longer observed today; therefore maybe we should abandon prohibitions against homosexuality.

Yet, the semen argument is faulty for similar reasons. The homosexuality laws are not part of ceremonial law, as can be seen from its severe penalty and the New Testament handling of homosexuality, in contrast to its treatment of ceremonial law. Also, any idea of double impurity, from semen emission by two males, would likely have been treated by a doubling of the length of impurity, followed by ceremonial washing (not death).

Yet, the most significant drawback to the semen argument is that there is no inferential connection between semen emission and the homosexual prohibition. Semen emission was acceptable in marital relationships, since it only required ceremonial cleansing of the lowest level. However, other sexual taboo laws involved the act of semen emission, such as bestiality (Lev 18:23; 20:15), adultery (Lev 20:10) and incest (Lev 18:6-18; 20:11-12), but clearly were viewed as defilement much beyond ceremonial uncleanness. So there is no necessary or causal connection between the semen-emission laws and homosexuality.

2. Polygamy and concubinage. Walter Wink argues for the cultural status of homosexuality texts based upon the cultural status of other biblical texts in the sexuality category.[103] He raises polygamy, levirate marriages and concubines, along with other examples, to show that sexual mores in Scripture are often culturally grounded. Obviously, these polygamy-levirate-concubine texts and the

---

[102]Scanzoni and Mollenkott, *Is the Homosexual My Neighbor?* pp. 64-65.
[103]Again, see Wink, "Homosexuality and the Bible," pp. 37-42.

homosexuality texts fall into the shared-topic domain of "sexuality." Furthermore, the former qualify as examples of texts with a significant cultural component. If so, perhaps as Wink argues, the latter homosexual texts should also be understood as culturally relative.

While Wink's shared-domain argument highlights some excellent examples of culture-based texts (or more accurately, texts with a significant cultural component), it falls short of making a convincing case for homosexuality. First, any two texts within Scripture can be grouped together using some kind of shared category between them. This should caution against hasty conclusions in cultural analysis based solely upon shared domains. Second, at most the polygamy and concubine texts (along with other examples in this domain) affirm that *some* biblical legislation in the sexual domain is culturally confined. However, this does not decide the case for homosexuality; all that it does is open the question. What has to be found is a necessary connection between the two areas being cited.

E. Evaluation of the criterion

A crucial concern in using the "closely related issues" criterion is that the various related issues be culturally confined themselves and (most importantly) have a close and substantive correlation to the issue at hand. Where the connection is only by means of a broad subject grouping, then the criterion invites fallacious reasoning. After all, a category can be made to cover almost any two items under the sun! The appeal to cultural components within a biblical portrait of "sexuality" is one genus removed from or one genus broader than the actual issue at hand, "homosexuality." At most, homosexuality advocates have demonstrated that *some* features of biblical sexuality are cultural. Their case would have been much stronger if they had demonstrated through "closely related issues" that certain components of a biblical development of "homosexuality" (not just "sexuality") were cultural. Thus the one-category-removed approach makes the homosexual case extremely weak. Ultimately, it is not persuasive.

On the other hand, the egalitarian arguments based on the "closely related issues" criterion do impact the *immediate* genus issue of "patriarchy." Comparatively, their arguments are much stronger. Nevertheless, egalitarians are prone to overstate just how far the evidence goes. These cultural components within the patriarchy of Scripture provide a good case for retooling patriarchy in our present-day application of the text. Maybe we should move to an egalitarian framework. But, maybe we should move to a much-improved kind of patriarchy (something like what I call "ultra-soft patriarchy" in chapter eight). While egalitarians may overstate how far the evidence leads with this criterion, patriarchalists are often guilty of ignoring its contribution altogether. Texts such as these make it difficult to hold to a static hermeneutic. While leaving the ultimate destination and application unresolved (either an ultra-soft patriarchy or an egalitarian conclusion), at the very least they support a redemptive-movement hermeneutic. Our contemporary application must carry the redemptive spirit of the text forward.

F. Summary

The "closely related issues" criterion provides significant data for the assessment of cultural components within the biblical text. The closely related issues surrounding the topic of patriarchy weigh heavily in favor of taking at least a redemptive-movement approach to the present-day application of biblical patriarchy. This may lead to either an ultra-soft patriarchy or an egalitarian conclusion. Egalitarians are prone to overstating how far the evidence necessarily leads; static-hermeneutic proponents have difficulty integrating these texts into their approach at all.

While pro-homosexuality scholars use the "closely related issues" criterion, their examples are far more dubious than the ones surfaced in the case of slaves and women. The primary liability is that they are one genus/category removed from the issue at hand (i.e., their examples engage the category of "sexuality," not "homosexuality"). At most, their examples lead to the conclusion that certain components of a biblical portrait of "sexuality" are cultural. But that is all. This only raises the question; it does not answer it. This one-category-removed line of argumentation is ultimately inconclusive and thus unpersuasive.

CRITERION 12: Penal Code

A. Statement

A prohibited or prescribed action within the text may be culturally bound (at least in its most concrete, nonabstracted form) if the penalty for violation is surprisingly light or not even mentioned.[104] To put the dictum another way: *the less severe the penalty for a particular action, the more likely it is of having culturally bound components.* The converse should also hold true: the more severe the penalty, the more likely it is that the prohibited or prescribed action reflects transcultural values. According to this broad approach, one would expect to find more transcultural items among those actions that receive the most severe penalties, and a greater presence of cultural components among those items where the penalty is minimal to nonexistent.

---

[104]Cf. Keener, *Paul, Women, and Wives,* p. 196.

Beyond this broad-sweep approach, a more refined assessment may be achieved through the comparison of legal penalties within one particular stratum of biblical codes (such as the household codes or submission lists). In areas where there is a significant divergence in severity of punishment yet a similarity in the nature of the "crime" itself, the divergence may be a subtle admission about the nature of the biblical expectations in this area. They may in part be culturally induced. The lighter penalty may be an indication that the values expressed in the text contain a significant cultural component and modifications are possible.

B. Neutral examples

Before exploring the viability of this criterion through neutral examples, it might be beneficial to develop a brief overview of the penal system. A survey of penal codes within the Bible reveals a wide spectrum of punishments and impurity restrictions placed on individuals for various actions. Ceremonial penalties have been added for completeness.

Capital punishment	Ambiguous intermediate category	Secondary punishment	Impurity restrictions (ceremonial)
death by fire/burning	"cut off" from the	childlessness	permanent confinement outside
death by stoning	covenant people[105]	sickness and disease	finement outside
death by sword, spear,	Yahweh "sets his	blinding or gouging	the camp
or arrow	face against . . ."	out the eyes	temporary confinement outside
death by beheading		flogging	the camp
		confiscating property	
		imprisonment	
		fines	*within the camp*
		making restitution	*major impurities:*
		reparation/guilt	people and cultic
		offering	contact
		disapproval/stigma,	restrictions
		but no legal penalty	*minor impurities:*
			cultic restrictions
			only

In addition, it might be helpful to list the various offenses that received capital punishment. Depending upon how they are grouped, approximately twenty-five offenses carried the death penalty:

☐ showing contempt for (cursing?) a judge or priest (Deut 17:12)

☐ striking (Ex 21:15) or cursing (Ex 21:17; Lev 20:9; Mt 15:4; Mk 7:10) or disobeying (Deut 21:18-21) a parent

---

[105]This penalty could range from death to sickness to excommunication.

☐ cursing[106] or disobeying (2 Kings 6:30-32; cf. Josh 1:18) the king

☐ cursing God (Lev 24:10-16, 23; 1 Kings 21:13)

☐ violations of (cultic) holiness boundaries[107]

☐ sabbath breaking (Ex 31:14-17; 35:2; cf. Num 15:32-36. Cf. Ex 4:24-26)

☐ witchcraft or sorcery (Ex 22:18; Lev 20:27; 1 Chron 10:13-14)

☐ sacrificing children to Molech (Lev 20:1-5)

☐ worship of a foreign god—idolatry[108]

☐ false prophecy (Deut 13:1-5; 18:20)

☐ unchastity (Deut 22:20-21; 22-24; cf. Gen 38:24)

☐ rape (Deut 22:25; Judg 19:25; 20:4, 13)

☐ adultery (Lev 20:10; Deut 22:22; cf. Lev 21:9; Ezek 18:6, 10-13)

☐ incest (only the most damaging forms) (Lev 20:11-12, 14)

☐ bestiality (Ex 22:19; Lev 20:15-16)

☐ homosexuality (Lev 20:13)

☐ kidnapping (Ex 21:16)

☐ abducting people for slavery (Ex 21:16; Deut 24:7)

☐ false witness in capital cases (Deut 19:16, 19)

☐ neglecting to fence in an animal that repeatedly gores or kills humans
    (Ex 21:28-31)

☐ intentional homicide, murder (Ex 21:12; Lev 24:17, 21; Num 35:16-21)

1. Capital cases. Despite the complexities of working with the capital punishment texts today, Christians generally agree on at least two things. First, divine displeasure was expressed against every single one of the capital offenses
listed above. These offenses carried severe penalties because they were abhorrent to the God of Israel and they were supposed to be abhorrent to the people
of Israel. There can be little question about God's evaluation of these actions
within the original culture. While Christians might debate the sustained applicability of certain details, at the more abstracted or principle level of "divine
displeasure" we can be reasonably assured that these actions did not please
Yahweh.[109]

Second, except for two cases (sabbath and cultic violations) where discontinuity between Testaments has pushed application to a principle level, divine
displeasure seems to carry over into today's setting against each of the other offenses. A preliminary assessment may be made on the basis of continuity and
discontinuity within Scripture. Cultic violations no longer *literally* apply be-

---

[106]Ex 22:28; 1 Sam 11:12-13; 2 Sam 16:5-14; 19:18b-23; 1 Kings 1:49-51; 2:8, 24; 21:10; Ezra 7:26.
[107]Ex 19:12-13; Lev 10:1-2, 8; Num 1:51; 3:10, 38; 18:7; Josh 7:25; 1 Sam 6:19.
[108]Ex 22:20; Lev 20:1-5; Num 25:5; Deut 13:6-11; 17:2-7; 2 Chron 15:13; Ezek 18:10-13.
[109]On the ladder of abstraction, see criterion 17.

cause there is no physical temple cult.[110] The sabbath laws would appear to no longer apply *literally* because of the change in covenants, old to new, the corresponding change in covenant symbols,[111] and the New Testament repeal of cultic days.[112] Yet aside from these two cases, all of the other twenty-three or so capital offenses would appear to carry God's displeasure today. There is nothing at least by way of obvious continuity-discontinuity issues[113] that suggest otherwise. As a Christian community we may quibble over contemporary application at a number of points: the form of execution, the implication of epochal changes, the implication of living in a pluralistic society, the selection of which offenses should make the death list today (all, some, or none), and the establishment of corresponding ecclesiastical penalties. Yet, aside from sabbath/cultic violations (where the nature of the crime has to be reconfigured for applicability today), there is little debate that God's displeasure still falls upon the remaining actions today.[114]

Therefore, our dictum holds true at the level of discovering *divine pleasure/displeasure*. At the most severe end of the penal code spectrum, we have examples of what is abhorrent to God. While we might advocate alternative penalties (in some cases), the important thing to note is that the list is highly transcultural at least at the level of understanding what God likes and dislikes.

2. Household codes and submission lists. In order to discuss household codes and submission lists in the New Testament, we will reproduce part of the biblical penal code that relates to authority figures in Israel. The death penalty was prescribed or carried out in the following cases of violating the authority of certain individuals:

☐ showing contempt for (cursing?) a judge or priest (Deut 17:12)

☐ striking (Ex 21:15) or cursing (Ex 21:17; Lev 20:9; Prov 20:20; Mt 15:4; Mk 7:10) or disobeying (Deut 21:18-21) a parent

☐ cursing[115] or disobeying (2 Kings 6:30-32; cf. Josh. 1:18) the king

---

[110]They still apply on a spiritual/moral level of ethical purity, but not on a physical level.

[111]Within Sabbath symbolism the aspect of covenant faithfulness would still apply today. But for Christians the symbols of our cult have changed, as has our covenant. Perhaps the Lord's supper would be one avenue of re-applying the dimension of covenant faithfulness today, as would be the celebration of God's creative hand through any number of means.

[112]For a good overview of the Sabbath issue, see Swartley, *Slavery, Sabbath, War & Women*, pp. 78-96. Cf. Donald A. Carson, *From Sabbath to Lord's Day* (Grand Rapids, Mich.: Zondervan, 1982); Paul K. Jewett, *The Lord's Day* (Grand Rapids, Mich.: Eerdmans, 1971).

[113]For a development of a continuity-discontinuity canon, see criterion 16.

[114]Even Christians who support covenant homosexuality today acknowledge divine disapproval upon other forms of homosexuality, primarily because of associated aspects such as covenant infidelity, idolatry, lust, abuse, pederasty, etc.

[115]Ex 22:28; 1 Sam 11:12; 2 Sam 16:5-14; 19:18b-23; 1 Kings 1:49-51; 2:8, 24; 21:10-13; Ezra 7:26.

☐ cursing God (Lev 24:10-16, 23; 1 Kings. 21:13)

Now we may compare these Old Testament penal codes to the New Testament submission lists. In the New Testament submission lists, obedience was to be shown to those in authority: husbands, masters, parents, elders and kings. At a later point in criterion 17, "Pragmatic Basis Between Two Cultures," we will assess these New Testament submission lists to determine their sustained applicability for the modern Christian (at least the applicability of the non-abstracted form of the text). What criterion 17 argues is that a pragmatic basis for the submission/obedience instructions existed in the original culture, but that pragmatic basis may (or may not) continue to exist in our culture today. A summary of the findings is as follows:

	Pragmatic basis in *original culture*	**Pragmatic basis in our** *contemporary culture*
wives to husbands	yes	no
servants to masters	yes	no
children to parents	yes	yes
church to elders	yes	yes
people to king	king and law aspect	law aspect only

An interesting pattern emerges. Upon examination of New Testament household codes, the two cases where pragmatic logic no longer sustains a literal continuation of the code in our culture are slaves and women.[116] Similarly, the "great omission" in the Old Testament penal codes is that of slaves and women. Israel had a very strict penal code when it came to the king/judges (cf. our law and courts), priests (cf. our elders) and parents (cf. our parents). But, no death penalty was prescribed for the insubordination of a slave or a wife. One might add, death was the penalty for a wife's insubordination in other ancient Near Eastern codes (cf. criterion 1.C.2).

3. Slaves. Slaves, then, did not receive the death penalty for insubordination. No penalties at all were legislated. This omission may be a tacit acknowledgment to the inherent difficulties in slavery as a sociological structure for human beings. When this penal-code discrepancy is linked with various redemptive elements in the legal texts related to slaves (e.g., refuge instead of reprisal for runaway slaves [Deut 23:15]) the pieces of the puzzle start coming together. The penal omission, like the redemptive elements of other slavery texts, may imply the cultural status of slavery.

---

[116]There is a partial carryover between the king (who is law) and law in our culture.

C. Women

What we have discovered from the range of neutral examples above is that the less severe the penalty for a particular action, the more likely it is of having culturally bound components. The lack of any penalty (even a light penalty) for female insubordination within Israel's penal code increases the likelihood of its cultural-component status.

Like slaves, women did not receive the death penalty for insubordination. Compared to the rest of the death penalty codes, this omission is striking and may be a clue to the underlying inequities within patriarchy as a sociological structure for human beings. The penal omission may be a backhanded admission to the cultural status of patriarchy, given the tentativeness shown toward its obedience formula for women relating to men.

D. Homosexuality

The law also prescribed its severest penalty for participation in various sexual acts, one of which was homosexuality. The list included

- [ ] unchastity (Deut 22:20-24; cf. Gen 38:24)
- [ ] rape (Deut 22:25; Judg 19:25; 20:4, 13)
- [ ] adultery (Lev 20:10; Deut 22:22; cf. Lev 21:9; Ezek 18:6, 10-13)
- [ ] incest (only the worst forms) (Lev 20:11-12, 14)
- [ ] bestiality (Lev 20:11-12, 14)
- [ ] homosexuality (Lev 20:13)

The placement of homosexuality on the death penalty list argues strongly for the ongoing applicability of divine displeasure against this act in any culture and at any time. The only way to modify the continuing force is to limit the focus of these Old Testament prohibitions. So the suggestion has been made that the biblical text addresses only noncovenant and nonmutual forms of homosexuality; thus it does not apply to the covenant, mutual-partner kind of homosexuality evidenced in our modern society. Granted, covenant fidelity is an important aspect of the sexual taboo lists. However, a number of criteria have already shown that the concern with homosexuality was much broader than simply a violation of covenant or simply an issue of the participant's passive/active status.[117]

Since we have before us the sexual taboo list, it might be helpful to interact with this covenant logic a little further. For example, the death penalty was also prescribed for bestiality. As with homosexuality, we might argue that the real issue is random and abusive bestiality. So one could alternatively suggest that a monogamous, covenant, caring relationship between one human and one animal

---

[117]Aside from earlier criteria, see also the important discussion in criterion 15.

would not fall under this sexual taboo. Obviously more is at stake in these sexual-taboo laws than covenant. With bestiality, as with homosexuality, one is breaking the "boundaries" of biological design and sexual order. Reproduction of species does not take place between an animal and a human; nor does it take place between two humans of the same sex. With bestiality one crosses the boundary between human and animal; in the act of homosexuality one breaks the structural boundaries between male and female. It is also these boundary lines, not covenant, which were important in the incest laws.[118] This structural approach to Israel's sexual-taboo laws will be developed further in another criterion below (cf. criterion 15).

E. Evaluation of the criterion

The penal code criterion is not without its difficulties. When applying the biblical code to modern Christians, we run into a mountain range of interpretive challenges. Whether we apply the codes in a one-to-one correspondence is dependent upon factors such as pluralism, the relationship between covenants, ethical and legal assessments, redemptive movement, etc. Also, our central dictum—the more severe a penalty, the less likely it will have cultural components within it—has exceptions. The most glaring exceptions on the severe end of the spectrum (death penalties) were the exceptions of Sabbath and certain cultic violations.[119]

We did not attempt to validate the lower end of the severity spectrum. In order to be complete, one would need to examine every law on the sliding scale of penalties listed above. Yet, such an extensive exploration is not necessary to make our case here. One may simply appeal to the host of cultic laws whose penalties are comparatively minor.

Despite these liabilities, the criterion does provide an approximate read on divine pleasure/displeasure related to a particular situation. At one end of the severity spectrum we are going to find more matters with cultural components than at

---

[118]The same could be said about incest laws, which often break the structural "boundaries" between parents and children or between various siblings. Also, the punishments are graded according to the distance from the immediate family circle: (1) death penalty, (2) "cut off," (3) childless, (4) disapproval, but no legal penalty. Interestingly, the death penalty is only prescribed against those cases that break the parent/child boundary (cf. Lev 18:6-18 and 20:11-12, 14). For a development of a structural approach to the interpretation of the sexual taboo laws in Scripture, see Jenson, *Graded Holiness*, pp. 144-45. For a similar sociological and structural approach to Old Testament ritual and laws, see Mary Douglas, *In the Wilderness: The Doctrine of Defilement in the Book of Numbers*, JSOT Supplement 158 (Sheffield: JSOT Press, 1993); Walter Houston, *Purity and Monotheism: Clean and Unclean Animals in Biblical Law*, JSOT Supplement 140 (Sheffield: JSOT Press, 1993).

[119]Cf. menstrual intercourse laws, which receive not a direct death penalty, but the second most severe penalty of being "cut off." Sometimes this meant death, while at other times it meant sickness or excommunication from covenant and community.

the other end. One would hope that the severest penal codes, those invoking the death penalty, expressed in a ritual fashion the negative values (and a positively stated counterpart) that lay at the heart of the Israelite society.

F. Summary

Overall, the penal code criterion is beneficial. It permits the interpreter to glimpse inside the Israelite community in order to discover what values were extremely dear and what values were peripheral. The taboos with the severest penalties expressed the essence of their religious convictions, at least in a negative way. Homosexuality is found on the death penalty list. As a part of the death list, one can almost certainly view homosexuality of the random-encounter kind as an ongoing sexual taboo for today. Yet, a further inference may even be drawn for covenant homosexuality. A comparison with other sexual taboos on the death list shows that the homosexual prohibition (as with bestiality and incest) were more concerned with structural boundaries than with the issue of covenant. So even covenant forms of homosexuality do not fair well under this criterion.

It is difficult to know how much weight to put on the omission of slaves and women from the Old Testament penal codes. At the very least, it serves as an interesting "wrinkle in the velvet"—a subtle variation which perhaps we do not want to make too much of. The omission does place the obedience hierarchy between men and women on more questionable grounds than in the various cases for which the death penalty was prescribed for insubordination.

CRITERION 13: Specific Instructions Versus General Principles

A. Statement

A component of a text may be culturally relative if its specific instructions appear to be at odds with the general principles of Scripture.[120] With this criterion we are asking the question, does the text appear to clash with the general principles of Scripture? Was the application in some measure a concession to or a reflection of the culture at that time? Our assumption here is that *specific statements within Scripture are more likely to be culturally confined in some aspect than general statements.* Conversely, the more general a statement is, the more likely it is transcultural in nature.

Christian scholars often identify universal norms with the moral nature of

---

[120]Swartley, *Slavery, Sabbath, War & Women*, p. 201; cf., Klein, Blomberg and Hubbard Jr., *Biblical Interpretation*, p. 411.

God.[121] God's communicable attributes (his justice, love, holiness, etc.) function as a good measure of that which is transcultural. One could easily develop this as a separate criterion. However, since its transcultural orientation relates to its broad expression of theological principles, I will subsume the moral nature of God under this specific-general criterion.

B. Neutral examples

1. Slavery. Slave owners in the United States valued the concession-based *specifics* of Scripture and argued their case primarily from those verses.[122] The same is true for the child labor debates in England. Abolitionists, on the contrary, began with the *broad principles* of Scripture and showed that slavery should be repealed on the basis of love and the ethics of equality in God's kingdom and in Jesus' new community.

For example, the broad principles of Scripture can be used to call for at least some movement in the slavery situation. Within the Israelite community God's people were supposed to grant their own Hebrew slaves a seventh-year release (Lev 25:39-43; cf. Jer 34:8-22). This was not required for non-Israelite slaves. By way of application, Christian slave owners might have been inclined to do the same at least for their *Christian* slaves.

The argument could be developed further. If we think about the broad ethical teaching of Jesus, "love your neighbor as yourself," then we are faced with legislation that should consistently be extended beyond a provincial domain to non-Israelite slaves as well. After all, Jesus defined "neighbor" in cross-cultural terms. From the broader principle, then, we have reinterpreted the specifics of Scripture for a contemporary application.

2. Gleaning laws. The Bible instructs farmers not to harvest the very edges of their fields or to pick their grapes a second time.[123] The leftover produce was for the poor to collect and eat. This practice no longer makes sense in our modern world. In rural settings today, the people who live close to farmers are other farmers. Most of our poor and hungry live in cities. So, if American or European farmers left grain in the fields for the poor to glean, most of it would go to waste.

---

[121]For example, see Tiessen, "Universal Moral Absolutes," pp. 193-94. Tiessen does well in drawing our attention to God's moral nature as a good place for pursuing absolutes. Unfortunately, his suggestion that we identify universals "by their basis in the moral nature of God" might be misleading. All of Scripture, even the cultural components, have their basis in God's moral nature. It might be helpful to qualify Tiessen's dictum to focus on God's nature *as expressed in its most general articulation.* For some of the strengths and weaknesses of theological analogy in cultural/transcultural analysis, see criterion 14.

[122]Keener, *Paul, Women, and Wives,* p. 193.

[123]E.g., Lev 19:9-10; 23:22. Cf. Klein, Blomberg and Hubbard Jr., *Biblical Interpretation,* p. 411.

Obviously, the broad principle of compassion for the poor remains transcultural; the specific laws of gleaning, however, must be assessed as cultural.[124] While this example does not illustrate the tension that sometimes arises between the general and specific features of Scripture (as with slavery above), it does support the basic general-specific dictum: general statements within Scripture are more likely to be transcultural than specific statements.

C. Women

When approaching the women's issue from this angle, we might ask some of the following questions: Does the power inequality between men and women violate a theology of justice? Is there a hint of inequity or unfairness about the treatment of women in the Bible? Is that inequity accentuated today because of the removal of many dependency aspects that fed the hierarchy in previous generations?

In contrast to the biblical culture, our contemporary culture generally endorses equality for women on every level: job opportunities, pay equity (equal work, equal pay between genders), marital equality (marriage rights, divorce laws, etc.), educational equality, property law and political equality. Is this not a fairer and more just social environment than the one that we find in the biblical text? In the case of marriage, would a shift from unilateral submission to mutual submission be a greater demonstration of love or a lesser demonstration of love? It would appear that the broad ethical principles of justice, love, fairness, compassion, etc. offer a rationale for change to, or at least further improvements in, the kind of treatment that women received in the biblical text.

A soft patriarchy position often answers this general principles critique with a response that women are of equal value to men, but should be functionally restricted and restricted somewhat in power, at least in a few areas. They argue that hierarchy does not necessarily mean inequality or inferiority. At the same time, they suggest that women should not be marginalized in marriages, churches and society any more than required. There is a sense of justice that quietly pushes their position.[125] Soft patriarchalists have endorsed the criterion, perhaps unknowingly, in moving away from certain biblical texts in their own journey from hard to soft patriarchy, but they are generally unwilling to see that it holds further implications for their position.

D. Homosexuality

The general principles criterion is an important one to think through, since those

---

[124]For a further discussion, see criterion 17.

[125]E.g., see John Piper, "A Vision of Biblical Complementarity," in *Recovering Biblical Manhood and Womanhood*, pp. 31-59.

who endorse a homosexual lifestyle often use it. A classic example of this argument is found in Scanzoni and Mollenkott's *Is the Homosexual My Neighbor?* Through the book's title and its internal discussion, the authors recall Jesus' parable about the Good Samaritan in which he asks the question, "Which one of these was the neighbor?"[126] This passage also recalls Jesus' summation of the Torah as, "Love your neighbor as yourself" (Lk 10:25-37). From the broad principle of loving one's neighbor Scanzoni and Mollenkott infer that a Christian response should ultimately be one that accepts homosexuality as an appropriate alternative form of sexual expression.[127]

At several points Scanzoni and Mollenkott's admonition is commendable. They suggest that the Christian community needs to rid itself of homophobia and unloving treatment of homosexuals. We have sometimes watched the physical and social plight of this community with callous hearts, applauding their pain as the judgment of God. Our stigmatization of homosexuals has led to an arm's length interaction with the homosexual community as a whole. This detachment has often left these people without a tangible expression of the love of Christ. Rather than being motivated by love for our neighbor, our stance against homosexuality has at times been driven by political motivations and self-righteous attitudes. With this sort of appraisal I can find little fault, except within myself.

However, the general principle of loving one's neighbor does not necessarily lead to accepting a homosexual lifestyle as an appropriate Christian option. Such an inference misunderstands the point of the parable. Jesus was teaching his followers to show love and compassion even toward those whom they would have great difficulty loving. To the question, "Is the homosexual my neighbor?" we should answer with a resounding "Yes!" But having given that answer, it hardly affirms the acceptance of homosexuality. The only implication coming from Jesus' words would be that we must act in a loving manner toward the homosexual person. Clearly Christ's words mean that we must break the fear barrier and love homosexuals as we would love other people and ourselves. Yet, Christ is not implying that the hearer should necessarily accept the Samaritan position on canon (holding only to the Pentateuch), or embrace their location for worship (Mount Gerizim instead of Jerusalem), or live in denial concerning their different lineage (not having a pure Jewish descent). The point of the parable is that, despite these factors and others, Christians must act with care and compassion toward all people.

It does not logically follow, however, that one should accept homosexuality.

---

[126]Mt 19:19; 22:39; Mk 12:31, 33; Lk 10:27; cf. Rom 13:9; Gal 5:14; Jas 2:8.
[127]See Scanzoni and Mollenkott, *Is the Homosexual My Neighbor?* pp. 1-11, 23.

We also have the example of Jesus' treatment of the woman caught in adultery.[128] While treating adultery as a sin, a perversion of appropriate sexual conduct, Jesus nonetheless acts in a loving manner toward the woman. In his loving actions he also focuses on her deeper needs. More than anything else, she needed to find forgiveness. Along similar lines, one may hold that premarital sex falls outside of a Christian sexual ethic, yet at the same time participate in a ministry of care and practical help toward unwed mothers (and fathers).

So the real question is, what is the loving thing to do? If a particular behavior incites God's anger to the point where habitual participants are susceptible to banishment from his kingdom, then what is the loving thing to do? In this case, it should be obvious. The loving thing to do would be to rescue the individual from destruction (negatively) and to invite them into the glorious kingdom of Christ (positively). The continued practice of bestiality and adultery, as with sustained homosexual activity, place one's participation in the kingdom at risk. It would be unwise to make any universal or broad-sweeping pronouncements about the eschatological destiny of homosexuals in light of a sliding scale of culpability that must engage the volitional question.[129] Yet, if some action or combination of actions has the potential for kingdom banishment, let alone divine displeasure, then loving my neighbor becomes a painful and tension-charged action. Silence is not love. A "live and let live" distancing is not love. Loving one's neighbor in this instance means caring for their entire well being—temporal and beyond—even if such act of interactive love has an extremely painful and straining side.

E. Evaluation of the criterion

Our interaction with this general principles axiom makes one thing quite obvious: it is not a straightforward criterion to apply. The criterion is susceptible to misuse. The most loving action or the greatest justice is not always readily obvious. Moving from highly abstract principles down into the concrete specifics of life often takes some work and willingness to dialogue on the potential for misjudgment. Therefore, it would be best to use the general principles assessment, in conjunction with other criteria, in a supplemental manner. Nevertheless, the criterion is extremely helpful in attempting to work through cultural analysis.

Having applied the general principles of love and justice to homosexuality, slavery and women, it becomes fairly clear that the homosexual issue differs significantly from the slavery/women issues. In the slavery/women discussion it

---

[128]Jn 7:53—8:11. Cf. Mt 9:10-11; 11:19; 21:31-32; Mk 2:15-16; Lk 3:12; 5:29-30; 7:34, 36-50; 15:1-2; 19:1-10.

[129]For a discussion of culpability see criterion 18.D.

might be better for us to talk about incremental improvements along a spectrum of "redemptive betters" or "comparative betters" instead of polarized morality, that is, the pristine righteousness of one option and the blackest evil of another. The women/slavery issues involve options that are on a graded scale. These options can be broken down into increments of that which is redemptively better than other options. When we view homosexuality in isolation from added complexities (rape, incest, multiple encounters, etc.), we see that a person either practices homoerotic acts or does not; thus, incremental assessment is not part of the equation.

Furthermore, whether one is a slavery advocate or an abolitionist, whether a strong patriarchalist, soft patriarchalist, ultra-soft patriarchalist or an egalitarian, the eschatological outcome is the same. Even though an ultimate ethic should always be sought, the individual who holds and practices these divergent views from strong patriarchy to egalitarianism never comes close within Scripture to getting banished from Christ's kingdom. Compared to the homosexual issue, the spectrum of alternatives in the slavery/women issues does not call into question one's salvation or eternal destiny.

F. Summary
The general-specific canon is a good one if used in conjunction with others. The general or broad principles of Scripture appear to favor movement from soft patriarchy to an egalitarian position, just as they favor movement from hard patriarchy to soft patriarchy. Granted, the need for movement is probably more pronounced in the latter case. The application of broader principles to the homosexuality texts should inform the way we treat homosexuals, but fails to argue for the acceptability of homosexual activity whether practiced in covenant forms or casual encounters.

6

INCONCLUSIVE CRITERIA

CRITERION 14: Basis in Theological Analogy

A. Statement
A component of a text may be transcultural if its basis is rooted in the character of God or Christ through theological analogy. This phenomenon within the biblical text may be referred to as "theologizing" or creating "theological analogies." The biblical author chooses to reinforce some feature of the text by drawing a theological or christological portrait that parallels the human life setting. At first glance, theological analogies within the text appear to argue for the ongoing application of a text in a transcultural fashion. However, the two sets of neutral examples below will reveal the faulty nature of such thinking.

B. Neutral examples
The first set of examples below (1-3) presents cases where theological analogy is used with instructions that have a transcultural status. The second set of examples (4-7) provides cases where theological analogy accompanies instructions that have a cultural-component status.

1. Love. Scripture instructs Christians to love one another in view of God's love. For instance, John admonishes believers, "Since God so loved us, we also ought to love one another" (1 Jn 4:11; cf. Jn 15:12). In other words, Christians are to act in love toward each other in a way that is like or comparable to God's love toward them.

2. Holiness. In a similar manner believers are called to a lifestyle of holiness based upon God's holiness. Echoing the words of Leviticus, Peter encourages his

Asia Minor congregations, "Be holy, because I [God] am holy" (1 Pet 1:16; cf. Lev 11:44-45; 19:2; 20:7). Christians are to pursue holiness that in some way reflects the holiness of their God.

3. Forgiveness. The act of human forgiveness is often tied to divine forgiveness. Paul exhorts the Ephesians, "Be kind and compassionate to one another, forgiving each other, just as in Christ God forgave you" (Eph 4:32).

Assuming that the call for Christian love, holiness and forgiveness is transcultural in nature (although I have not made the case here), these examples show that theological analogy often accompanies instructions with a transcultural status. One might be inclined to think that this would always be the case. However, the next set of examples demonstrates that theological analogy can also accompany instructions with a cultural-component status.

4. Slavery. Slavery proponents frequently argued from theological and christological analogies in the text.[1] The material from which they could make their case is quite extensive (e.g., Eph 6:5-9; Col 3:22—4:1; 1 Pet 2:18-25). For example, God is pictured as a "lord" or "master" in heaven who directs the affairs of his people, like an earthly master would govern his slaves. Also, Christ himself is portrayed as the slave *par excellence.*[2] Following instructions for slaves to "submit to their masters," Peter builds an analogy between the slaves he is addressing in the church community and Christ who functioned as the greatest of all servants.

In view of these theological analogies, pro-slavery advocates argued that slavery should continue to be practiced. Slavery was viewed as an abiding and eternal principle because the Bible portrays Christ as a slave/servant in the texts that discuss slavery. However, if slavery should be assessed as cultural within Scripture (a position developed above), then obviously theological analogy at times accompanies biblical instructions with a dominant cultural component.

5. Monarchy. In the past, proponents of monarchy used theological analogy to sustain their beliefs in a monarchical form of government. After all, God and Christ are frequently presented as ruling kings (e.g., 1 Tim 6:15; Rev 17:14; 19:16). Along with the biblical instructions to submit to the king, it was argued that only a monarchy properly represented God's sovereign reign over the earth.

Today most Christians would consider monarchy as a cultural component within the pages of Scripture. While I will not develop the case for its cultural status here, such a case can be easily constructed.[3] If so, then we once again en-

---

[1]See Willard M. Swartley, *Slavery, Sabbath, War & Women: Case Issues in Biblical Interpretation* (Waterloo, Ontario: Herald, 1983), pp. 33-37, 46-50.

[2]1 Pet 2:18-25; cf. Is 53:4-7, 9, 12. Peter draws from Isaiah's fourth servant song.

[3]Monarchy was clearly a secondary preference for Israel. See 1 Sam 8:5; cf. Deut 17:14-20.

counter a situation where theological analogy accompanies a sociological form within the text that is cultural.

6. *Primogeniture*. Scripture often theologizes firstborn social customs. For instance, the exalted status of Christ is frequently patterned around the special status given to the firstborn.[4] Just as the firstborn son had certain privileges and honor in the customs of the biblical world, so also Christ enjoys a firstborn status in a theological sense. It could be argued from this analogy (though wrongly so) that firstborn customs themselves are transcultural and should be practiced today. But this is hardly the case; in our society there is good reason for a different kind of practice.[5]

7. *Right-handedness*. Within its social world the Bible viewed right-handedness from a favored vantage point. Right-handedness pictured strength, whereas left-handedness portrayed weakness. As one might expect, a right-handed analogy was used to depict the strength of God's actions and of Christ's enthronement. While I do not develop the case here,[6] there is good reason why most Christians would consider the right-handed portrait within Scripture as having an extensive cultural component within it.

8. *Summary*. The former examples (1-3) illustrate where theological analogy is used in conjunction with transcultural instructions; the latter examples (4-7) show its use in areas where the biblical instructions or concepts reflect a cultural component. Unless one is prepared to argue that slavery, monarchy, primogeniture practices and right-handed preference should be transcultural values, then the implication should be clear. One cannot automatically assume the transcultural status of a biblical instruction simply because it is supported by theological analogy.

Looking at these two sets of examples helps develop a double-sided guiding principle. To the extent that the theological analogy is direct and in a sense "literal" in its overlap of the human and divine, it is more likely to endorse transcultural concepts. In a (more) "literal" sense God *is* a lover, a forgiver and one who is holy. On the other hand, to the extent that the theological analogy is less direct and less literal, it is more prone to reflect cultural concepts. God is *not* literally a slave, a monarch, a firstborn or a right-handed individual. When the biblical text addresses human sociological structures, there is a significant possibility that the theological analogy is intended to motivate behavior within existing structures without necessarily endorsing the structures themselves as transcultural.

---

[4]E.g., Col 1:15-18; Rom 8:29; Heb 1:6; cf. Ps 89:27; Ex 13:1-16.
[5]For an extended discussion of primogeniture customs see criterion 7.
[6]For a partial development of left- and right-handedness see criterion 3.B.1.

C. Women

1. Christ as a husband who loves his wife. When discussing marital relationships in Ephesians 5:22-33, Paul introduces a christological analogy. He compares the relationship between husband and wife to the relationship between Christ and the church. Paul instructs wives to submit to their husbands even as the church submits to Christ's headship, and husbands to love their wives even as Christ loved the church in a sacrificial and servant-like manner. First Corinthians 11:3 presents a similar picture of theological analogy where the sociological elements of headship are assumed: God is the head of Christ, Christ is the head of man, and man is the head of woman. From biblical theology it would seem that the unstated or assumed comparatives in the passage run along the following lines: God is the "father-head" over Christ (the son), Christ is the "husband-head" over man/church (the bride),[7] and, correspondingly, man is the "father-head" and "husband-head" over woman (unmarried and married women respectively).

The theological "head" analogy within Ephesians 5 (and its more cryptic expression in 1 Cor 11) has sometimes persuaded Christians toward transcultural conclusions about gender hierarchy. This kind of thinking is certainly understandable, for it would appear that the sociological forms on earth are inextricably tied into the structures of heaven. However, based upon the neutral examples cited above, these transcultural conclusions are not well founded. The texts of Ephesians 5 and 1 Corinthians 11 fall into the second set of examples illustrated in the neutral section above. Surely, if we can learn anything from the slavery and monarchy debates of the past (not to mention the other examples cited above), it would be that theological analogy can just as easily append cultural-component injunctions in Scripture as it can transcultural instructions.

While the head analogy may contain elements of authority and rightful ownership of glory,[8] this does not mean that it has or should have transcultural implications for gender relationships. The theological analogy may simply have been applied to an existing cultural form in order to motivate behavior within that form. If Paul had been addressing an egalitarian culture, he may have used the very same christological analogy (with its transcultural component) and reapplied it to an egalitarian relationship between husband and wife. He would simply have encouraged both the husband and the wife to sacrificially love one

---

[7]Paul may also be drawing upon the Christ as monarch imagery (the one who is head over all).

[8]I tend to agree with patriarchalists on the lexical study. Schreiner presents a good review of the evidence for understanding "head" to have an authoritative component to its meaning in 1 Cor 11:3-5 (and Eph 5:23-24). See Thomas R. Schreiner, "Head Coverings, Prophecies and the Trinity," in *Biblical Manhood and Womanhood: A Response to Evangelical Feminism*, ed. John Piper and Wayne Grudem (Wheaton, Ill.: Crossway, 1991), pp. 127-28.

another: as Christ sacrificially gave himself for the church, so ought husbands and wives to love and serve each other. In fact, at times Paul applies the same servant Christology to mutual submission contexts that he does to unilateral submission situations.[9]

In sum, theological analogy is no guarantee that all components of the sociological structure to which it is applied should be ongoing. The theological analogy will always retain a transcultural principle on the God/Christ side of the analogy. Yet, this more-abstracted principle may require a new form of application in a different setting without necessarily locking all aspects of the original sociological form itself into unchanging categories.

2. God as a husband who disciplines his wife. The story of Gomer is recorded in Hosea 1:1—3:5.[10] It is a wonderful love story between the prophet Hosea and his wife Gomer which functions as a picture about Israel's relationship to God. So while the prophet and his wife may be historical, the marriage dramatizes the covenant relationship between Yahweh and his people. In Hosea 1:2 God instructs the prophet Hosea to find a promiscuous woman as his wife. Hosea takes a wife, Gomer, and she bears three children whose names speak of the sad condition of Israel's relationship to Yahweh. In this analogy Hosea plays God's role as husband, while Gomer parallels in the role of Israel as wife.

For our purposes, I will focus on the husband's treatment of his wife. Two elements are particularly problematic in the analogy for the modern reader: the husband vows to "strip his wife" and "physically confine" her. Unless Gomer puts away her sexual promiscuity, Hosea will take action against his wife:

I [Hosea] will strip her [Gomer] naked
    and make her as bare as on the day she was born;
I will make her like a desert,
    turn her into a parched land,
    and slay her with thirst. . . .

Their [the children's] mother has been unfaithful
    and has conceived them in disgrace. . . .

Therefore I will block her path with thornbushes;
    I will wall her in so that she cannot find her way. . . .

Therefore I will take away my grain when it ripens,
    and my new wine when it is ready.

---

[9]In the epistle to the Philippians, Paul can just as easily apply the same christological-submission theology along egalitarian lines when he calls for mutual, not unilateral, submission (Phil 2:1-11).

[10]For a probing treatment of the Gomer story, see Alice O. Bellis, *Helpmates, Harlots, Heroes: Women's Stories in the Hebrew Bible* (Louisville: Westminster John Knox, 1994), pp. 178-83.

> I will take back my wool and my linen,
>   intended to cover her nakedness.
>
> So now I will expose her lewdness
>   before the eyes of her lovers;
>   no one will take her out of my hands.[11]

In another setting we might read this story and think nothing about the way in which the husband treats his wife. Since the whole thing is an analogy, we can easily think about the entire exchange between the husband and wife as simply an act of divine judgment. God has the right to judge and punish sin. Furthermore, today we can hardly conceive of a husband doing such things to his wife, even if she is unfaithful. So our minds say, "Ah, it's not real. It's just an analogy. The story extends God's right as judge into the marital realm. He must be acting as a judge, not as a husband."

But, the text is not really talking about a judge. The main actor is a husband, a husband who disciplines his wife for her promiscuity. As difficult as it is to believe for the contemporary reader, the husband vows to physically strip his wife naked and physically confine her.

The dilemma with theological analogy should be apparent. We cannot use the theological analogy in Ephesians 5 to endorse that material as completely transcultural without doing the same in Hosea 2. In both cases the analogy reflects an existing social reality in the husband-wife relationship without necessarily prescribing patriarchy itself or even the form of patriarchy depicted within the text as transcultural.

D. Homosexuality

It appears that the "theological analogy" criterion is not applicable to the homosexual issue. There are no theological or christological analogies used in the homosexuality texts to affirm the prohibitions.

Some might be inclined to work from the heterosexual metaphor, which Scripture uses to describe God's relationship to his people particularly within the marriage portrait. Due to the dubious nature of theological analogy (as argued above), it would be unwise to lean too heavily on this material for developing an ethic regarding same-sex practices.

E. Evaluation of the criterion

Some theologians would suggest that all human language that describes God uses

---

[11]Hos 2:3, 5-6, 9-10. Cf. primary parallel texts in Jer 13:20-27; Ezek 16:32-42; 23:22-30; secondarily compare Is 47:3; Nahum 3:5-6.

analogy. Even in commands as direct and simple as love, be holy and forgive—based upon God's intrinsic character—there exists a human element to the comparison that cannot be transferred to God. In a limited way I agree with this perspective, since God's love, holiness and forgiveness are going to differ slightly from ours. Yet, these examples—love, holiness and forgiveness—evidence a large amount of direct, reality-based overlap between the human and the divine spheres. The degree of discontinuity in the analogy is so minimal that it is almost nonexistent. The degree of reality-based overlap or continuity is so high that one almost forgets that an analogy is being drawn.

I do not wish to enter into a philosophy of language discussion. Rather, I simply point out, based upon the two sets of neutral examples above, that the degree of direct or literal overlap between the human and divine is far more extensive in the first set of examples than in the second. As noted above, it makes sense to say that God literally loves, literally forgives and is literally holy. The extent of the actual or reality-based overlap between human and divine is so extensive that we can talk in these terms. On the other hand, it would not be correct to say that God is a literal king, a literal servant/master or a literal firstborn, or is literally right-handed. Here it is helpful to insert our English word *like*. In other words, the amount of discontinuity in the analogy is far more pronounced in this second set of examples.

The use of theological analogy in the women texts falls into this second non-literal and less-direct category. Within the women texts, God is not a literal husband. Thus the theological analogies within the women texts should not be used to argue the case for the transcultural status of patriarchy. Slavery, monarchy, primogeniture and left- or right-handed preference—examples of human sociological structures—teach us that in these nondirect cases, theological analogy reveals very little about the cultural/transcultural status of a biblical text.

F. Summary

One might have hoped that theological analogy would always provide a sure indicator that something is transcultural. However, it does not. To the degree that something exhibits a more direct and literal correlation (love, holiness, forgiveness, etc.), it increases the likelihood of its transcultural status. However, to the degree that something is less direct and less literal in its correlation with God (God functioning as slave/master, as firstborn, as husband/wife, as a right-handed person or as king), it increases the potential for the analogy to contain significant cultural components. Thus the presence of theological analogy itself does not produce transcultural conclusions. When theological analogy enters the realm of human sociological structures, it often illustrates and motivates behavior within existing sociological relationships. Yet, it says virtually nothing about whether a particular sociological structure should be ongoing.

CRITERION 15: Contextual Comparisons

A. Statement
A text or something within a text may be transcultural to the degree that other aspects in a specialized context, such as a list or grouping, are transcultural. Conversely, a text or something within a text may be culturally bound to the degree that other aspects in a specialized context are culturally bound. In this book, with its focus on the women's and the homosexual issues, the contextual aspect of lists or groupings becomes fairly important. However, in a broader use of this criterion, other linking aspects within the literary context may be suitable.

B. Neutral examples
In the following examples I will bracket items in the lists or groupings that pertain to either the case study of women or of homosexuals. The lists contain sufficient other examples that are neutral in order to make the point about how the criterion functions.

   1. Mixture texts. In Deuteronomy 22:9-11 there is a grouping of mixture texts: "Do not plant two kinds of seeds in your vineyard. . . . Do not plow with an ox and a donkey together. Do not wear clothes of wool and linen woven together." While some ongoing principles could be derived from these texts, the grouping or cluster brings together a number of texts that today are considered cultural.

   2. Vice and virtue lists. Both the Old and New Testaments contain a significant number of what scholars call vice and virtue catalogues.[12] They usually represent a listing of core values, practices, attitudes and character traits that the author wants the reader either to shun or to embrace. A quick glance at the items in these lists should convince anyone of their strong transcultural leanings.

Proverbs 6:16-19	Jeremiah 7:9	Ezekiel 18:10-13
pride	stealing	eating at mountain shrines
lying	murder	defiling a neighbor's wife
bloodshed	adultery	oppressing the poor
wicked schemes	perjury	committing robbery
acts of evil	burning incense to Baal	not returning a pledge

---

[12]For an introductory discussion of vice and virtue lists, see James L. Bailey and Lyle D. Vander Broek, *Literary Forms in the New Testament: A Handbook* (Louisville: Westminster John Knox, 1992), pp. 65-68.

false witness
stirring up dissension

following false gods

idolatry   detestable acts
usury/excessive interest

Ezekiel 18:5-9
not eating at shrines
not looking to idols
not defiling neighbor's wife
not lying with a woman
 during her period
not oppressing anyone
returning a pledge
not committing robbery
giving food to the hungry
providing clothes
not lending at usury
not taking excessive interest
withholding from wrong
judging fairly
following God's decrees
keeping God's laws

Ezekiel 18:15-17
not eating at shrines
not looking to idols
not defiling neighbor's wife
not oppressing anyone
not requiring a pledge
not committing robbery
giving food to the hungry
providing clothes
withholding hand from sin
not taking excessive interest
keeping God's laws/decrees

Ezekiel 22:6-12
treating parents with contempt
oppressing the alien
mistreating orphans/widows
despising holy things
desecrating the sabbath
slander   bloodshed
eating at shrines
committing lewd acts
dishonoring father's bed
violating women during
 period
adultery
defiling a daughter-in-law
violating a sister
accepting bribes
taking excessive interest
unjust gain by extortion

Hosea 4:2
cursing
lying
murder
stealing
adultery

Matthew 5:3-10
poor in spirit
mourn
meek
hunger for righteousness
merciful
pure in heart
peacemakers
persecuted for righteousness

Mark 7:21
evil thoughts
sexual immorality
theft   murder
adultery   greed
malic   deceit
lewdness   envy
slander   arrogance
folly

Romans 1:24-32
worship of images
sinful desires
sexual impurity
[homosexual acts]
every kind of wickedness
evil   greed
depravity   envy
strife   deceit
malice   gossips
slanderers   God-haters
insolent   arrogant
boastful   inventing evil
disobedient to parents
senseless   faithless
heartless   ruthless

Romans 13:13-14
orgies   drunkenness
sexual immorality
debauchery   dissension
jealousy   sinful desires

1 Corinthians 6:9-10
sexually immoral
idolaters
adulterers
[male prostitutes]
[homosexual offenders]
thieves   greedy
drunkards   slanderers
swindlers   debauchery

1 Corinthians 5:9-11
sexually immoral
greedy   swindlers
idolaters   slanderers
drunkards

1 Corinthians 12:20-21
quarreling
jealousy
outbursts of anger
factions   slander
gossip   arrogance
disorder   impurity
sexual sin

Galatians 5:19-20
sexual immorality

Galatians 5:22-23
love

Ephesians 4:31-32
bitterness

impurity
debauchery
idolatry
witchcraft
hatred
discord
jealousy
fits of rage
selfish ambition
dissension
factions
envy
drunkenness
orgies

joy
peace
patience
kindness
goodness
faithfulness
gentleness
self-control

Ephesians 5:3-4
sexual immorality
impurity   greed
obscenity   foolish talk
coarse joking

rage
anger
brawling
slander
malice
be kind
compassionate
forgiving

Philippians 4:8
true   noble
right   pure
lovely   admirable
excellent or praiseworthy

Colossians 3:5-9
sexual immorality
impurity   lust
evil desires   greed
anger   rage
malice   slander
filthy language
lying

Colossians 3:12-14
compassion
kindness
humility
gentleness
patience
bearing with each other
forgive   love

1 Timothy 1:9-10
lawbreakers   rebels
ungodly   sinful
unholy   irreligious
those who kill parents
murderers   adulterers
[perverts]   slave traders
liars   perjurers

2 Timothy 3:2-5
lovers of themselves
lovers of money
boastful   proud
abusive
disobedient to parents
ungrateful   unholy
without love   unforgiving
slanderous
without self-control
brutal
not lovers of good
treacherous   rash
lovers of pleasure
not lovers of God
form of godliness
denying its power

James 3:17
pure
peace-loving
considerate
submissive
full of mercy
good fruit
impartial
sincere

1 Peter 4:3
debauchery
lust
drunkenness
orgies
carousing
detestable idolatry

Revelation 9:20-21
murders   magic arts
sexual immorality
thefts

Revelation 21:8
cowardly   unbelieving
vile   murderers
sexually immoral
magic arts
idolaters   liars

Revelation 21:15
[dogs?]   magic arts
sexually immoral
murderers   idolaters
practice falsehood

Virtue and vice catalogs

The most significant contribution of these vice/virtue lists to our study is their tremendous weighting toward transcultural issues. Of course, homosexuality is one component of the vice lists. Of further interest, however, is denouncement of slave traders in 1 Timothy 1:10. This Timothy text continues to stand as a lasting memorial to something transcultural within the slavery texts.

3. New Testament household codes/submission lists. Within the New Testament household codes/submission lists, the believing community is instructed to submit to various authorities within the ancient world. Rather than replicating all of the lists, the lines of submission and obedience may be indicated in summary fashion:[13]

people/subjects	submit to/obey	the king/emperor
[wives]	submit to/obey	[husbands]
children	submit to/obey	parents
slaves	submit to/obey	masters
congregation	submit to/obey	elders

These household codes/submission lists contain a mixture of what is cultural and what is transcultural. Setting aside the husband/wife example (i.e., a patriarchal marriage), I have argued elsewhere that two items within these lists are culture bound (monarchy and slavery) while two items reflect transcultural hierarchies (children/parents and congregation/elders) (see criterion 17.B.2-4).

4. Sexual taboo lists within the holiness code. The holiness code of Leviticus 18:1—20:27 contains a number of prohibitions related to sexual intercourse. The grouping of sexual taboos includes incest, menstrual intercourse, adultery, homosexuality and bestiality. The sexual taboo lists are found in two distinct groupings. Their organizational strategies should unfold in the following comparison:

Leviticus 18:6-23	**Leviticus 20:10-21**
incest—close relative (v. 6)	adultery—neighbor's wife (v. 10)*
incest—mother (v. 7)	incest—father's wife (v. 11)*
incest—father's wife (v. 8)	incest—daughter-in-law (v. 12)*
incest—sister (v. 9)	[homosexuality—prohibition (v. 13)]*
incest—son/daughter's daughter (v. 10)	incest—woman and her daughter (v. 14)*
incest—daughter of father's wife (v. 11)	bestiality—prohibition (vv. 15-16)*
incest—father's sister (v. 12)	
incest—mother's sister (v. 13)	
incest—father's brother's wife (v. 14)	incest—sister (v. 17)**
incest—daughter-in-law (v. 15)	menstruation—no sexual relations (v. 18)**
incest—brother's wife (v. 16)	
incest—woman and her daughter (v. 17)	
incest—wife's sister while wife alive (v. 18)	incest—father or mother's sister (v. 19)***
	incest—aunt (v. 20)***
	incest—brother's wife (v. 21)***
menstruation—no sexual relations (v. 19)	
adultery—neighbor's wife (v. 20)	
Molech–no sacrifice of children (v. 21)	
	Levels of punishment
[homosexuality—prohibition (v. 22)]	*death penalty
	**cut off/excommunication
bestiality—prohibition (v. 23)	***infertility

---

[13]Eph 5:21—6:9; Col 3:18—4:1; 1 Tim 2:8—6:2; Tit 2:1-10; 1 Pet 2:11—3:7; 5:1-5.

The reason for grouping the sexual intercourse laws in these two different orders relates to which is in focus: the *category* (Leviticus 18) or the *punishment* (Leviticus 20).

C. Women

An evaluation of the women's issue must take into account the contextual setting of the New Testament household codes/submission lists. The commands for women to submit to/obey their husbands fall within a clustering of several other such commands. As pointed out above, two of the items within these submission lists are culture bound (monarchy and slavery) while two are transcultural (children/parents and congregation/elders) (see criterion 17.B.2-4). Such a finding establishes the degree to which other items within the composite list are likely to be cultural or transcultural. Putting aside the husband/wife case, the other items are evenly split. This certainly opens the question of cultural relativity for the husband/wife scenario. But that is all; an even split within the grouping does not give us a greater leaning one way or the other.

D. Homosexuality

The homosexual texts will once again be assessed from two categories—casual and covenant—in order to pursue our contemporary questions. As applied to casual homosexuality, the contextual/lists criterion clearly favors a transcultural understanding of the biblical prohibitions. Out of the hundreds of items in the vice and virtue lists, an extremely high percentage of them reflect transcultural values. The degree of transcultural consistency within these lists is impressive. With very few exceptions,[14] almost all of the items in the vice and virtue lists would be considered issues that retain an ongoing status. In view of the repeated inclusion of homosexuality within the vice lists,[15] the case for not accepting homosexuality in general for today is extremely strong.

When applied to covenant homosexuality, findings from the lists/contextual criterion are no less weighty. The vice lists provide little help with covenant homosexuality, since the terms used *may* focus on a particular type of homosexual-

---

[14]The probable exceptions within these vice/virtue lists are profaning the Sabbath, defiling the holy things and having sexual intercourse during menstruation. Some of these would retain an aspect of continuing application today, but with major modifications. For a discussion of the prohibition of sexual intercourse during menstruation, see criterion 11.D.1.

[15]See the vice lists above: Rom 1:24-32; 1 Cor 6:9-10; 1 Tim 1:9-10. Rev 21:15 may refer to male prostitution with the pejorative term "dogs."

ity and there is insufficient contextual data to argue otherwise.[16] On the other hand, the sexual taboo lists in the holiness code (Lev 18:1—20:27) offer a more reliable source for evaluating covenant homosexuality. The major interpretive issue within the holiness code is whether the nature of the homosexuality being prohibited is specific (in relation to pagan cult practices) or general (a man sleeping with another man regardless of setting).

Advocates of a specific type of homosexuality within the holiness code (Lev 18:22) appeal to the presence of the Molech prohibition, which immediately *precedes* the homosexual prohibition in verse 21.[17] Notice where the Molech prohibition comes in Leviticus 18:6-23:

- ☐ incest (vv. 6-18)
- ☐ menstruation (v. 19)
- ☐ adultery (v. 20)
- ☐ children to Molech (vs. 21)
- ☐ homosexuality (v. 22)
- ☐ bestiality (v. 23)

After mentioning the cult practice of sacrificing children to Molech (v. 21), perhaps the author reflects upon another practice within pagan cults, namely, homosexual prostitution (v. 22). Consequently, the prohibition of Leviticus 18:22 might be more narrowly applied today against cult or prostitution-type homosexuality.

While the cultic argument is a tenable one,[18] it is by no means the most probable explanation. Another understanding of the organization of Leviticus 18 is more likely.

The placement of the Molech verse within the sexual intercourse list is probably related to the nature of the category groupings. Notice that the Molech verse comes immediately *after* the category of heterosexual intercourse and immediately *before* non-heterosexual intercourse.

---

[16]The one exception, perhaps, might be the vice list in Rom 1:24-32 where homosexuality is juxtaposed with "natural" sexuality (i.e., heterosexuality). It could be argued that this broad contrast would encompass even covenant homosexuality.

[17]Some homosexuality advocates limit the kind of homosexuality addressed in Leviticus 18—20 by suggesting that it is related to pagan cult prostitution and idolatry. The basis for this appeal is rooted in the opening verses about the Canaanite nations (Lev 18:1-5; cf. 18:24-30) and the mention of Molech (Lev 18:21; 20:1-5). For example, see Letha D. Scanzoni and Virginia R. Mollenkott, *Is the Homosexual My Neighbor? A Positive Christian Response,* 2d ed. (San Francisco: HarperCollins, 1994), pp. 63-66; Thomas Horner, *Jonathan Loved David: Homosexuality in Biblical Times* (Philadelphia: Westminster Press, 1978), pp. 71-85; Stephen F. Bigger, "The Family Laws of Leviticus 18 in their Setting," *Journal of Biblical Literature* 98 (1979): 202-3; N. H. Snaith, *Leviticus and Numbers,* CB (London: Thomas Nelson, 1967), p. 126.

[18]For biblical references to male cult prostitutes, see Deut 23:17; 1 Kings 14:24; 15:12; 22:46; 2 Kings 23:7; Job 36:14; and possibly Rev 22:15.

incest (vv. 6-18)	*heterosexual* intercourse
menstruation (v. 19)	*heterosexual* intercourse
adultery (v. 20)	*heterosexual* intercourse
———	
sacrifice of children to Molech (v. 21)	
———	
homosexuality (v. 22)	*nonheterosexual* intercourse
bestiality (v. 23)	*nonheterosexual* intercourse

The point of locating a verse about the sacrifice of children to Molech where it comes in the list (Lev 18:21) emerges from this configuration. To begin with, it is rather unusual in a list of seventeen sexual intercourse prohibitions to have that list interrupted by a prohibition that is *not* about sexual intercourse. But its placement within the list makes sense once one recognizes its connection to offspring from sexual intercourse. Heterosexual intercourse produces offspring; homosexual intercourse and bestiality do not produce any children. Thus the prohibition against sacrificing one's offspring to Molech is appropriately located after a discussion of heterosexual intercourse, which could potentially result in such an act. Subsequently, the author finishes the list with two remaining intercourse taboos where offspring are not involved. This explanation seems far more likely than the foreign cult view. The connection between Molech and the intercourse list is primarily with the heterosexual relationships, mentioned earlier in the list, due to the offspring that comes from those relationships. It relates to homosexuality and bestiality only as a transitional marker that naturally distinguishes between offspring-bearing intercourse and intercourse that produces no offspring. The author may well have cult-prostitution homosexuality in view but only as one kind of homosexuality, along with other expressions which fit within this wider sense of the homosexual prohibition. The author's organizational categories relate to offspring and a distinction between heterosexual intercourse and nonheterosexual intercourse.

In addition, the composer of the holiness code appears to have a broader understanding of homosexuality in view of the comparative terms used in the prohibition. The prohibition compares homosexual intercourse with heterosexual intercourse: "If a man lies with a man *as one lies with a woman,* both have done what is detestable" (Lev 20:13; cf. 18:22). The concern of the author within this verse reflects the larger organization of the entire passage. The dominant concern with homosexuality (as with bestiality) is that it breaks from heterosexual patterns. The point of the organizational structure for the list as a whole thus reinforces the comparative point within the verse.[19]

Here is where the context/list criterion makes a contribution. First, it suggests that the organizational principle behind the list is most likely heterosexual versus nonheterosexual intercourse, with the Molech comments forming a nice transition. If this structural analysis betrays something of the author's intent, then covenant homosexuality seemingly fits within the instructions. Second, a comparison of the homosexual prohibition with other elements within the grouping reveals that the lack of covenant and the lack of equal-partner status are simply not substantive issues. The primary issue appears to be one of appropriate sexual boundaries. The incest laws, for example, are primarily arranged around crossing the boundary of parent and child. The severity of punishment in the incest cases relates to the degree to which one violates that significant parent-and-child boundary (Lev 20:11-12, 14, 17, 19-21). After the incest laws in the list of Leviticus 18, one enters into yet another boundary issue, namely, the boundary between heterosexual and nonheterosexual relationships. In sum, the author's concern is rooted in maintaining sexual boundaries between humans and animals, and between parents and children, as well as maintaining sexual boundaries between people of the same gender. Third, it is significant for our analysis that the elements of the sexual taboo list are predominantly transcultural. These three contextual/list considerations weigh heavily against accepting covenant or equal-status homosexuality today.

While on the topic of sexual boundaries, a discussion of Deuteronomy 22:5 might shed some illustrative light on the issue. This Deuteronomy text prohibits cross-dressing: "A woman must not wear men's clothing, nor a man wear women's clothing, for the Lord your God detests anyone who does this." The verse appears to be a symbolic or external-ritual prohibition that correlates with homosexuality. Obviously the specific substance of gender distinctions expressed through clothing is cultural, and subject to change. Yet, most societies retain some kind of dress distinction between men and women. Many Old Testament commentators regard this text as a prohibition against transvestite activity (dressing and acting like the opposite sex) *and* a primary forum in which it would be expressed, namely, homosexuality.[20] This Deuteronomy text illustrates, along with the holiness code material, that a covenant or equal-status expression of homosexuality (or the lack of these adjectival qualifiers) makes

---

[19]One might also examine the parallel passage of Leviticus 20, which is organized around descending levels of punishment. Even though the sacrificing of children to Molech receives the *same level of penalty* as homosexuality (i.e., death), it is split off from homosexuality and placed ahead of the sexual taboo list in a separate discussion (Lev 20:1-5).

[20]Peter C. Cragie, *The Book of Deuteronomy* (Grand Rapids, Mich.: Eerdmans, 1976), pp. 287-88.

little difference to the biblical concerns about homosexuality. Just as incest laws are designed out of a concern not to cross parent-child lines, so also the homosexual codes appear to be given in order to retain appropriate sexual lines between male and female.

Such a structural perspective speaks against any type of homosexuality today. Within a biblical framework, the issue that the biblical writers have with homosexuality is not really about covenant or the lack of it; it is not really about the equality or lack of equality between the two individuals. The deepest issue for the biblical authors was the breaking of sexual boundaries between male and female. Until God redesigns the physical/sexual construction of male and female, this distinction or boundary continues to influence our contemporary world.

E. Evaluation of the criterion

The most significant drawback to the contextual comparisons criterion, at least as developed along the line of list analysis, is the mixed nature of the outcomes. In none of the three major illustrations (household codes/submission lists, vice/virtue lists and sexual-intercourse lists in the holiness code) could I make an *absolute* pronouncement about every item on the list. Even in groupings that were almost completely transcultural (vice/virtue lists and sexual intercourse lists), there were still one or two elements that would be considered to have a cultural-component status. So the assessment of a list as a whole provides no *absolute* assurance about each particular element within. Nevertheless, it offers a sense of probability about the individual components within the list. If the criterion is used in this qualified sense of "weighted probability," then it can make a significant contribution in our quest for cultural/transcultural assessment.

F. Summary

The contextual comparisons criterion utilizes parallel features within a list or grouping in order to analyze one particular element being studied. Besides giving the interpreter a basis on which to evaluate authorial concerns for the list, it also provides valuable insight into the degree to which the list *as a whole* reflects cultural or transcultural concerns. Unfortunately, the even split within the household codes offers no help in assessing the patriarchy of the husband/wife instructions as either a cultural or transcultural. On the other hand, the vice/virtue lists and the sexual intercourse lists are extremely valuable in analyzing the status of the homosexuality prohibitions. The nature of these groupings within Scripture argues strongly against accepting either casual or covenant homosexuality within a Christian sexual ethic. While the analysis of a list as a whole does not make an absolute case for any one particular element, the high proportion of transcultural elements within the vice lists and the sexual intercourse lists increases the likelihood of the homosexuality prohibitions being transcultural as applied to both casual and covenant forms.

CRITERION 16: Appeal to the Old Testament

A. Statement

A practice within a New Testament text may or may not be transcultural if appeal is (or could be) made to the Old Testament in support of that practice. Continuity between Testaments offers no assurance of transcultural status. On the other hand, discontinuity between Testaments is a fairly reliable indicator that a practice/text has a significant cultural component within it. When a New Testament text repeals an Old Testament practice, it is almost a certain indication of cultural-component status. In other words, continuity between the Testaments provides inconclusive results, whereas discontinuity offers reasonably conclusive results.

An interpreter might be inclined to think that something in the New Testament that enjoys Old Testament support should be considered transcultural. However, such is not the case. What we will discover is that continuity between Testaments does not offer assured results in the process of cultural/transcultural assessment. The two sets of neutral examples below will reveal the different approach one must take with discontinuity cases compared to continuity cases.

B. Neutral examples

The first set of neutral examples (1-3) presents cases where there is discontinuity between the Testaments. The second set of examples (4-8) provides cases where there is continuity between the Testaments.

1. Sacrifices. Within the Hebrew Torah, Leviticus provides numerous instructions about offering animal sacrifices as a means of approaching a holy God. The New Testament obviously discontinues these practices on a literal level (e.g., Heb 10:1-18). Rich aspects of theology from the Old Testament sacrifices still apply to the modern Christian, but there is a clear discontinuity at the most concrete level of the text.

2. Food laws. Like Old Testament sacrifices, the food laws and the ritual purity laws of Israel are repealed for the Christian community (e.g., Acts 10:1—11:18; Gal 2:11-14). Once again, these components of Old Testament theology contain wonderful underlying principles that can and should be applied within the Christian community. However, the cross-Testament discontinuity is a fairly reliable indicator that these Old Testament texts contain significant culture-locked components within them.

3. Circumcision. While the Old Testament instructions for circumcision expressed a core value and boundary marker within Israel, the Christian "people of God" no longer retain this physical practice (e.g., Acts 15:1-35; Gal 5:2; 6:12-14). The theology of circumcision at an abstracted, principle level does continue to influence Christian thinking in profound ways. However, the literal practice of foreskin removal has been abandoned. As with sacrifice and food laws, the discontinuity between Testaments yields a reliable basis for positing that the Old Testament circumcision texts contain significant cultural-bound components.

Having surveyed this set of discontinuity examples (1-3), one might be inclined to think that the converse is true for continuity cases. In other words, if discontinuity is a good indicator of cultural-component status, maybe continuity between Testaments is a reliable indicator of transcultural status. There is no doubt that the chance of finding something transcultural is far better in continuity material rather than in discontinuity material. That much is true. However, the next set of continuity examples (4-8) will demonstrate that the continuity side of the question contains numerous examples with a cultural-component status. Even direct reliance of the New Testament writers upon Old Testament precedent does not provide assurance of transcultural status.

I will not make a case here for assessment of the following examples. Fortunately, these are examples that carry fairly widespread agreement about their cultural-component status. A limited case is developed for most of these examples at other points within this book.

4. Slaves and masters. Several slave/master texts within the New Testament rely heavily on the Old Testament for their formulation of ideas and words. The following sources illustrate the conceptual and verbal dependence of New Testament writers upon the Old Testament for shaping their instructions about slavery:

NT message:	**OT tradition:**
Eph 6:9	Job 31:13
Col 4:1	Lev 25:43, 53
1 Pet 2:22	Is 53:9*
2:23	Is 53:7*, 9; cf. 53:6, 12
2:24a	Is 53:12*; cf. 53:4
2:24b	Is 53:5*
2:25	Is 53:6*

During the slavery debate of the 1800s, Christians were sometimes confused by this appeal to the Old Testament and by the basic continuity between the Old

Testament and New Testament ideas on slavery ideas. Some employed this continuity as an argument for the transcultural status of the practice.[21] Unfortunately,
the use of Old Testament traditions, either conceptually or verbally, does not ensure transcultural outcomes.

5. *Kings and subjects.* As with the slavery material, the monarchy texts within
the New Testament derive their message largely from the Old Testament:

NT message:	OT tradition:
1 Pet 2:13-14	Eccles 8:2-6
2:17	Prov 24:21-22*
Rom 13:1a	Eccles 8:2-6
13:1b	Prov 8:15-16*; cf. Dan 2:21; 4:17
	(Cf. Jn 19:11)
13:4	Is 45:1
13:5	Prov 24:21-22

The monarchy debates within Christendom were likewise clouded by the support of the New Testament message with Old Testament tradition. This aspect of
continuity and reliance upon the Old Testament, along with other considerations,
led many to see the need for continuing the monarchy.

6. *Lifting up holy hands in prayer/worship.* The New Testament instructions (1
Tim 2:8; cf. Lk 24:50) about lifting up hands in worship rest squarely upon Old
Testament exhortations and practices.[22] While no verbal citation takes place, the
source of the New Testament instructions is clear. Continuity between the Old
and New Testaments might persuade some that these traditions are transcultural
and binding. I will not take the time to make the case here. Nevertheless, a more
feasible analysis is that the external form is cultural while the inner/attitudinal
component is transcultural. If so, then continuity between Testaments does not
assure transcultural outcomes.

7. *Holy kiss.* The repeated New Testament command for believers to greet one
another with a holy kiss[23] finds considerable support within the Old Testament.[24]
Such was the practice of the saints of old. The apostolic instruction to the early
church carries on that kissing tradition from the Old Testament as well as from
the traditions of Jesus, who himself casts a positive light on the practice (Lk
7:45). This kind of continuity and precedent in tradition has caused a few within

---

[21]Swartley, *Slavery, Sabbath, War & Women,* p. 47.
[22]Ezra 9:5; Ps 24:4; 28:2; 63:4; 134:2; 141:2; Lam 2:19.
[23]Rom 16:16; 1 Cor 16:20; 2 Cor 13:12; 1 Thess 5:26; 1 Pet 5:14.
[24]Gen 27:27; 29:11, 13; 33:4; 45:15; 48:10; Ex 4:27; 18:7; 1 Sam 20:41.

the modern Christian community to continue such practices.

8. Foot-washing traditions. The practice of foot washing is firmly rooted in Old Testament traditions.[25] Within the newly emerging church, Jesus commanded his followers to "wash one another's feet" (Jn 13:14; cf. Lk 7:44). About a generation later, Paul gave similar instructions about "washing the feet of the saints" (1 Tim 5:10). Only a very limited number of Christians continue this ancient world practice in the modern church. The continuity between the Old Testament practice, Jesus' command and Paul's instructions is impressive. Unfortunately, this continuity in tradition simply clouds the issue of cultural assessment. While having a powerful transcendent dimension of application for today, as do all cultural-bound texts, the practice of foot washing itself probably should be considered cultural.[26]

Interestingly, we have much greater assurance of transcultural substance within the foot-washing materials where they cut against the original culture. What stands out in dramatic contrast to Old Testament tradition and standard protocol of the day is the idea of a great rabbi washing his disciples' feet.[27] It was unthinkable for a master to wash a slave's feet. Thus the reversal of roles, modeling a servant spirit for leaders, is a major transcultural component to the text. What gives us a credible read on the transcultural application of the passage is not where it is has the support of former tradition, but where is breaks with the Old Testament and with the surrounding cultures. Once again, the usefulness of the opposition criterion is confirmed (see criterion 10).

C. Women

The patriarchy of Old Testament tradition serves as both precedence and appeal basis for the apostolic writers as they make exhortations to their communities.[28] While one might have hoped that continuity with Old Testament traditions would provide a transcultural indicator, such expectations are not well grounded. The second set of neutral examples above (4-8) suggests that continuity between Testaments provides unstable grounds for cultural/transcultural assessment. The results are inconclusive.

D. Homosexuality

The perspective on homosexuality between the Testaments is fairly uniform. The

---

[25]Gen 18:4; 19:2; 24:32; 43:24; Deut 33:24; Judg 19:21; 1 Sam 25:41; 2 Sam 11:8.

[26]For a limited development of the basis for my cultural-component assessment of foot washing, see criterion 17.B.1, p. 211.

[27]Notice Peter's reaction to Jesus as teacher/rabbi washing his feet (Jn 13:8-9).

[28]For an appeal basis, see 1 Cor 14:34; 1 Tim 2:14-15; 1 Pet 3:5-6.

Old Testament tradition provides a verbal and conceptual basis for the formulation of the apostolic message. Nevertheless, such continuity in and of itself offers little assurance of an item's transcultural status. Again, the neutral continuity examples above (4-8) confirm this guarded approach.

E. Evaluation of the criterion

Moving across epochs in salvation history obviously raises the tension of continuity and discontinuity. When wresting with the application of the Old Testament, one must interact with two common fallacies:

First fallacy: *Only* those particulars of the Mosaic law that the New Testament *expressly sanctions* apply to New Testament believers.

Second fallacy: Christians are bound to obey *all* those particulars in the Mosaic law that the New Testament does not *expressly abrogate.*

The first fallacy is typical within Lutheran camps, while the second fallacy reflects a popular expression of Reformed ideas. There are a number of reasons why both dictums are false and need to be rejected.[29] I am not about to enter into a full discussion regarding all of the reasons why these two popular adages are fallacious. Nor am I going to establish a more durable and alternative dictum about how the Old Testament relates to the modern Christian. Such is beyond the scope of this work.

Rather, I would like to make a couple of comments about the way in which cultural analysis influences these continuity/discontinuity discussions. First, the two popular sayings mentioned above are faulty because, among other things, they overlook the question of culture. As shown in the neutral continuity examples above (4-8), the New Testament sometimes does sanction a particular Old Testament practice that should not be seen as binding today. Or, to put it another way, sometimes the New Testament fails to abrogate some aspect of the Old Testament that, because of the cultural dimension of both Testaments, should be limited in its application today. Therefore, whatever hermeneutical grid one adopts for the relationship of the Old Testament to the contemporary Christian, it must

---

[29]For the problems involved in these two popular adages see the excellent treatment by Knox Chamblin, "The Law of Moses and the Law of Christ," in *Continuity and Discontinuity: Perspectives on the Relationship Between the Old and New Testaments*, ed. J. S. Feinberg (Wheaton, Ill.: Crossway, 1988), pp. 200-201. A much broader development of the topic may be found in Wayne G. Strickland, ed., *The Law, The Gospel, and the Modern Christian: Five Views* (Grand Rapids, Mich.: Zondervan, 1993), pp. 1-406.

add the component of cultural analysis. Along with other considerations, cultural/ transcultural assessment must qualify any paradigm one constructs for that which continues to be binding between the covenants.

Second, the discontinuity side of our traditions criterion works far better than the continuity side. Most within the debate over the Mosaic law and the modern Christian would agree that what is abrogated in the New Testament serves as a good basis for discontinuity today. The first set of neutral discontinuity examples (1-3) provides sufficient evidence to this end. Both sides of the continuity/discontinuity debate agree at least upon this one point. For cultural/transcultural assessment, these discontinuities across the face of salvation history seem to consistently reflect a significant cultural component within them. So while discontinuity between epochs provides a fairly reliable indicator for assessing something as cultural, continuity is not a valid basis for determining what is transcultural.

The homosexual issue and the women's issue lie on the continuity side of the equation. So, for purposes of this book, in our interaction with questions of continuity/discontinuity between the Testaments we will have to be content with a moot conclusion. We cannot apply continuity findings within Scripture with any assurance to the discussion of cultural/transcultural assessment.

F. Summary
Continuity between Testaments, whether by ideological precedence or verbal appeal, is not a reliable indicator for discovering that which transcultural. This line of reasoning in the past cases of slavery and monarchy proved to be faulty. Consequently, the traditions criterion should not be applied in the case of women and homosexuality texts, which both evidence continuity. Even if earlier biblical tradition supports apostolic teaching, through precedence or appeal, that does not assure us of its transcultural status. In a similar manner, examples such as the lifting up of hands, the holy kiss and foot washing show that connectivity between Testaments may actually skew our search for the transcultural.

Nevertheless, *discontinuity* between epochs in salvation history does provide a reliable basis for assessment of that which is of a cultural-component status. When testing other items within Scripture, beyond homosexuality and patriarchy, the aspect of epochal discontinuity plays a significant role in the application process. Unfortunately, most of the women's material and all of the homosexual material reflects a continuity perspective. For our purposes, then, the criterion is inconclusive.

Part Three

EXTRASCRIPTURAL CRITERIA

7

PERSUASIVE EXTRASCRIPTURAL CRITERIA

CRITERION 17: Pragmatic Basis Between Two Cultures

A. Statement

A component of a biblical imperative may be culturally relative if the pragmatic basis for the instruction cannot be sustained from one culture to another. The converse is that a biblical command is more likely to be transcultural in its articulated form to the extent that the pragmatic factors are themselves sustainable across various cultures. When moving between two cultures, the lack of a sustained pragmatic basis serves as a signal that something might be cultural, while continuity in pragmatics raises the probability that something is transcultural.

It is important to recognize that pragmatic factors played at least a limited role in shaping the biblical text. Some Christians do not want to see any pragmatic rationale in the formation of the biblical text; others will argue that the whole of a particular biblical instruction is based on pragmatic considerations. The former method assumes a view of Scripture that lacks incarnation and reality; the latter turns Scripture into little more than a pragmatics manual. A more balanced approach sees pragmatic factors as a series of "clues" in the process of trying to sort out what is cultural and what is transcultural within any given biblical instruction. Culture-based or situation-based pragmatics often give us clues about what within a biblical imperative is the cultural form or situational expression of the transcultural principle that is embedded within the text. In other words, when the nonmoral, pragmatic factors are limited by culture or situation, they give the basis not for the *entire* biblical command or imperative but for the cultural *component* within the imperative.

Our discussion of a *pragmatic* basis needs to be clearly distinguished from the *ultimate* basis that underlies every biblical command and imperative. The ultimate basis for a command is rooted in the character/will of God and his covenant concerns for humanity. That ultimate basis becomes the grounds for the underlying transcultural principle or principles that are embedded within the biblical text. In turn, the abstracted principles as they move down the ladder of abstraction toward expression in the real world are often impacted by culture-based pragmatic factors. As they reach their finalized expression, pragmatic factors often produce the culture-bound component of a biblical command.

Leviticus 19:10 ("Do not reap the very edges/corners of your field") offers a good opening illustration of how pragmatic factors help us discover where the line is between cultural and transcultural components. It also illustrates how pragmatic factors affect the lower end of the ladder of abstraction:

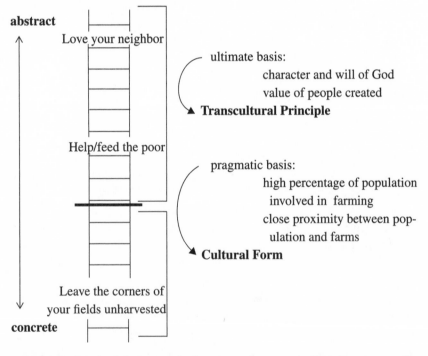

Nonmoral pragmatic factors tend to shape the most concrete "on the page" expression or form of a biblical command. Pragmatic factors often uncover the rationale for the "down the ladder" components of a biblical command, whereas the ultimate rationale provides the basis for "up the ladder" components of a biblical command. The pragmatic factors related to the original setting of the command of Leviticus 19:10 are at least twofold:

☐ high percentage of the original population involved in farming

☐ close proximity between the population base and the farms

These two pragmatic factors were part of the original setting, but they are not part of the agricultural and social configuration of our modern world. In our modern setting, the percentage of the population in cities is much greater, and the farms are sometimes hundreds of miles removed from the people. If modern farmers were to leave the corners/edges of their fields unharvested, the grain would simply rot. Thus the pragmatic basis of the Leviticus text is lost in our setting. When moving between two cultures, the lack of sustained pragmatics serves as a clue to the cultural component of the biblical text. When the bottom drops out of the pragmatic basis between two cultures, the Christian interpreter should prepared to say, "Hmm, maybe I should move up the ladder of abstraction to discover what is transcultural in this biblical command."

On the other hand, a sustained continuity of pragmatics between two cultures increases the likelihood that the on-the-page command should be viewed within a transcultural category. When the pragmatic basis continues to hold up between two cultures, the Christian interpreter should be inclined to say, "Perhaps I should *not* move up the ladder of abstraction in order to discover what is transcultural in this biblical imperative." The interpreter may well already be there. Examples of both culture-locked pragmatics and crosscultural (or universal) pragmatics will be surfaced in the neutral examples below.

B. Neutral examples

1. Washing one another's feet. Jesus gave his disciples the command that they "should wash one another's feet" (John 13:14). There is a pragmatic basis or rationale that allows for this command to make greater sense in the original setting than in ours:

☐ transportation by foot

☐ barefoot or sandals as footwear

☐ lack of running water

☐ dusty streets/paths and an extremely hot climate

These pragmatic elements disappear as one moves into most modern settings. Consequently, the literal foot-washing aspect of Jesus' instruction should probably be understood as cultural. We then move up the ladder of abstraction to "service" and "role reversal in leadership" (leaders serving with the attitude of servants) as the transcultural component within the command.

2. Children's obedience/submission to parents. The Bible instructs children to "obey/submit to" their parents (e.g., Eph 6:1; Col 3:20). There are several reasons (pragmatic factors) why this command makes sense both in the original culture and in our setting:

☐ knowledge/education differential
☐ character maturity differential
☐ physical strength differential
☐ economic dependence
☐ vulnerability (related to the above)

We can logically expect there to be *some* dimension of hierarchy between children and parents in all cultures (though the degree and implementation may vary) because there are differentials in dependency, which naturally facilitate and explain the hierarchy.

Yet I would not advocate, as some Christian teachers do, that adult children should "obey/submit to" their parents for the whole of their lifetime. Here it is not the culture that has changed so much as the situation or circumstances. A similar process happens in application whether talking about situation-based pragmatics or culture-based pragmatics. With adult children these pragmatics no longer exist. When we lose the pragmatics, we should be willing to move up the ladder of abstraction in our application of the biblical text. Thus an application of these texts to grown adults should perhaps be one of honor for their parents but not a relationship of lifelong submission and obedience. Thus "submit/obey" is situational (comparable in essence to cultural) in the parent-children relationship, whereas "honor" is trans-situational (comparable to transcultural).

3. People's obedience/submission to king/emperor. Scripture instructs Christians to "obey/submit to" the king/emperor (e.g., 1 Pet 2:13). There are several reasons (pragmatic factors) why this command made sense in the original culture:

☐ The king's word was the law.
☐ The masses were often poorly educated, so decisions were made by the elite.
☐ Wealth was narrowly distributed.
☐ Many lived a hand-to-mouth existence with little involvement in politics.

In modern democratic societies this pragmatic basis has changed significantly. In our culture it is the government-enacted law, not the word of the leading politician (president or prime minister), that should be obeyed. This change in pragmatics alone (not to mention the others) should push us up the ladder of abstraction to something like "honor leaders" within our modern setting. But, in a democracy we obey the law; we do not obey our elected officials in some kind of submissive, hierarchical relationship. The discontinuity in pragmatics between the original culture and ours gives us an important clue in being able to identify the culture-based component of the biblical text.

4. Congregational obedience/submission to elders. Biblical texts call for the congregation to "obey/submit to" the elders who lead them (e.g., 1 Pet 5:1-5). Once again, several pragmatic factors provide a basis or rationale for why this command made sense in the original culture:

☐ Knowledge: Elders were generally more theologically educated.

☐ Qualifications: Their character quality has been tested over time, etc.

☐ Age and experience: They have seen/done more, contributing to their wisdom.

☐ Length of time as a believer: Their faith has been tested by time.

On the whole, these pragmatic factors in the congregation-elder relationship apply to churches in every culture and setting. They are not limited to the original setting. One might expect a congregational government to soften the hierarchy, although such is not always the case. Also, the degree of hierarchy will vary from church to church depending upon the degree of differential in the above factors. Empowerment models of leadership may change the way that leaders facilitate the development of people in their care. Thus one might expect modifications on the theme. Nonetheless, in all congregations some measure of hierarchy is naturally formed through these factors that contribute to power differentials, whether or not Scripture gives any instructions in this area. The sustained continuity in pragmatic factors between cultures suggests that one *not* move up the ladder abstraction. The command in its on-the-page stated form should probably be seen as transcultural. The abstracted idea of honoring church elders should continue to carry the more concretized element of substantive hierarchy due to the cross-cultural continuity of these pragmatic factors. They provide a clue that the hierarchy itself probably has transcultural weight in this instance.

C. Women's obedience/submission to men

Scripture instructs wives to "obey/submit to" their husbands (e.g., Eph 5:22; Col 3:18; 1 Pet 3:1, 6). There are several reasons (pragmatic factors) why this command made sense in the original culture:

☐ lack of knowledge/education

☐ lack of social exposure/experience

☐ lack of physical strength: greater reliance upon male strength in an agricultural society

☐ economic dependence: most of the economy and earning potential dependent upon males

☐ marital-age differential: young girls (ages 12-14) marrying older males[1]

Each of these factors in the original setting built a natural or understandable hierarchy between men and women, whether or not Scripture had anything to say on the matter. The differential between men and women in knowledge, social exposure, strength, economics and age as marriage "partners" created its own hierarchy. With one exception (strength differential) all of these factors are culture-based pragmatics. When the pragmatics give way between two cultures, we should be willing to move up the ladder of abstraction.

The most problematic factor to sort out in this list of five pragmatic factors is the physical strength differential between males and females. On the one hand, there exists a "difference between two worlds" to which egalitarians can appeal, namely, the fact that in our modern world physical strength is no longer required as it was in the ancient world. Any dependency scenario created by this strength differential no longer fits our modern world. Maybe this difference between worlds offers us an important clue leading to egalitarian conclusions. On the other hand, there exists a "continuity between two worlds" to which patriarchalists can appeal, namely, the ongoing strength differential between men and women. In general, men appear to have had greater body strength than women in the ancient world.[2] This male-female distinction carries over to our modern world. So perhaps this continuity between worlds yields a creative-design clue that should guide us to patriarchal conclusions.

Somehow we must choose between these divergent clues and their respective paths. Several considerations demonstrate the fallacy of using the physical-strength differential between males and females to support a universal gender hierarchy. First, there is simply too much overlap between categories to make a persuasive argument. Some women are stronger than some men. Many women are of comparable strength to many men. Thus this gender generalization yields only mixed data without any universal consistency (unlike the case in the child-parent discussion above and the homosexuality discussion below). Second, there is a significant difference in physical strength between men themselves. Does this infer that the physically strong men should be the leaders, while physically weaker

---

[1]For a helpful survey of the differential in marital ages between genders, see Craig Keener, *And Marries Another: Divorce and Remarriage in the Teaching of the New Testament* (Peabody, Mass.: Hendrickson, 1991), pp. 73-74. The age spread ranged from about five to fifteen years, depending upon which ancient world culture one looks at. This age difference placed Roman, Greek and Jewish men in an automatic culture-based hierarchy in their marriages.

[2]While I cannot support this with ancient medical records, writers in biblical times seem to have had a perception of women as physically weaker than men. E.g., within biblical literature compare the military taunts about women warriors (Is 19:16; Jer 50:37; 51:30; Nahum 3:13) and Peter's comment about wives as the weaker partner (1 Pet 3:7).

men should be disqualified from leadership? Probably not. If not within a gender grouping, then why between genders? Third, physical-movement skills often outweigh brute physical strength. A featherweight person with martial arts skills can easily best someone two or three times their physical strength. If this physical-skill component is factored into the strength equation, the amount of overlap between genders (first point) becomes even more pronounced. Fourth, microevolutionary development often produces physical-strength differentials for humans and animals. For instance, the differences in physical strength and body sizes between different people groups and races are explained on this basis. Evolutionary development, due to genetic adaptation and environmental factors, has played a primary role in the history of body size within the human species. Fifth, the strength/size differences between races holds another implication for our gender question, namely, the feasibility of using these differences for establishing hierarchy. Should we look across various people groups—Asians, whites, blacks, etc.—and propose some kind of racial hierarchy on the basis of these race strength/size differences? Such a conclusion would not be a convincing one. If not with race, then why with gender? Sixth, the factor of physical strength simply should not enter into the question of leadership. If we permit brute physical strength to define leadership roles, then our boardrooms would only include professional weight lifters, football players and all-star wrestlers! I am not mocking physical strength—it has its advantages and its liabilities. My point is simply that there is no logical connection between physical strength and some kind of innate leadership hierarchy. At most, physical strength may affect a minuscule number of roles where brute strength is required. Yet even here, gender crossover cautions against making any universal statements.

Let us summarize the pragmatics-between-two-cultures criterion as applied to women. One of the five pragmatic factors (strength differential) *does* carry over between cultures in a loose fashion but should not influence the question of leadership capabilities and hierarchy. The other four pragmatic factors (differentials in education, social exposure, economics and marital ages) *do not* carry over to our modern setting and yet they did affect and should continue to affect the question of leadership capabilities and hierarchy. Consequently, when the pragmatic basis that sustained gender hierarchy no longer exists as one moves between cultures, the interpreter has to be willing to move up the ladder of abstraction. If the component of hierarchy within the command is cultural (as it would appear to be), we should probably move up the ladder of abstraction to a nonhierarchical type of "honor" and "respect" for a wife to show her husband. This remains the transcultural, binding component to the instruction. In other words, the higher transcultural principle of honor/respect/mutual submission binding on *all* human

beings was likely given a culturalized form as the principle moved down the ladder of abstraction into an ancient world setting where pragmatic factors placed
hierarchy into the equation for women. However, the lack of a sustained pragmatic basis for the hierarchal component of the command should impel us to rethink our application of the text today.

Before moving to the homosexuality issue, it is worth noting that this five-fold
rationale for a male/female hierarchy in the original culture was the result of factors almost identical to those related to children. Compare this rationale with the
earlier parent-child discussion. The only distinction would be that the hierarchy-
creating differentials were less pronounced in the case of women than in the case
of children. The differentials relating to children will remain in all cultures until
the eschaton (except for fully grown, adult children relating to their parents) because these differences are absolute given the maturational development of all
children. However, the differentials relating to women are/were culturally not
universally established. As with adult children, the lack of continuity in pragmatics should cause one to move up the ladder of abstraction in attempting to discover the transcultural component as we apply the submit/obey texts for women
today.

D. Homosexual prohibitions

Scripture instructs the covenant community not to be involved in homosexual activity (e.g., Lev 18:22; 20:13). There are several reasons (pragmatic factors) why
such a command made sense in the original culture:

☐ *Sexual* design: The creative architecture of male and female sexuality with its
part-and-counterpart configuration argues against same-sex relationships. For example, the design of male and female anatomy facilitates sexual intercourse
through the shape and interface of sexual organs (penis and vagina), the nature of
the vaginal tissue (anal tissue is more easily damaged by intercourse than vaginal
tissue), the placement of stimulus receptors (e.g., clitoris) and the vaginal secre-
tion of lubricants for intercourse. Two males or two females can function sexually. They can produce sexual arousal and climax but not in a way that utilizes the
natural, complementary design of body parts.

☐ *Reproductive* design: The mutually completing contribution of male-and-female chromosomes, the egg-and-sperm, etc. argues against gay and lesbian relationships.

☐ *Nurturing* design: The physical design of breasts, their function with nurturing
and comforting infants, and the benefits of breast milk for a strengthened immune
system argues against homosexual relationships and for heterosexual relationships where the mother can, if possible, breast-feed her children.

☐ *Survival* of the human race: The continued survival of a species depends upon heterosexual activity. This is why homosexuality remains an anomaly within any species where survival is viewed as a good value.

Each of these pragmatic factors crosses cultural and temporal boundaries— they enter our world today. When moving between two cultures, continuity in pragmatics raises the probability that the instruction in its stated form is transcultural.

Of these four factors, the one contested point is the survival/propagation of the human race. Obviously the ancient world and the modern world no longer look the same when thinking about population and survival issues. The struggle has been reversed: overpopulation, rather than the survival of the human species, is the problem of our day. Homosexual proponents frequently appeal to this "difference between two worlds" for the modern acceptability of a gay or lesbian lifestyle. For example, in a thought-provoking article on "Homosexuality and the Bible" Walter Wink argues the case for homosexuality within a Christian ethic based on survival or ecology issues: "In an age of overpopulation, perhaps same-sex orientation is especially sound ecologically!"[3] When presented with this type of reasoning, I acknowledge a certain *prima facie* persuasiveness to the argument. It does capture a significant difference between the two worlds across which Christians are attempting to apply the text. I grant that something has to change based on this difference between worlds. Yet, I am not persuaded that the change should be the acceptance of same-sex lifestyles.

There are several reasons why this overpopulation argument is faulty when developing a case for homosexuality. First, even Wink would have to admit that propagation of the human race is *still* a significant value, only that it takes on a less-pressing status than in biblical times and now has the added complexity of needing to balance propagation of human beings with population control. So the value has not vanished completely; it remains a transcendent, albeit reduced, value for the human race even in our day of overpopulation. Second, it is one thing to limit the degree of procreation within male-female sexuality in order to control population growth; it is quite another to approve of homosexuality because of its nonprocreative benefit. The former advocates a strategy of minimalist modifications of natural reproductive-sexuality patterns; the latter invokes far greater alterations. Third, Wink and others generally do not posit

---

[3]Walter Wink, "Homosexuality and the Bible," in *Homosexuality and Christian Faith: Questions of Conscience for the Churches* (Minneapolis: Fortress, 1999), p. 41. See also Wink's discussion on p. 35.

and weigh all of the alternative solutions for addressing our overpopulation problem. The overpopulation problem simply does not make every feasible solution to that problem a good moral choice or even the best/better choice among alternatives. One might want to reflect first upon other means of controlling population, rather than in an isolated assessment declare that homosexuality is now "natural" given our current circumstances. Fourth, the overpopulation problem does not make all expressions of nonprocreative sexuality right and honorable before God. Should we now accept bestiality because of its nonprocreative benefit? What about the newly emerging world of virtual-reality simulators, computer-generated robotics and high-energy sound and graphics? The third-millennium world will surely create various types of nonprocreative, human-simulated sexuality surpassing aspects of sexual pleasure known to a former world. Do we accept this new sexuality because of its nonprocreative benefit? Or, what about the validity of "outer-course" (as opposed to intercourse), a form of sexual expression for teenagers that is now taught in many public schools? Our problem with overpopulation is a serious one, but such a problem hardly validates any and every nonprocreative form of sexuality. In sum, our population predicament is not a viable argument for same-sex relationships. A case for homosexuality as an acceptable Christian lifestyle must be established on other grounds.

Aside from the above liabilities, the Achilles' heel to Wink's overpopulation argument is that it generates (unwittingly) a new breed of discrimination against gays and lesbians. Wink's homosexuality-based-on-overpopulation reasoning only works if one assumes that same-sex couples are not going to have any children. Surely he is not prescribing a discriminatory measure against all homosexual couples, disallowing them the use of artificial insemination (for lesbians) or the use of third-party wombs (for gays) to have families. I do not think Wink would be prepared to say that. Yet, his limiting-the-population argument clearly implies such a position and, in fact, only carries logical merit if it were the case. If one grants the acceptability of same-sex relationships, should it not follow that homosexual couples be permitted to form families and produce offspring along these alternative lines? If so, then the overpopulation argument fails, for we come right back to square one—the urgent global need to set limits on *all* procreative activity, even within that which is unnaturally or alternatively possible for homosexual relationships.

Homosexuality proponents sometimes argue that artificial insemination or third-party contributions for heterosexual families set precedents for accepting alternative reproductive methods for gays and lesbians. Granted, the abnormality of alternative routes for heterosexual infertility raises a clear ethical dilemma since it too departs from natural means. However, its departure attempts to "fix" a natural process that has become "broken" due to infertility problems. Such is not the case with alternative reproduction routes for homosexuals. Artificial childbirth for homosexual couples is not an attempt to restore a natural process that has broken down. The natural reproductive organs of most homosexuals work just fine. Rather, they use "unnatural" reproduction patterns for the sake of sustaining "unnatural" sexual patterns. (I use the word *unnatural* in the sense of contravening the complementary male-female reproductive and sexual physiology mentioned above.) Homosexual reproductive routes utilize a double departure from nature, compared to a singular departure in the case of heterosexual infertility. Also, the motivation for the act is completely different—it is not intended to fix what is broken, as is the case with heterosexual infertility, but to have children in relationships that were/are clearly not designed for that purpose.

The very fact that gay couples have to employ a third-party womb/egg and lesbian couples must use third-party sperm should tell us something about the magnitude of departure from natural processes. Furthermore, if one of the homosexual partners contributes the egg or sperm, it produces offspring with a biological imprint from only one parent within the same-sex partnership, not both. This raises certain affinity tensions between parents and between parents and children, especially since the selection of donor input would have been a matter of active choice (in most cases) not passive default as in the case of heterosexual infertility.

Let us summarize the pragmatics-between-two-cultures criterion as applied to homosexuality. The fourfold rationale developed above (sexual design, reproductive design, nurturing of infants and continued propagation of the human race) increases the probability that the on-the-page form of the biblical prohibition should carry weight across various cultures. There is no need to move up the ladder of abstraction. In fact, the universality of these factors lends weight to understanding the underlying principle of distinction of gender, in a complementary and noninterchangeable sense, as an ongoing value within a Christian sexual ethic. Three of the considerations apply as much in our modern culture as they did in the original setting. A fourth, propagation of the human species, still applies to our modern world as a sustained value, though with lesser weight. For several reasons, developed at length above, the argument for accepting homosexuality based upon current population patterns is a faulty one.

It does not really matter to which culture a person travels. These four pragmatic factors, with a qualified weighting on the fourth factor, are going to be universally present. In view of contemporary discussions, it is important to note that this pragmatic rationale applies to both casual and covenant forms of homosexuality. It also matters little whether participants are equal-status partners or in some kind of active/passive relationship. Those who argue for covenant, equal-partner homosexuality as a feasible Christian lifestyle for today cannot adequately account for these factors that transcend culture. These pragmatic factors are persuasive not only across cultures, but also across various forms of homosexuality.

E. Evaluation of the criterion

This criterion invites confusion if not understood correctly. When talking about the pragmatic basis for a biblical command, one might easily get the idea that the pragmatic is the *sole* basis for the command. However, such is not the case. The pragmatic factors serve as the rationale for the most concretized form or the most situation-specific component of the biblical command. The pragmatics, whether culture-based or transcultural in nature, do *not* provide the ultimate basis or rationale for the moral obligation within a biblical command. It is important to keep this distinction in mind and to work with both the pragmatic basis and the ultimate basis (as well as underlying principles) in order to sort out the cultural and transcultural components within a biblical text.

Despite its openness to confusion, the "pragmatic basis" criterion is a good one. Along with other criteria, it causes one to wonder about the feasibility of retaining a mandatory hierarchy in the male/female domain. Social factors clearly shaped the rationale for biblical injunctions. Culture quietly informed the direction of the biblical text, often without any open articulation. When the culture changes and the pragmatic basis is missing, it is a fairly reliable indication that the articulated form of the biblical injunction (though not the entire injunction) is culturally rooted. One must be willing to move up the ladder of abstraction in order to discover the transcultural principle(s) embedded in the biblical text.

F. Summary

The "pragmatic basis between two cultures" criterion provides a helpful grid through which to interpret and apply Scripture. When a biblical command is tracked from one culture to another, the lack of a sustained pragmatic basis serves as a signal that something might be cultural, while continuity in pragmatics raises the probability that the instruction in its stated form is transcultural. The criterion strongly suggests the cultural relativity of the male/female hierarchy; on the other hand, it provides a persuasive argument against permitting homosexuality as an acceptable Christian lifestyle, even in a covenant or equal-partner form.

CRITERION 18: Scientific and Social-Scientific Evidence

A. Statement

A component of a text may be culturally confined if it is contrary to present-day scientific evidence. Should scientific or social-scientific research produce evidence that conflicts with the text, then it may be that the particular affirmation in the biblical text reflects a cultural or time-locked perspective. This may signal possible cultural components within a text and prompt us to move up the ladder of abstraction in order to discover the underlying transcultural principle. By definition, scientific evidence requires that something can be tested through repeated observation or experimentation. Such testing is a part of physical sciences like physics, chemistry and biology, but also a core facet of social sciences like psychology, sociology and anthropology.

As the reader will see in the examples to follow, two kinds of scientific data emerge:

absolute scientific/social-scientific data   relative scientific/social-scientific data

Absolute scientific data is observational or experimental evidence that would hold true in any culture and time (e.g., the case of cosmology and the case of reproductive models for women). *Relative* scientific data is observational or experimental evidence that would hold true only within a given culture and time (e.g., an assessment within a particular culture of women as child-like leaders or of women as more easily deceived than men). These social assessments may be true and accurate within a particular culture, but they are associative, culture-based matters not inherent to gender itself. While it is important to recognize a distinction between absolute and relative scientific evidence, both assist the church in setting limits on the application of a particular text as it relates to today. In general, absolute scientific evidence plays a greater role in the physical sciences, whereas relative scientific evidence surfaces more frequently in the social sciences, where certain observations may pertain to one people group but not to another.

B. Neutral examples

1. Geocentric versus heliocentric models. Scripture depicts a geocentric or

earth-centered model of the universe. The earth is placed on a stationary foundation in a central location with other luminous bodies revolving above it.[4] With the
earth in the middle, the larger universe is constructed in three stories: "above,"
"on" or "below" the earth.[5] Although expressed in different ways, these three cos-
mic levels are known as the heavens, the earth and the underworld.[6] This geocentric perspective reflects the assumed cosmology of the day. The Bible does not
magically jump ahead of its time to make discoveries that a Newton or Galileo
could have found out about if only they had studied its pages more closely.

    While the geocentric component of biblical cosmology is cultural, the cosmol-
ogy texts still retain important transcultural elements. A geocentric universe accurately portrays a metaphysical or theological reality in terms of God's care and
providence for his people.[7] Also, at least in part these texts reflect phenomenological language (what a person actually sees). God's Spirit worked in the production of the text through language common to everyday people. Thus we might
summarize biblical cosmology by saying that the geocentric component is cultural; the theological and phenomenological components are transcultural.

    For many years the cultural component of biblical cosmology remained inex-
tricably bound together with the phenomenological and the theological components. Science has performed a great service in helping us assess the nature of
these biblical texts. Aside from phenomenal and theological truth, the church had
wrongly assumed a transcultural or absolute cosmological reality being expressed within the geocentric component of these texts.[8] Scientific evidence
eventually played a crucial role in helping the church determine what aspects of
the cosmological portrait were cultural and what aspects were transcultural. We

---

[4]1 Sam 2:8; 1 Chron 16:30; Job 9:6; 38:4-7; Ps 18:15; 19:2-5; 24:1-2; 75:3-4; 82:5; 93:1; 96:10;
102:25; 104:5-9; Prov 8:27-29; Is 24:18; 51:13, 16; Jer 31:37; Zech 12:1. Like a temple, the earth
was depicted as having a secure foundation and pillars. The earth itself rested upon pillars sunk deep
into the primeval sea below.

[5]E.g., Rev 5:3, 13; 9:1-2; 11:7; 17:18; 20:1-3. A shaft or tunnel connects the underworld to the earth.
Passages dealing with the netherworld typically describe the journey as "going down" into that region, e.g., Gen 37:35; 42:38; 44:29, 31; Num 16:30, 33; Deut 32:22; Ps 49:15; 55:16; Job 7:9; 17:16;
21:13; 1 Sam 2:6; 1 Kings 2:9; Is 14:11, 15; Ezek 31:15-17; 32:27. Cf. the similar aspect of descent
in the expression, "those who go down into the pit," e.g., Ps 28:1; 30:4; 88:5; 143:7; Prov 1:12; Is
38:18; Ezek 26:20; 31:14, 16; 32:18, 24-25, 29-30.

[6]Ex 20:4; Deut 5:8; 33:13-16; Ps 115:16-17; 135:6; Prov 8:27-32. For a brief overview of the biblical
texts see R. A. Muller, "World," in *The International Standard Bible Encyclopedia,* ed. Geoffrey W.
Bromiley (Grand Rapids, Mich.: Eerdmans, 1988), 4:1112-16.

[7]For a probing discussion about geocentricity and theology, see Francis Watson, *Text, Church, and
World: Biblical Interpretation in Theological Perspective* (Grand Rapids, Mich.: Eerdmans, 1994),
pp. 148-50.

[8]Luther, Calvin, Melanchthon, Owen, etc. anchored their geocentric and stationary-earth views on
biblical statements.

must not lose grasp of the text's metaphysical reality and phenomenological basis, but neither should we forget how scientific evidence awakened us to previous assumptions about the portrait that were cultural. As an interpretive community we do well to confess our fallibility about determining what it is that Scripture infallibly affirms.

2. *Flat earth versus round earth.* The combined explorations of Columbus, Cabot, da Gama, Vespucci, Drake, Cortez and others eventually proved that the earth was round. The church had difficulty accepting this revelation because the Bible incorporated a "flat earth" view of the world, with a typical "four corners" perspective (e.g., Gen 1:6-7; Ps 75:3; Rev 7:1).

In time, the findings of Copernicus, Galileo, Columbus and others forced the church to recognize that Scripture accommodated itself to the cosmology of its day. It adopted a cosmology that reflected the time and culture in which it was written. For today's generation familiar with shuttle flights and space photography, it is no longer possible to affirm the biblical text where it presents a flat earth, a stationary earth or a geocentric universe. While we should not force contemporary scientific expectations upon the text, neither do we want to overlook its utilization of culturally appropriate perspectives.

C. Women

1. *Women as reproductive gardens.* The biblical model of reproduction is heavily influenced by its agrarian culture. A woman provides the "soil" into which a man planted the "seed" of the miniature child *(homunculus)* to grow for nine months (Gen 38:9; Lev 15:16-18, 32). As in the harvesting of crops, at birth the child is known as the "first fruits" (Ps 78:51; 105:36) or "fruit"[9] of the wife's garden/womb. Furthermore, infertility is always connected with the woman (not the man). A woman's barren womb was equivalent to desert-like soil conditions.[10]

The church was very slow to accept the emerging scientific evidence about reproduction because the agrarian reproductive model was so deeply ingrained. The transition from an agricultural model to a scientific model was not an easy journey. Through the sperm and egg, the male and female contribute equally to the genetic makeup of the child. The male and female each provide 23 chromosomes for the creation of a new fetus.[11] Also, male infertility accounts for a sig-

---

[9]Deut 7:13; 28:4, 11, 18, 53; Mic 6:7; cf. Ps 128:3.

[10]Consider the numerous references to "barren" women in Scripture; there are no references to "barren" men.

[11]First Corinthians 11:12 (with its two different Greek prepositions, "from" and "through") may reflect a cultural component within its procreation argument. For a discussion of 1 Corinthians 11:12, see appendix D.

nificant share of the problem of not having children. As on other occasions, Christians had mistakenly invested too much transcultural or absolutized meaning into the text. A tight agricultural analogy—the man provides the totality of the new life in seedling form while the woman provides only the fertile environment for its growth—reflects a culture-based component within the text.[12] The text's actual transcultural component is reflected in its broader comparative ideas—the creation and sustenance of new life. Thankfully, scientific investigation has helped us distinguish between the cultural components and the transcultural components when reading the reproductive texts.

2. *Women as poor leaders.* The prophet Isaiah hurls caustic remarks at Israel's leaders: "Youths [children] oppress my people, women rule over them! O my people, your guides lead you astray; they turn you from the path" (Is 3:12). The scope of Isaiah's rebuke is much broader than religious leaders; he is also chiding political, judicial and business leaders.[13] It is not that Israel literally had children or women leading them; his words are figurative: "It is *as if* youths/children oppress . . . women rule." So Isaiah compares the current male leaders to what it would be like if women or children were in leadership. The picture is not a complimentary one. In today's jargon the text conveys the perspective that "women make lousy leaders!"

While there may well have existed a social-scientific basis to Isaiah's observations about women in his day (due to associative factors that affected the lives of women), it would be difficult to show that such is the case today. In our modern context, women make tremendous contributions at the highest levels in contemporary politics, business, science, technology, education, judicial process, etc. To suggest some kind of *absolute* social science data behind Isaiah's statement (rather than *relative* social science data) is extremely difficult in view of the contribution of women to leadership in North America and Europe during the past hundred years. While the specific gender component of the Isaiah text is cultural, the broader underlying transcultural principle remains in force today: childish or immature persons make poor leaders.

3. *Women as more easily deceived than men.* The text of 1 Timothy 2:14 reads, "And Adam was not the one deceived; it was the woman who was deceived and

---

[12]Before the scientific discoveries in this area, Jewish and Christians readers of the biblical text certainly understood the reproductive analogy within the typical agrarian framework without being able to distinguish between its cultural and transcultural components. To say anything about authorial intent is speculative. Obviously, the divine author understood the cultural/transcultural distinction. Yet, it would seem to be special pleading to suggest that somehow in the human authors' minds the cultural and the transcultural components were clearly separated.

[13]Note the broader context of Is 3:2.

became a sinner." The traditional interpretation of this verse has been that women are more easily deceived than men (see appendix B for a history of interpretation sketch). On the basis of 1 Timothy 2:14 the church has viewed women as more gullible than men due to their supposed lesser intellectual and critical-thinking capacity. For many years the church taught that women were given to silly and emotional speech and not to the kind of rational judgment possessed by men. As shocking as this sounds to the modern ear, it is important to realize that Paul's words in 2:14 have been understood in this sense for hundreds of years. Due to its longevity, the view that women are more easily deceived than men might almost be called the "canonized teaching" of the church.

On this historical point, there is no disagreement. Both egalitarians and patriarchalists agree concerning what has constituted the traditional teaching of the church: 1 Timothy 2:14 taught that women are more easily deceived than men due to an inferior capacity to understand and make sound judgments. In addition to examining my own Appendix B at the end of this book, one might also read Daniel Doriani's "History of the Interpretation of 1 Timothy 2" (written by a patriarchalist).[14] In the last hundred years many interpreters, both egalitarian and patriarchalists, have departed from the traditional interpretation, and for good reason. It is very difficult to reconcile this rendering of the text with what we experience in the Western world.

Nevertheless, a number of patriarchal scholars are returning to the traditional position. They are to be commended for courageously following their exegetical convictions. In one of the finest *exegetical* treatments of 1 Timothy 2 available today, the authors of *Women in the Church: A Fresh Analysis of 1 Timothy 2:9-15*[15] develop the text in its lexical and grammatical aspects in much the same way as I would be inclined. In addition, when discussing 1 Timothy 2:14, they argue for the historical exegesis of that text in a most convincing fashion. In their view (as well as mine), the traditional rendering is the most supportable reading of the text. Rather than duplicating their efforts, I would encourage readers to see particularly the chapters by Schreiner[16] and by Doriani[17] as they develop 2:14. From an exegetical standpoint, the book makes a masterful and lasting contribution to the discussion of this passage.

---

[14]Daniel Doriani, "History of the Interpretation of 1 Timothy 2," in *Women in the Church: A Fresh Analysis of 1 Timothy 2:9-15*, ed. Andreas J. Köstenberger, Thomas R. Schreiner and H. Scott Baldwin (Grand Rapids, Mich.: Baker, 1995), pp. 213-67.

[15]Andreas J. Köstenberger, Thomas R. Schreiner and H. Scott Baldwin, eds., *Women in the Church: A Fresh Analysis of 1 Timothy 2:9-15* (Grand Rapids, Mich.: Baker, 1995).

[16] Thomas R. Schreiner, "An Interpretation of 1 Timothy 2:9-15: A Dialogue with Scholarship," in *Women in the Church*, pp. 105-54.

[17] Doriani, "History of the Interpretation of 1 Timothy 2," pp. 213-67.

What I find most problematic with Schreiner and Doriani's approach, however, is their *modification* of the traditional understanding of 1 Timothy 2:14. Clearly they wish to present their view as the "historic position" of the church, but their modification makes it far from the historic position. They argue that this verse basically means that "women are more easily deceived than men" (following in the church tradition), but then they modify the rationale that was clearly articulated. The church had consistently understood the verse to mean that women are more easily deceived *because of a fundamental difference between men and women in rational or intellectual capacity.* Early church interpreters express this capacity difference in a variety of ways, but the perspective is generally the same. Appendix B and Doriani's historical survey show this to be the case. However, Schreiner and Doriani attempt to "clean up" the historical interpretation of its more offensive components. Thus, they are careful not to say that women have a lesser intellectual capacity than men (as was the historic teaching of the church). Rather, they emphasize a difference between men and women in terms of "inclination," "proclivity," and "constitution." Here is a sampling of Schreiner and Doriani's nuanced position (italics mine):

> Generally speaking, *women are more relational and nurturing and men are more given to rational analysis and objectivity. Women are less prone than men to see the importance of doctrinal formulations*, especially when it comes to the issue of identifying heresy and making a stand for the truth. Appointing women to the teaching office is prohibited because *they are less likely to draw a line on doctrinal non-negotiables*, and thus deception and false teaching will more easily enter the church.[18]

> What concerns him [Paul] are the consequences of allowing women in the authoritative teaching office, for their gentler and kinder nature inhibits them from excluding people for doctrinal error. There is the danger of stereotyping here, for obviously some women are more inclined to objectivity and are "tougher" and less nurturing than other women. *But as a general rule women are more relational and caring than men. This explains why most women have many more close friends than men.*[19]

I must applaud this "revised historic" position on its exegesis of the text. There is much that I find attractive in the position. The fact that these authors have returned to at least part of the traditional position (women are more easily deceived than men) is admirable. In one or two respects I think they are right. Their case is both historically and exegetically persuasive. And, inasmuch as they affirm complementary functions for men and women (biological differences should result in *some* functional differences between men and women

---

[18]Schreiner, "An Interpretation of 1 Timothy 2:9-15," p. 145.
[19]Ibid., pp. 145-46.

[see chapter eight]), their arguments are quite engaging.

Although their view has tremendous strengths, permit me to raise difficulties with the revised historic position through a series of questions. *First, has not the revised historical position utilized a social-scientific canon in its interpretive process?* As with my own work, I suspect that it is also the gulf between the historic view and our present experience with men and women that is determining what proponents of the revised historic view have decided to remove from the church's historic position. Similar to the majority of soft patriarchalists who have completely dismissed the traditional position on social-scientific grounds, the revised historical position "cleans up" the traditional view based upon their own social-scientific awareness. Every view, including my own, utilizes the scientific or social-scientific criterion to determine how the verse should be understood.

Second, is not minimizing educational differences (and other cultural factors) "because Paul does not say this" somewhat unfair? For one thing, the text does not say that "women are more easily deceived than men"; that is interpretive. Also, the text does not say, "the reason women are more easily deceived than men is because they are more relational"; that also is interpretive. So while it is true that Paul does not mention "educational factors" and other social-based factors that impact deception, neither does he talk about "relational factors." Every interpretation of 1 Timothy 2:14 has to fill in the blanks in some fashion.

Third, would tough/detached men and tender/relational women really have been on Paul's mind in a declaration that women are more easily deceived than men? Schreiner and Doriani's tough/tender thesis amounts to an overblown and forced stereotype of women and men. Even so, these considerations probably played a minuscule role in obstructing one's decision-making capabilities compared to other factors in Paul's day. It is far more likely that Paul had in mind gender-related factors of much greater impact on the question of deception. Rather than deducing through ancient writers what the views on gender differences were in Paul's day, Schreiner and Doriani take a current psychological perspective to figure out what Paul might have been thinking back then. In Schreiner's article there is extensive reference to ancient Greco-Roman and Jewish writers to determine what Paul might have had in mind when discussing women's attire in 1 Timothy 2:9-10 (e.g., Juvenal, Plutarch, Josephus, Mishnah, Talmud, Apocrypha, Pseudepigrapha). However, when it comes time to determine what Paul might have in mind when talking about women being more easily deceived than men in 1 Timothy 2:14, there is complete silence about the cultural perspective. The silence is deafening. In fact, without that silence the revised-historic position stands little chance of making its case.

In our quest to discover what Paul might have been thinking, a biblical text like Isaiah 3:12 offers a more suitable starting place than pop psychology. As noted earlier, Isaiah lumps women together with children and youths in order to depict the poor quality of leadership in Israel. The poetic parallelism brings women and youths/children into a close association (emphasis added):

> *Youths [children]*[20] oppress my people,
> *women* rule over them.
> My people, your guides lead you astray;
> they turn you from the path.

What Paul had in mind in 1 Timothy 2:14 probably differs little from what Isaiah had in mind when talking about women in Isaiah 3:12. Isaiah was speaking about women leaders in general (society), while Paul was talking about women leaders in the congregation (church). The sphere was different, but the point was much the same: women make poor leaders! Through examining the Isaiah text we come much closer to discovering a credible rationale—women had similar liabilities in leadership to the liabilities of youths/children in leadership. The prophet Isaiah was hardly worried about women being more relational. As laid out in the "pragmatic basis between two cultures" criterion (criterion 17), the shared liabilities between ancient women and children/youths created a natural hierarchy in both situations. These culture-based factors are especially pertinent to the issues of deception and gullibility. In ancient cultures like Isaiah's, both women and children shared similar liabilities: the lack of knowledge and education, less social exposure and breadth of experience, and a significant (marital) age differential.[21]

It is understandable why Isaiah lumps together women and youths/children as poor leaders. Isaiah's perspective on women, in giving them a capacity status close to children, is a common theme within Scripture[22] and an emphasis found in readily available research on ancient women.[23] Not surprisingly, Schreiner and Doriani never mention this Isaiah text, or the broader scriptural theme, or the pertinent ancient texts bearing on this subject.

Finally, is there sufficient social-scientific evidence for the "relational thesis"? For several reasons, the data used to support the relational thesis are not credible. One crucial liability is that the proponents have not isolated innate gender factors from cultural ones. Studies by Myers-Briggs on gender and "thinker

---

[20]Cf. the emphasis on children/babes as leaders in Is 3:4.

[21]Not only was there was an age differential between parents and children, a significant age difference often existed between males and their younger female spouses.

[22]See the scriptural texts discussed under criterion 11.C.

[23]For two helpful works in this area, see Tal Ilan, *Jewish Women in Greco-Roman Palestine* (Peabody, Mass.: Hendrickson, 1996) and Craig S. Keener, *Paul, Women, and Wives* (Peabody, Mass.: Hendrickson, 1992).

versus feeler" traits (roughly comparable to rational vs. relational) do place more women in the "feeler" category. But, over the years the statistics have changed; a greater number of men are becoming relational, which indicates that social conditioning plays a considerable role in this area.[24] Second, while general observations can be made, too much gender crossover exists to make any binding endorsements about roles for men or women. If it is true that relational people are more vulnerable to deceit, then why not choose men and women as leaders who are more rational and less relational? The significant gender crossover should logically lead soft patriarchalists to a personality conclusion, not a gender conclusion. A limitation on relational-type people in leadership would retain the authorial intent of the passage in a more informed generation (i.e., one with sophisticated tools for assessing such traits). Third, and most importantly, the assumed link between "relational women" and "vulnerability to deception" has not been established. If there is a connection between relational women and deception, then scientific testing today could easily verify that women are more easily deceived than men. However, the research shows that gender is not a significant issue in detecting deception (and in some cases women do a marginally better job). Instead, social-scientific studies on deception—surveyed in appendix C—indicate that the crucial factors in making a person more vulnerable to deception are the following:

☐ crosscultural nuances

☐ age*

☐ experience*

☐ broad versus sheltered social exposure*

☐ intelligence

☐ knowledge/formal education*

These factors, especially the ones with an asterisk (*), sustain a cultural thesis for why women in Paul's day were generally more easily deceived than men. Women in patriarchal societies generally married at a younger age than men, were not permitted the range of experiences and social exposure of men, and were often restricted in their formal education. It is not simply a wild hunch, then, that women in Paul's day would have been generally more vulnerable to deception because of these associative factors. (For a survey of scientific research on deception, see appendix C.)

---

[24]Isabel Myers-Briggs and Mary H. McCaulley, *Manual: A Guide to the Development and Use of the Myers-Briggs Type Indicator* (Palo Alto, Calif.: Consulting Psychologists Press, 1985), pp. 149-50. Not only is there significant overlap between genders in this area (30-40 percent), but the change over time in males being more characterized by T/thinking and females by F/feeling has been quite significant.

In sum, I agree with both the historic and the (new) revised-historic view of 1 Timothy 2:14 that Paul is saying that "women are more easily deceived than men." That is by far the most straightforward and persuasive reading of the text. The historic position places a limitation on women due to their being intellectually inferior to men, whereas the revised-historical position wants to say that women are more relational than men and thus they lose objectivity. Unfortunately the revised-historic modification of the historical view, by what they judge as misogyny in the historic view, is not convincing. It amounts to using social-scientific data about women today to dismiss what the church (and I think Paul) was correctly saying about women in a former day. For the revised position to say that the church (or Paul or Isaiah) was wrong about women's intellectual inferiority is heavily anachronistic. It is to read our present findings back into church history and into Paul's words. In fact, the research tells us that the social situation of women in Paul's day (and for many years afterwards) makes statements about lesser intellectual performance a valid concern from a cultural perspective.

The best solution, then, is not to discount the historical teaching of the church but to say that the social data has changed from Paul's day to ours. The degree to which one is deceivable or gullible relates primarily to a combination of factors such as upbringing (sheltered or broad exposure), age, experience, intelligence, education, development of critical thinking, economic conditions and personality. Spanning centuries, whether in Paul's or Isaiah's culture, many of these factors functioned in an associative way to make women more easily deceived than men. In our culture, however, gender is simply not a viable explanation for this "greater deception" phenomenon. So the text was suitable and accurate in its day due to cultural factors of an associative nature. Applying 1 Timothy 2:14 today, however, requires that we move up the ladder of abstraction and work with the underlying transcultural principle: *seek teachers and leaders who are not easily deceived.*

When presenting this material in a live forum, at this point in the lecture I inevitably am asked the question, "How could these cultural factors (education, social exposure, marriage differential, etc.) have influenced Eve in the garden?" The question is an excellent one since it usually means that people have been following the argument with genuine reflection and forethought. However, the question also reflects several false assumptions. First, it assumes that cultural factors did not play a role in the shaping of the creation narrative. This assumption has been countered in criterion 6 by looking at actual components within the narrative itself. Second, it assumes that the author's perspective in the opening chapters of Genesis is completely isolated from later epochs or dispensations in salvation history. Criterion 7.D has challenged this assumption in a discussion on the perspective of "protology" and how that perspective parallels the accommodation or time-displaced language of "eschatology." Third, and most specifically pertinent to 1 Timothy 2:14, it assumes that the use of the Old Testament by a New Testament writer must follow along the lines of grammatical-historical exegesis. However, instead of connecting every aspect of the New Testament situation to the garden, Paul is likely developing a simple analogy between Eve and the women at Ephesus (and beyond Ephesus). With analogy there will always be aspects that are similar and aspects that are dissimilar. Paul's point of similarity with the Old Testament is the greater deception of women compared to men. Beyond this similarity component, one should not push other aspects of the New Testament situation back into the Old Testament setting. The hazardous nature of such an approach is confirmed by the broader discipline in biblical studies known as "the use of the Old Testament in the New Testament."[25] One should not expect to be able to read all components of the New Testament context and setting back into the Old Testament text. Such an approach introduces a faulty assumption about how the New Testament writers wove the Hebrew tradition into their own materials.

D. Homosexuality

Some argue for same-sex lifestyles based upon the findings of social sciences and biology. Since environmental and biological factors influence sexual orientation, then perhaps one's sexuality is beyond an individual's control and simply a matter of destiny. As the argument goes, if forces external to one's own volition influence homosexual behavior, maybe the behavior should be considered natural and good. Accordingly, the Christian community should accept homosexual relationships today.

---

[25]For helpful discussions of the use of the Old Testament in the New Testament, see E. Earle Ellis, *The Old Testament in the Early Church* (Grand Rapids, Mich.: Baker, 1992); idem, *Paul's Use of the Old Testament* (reprint, Grand Rapids, Mich.: Baker, 1981); Douglas J. Moo, *The Old Testament in the Gospel Passion Narratives* (Sheffield: Almond Press, 1983); G. K. Beale, ed., *The Right Doctrine from the Wrong Texts: Essays on the Use of the Old Testament in the New* (Grand Rapids, Mich.: Baker, 1994); Donald Juel, *Messianic Exegesis. Christological Interpretation of the Old Testament in Early Christianity* (Philadelphia: Fortress, 1988); Richard N. Longenecker, *Biblical Exegesis in the Apostolic Period* (Grand Rapids, Mich.: Eerdmans, 1975); Darrell L. Bock, *Proclamation from Prophecy and Pattern: Lucan Old Testament Christology* (Sheffield: JSOT Press, 1987); William J. Webb, *Returning Home: New Covenant and Second Exodus as the Context for 2 Corinthians 6.14—7.1* (Sheffield: JSOT Press, 1993); Craig A. Evans and James A. Sanders, eds., *Paul and the Scriptures of Israel* (Sheffield: JSOT Press, 1993); Leonhard Goppelt, *Typos: The Typological Interpretation of the Old Testament* (Grand Rapids, Mich.: Eerdmans, 1982). Any of these studies (and numerous others) demonstrate that it is extremely dubious to read all of the components of the New Testament context back into the Old Testament setting. For an introduction to the field, see Moises Silva, "The Old Testament in Paul," in *Dictionary of Paul and His Letters*, ed. G. F. Hawthorne, R. P. Martin and D. G. Reid (Downers Grove, Ill.: InterVarsity Press, 1993), pp. 630-42.

Environmental factors can clearly play a role in shaping sexual preference.[26] One can readily understand, for example, how two females who previously experienced abusive heterosexual marriages (or abusive fathers in their childhood) might find a lesbian relationship an appealing and fulfilling alternative. Likewise, a child who is seduced by a same-sex adult may develop a lasting disposition toward homoerotic behavior. Early learning experiences help children define their sexual identity. Again, some studies have shown that relational distance between the same-sex parent and the child (i.e., strong estrangement in the father-son or mother-daughter relationship) produces a longing for same-sex closeness, which in later years may be fulfilled through homosexual relationships.

Biological factors also appear to influence erotic orientation. While biological research into homosexual behavior is growing rapidly,[27] three major areas dominate the inquiry: hormones, brain structures and genetics. One avenue of research suggests that hormones may play a significant role in sexual orientation. Hormonal manipulations in animals, particularly in prenatal animals, have been shown to produce a greater degree of homoerotic preference. Similarly, cases of genital abnormalities in humans have been linked to prenatal hormone variations (e.g., enzyme defects can overexpose the fetus to male hormones). Females born with external male-genital features, even though these abnormalities are surgically corrected, in later life enter into lesbian relationships at a rate much beyond that of the general population. Along different lines, some studies suggest that variations in certain brain structures are somehow related to sexual orientation (e.g., the anterior hypothalamus in homosexual males has a configuration more like heterosexual females than heterosexual males; the suprachiasmatic nucleus is nearly twice as large in homosexual men as in heterosexual men).[28] A third area of biological inquiry is genetics. For instance, genetic mutations in fruit flies have produced a higher incidence of homoerotic behavior. While human genetics is far more complex than fruit flies,

---

[26]For an introduction to environmental/societal factors, see Stanton L. Jones and Don E. Workman, "Homosexuality: The Behavioral Sciences and the Church," in *Homosexuality in the Church,* ed. Jeffrey S. Siker (Louisville: Westminster John Knox, 1994), pp. 100-103. See also articles in the next footnote.

[27]For an introduction to biological factors, see ibid., pp. 98-111; Chandler Burr, "Homosexuality and Biology," in *Homosexuality in the Church,* pp. 116-34; Stanton L. Jones and Mark A. Yarhouse, "Science and the Ecclesiastical Homosexuality Debates," *Christian Scholar's Review* 26:4 (1997): 446-77; idem, "A Critique of Materialist Assumptions in Interpretations of Research on Homosexuality," *Christian Scholar's Review* 26:4 (1997): 478-95; Heather Looy, "Taking Our Assumptions Out of the Closet: Psychological Research on Homosexuality and Its Implications for Christian Dialogue," *Christian Scholar's Review* 26:4 (1997): 496-513; James R. Beck, "Evangelicals, Homosexuality, and Social Science," *Journal of the Evangelical Theological Society* 40:1 (1997): 83-97.

[28]This variance in suprachiasmatic nuclei may be due to the homosexual behavior itself (i.e., as an effect from the behavior, not a cause).

studies of adoptive brothers, dizygotic twins and monozygotic twins indicate a genetic component of homosexuality. (As we move from one of these categories to the next, there is an increase in the correlation of fraternal homosexuality.) This information may confirm some kind of genetic connection to homosexual behavior in people. All of these studies are in the process of being critiqued and validated. While hormones, brain structure and genetic variations do not account for all cases of homosexual behavior among humans, these biological considerations appear to be factors in a significant number of cases.

Once the physiological link with homosexuality has been established (as it seems to have been), it is often difficult to determine *the degree* of influence a particular biological component has on the behavior, due to the difficulty of isolating that one factor from other environmental or biological factors. Some speak of little to no biological influence; others frame the relationship between homosexual biology and behavior in strong, deterministic terms. However, most suggest some kind of moderating influence that could be described as a predisposition to the behavior, which in different individuals could range from mild to strong.[29]

That genetics influence but do not determine behavior may be illustrated by research on children's television viewing habits. A recent study provides evidence of "significant genetic influence on individual differences in children's television viewing."[30] Their findings concerning television viewing had nearly the statistical weight of the homosexual genetics study about twins (cited above).[31] No one would seriously argue that our genes make us sit in front of a television set. Yet, a person may have a greater or lesser predisposition toward television as a stimulus due to their genetic makeup.

However, the influence of nonvolitional forces upon *any* human action is no help in determining the ethical status of that action. In the sexual domain, many forms of erotic expression are likely influenced by a combination of these "external" factors. A case could be made for various environmental and biological influences on one's sexual preference toward pornography, sex with young children (whether homosexual or heterosexual), sex with animals, sex with corpses, violent sex, rape, incest, etc. Beyond the sexual domain, many other human actions are heavily influenced by environmental and biological factors (e.g., alcoholism, eating disorders, gambling, domestic violence, verbal abuse, depression, suicide).

---

[29]For an example of this moderating approach, see John Money, *Gay, Straight, and In-between: The Sexology of Erotic Orientation* (Oxford: Oxford University Press, 1988).

[30]R. Plomin, R. Corley, J. C. DeFries and D. W. Fulker, "Individual Differences in Television Viewing in Early Childhood: Nature as Well as Nurture," *Psychological Science* 1 (1990): 371.

[31]Jones and Yarhouse, "Science and the Ecclesiastical Homosexuality Debates," p. 467.

While studies have not been carried out in all of these areas, biological influences, as well as social causes, have been linked to alcoholism,[32] antisocial disorders[33] and certain sexual offenses.[34]

By themselves, these negative examples of nonvolitional influence do not demonstrate that homosexuality is evil or wrong. Similar considerations also influence neutral or positive behaviors (e.g., left-handed preference). Nevertheless, what they do show is that environmental and biological factors are not sufficient grounds for assessment of any behavior. To the degree that these external or nonvolitional factors influence one's actions, they moderate the degree of personal culpability (or personal credit in the case of a good behavior) but they do not change the assessment of the behavior itself.

E. Evaluation of the criterion

Although the relationship between science and biblical interpretation is a complex one,[35] it is hard to escape the conclusion that cultural accommodation played a significant role in a variety of biblical texts. In the women texts current social-scientific data should help us limit what applicational meaning should be derived from a text like 1 Timothy 2:14, as understood along traditional lines. Whether one is a revised traditionalist (and limits the "intellectual inferiority" component) or an egalitarian (and limits both the "intellectual inferiority" and the "more easily deceived" component) social-scientific evidence plays a significant role. Similarly, the remaining majority of soft patriarchalists who have abandoned the traditional view altogether, and adopted far more convoluted interpretations of the passage, have likewise shifted their understanding based on social-scientific data. They cannot live with the dissonance between the traditional position and what they see in the world around them. What should be abundantly clear is that all views are interacting with the scientific and social-scientific criterion to inform their understanding of 1 Timothy 2:14.

F. Summary

The "scientific and social-scientific evidence" criterion has played a major role over the years in helping the church assess what is cultural and what is transcul-

---

[32]K. Kendler, A. Heath, M. Neale, R. Kessler and L. Evans, "A Population-Based Twin Study of Alcoholism in Women," *Journal of the American Medical Association* 268 (1992): 1877-82.

[33]P. B. Sutker, F. Bugg and J. A. West, "Antisocial Personality Disorder," in *Comprehensive Handbook of Psychopathology*, eds. H. Adams and P. Sutker, 2d ed. (New York: Plenum, 1993), pp. 337-69.

[34]Sherwood O. Cole, "Reflections on Integration by a Biopsychologist," *Journal of Psychology and Theology* 24 (1996): 292-300.

[35]For a helpful evangelical discussion, see Vern S. Poythress, *Science and Hermeneutics: Implications of Scientific Method for Biblical Interpretation* (Grand Rapids, Mich.: Zondervan, 1988).

tural within a text. Current sociological data make it very difficult to affirm only a transcultural component to biblical statements made about women being poor leaders (Is 3:12) or more easily deceived than men (the traditional interpretation of 1 Tim 2:14). In an associative sense (not with regard to gender as an isolated component), what these texts affirm about women was correct and reliable in the original setting. Within the ancient world setting, a text like 1 Timothy 2:14 is understandable: the greater vulnerability of women to deception (compared to men) was a valid concern for cultural reasons. When bringing this verse into our modern world, one should acknowledge the culture-based perspective on deception within the text and apply its concerns to *both* genders today. Recent social-scientific studies indicate that gender is not a factor in terms of what makes one more vulnerable to deception. In applying the text today, then, we must move up the ladder of abstraction to the transcultural principle underlying the text, namely, that persons who are easily deceived should not be the leaders or teachers within the congregation. Only then do we adequately retain the original intent of the text as spoken within its social context. Scientific research on deception (see appendix C) is a helpful indicator for us today that something within Scripture may have a time-locked or cultural component.

Depending upon the individual person, environmental and biological factors may play a significant role in influencing (though not determining) their sexual behavior. However, the impact of environmental and biological factors upon any human action is not a sufficient basis for determining whether or not the action itself is right or wrong. Too many cases exist where environmental and biological factors influence actions that are clearly wrong. To the degree that these nonvolitional factors influence one's actions, they moderate the degree of personal culpability, but they do not change an assessment of the behavior itself.

8

WHAT IF I AM WRONG?

Some decisions in life are of the difficult 60/40 sort, where good evidence stacks up on either side. Other decisions are of a clearer 90/10 type. I am reasonably convinced of all I have written within this book. However, that does not mean that I am equally convinced about each detailed finding. As with every interpretive decision, one must carefully weigh the competing evidence and make the best assessment possible. Even so, it is often a healthy and insightful exercise to reflect at length upon what one considers their point of least strength, or greatest weakness, is. After isolating the greatest weakness, one might ask the question, "What if I am wrong?" The results of such a reflection permit one to develop a default position—the position that one would take should they be wrong at their most vulnerable spot.

Rethinking 1 Timothy 2:13 from a Transcultural Viewpoint
I am prepared to ask this chapter's reflective question about one aspect of my findings, namely, my assessment of 1 Timothy 2:13. While I find a cultural-component assessment of 1 Timothy 2:13 more compelling than assessments finding it to be completely transcultural, I will be the first to admit that I might be wrong. The amount of available material for assessing the situation either way is marginal. In view of the lack of conclusive data plaguing both egalitarian and patriarchal developments of this verse, it might be worthwhile for me to ponder the possibility that I am wrong. Several thoughts come to mind.

1. Paul's application does not equal Moses' principle.
Assuming that God intended Eden's creative order to have transcultural implica-

tions, that does not necessarily mean that women should be restricted from having a pastoral teaching ministry today. Genesis does not say that women cannot teach men. If one accepts a transcultural dimension to the garden's patriarchy, the most that can be said is that *man should have some kind of greater honor or prominence than woman*. Paul applied the principle of the Genesis text within his day and culture. But Paul's use of the Genesis text in restricting women from teaching is an application of the principle, not the principle itself. If we have discovered anything with surety in the cultural journey within this book, it is that different cultures would apply the degree of patriarchy in greater or lesser strengths (see criterion 11). Some of the patriarchy found within Scripture, while redemptive relative to its original setting, is abhorrent from a contemporary Christian perspective and should not be practiced today.

Generally speaking, in our Canadian, American and European cultures male honor is no longer threatened by having a woman teach. This may be amusingly illustrated by the way in which soft patriarchal denominations will often invite a woman to come and develop her views of what the Bible says about women. She will teach a mixed gathering of men and women that women ought not to teach men "as senior pastors" (a subtle qualification of the Timothy text). Aside from the obvious irony, the experience itself suggests that a woman teacher does really not dishonor men in our culture. Thus, even if one views the Genesis "male honor" principle as transcultural, its application is going to differ in different cultures. The apostle Paul applies the primogeniture principle in his culture. But his application does not equal the principle itself.

2. 1 Timothy 2:14 is almost certainly a cultural-component text.

Paul's restriction on women teaching men is based upon two arguments—the primogeniture argument of 1 Timothy 2:13 and the deception argument of 2:14. While I am willing to write a "what if I am wrong" section about 2:13, I am not inclined to do so for 2:14. The evidence is very strong for taking 2:14 as cultural (see criterion 18.C.3), that is, the text has a significant cultural component (beyond its underlying transcultural principle). In this case, Paul had two considerations that led him to restrict women from teaching. While the first might be transcultural, the second is almost certainly cultural.

If this kind of scenario is feasible, then we have to ask if the weight of Paul's one argument by itself can sustain the restriction on women teaching. Are the two arguments independently persuasive in establishing the restrictions on women teaching, or are they cumulative in their support of the restriction? If one of Paul's two arguments has a significant cultural component to it, then the apostle may well have lightened his restriction considerably in another setting and circumstance. If this "one out of two" consideration is paired with our "application, not principle" comments above, then even a transcultural read of 2:13 should take the implications for women today to a much softer expression of patriarchy than what is prescribed in 2:11-12 for the Ephesus congregation.

3. Creative-order prominence is a light (not heavy) value in Scripture.
I have catalogued the breakouts to creative-order logic in Scripture (criterion 7.C.1). The sheer number of them is impressive. At the very least, these breakouts show that creative-order prominence was a rather light value in Scripture. If the numerous breakouts are merely exceptions to the rule and nothing more (as patriarchalists must insist), then the exceptions at the very least say something about the strength of the value being affirmed. Primogeniture was easily overthrown for more important considerations, namely, a person's leadership capability, proven character and heart for God. One has to ponder whether a good number of exceptions should be allowed today on this basis as the concept is related to women. Also, since the teaching of 1 Timothy 2:14 (women are more easily deceived than men) contains a significant cultural component, one cannot help but wonder how much that perspective dampened the leadership opportunities for women in Paul's day. The competing value of leadership capability, which often flipped creative-order patterns within Scripture, would not have been able to speak as loudly back then on behalf of women as it could today.

Even if primogeniture logic should be viewed as transcultural, the numerous exceptions surely give us a Scriptural framework for seeing it as a light value for the covenant people. It was/is not a heavyweight value as some would lead us to believe today, especially those who attempt to make it part of confessional statements. Rather, it is a value that often took, and should often take, a back seat to other considerations.

4. Even the light-value weighting of creative-order prominence in Scripture is itself accentuated by culture-based factors.
Criterion 7.C.2 has shown how certain culture-based factors drove primogeniture or creative-order prominence in the ancient world. These factors—land inheritance, farming and livestock concerns, physical property rather than liquid financial resources, large families, survival issues, etc.—are no longer a determinative part of our modern world. These pragmatic factors existed in the original culture, but they no longer play a role in our lives (see criterion 17, "Pragmatics Between Two Cultures"). This consideration must be factored into any contemporary application scenario. If primogeniture values should be transcultural in some fashion, then at the very least we should concede that culture-based factors have

strengthened or accentuated the application of these values within the ancient world. Consequently, an application of creative-order prominence for our modern world must not only take into consideration its light weight configuration within Scripture (see point 3 above), it must also consider an appropriate reduction of this light-weight perspective even further for our contemporary setting. Some of its light-weight strength within the biblical text is surely attributable to cultural factors.

5. Paul's logic is sibling logic, not parent-child logic.
Earlier I argued that the hierarchy in parent-child relationships, which Scripture endorses, should be granted transcultural status (criterion 17). Children are called upon to "obey," "submit to" and "honor" their parents. Even in coming to this conclusion, I do *not* support a view held by some that children today as *grown* adults should obey and submit to their parents. The changes in family structures between biblical times and today, aside from a host of other maturational considerations, make such an application of the text rather strained. For grown children, I would advocate honor for an ongoing relationship of grown children to their parents, but not an obedience or submission framework.

If this kind of cultural and maturational modification is needed in the parent-child relationship, how much more for prominence patterns on the sibling level where there is not the weight of intergenerational priority. If one views primogeniture as having an ongoing impact on spousal relationships, surely this does not lead to the conclusion that a wife still must obey and submit to her husband today (unless we are speaking of mutual submission). Even a patriarchal viewpoint that takes 1 Timothy 2:13 as transcultural must be open to *the degree* of hierarchy within Scripture being shaped by cultural factors. This mixed-package framework would accept a combination of both cultural and transcultural factors: the primogeniture or creative-order ideas of Genesis would be considered transcultural in the principle sense of honor, but the degree of primogeniture/patriarchy with its large margins of social-power differences between men and women would be viewed as culturally defined.

Like it or not, the factors that built up a hierarchy in biblical times (financial dependency, educational differences, earning potential, social exposure, age differences, etc.) are no longer present in our culture (see criterion 17.C). Consequently, it is somewhat naïve to practice the same degree of hierarchy indicative of the biblical times. Given the changes between the original culture and our modern culture, the submit-and-obey framework is simply no longer defensible as a prescriptive form for husband-and-wife relationships. Even patriarchalists today should acknowledge that changes between the biblical culture and ours have and should flatten the hierarchy considerably. If "honor" retains a minimalist hierarchy between grown children and their parents today (a change from "obey" due to maturational considerations), then it makes even greater sense that "honor" should be the minimalist nature of the hierarchy today between husband and wife. Just as children grow up and move from submission/obedience to an honor framework, so also women in a cultural sense have "come a long way" from where they were when the ancient text was written. Rather than living in denial, a patriarchal application of the Timothy text needs to reflect the reality of those changes. If we recognize the need to transform the submit/obey injunctions within the parent-child relationship, how much more so is this true for prominence patterns on the sibling-type level where the rationale for hierarchy is far less.

6. Galatians 3:28 has sociological implications that need to be heard.
I am still convinced that Galatians 3:28 speaks with transcultural and profound force to the need for equality between men and women. The equality carries sociological as well as salvific implications. Given the radical nature of Paul's "neither male, nor female" pronouncement within its original setting, there should be little doubt that we ought to champion the value of equality to its fullest. Should some kind of "male prominence/honor" value be sustained as well (as a comparatively light value in Scripture), we would then apply the male creative-order prominence principle in a way that would have the least detrimental effect upon male-female equality.

7. At the very least, a redemptive-movement hermeneutic invites change toward a better expression of patriarchy than is often seen in Scripture.
Even if one assumes a transcultural dimension to primogeniture logic, and thus an ongoing application of patriarchy, a redemptive-movement hermeneutic must speak to the application of these values today. As developed at length within this book, a redemptive-spirit approach argues that we must move toward a better, more fully realized ethic in our treatment of women—one that picks up on the underlying spirit of Scripture and permits it to influence our own application process beyond the confines of the original setting. For me, this amounts to a "Wittenberg Door" issue—an issue of significant magnitude—as the church wrestles with the application of 1 Timothy 2 in our modern context.

8. Summary
In sum, these "what if" reflections draw together a number of musings were I to concede a completely transcultural force to 1 Timothy 2:13. Granting this tran-

scultural perspective on this verse, the application for today should still be markedly different from where Paul takes it in 2:11-12. Even if one affirms a completely transcultural approach to 2:13, the seven arguments above raise considerations for significantly modifying the *application* of the Timothy text in our time and setting. Even for patriarchalists, such considerations need to influence the way 1 Timothy 2 is lived out today.

Two Redemptive-Movement Models: Complementary Egalitarianism and Ultra-Soft Patriarchy

As the culmination of this reflective discussion, I will now sketch out a position called "complementary egalitarianism" for those who view the creative-order logic of primogeniture as having a cultural-component status. Correspondingly, I will lay out what an "ultra-soft patriarchy" position might look like for those who view the creative-order logic of primogeniture as completely transcultural, but agree with some or all of the seven considerations just presented. In many respects, the application of 1 Timothy 2 is going to be very similar for both complementary egalitarians and ultra-soft patriarchalists. The only difference is whether there should be a dimension of *symbolic honor* granted to one gender over the other. Perhaps this will offer a forum for future ecclesiastical harmony.

Complementary egalitarianism
Complementary egalitarianism is an appropriate title for the form of egalitarian position developed within this book. On the one hand, it differs from secular egalitarianism in the sense that interdependence and mutual submission are the pursued values instead of extreme independence and autonomy. On the other hand, it differs from some forms of Christian egalitarianism in that it applauds the recognition of biological, psychological and social differences between males and females. Men and women can and should function in "complementary" ways. The component that complementary egalitarianism seeks to remove from the gender-differentiation equation is that of a power differential based solely upon gender and any role differentiation related to that power differential. Nevertheless, I would continue to argue for role distinction based upon biological differences between men and women. For instance, the most discernible differences between men and women (i.e., biological differences) should argue for a greater participation of women in the early stages of child rearing. This is not to discourage the involvement of men; it is simply to recognize, for example, the benefits of breast-feeding during early infant formation.

In other areas of psychological and social differences between men and women, the proportional contribution of nature and nurture cannot be clearly determined. So here we need to tread softly. We should acknowledge psychological and social differences, but not let them carve a definitive outline of distinctive gender roles. Only nature-based, not nurture-based, etiology makes a sufficient case for going any further. Even then, an interdependence model, rather than gender exclusion, may be a better way to handle the data. One might also caution against the use of gender differences in psychological and social studies for creating definitive roles, since there is often significant overlap between genders in these areas. Unlike biological differences that are universal, psychological/social differences between genders overlap considerably.[1] Both the unanswerable nature-nurture question and the mixed data from psychological and social findings suggest that attempts at role differentiation on such a basis are dubious at best.

Ultra-soft patriarchy

A redemptive-movement hermeneutic does not mean that one has to automatically nor necessarily adopt an egalitarian position. A redemptive-spirit approach clearly pushes that direction. But how one sorts out the cultural status of various components of the Genesis material, as discussed by Paul, will probably permit one in good conscience to "cross the line" or to "keep one step back from the line." For those who are convinced of a redemptive-movement hermeneutic, yet feel the data tip the scales in the direction of patriarchy, it is still a much-needed step to apply a redemptive strategy *within* a patriarchy framework.

In theory what one would be looking for, then, is a model that minimizes the liabilities of patriarchy as much as possible while keeping a measure of greater deference and honor. Given this blend of *redemptive spirit* and *retained patriarchy*, patriarchalists should be inclined to the possibilities of an ultra-soft patriarchy. This kind of patriarchy would accept the good value of equality even with much of its social and functional implications, but keep something of a special, symbolic honor for men in order to comply with that value as well.

At least in an analogous way, the creative-order argument by Paul reflects primogeniture customs that accentuate a kind of social-honor logic within that culture. If one sees primogeniture as transcultural, surely it still leaves open the question of whether the degree or weight of creative-order deference should be viewed as cultural. My reasons for questioning the weight given firstborn logic as it influences the sphere of patriarchy can be readily captured by reviewing criteria

---

[1]Virtually all women have wombs and breasts. By way of contrast, psychological gender testing produces mixed findings. Despite broad trends, some women are more rational/thinker types than some men, and some men are more relational/feeler types than some women. Also, current studies have shown that the percentages in these categories have shifted considerably over the years, indicating a major conditioning component not inherent to gender.

7, 11 and 18. These criteria surface much material that argues that at least the *weight* of biblical patriarchy is cultural, if not patriarchy itself. Also, the six other "what if" considerations in this chapter should significantly alter the application of 1 Timothy 2 even for those who wish to retain some form of patriarchy today.

So what might ultra-soft patriarchy look like? Well, an analogy might be the best way to start the wheels turning without prescribing my own concrete solutions. As an illustration I will draw upon the Old Testament inheritance laws, which honored the firstborn above the other siblings. Here we have an example of creative-order prominence. When speaking with several pastors, I asked how many of them had wills for their estates. They all did. Then I asked how many of them had designated a "double portion" of their inheritance for their firstborns, an implied scriptural practice based upon creative-order values. None of them had. As the discussion ensued, it became evident that a "blended approach" was possible—one that retained deference to the firstborn logic, while infusing the benefits of equality. Combining creative-order values along with the value of equality among siblings, a family might make the firstborn the executor of the will but have an equal distribution of the funds and property. It does not take much imagination to apply something of this blended model to the home and church. An equal power differential could be developed in the home and church (i.e., not restricting women in the decision-making process or from offices based solely upon gender), while at the same time granting men a certain level of *symbolic* honor for their firstborn status within the human family. I could list a dozen ways this symbolic honor could take shape and form without restricting the roles of women and without imposing a substantive power differential between genders. However, I will leave this creative brainstorming to my reader.

A Forum for Harmony
Complementary egalitarianism and ultra-soft patriarchy provide a forum for harmony and healing within the church. It is with this goal in mind that I have included these what-if-I-am-wrong reflections as my final chapter. I hope they will awaken a spirit of reconciliation between egalitarians and patriarchalists. Those patriarchalists who embrace a redemptive-spirit approach, along with other aspects of this seven-fold reflection (see points 1-7 above), should recognize the feasibility of movement within their position toward an ultra-soft patriarchy. From a practical and theological standpoint the "complementary egalitarian" position proposed in this book is very close to the position of "ultra-soft patriarchy with a redemptive-movement hermeneutic." These two positions, though they bear egalitarian and patriarchal within their labels, are much closer to one another than either is to the kind of patriarchy found in *Recovering Biblical Manhood and*

Womanhood.[2] Unfortunately, the patriarchy of Piper and Grudem's classic work is hindered by its use of a static hermeneutic for applying Scripture.[3] Patriarchalists who embrace a redemptive-movement hermeneutic and a number of the other sevenfold considerations have considerable room to move beyond the patriarchy advanced by Piper and Grudem.

---

[2]John Piper and Wayne Grudem, eds., *Recovering Biblical Manhood and Womanhood: A Response to Evangelical Feminism* (Wheaton, Ill.: Crossway, 1991).

[3]Cf. the static hermeneutic developed by Yarbrough and Brown in *Women in the Church: A Fresh Analysis of 1 Timothy 2:9-15,* ed. Andreas J. Köstenberger, Thomas R. Schreiner and H. Scott Baldwin (Grand Rapids, Mich.: Baker, 1995). Aside from the tender-tough thesis, the exegesis by Schreiner, Baldwin, Köstenberger, etc. is persuasive and will make a lasting contribution. On the other hand, the best that can be said about the hermeneutical chapters is that they do not match the quality of work found in the rest of the volume.

Conclusion

ARRIVING AT A BOTTOM LINE

A journey into the world of culture is a fascinating one. As mentioned at the outset, everything within Scripture is cultural in the sense that the Bible represents God's communication to human society through cultural forms. All communication takes on a cultural dimension. In this book, however, I am not simply interested in that broad sense of culture as human behavior expressed in social forms, customs, patterns, values, rituals, taboos, and so on. Rather, the book approaches culture as an aspect of the hermeneutical process. In this sense, then, I have attempted to distinguish between two features within the text: that which is "culturally confined" and that which is "transcultural." Here we are talking about the *application process* in hermeneutics and asking the questions of what aspects of the text we should continue to practice and what aspects we should discontinue or modify due to differences between cultures.

Beyond terminology issues, one key matter is utterly crucial to understanding cultural analysis. Some might get the impression that cultural analysis is more interested in listening to our modern culture than in listening to Scripture. I understand how this impression can develop, since cultural analysis requires interaction with our contemporary culture. However, this impression does not reflect reality. In fact, nothing could be further from the truth. Of course, I must thank our modern culture for raising the issues addressed in this book. But our culture only *raises* the issues for me; it does not *resolve* the issues. When it comes to cultural assessment, it matters little where our culture is on any of the issues discussed in this book! Scripture, rather than contemporary culture, always needs to set the course of our critical reflection.

Let me summarize my conclusions, then, in a way that places appropriate distance between them and our culture. If our modern culture were at some point in the future to accept slavery, it would not influence my conclusions to the slightest degree. I would still be an abolitionist. If our modern culture were to embrace an extremely strong form of patriarchy down the road, it would not change my thinking at all. I would still affirm either ultra-soft patriarchy or complementary egalitarianism (my own preference being for the latter). If our culture eventually accepts homosexual lifestyles with their complete and unreserved blessing, such a position would not alter my conclusions. I would still advocate a heterosexuality-only position as a Christian sexual ethic. I do not wish to encourage a callous attitude toward our culture. My point is simply that our modern culture must not determine the outcome of any cultural/transcultural analysis of Scripture.

Criteria for Cultural Analysis
Determining what should be assessed as cultural components within a biblical text in contrast to transculturally enduring aspects is no easy task. Some examples are widely accepted. For instance, most of the Western church no longer practices what Scripture says (at a nonabstracted, concrete level) about head coverings, holy kisses, foot washings, hairstyles, slavery, and so on. But we have not been particularly clear in explaining why we have discontinued certain practices yet continued others. The lack of explanation and consistency has often left thorny problems for the next generation of Christians. We pass on to them both the Scriptures themselves and our assessment of what to practice and what not to practice within those Scriptures, but without a clear guide as to how those decisions have been reached. This book attempts to provide a collection, in one volume, of the various criteria that can be used in cultural analysis. In order to make the process more objective, I have attempted to establish each criterion from neutral examples before moving to two of today's more debated topics—women and homosexuals.

In this respect, the book has been designed as a tool for the application process in hermeneutics. Although my focus has been primarily on slaves, women and homosexuals, the various criteria may be used as a grid to explore any aspect of Scripture where one might suspect or question the impact of culture. I have used this material in a hermeneutics course for several years. My students have utilized these criteria, along with a redemptive-movement hermeneutic, to explore the question of cultural assessment in a wide variety of issues, for example, war, clothing taboos, government, circumcision, alcohol, child rearing practices, dancing, transvestism, polygamy, church offices, reproductive technologies, capital punishment, Sabbath and animal rights. While not a complete or final grid for cultural analysis, this book should provide at least a starting point for solid discussion of these perplexing applicational problems. I have personally enjoyed much of what my students have written as they have applied this material to different issues. It is my hope that this book will function as a resource for exploring many other areas beyond the three major topics discussed in this work.

Slaves

Our analysis of the slavery texts has led to a fairly firm conclusion that the sociological structure of slavery along with much of the legislation related to slaves should be viewed as culturally relative. In many respects this perspective has become a given within the contemporary church of Western culture and is now almost a global Christian perspective. The way that the Bible deals with slaves, as well as numerous other topics, should convince us of the influence of culture on the formation of the text. Scripture does not present a "finalized ethic" in every area of human relationship. God challenges his covenant people to act redemptively in the area of slavery (e.g., release for Hebrew slaves every seventh year, provisions upon release, limitations on beatings, slave-free equality statements). The text takes us on a journey that clearly involves restoration of the society to which it was given. However, to stop where the Bible stops (with its isolated words) ultimately fails to reapply the redemptive spirit of the text as it spoke to the original audience. It fails to see that further reformation is possible and that further reformation must happen in order to fulfill the spirit-based component of meaning within the text's words.

While Scripture had a positive influence in its time, we should take that redemptive spirit and move to an even better, more fully-realized ethic today. When reading the slavery texts, the contemporary Christian should awaken to the dimensions of justice left unfulfilled in the past and in our present context. There are still aspects of the biblical scene that require further redemption (e.g., treatment of human beings as property, non-release of foreign slaves, the use of slaves for reproductive purposes, inequity in rape legislation for slaves). The abolition of slavery and its many related injustices should be a passionate value of modern Christians. Furthermore, the spirit of creating a more just work world, which lies *within* the slavery texts (not the isolated stipulations on the surface), is what should be carried forward into the modern workplace today. While frequently made in contemporary preaching, a one-to-one correspondence between the slave-master relationship and today's employee-employer (e.g., a submission framework) grossly distorts the application process. Such a practice forgets that the text should be brought forward from the original slavery situation. It ignores the new situation of a contractual framework for work relationships today and completely fails to reapply the most important component of the biblical text—its underlying spirit.

Women

Having completed a cultural analysis of the texts concerning women, it is reasonable to say that much of the portrait of patriarchy within Scripture contains culturally bound components and is not uniformly transcultural in nature. Through the writers of Scripture, God brought about significant improvement in the social situation of women relative to the original setting. But that improvement needs to continue today. While the biblical text spoke redemptively to its generation, we would not want to advocate much of the legislation we find in Scripture concerning women. Like the slavery issue, we need to reapply the spirit of the text and attempt to make things fairer and more equitable for women in our time. As I have argued, we need to reform the biblical legislation about women in many areas within Scripture (e.g., adultery, inheritance, rape, property concepts, virginity expectations, divorce, treatment of women in war). Our ethic needs to embrace the renewing spirit of the original text (in its social setting) and move to an even more equitable and just treatment of women today. Without a doubt, we should do whatever we can to de-marginalize women in our contemporary Western setting.

Such a perspective leaves little place for the ultra-strong patriarchy of days gone by. Yet, it still does not entirely answer the question of whether we should move to an ultra-soft patriarchy or further to an egalitarian position. When the various cultural criteria are applied to the women texts, the bulk of the data appear to favor an assessment of patriarchy as culturally relative. However, the outcome is not entirely conclusive. The signals within Scripture concerning creation patterns are somewhat mixed. On the one hand, the original creation material seems to retain at least implied echoes of patriarchy. On the other hand, egalitarian ideas appear to be embedded in second creation texts. Patriarchalists tend to minimize the egalitarian spirit of second creation texts, while egalitarians often ignore or dismiss the patriarchy of the original creation texts. Ultimately, both groups must prioritize one feature of Scripture over the other in order to establish their position.

Obviously there exists a crucial difference between slavery and patriarchy. The former is not found in the creation story, while the latter, perhaps in implicit ways, is. Those who support a patriarchal perspective for today make much of this point. The observation itself is a good one. Yet, there are several reasons why we should not be quick to use the original creation story in affirming patriarchy for today. First, the patriarchy in the pre-Fall material is at best implicit (embedded in quiet, background features of the narrative), not explicit disclosure. Patriarchy only becomes explicit after the Fall. Second, the patriarchal elements in the creation narrative in Genesis may tell us more about the audience to whom the story is being told than about the original event itself. The patriarchal aspects of the story may have been a way to accommodate the story to the patriarchy of the Exodus generation and beyond. Most Christians are familiar with this accommodation phenomenon in eschatology, where the projections of the future are often cast in terms that are understood to the present audience. Some of these projected-into-the-eschaton elements will not likely be part of a future reality (e.g., rebuilding the temple wall of partition between Jew and Gentile that Christ has previously torn down). Perhaps this kind of audience accommodation found in eschatology is also a part of biblical protology. Third, if the patriarchal elements of the story were a part of the original event and intended for the benefit of the first generation of human beings, it does not necessarily follow that we should practice them today. There are a number of aspects of the original story that the Christian community no longer practices (at the nonabstracted level), for they contain cultural components within them. Thus the inclusion of something in the creation story does not automatically make it transcultural, as some would suggest. Fourth, the rationale for implicit patriarchy in the Genesis story may have been closely tied to the agricultural setting to which the account is directed. If this is so, then such a rationale fails to carry over to us today. Fifth, it appears that Paul's argumentation in 1 Timothy 2 is based upon two underlying assumptions which themselves contain significant cultural components: (1) the assumption of primogeniture customs for establishing honor (2:13) and (2) the assumption that women are more easily deceived than men (2:14). Perhaps women should be permitted to teach in cultures where these underlying assumptions no longer apply in quite the same way. Once the cultural component within these verses is identified, one must move up the ladder of abstraction (see criterion 7, 17 and 18.C.3) and reapply the transcultural principles contained within these texts. The underlying principles that carry ongoing transcultural application today needs to be directed toward both genders, not simply women, in the selection of teaching leadership within a congregation: choose leaders and teachers who are worthy of high honor within the congregation (2:13) and choose leaders and teachers who are not easily deceived (2:14). The church will be forever strengthened through the enduring application of the text in this manner. Finally, the second-creation material in the New Testament, as mentioned above, appears to displace or supersede the patriarchy found in the first-creation story.

Given the ambiguity of the creation material in terms of its ongoing applicability, we would do well to exercise charity toward those who read that data differently (i.e., toward both those who wish to retain some modified application of patriarchy in an ultra-soft form and those who wish to embrace an egalitarian framework). Similar to eschatological issues where the biblical evidence is not entirely clear, the Christian community needs to maintain a healthy respect for divergence of perspective. To do otherwise embraces a kind of interpretive arrogance not becoming of Christ's kingdom. *Nonetheless, what should be clear is that a redemptive-movement hermeneutic beckons for change.* Those Christians who wish to retain some form of patriarchy should strive to make the patriarchy of tomorrow more just and equitable than the patriarchy of today and certainly much improved from the patriarchy of the biblical text. In this respect I encourage my reader toward either a "complementary egalitarian" approach or an "ultra-soft patriarchy" approach (see chapter eight). While my own preference is be the former, I recognize that the latter as a significant possibility. Both positions embrace a redemptive-movement hermeneutic while living with interpretive humility between now and the eschaton.

Homosexuals

Analyzing the homosexuality texts with the canons of cultural analysis has been an enlightening task. While some Christians advocate covenant/equal-status homosexuality as an appropriate expression for human relationships today, the results of this study would argue against such a position. The same canons of cultural analysis, which show a liberalizing or less restrictive tendency in the slavery and women texts relative to the original culture, demonstrate a more restrictive tendency in homosexuality texts relative to the original culture. Furthermore, the biblical texts not only hold an aversion to associative features (e.g., rape, pederasty), they appear to voice a concern about the more basic or core issue of same-gender sexual acts themselves (i.e., male with male; female with female). Once this factor is paired with finding a more restrictive movement within Scripture compared to the surrounding cultures, the covenant homosexual argument fails to be persuasive. Virtually all of the criteria applicable to the issue suggest to varying degrees that the biblical prohibitions regarding homosexuality, even within a covenant form, should be maintained today. There is no significant dissonance within the biblical data.

A comparison of homosexuality with other sexual-intercourse prohibitions in Scripture reveals that the lack of covenant or the lack of equal-partner status is simply not a substantive issue. The core issue in the Leviticus code appears to be one of appropriate sexual boundaries. For example, the incest laws are primarily arranged around crossing the boundary of parent and child. Similarly, the bestiality laws are interested in setting sexual boundaries between humans and animals. Along these structural lines, the homosexual prohibitions celebrate the good value of intercourse between male and female, yet disallow intercourse between members of the same sex. In all three cases, then, the biblical author's concern is rooted in maintaining sexual boundaries—between humans and animals, between parents and children, as well as between same-sex participants. I must applaud recent studies that have shown unequal-status and active/passive aspects to be a culturally sustained component of an ancient world portrait of homosexuality.[1] But interjecting equal-status or covenant into the equation fails to sidestep the problem. It amounts to a highly reductionistic reading of the biblical texts. The deepest issue for the biblical authors was the breaking of sexual boundaries between male and female. Until God redesigns the physical/sexual construction of male and female, this distinction or boundary continues to influence our contemporary world. While a greater understanding of nonvolitional components—biological and environmental—confirms the need for an appropriately nuanced approach (scaled culpability), it hardly overturns the physiological facts of being male or female and does not alter the grounds for ethical reasoning about right relationship between persons who remain male and female under God's creative and recreative purposes.

The cultural environment and Israel's theocratic setting may have influenced the severity of the Old Testament penal code, which called for the death penalty for homosexual behavior. Yet, the inherent *negative assessment* of homosexual activity itself retains a transcultural dimension. Thus, at least this prohibitive aspect of the homosexuality texts should be viewed as transcultural and applied as such within the Christian community today. Although it is not a popular stance today, only by retaining heterosexuality as normative and homosexuality as aberrant do we perpetuate the redemptive spirit of that text, as it was invoked in the original setting. We need to journey with the redemptive spirit of the text and always move in a direction toward which the whole of Scripture taken together points.

Nevertheless, our continued negative assessment of homosexuality today should take into consideration several differences between the original setting back then and the contemporary setting today. One significant difference is the present move toward covenant homosexuality. The stigma of homosexuality in the Bible was often increased beyond the stigma associated with the same-sex act

---

[1]E.g., Martti Nissinen, *Homoeroticism in the Biblical World: A Historical Perspective* (Philadelphia: Fortress, 1998).

itself due to associative events sometimes related to homosexual activity (e.g., pederasty, rape, multiple partners, lust, pagan idolatry). While continuing a negative assessment of homosexuality today, even of its least offensive form, the Christian community should reserve its greatest denouncement for the vilest forms of homosexual activity. A second cultural difference is the increased awareness today of various environmental and biological influences in shaping sexual preference. While these influences should not overturn a negative assessment of same-sex relationships, they should clearly give us a greater degree of compassion for those who struggle with homosexual feelings and behavior. The journey to a heterosexual or an abstinence lifestyle may be a very difficult one. These influences also introduce a sliding scale of culpability—a standard feature of other areas of biblical ethics—since volitional questions enter the equation. Only God knows the volitional configuration for each individual person. Finally, the heterosexual hypocrisy of the church in the Western world at times appears to be even more pronounced than the original setting. It appears that adultery, pornography and other aberrant forms of heterosexuality plague the Western church in epidemic proportions. This difference between two worlds surely influences our application of the homosexuality texts. The Christian community, while *talking* about upholding high ethical standards regarding homosexual activity, is *failing* to live out its ethical standards with regard to heterosexual activity. Until the church starts truly living out its heterosexual ethic, we undermine anything we have to say to the homosexual community about its sexual ethic.

Comparing Case Studies: Women's Issue versus Homosexual Issue

If the proposed cultural assessment has validity, then this study has significant comparative value. The comparative outcome is this: *the homosexual texts are in a different category than the women and slavery texts.* The former are almost entirely transcultural in nature, while the latter are heavily bound by culture. One of the strengths of this book's parallel case study approach is that it brings into clearer focus issues that people often confuse and blur together. Provided the findings are sound, they should expose the fallacy of some popular misconceptions. For example, some patriarchalists are worried that openness on the women's issue will lead to acceptance of homosexuality. This claim forms a knee-jerk responsive echo to homosexual advocates who say that the cultural dimension of the women and slavery texts should lead to the acceptance of homosexuality. If this work has demonstrated anything, however, it has shown the fundamental difference between the women's issue and the homosexuality issue. Regardless of perspective, it is necessary to ask the obvious question, "If we are able to take slavery and women texts as culturally bound (within much of their non-abstracted formulation), then why not the homosexuality texts?" This book provides the "why not" to that question.

Furthermore, the dialogue between issues adds a much-needed corrective to the current debate over the women's issue. Some patriarchalists, for example, applaud patriarchy as a means of distinction between genders. They mourn the loss of patriarchy today, since it undermines the Christian value of gender distinction. To a large extent, they are right. Even Christian egalitarians should affirm the positive benefit of gender distinction within patriarchal arguments. Our discussion of Deuteronomy's transvestite text shows how it functions as an external-ritual counterpart to the homosexuality texts. Both the homosexuality texts and the transvestite text are concerned about the social boundaries of gender. Both celebrate gender differences. So it is understandable why many Christians (whether patriarchal or egalitarian) sense a loss over today's softening or removal of patriarchy. A biblical perspective on gender calls for "men to be men" and "women to be women." Gender distinction needs to be celebrated as a transcultural value within the Christian community. As shocking as it might sound to some patriarchalists, egalitarians need to be complementarians too—in the sense of affirming gender differences and cooperative roles based on those differences.

Yet, our theological reflection must go a little further. It is one thing if a good value sustains gender differentiation; it is quite another if gender distinction is propped up by a damaging or faulty value. Without talking about the touchy topic of hierarchy, this problem may be illustrated through the related matter of male ownership of females. Scripture often views women as the property of the male (see discussion under the women texts). Such an ownership framework sustained the good value of gender distinction, but it did so at too high a price. Both egalitarians and patriarchalists should denounce an ownership framework between the male and female today; it falls far short of an ultimate redemptive ethic. Other areas should also be acknowledged as less-than-ideal ways of celebrating a distinction between men and women (e.g., the biblical perspective and legislation on adultery, inheritance, rape, virginity expectations, divorce). The inequities in these areas also sustained the good value of gender distinction, but better ways of sustaining that distinction should be sought and implemented today.

A Hermeneutic of Cultural Analysis

In order to account for the impact of culture upon the formation of Scripture, we must embrace a *redemptive-movement hermeneutic*. Without this interpretive framework we fail to answer the criticisms of those who rightfully find abhorrent things within the sacred text. If a static or completely-realized hermeneutic is adopted, the criticisms of secular ethicists go unanswered, for they are quick to point out the pitfalls in biblical legislation. Without the kind of hermeneutic proposed in this book our evangelistic efforts are muffled if not completely muted. We have no answer for the seeker who struggles with certain unsightly portraits within the pages of the Bible.

In addition to harming evangelistic efforts, we do irreparable damage within our community of faith without a redemptive-movement hermeneutic. We set up unnecessary roadblocks to retaining one's faith. We place in the path of a new inquisitive generation stumbling blocks to believing in the inspiration of Scripture. Many evangelical Christians would struggle with seeing a "top down" dimension to Scripture if this kind of redemptive-movement hermeneutic were not part of their pilgrimage and understanding. Cultural assessment is an essential component if we are to adequately account for the less-than-ultimate ethic of Scripture. Yet, as emphasized in this work, the issue is one of perspective. It is *not* as some critics have said, that Scripture is sexist or repressive regarding slaves and women. That is to talk about Scripture in a vacuum, devoid of its original social context or cultural backdrop. Such is an anachronistic reading of the text! Relative to when and where the words of Scripture were first read, they spoke redemptively to their given communities. Yet, to stay with the isolated words of the text—the words understood apart from cultural and canonical movement—leads to an equally tragic misreading. It looses a sense of their underlying spirit. It mutes the component of meaning through which the biblical words continue to speak with transforming power, as they did in the original setting, to the question of application for the modern world. It keeps us from experiencing the very heart of Scripture within our generation.

Some suggest that the kind of redemptive-movement hermeneutic proposed in this book is nothing more than self-congratulatory Western thinking. They argue that a redemptive-movement hermeneutic is produced from the prideful and subjective introspection of Western Christianity. Some of their concern is well founded. I would not want to see the diversity of Christianity around the world replaced by a monolithic Western package. Nevertheless, much of their perspective succumbs to false humility. While determining what exactly a better ethic would look like is not always easy, that should hardly dissuade us from pursuing such a goal. At most, it should cause us to be humble in our conclusions for a particular area. Also, the alternative (a static hermeneutic) actually does work from an assumption of relative betters, especially when the playing field is already constructed for those using a static hermeneutic within the text. Those who use the static approach are reluctant to examine our contemporary landscape and ask the hard questions. For example, they are afraid to ask, Where does the ethic of our contemporary setting *surpass* Scripture's unrealized ethic, as seen in the isolated words on its pages (i.e., where the ethic of the contemporary setting *goes beyond* Scripture's unrealized ethic)? The static alternative ultimately leads to a hollow or empty fulfillment of Scripture within our generation, for it leaves behind the spirit of the text. It produces a generation of gridlocked Christians.

So why would God adopt a partially realized ethic in the formation of Scripture? I have suggested that God utilized this kind of redemptive-movement strategy for several reasons. *Pastoral:* to "stretch" the covenant people as far as they could go (like an elastic band), but not wanting them to "snap." Change is always difficult. God brings his people along in ways that were feasible adaptations. *Pedagogical:* to take people from where they are (the known) and help them move to a foreseeable future (the unknown) that has enough continuity with the present so that they can find their way into the preferred future. *Evangelistic:* to make the Christian lifestyle evangelistically winsome to unbelievers. The reform was enough to better existing sociological structures, but not so radical that it would jeopardize other aspects of Christian mission or overtly threaten governmental structures. *Competing values:* to sustain other good values at least temporarily within a less redemptive framework. For example, slavery functioned as something of a social welfare net; male ownership of females helped support the good value of gender differentiation. Gender differentiation and helping the poor are good things. However, a redemptive-movement hermeneutic argues that these good values need to be sustained through a non-embedded framework if at all possible. *Soteriological:* to deal with humanity's sinful and stubborn condition. Reform does not come easily to a dark side within fallen humanity. God's revelation took measured steps (not unrealistic leaps) in the progressive sanctification of social structures.

I hope that the hermeneutic proposed in this book will bring a dimension of reconciliation between egalitarians and patriarchalists. Those patriarchalists who embrace a redemptive-movement approach should recognize the feasibility of movement within their position toward an ultra-soft patriarchy (see chapter eight). From a practical and theological standpoint the "complementary egalitarian" position proposed in this book is very close to the position of "ultra-soft patriarchy with a redemptive-movement hermeneutic." Interestingly enough, these two positions, though they bear egalitarian and patriarchal within their labels, are much closer to one another than either is to the kind of patriarchy found in *Recovering Biblical Manhood and Womanhood*.[2] Unfortunately, the patriarchy of Piper and Grudem's classic work is hindered by its use of a

---

[2] John Piper and Wayne Grudem, eds., *Recovering Biblical Manhood and Womanhood: A Response to Evangelical Feminism* (Wheaton, Ill.: Crossway, 1991).

static hermeneutic for applying Scripture.[3] Patriarchalists who endorse a redemptive-movement hermeneutic have considerable room to move beyond the patriarchy advanced by Piper and Grudem.

In sum, the case studies developed in this book support a redemptive-movement hermeneutic. If the original readers of Scripture lived out its isolated words, by virtue of their cultural context, they lived out the redemptive spirit of the text for that generation. For us, however, it is a different story. For us the redemptive spirit does not always come automatically because the applicational context has changed. We must journey beyond any surface-level appropriation to an application of the text that captures its meaning in cultural and canonical context—an application that honors its underlying spirit. Our task is not to lock into an ethic that has been frozen in time, but to pursue an ultimate ethic, one reflected in the redemptive spirit of Scripture. As a community born to the twenty-first century, we must not be limited to a mere enactment of the text's isolated words.[4] It is our sacred calling to champion its spirit.

---

[3]Likewise, the static hermeneutic developed by Yarbrough and Brown in *Women in the Church: A Fresh Analysis of 1 Timothy 2:9-15* (ed. Andreas J. Köstenberger, Thomas R. Schreiner and H. Scott Baldwin [Grand Rapids, Mich.: Baker, 1995]) is entirely unconvincing. On the other hand (with the exception of the tough-tender thesis), the exegetical chapters by Köstenberger, Schreiner and Baldwin make a persuasive and lasting contribution.
[4]While it should be fairly clear in this sentence, the expression "isolated words" refers to "words understood *in isolation* from their cultural-movement and canonical-movement context." For further discussion, see chapter two.

Appendix A

MAN CREATED FIRST &
PRIMOGENITURE ASSUMPTIONS
The Traditional Interpretation of
1 Timothy 2:13

John Chrysostom (347-407): "What has this to do with women of the present day? *It shows that the male sex enjoyed the higher honor. Man was first formed; and elsewhere he shows their superiority.*[1] 'Neither was the man created for the woman, but the woman for the man.' (I Cor. Xi. 9.) Why then does he say this? He wishes *the man to have the preeminence* in every way; both for the reason above [i.e., Adam first formed], he means let him have precedence, and on account of what occurred afterwards."[2]

Augustine (354-430): "Now, if the woman was not made for the man to be his helper in begetting children, in what was she to help him? She was not to till the earth with him, for there was not yet any toil to make help necessary. If there were any such need, a male helper would be better, and the same could be said of the comfort of another's presence if Adam were perhaps weary of solitude. How much more agreeably could two male friends, rather than a man and woman, en-

---

[1] All bracketed explanatory comments and italics are mine.
[2] John Chrysostom, "Homilies on Timothy (Homilies 8-9)," in *A Select Library of the Nicene and Post-Nicene Fathers of the Christian Church, First Series*, ed. Phillip Schaff (1886-1890; reprint, Grand Rapids, Mich.: Eerdmans, 1976), 13:435.

joy companionship and conversation in a life shared together. And if they had to make an arrangement in their common life *for one to command and the other to obey in order to make sure that opposing wills would not disrupt the peace of the household, there would have been proper rank to assure this, since one would be created first and the other second,* and this would be further reinforced if the second were made from the first, as was the case with the woman."[3]

Erasmus (1466-1536): "As it is the responsibility of the mind to rule, of the body to obey, so a wife ought to hang on her husband's nod. Why do we reverse divine order? *Adam was created first; Eve was then created for his sake.* Why should impudence put second what God wanted to be first?"[4]

Martin Luther (1483-1546): "God himself has so ordained that man be created first—first in time and first in authority. His first place is preserved in the Law. Whatever occurs first is called the most preferable. *Because of God's work, Adam is approved as superior to Eve, because he had the right of primogeniture.*"[5]

John Calvin (1509-1564): "He accordingly shows that, although mankind had stood in their first and original uprightness, the true order of nature, which proceeded from the command of God, bears that women shall be subject. . . . *Yet the reason which Paul assigns, that woman was second in the order of creation, appears not to be a very strong argument in favor of her subjection*; for John the Baptist was before Christ in the order of time, and yet was greatly inferior in rank. But although Paul does not state all the circumstances which are related by Moses, yet he intended that his readers should take them into consideration. Now Moses shows that the woman was created afterwards, in order that she might be a kind of appendage to the man; and that she was joined to the man on the express condition, that she should be at hand to render obedience to him. (Gen. ii. 21.) Since, therefore, God did not create two chiefs of equal power, but added to the man an inferior aid, the Apostle justly reminds us of that order of creation in which the eternal and inviolable appointment of God is strikingly displayed."[6]

---

[3] Augustine, *The Literal Meaning of Genesis,* vol. 2, trans. John Hammond Taylor, in *Ancient Christian Writers,* ed. Johannes Quasten, Walter J. Burghardt and Thomas C. Lawler (New York: Newman, 1982), 42:75.

[4] Erasmus, "Paraphrases on the Epistles to Timothy, Titus, and Philemon," trans. John J. Bateman, in *Collected Works of Erasmus,* vol. 44, ed. R. D. Sider (Toronto: University of Toronto Press, 1993), p. 17.

[5] Luther, "Lectures on 1 Timothy," in *Luther's Works,* vol. 28, ed. Hilton C. Oswald (St. Louis: Concordia, 1973), p. 278.

[6] John Calvin, "The First Epistle to Timothy," in *Calvin's Commentaries* (reprint, Grand Rapids, Mich.: Baker, 1981), 21:68-69.

Thomas Gataker (1574-1654): "The man was first created . . . and *therefore the man has the birthright* (1 Tim 2:13)."[7]

Johann Albrecht Bengel (1687-1752): "The reason which applies to the first man, holds good for all men; and that which applies to Eve, holds good for all women. Again, what is said of the salvability [safety] of the woman, ver. 15, is also appropriate to be understood of the first woman . . . *first; so that the woman was created for him,* 1 Cor. xi. 8. 9."[8]

John Gill (1697-1771): "All this while Eve was not as yet formed, but after this, then Eve. She was formed out of him, was made out of one of his ribs; and was formed for him, for his use, service, help, and comfort; and here lies the strength of the apostle's reason, why the woman should be in subjection to the man: *not so much because he was made before her: for so were the beasts of the field before Adam; and yet this gave them no superiority to him*; but because she was made out of him, and made for him. See 1 Cor. xi. 8, 9."[9]

John Wesley (1703-1791): " 'First'—*So that woman was originally the inferior* [in rank or status]. She was inferior too in bodily strength."[10]

Patrick Fairbairn (1805-1874): "For Adam was first formed . . . then Eve; *the precedence in time implying superiority in place and power.* The relation in this respect is still more strongly marked in the Epistle to the Corinthians: 'For the man is not of the woman, but the woman of the man; for also the man was not made for the sake of the woman, but the woman for the sake of the man.' Thus did God in the method of creation give clear testimony to the headship of man— to his right, and also his obligation, to hold directly to God, and stand under law only to Him; while woman, being formed for his helpmate and partner, stands under law to her husband, and is called to act for God in him."[11]

C. J. Ellicott (1819-1905): "*The argument from priority of creation . . . requires the subsidiary statement in 1 Cor. xi. 9.*"[12]

Henry P. Liddon (1829-1890): "Adam was first formed; then Eve. *This prior-*

---

[7]Thomas Gataker, *Certaine Sermons* (London: n.p., 1635), 2:188-89.

[8]Johann Albrecht Bengel, "On the First Epistle to Timothy," in *Gnomon of the New Testament,* vol. 4, ed. Andrew R. Fausset, trans. James Bryce (1759; reprint, Edinburgh: T & T Clark, 1860), pp. 253-54.

[9]John Gill, "1 Timothy," in *Gill's Commentary,* vol. 6 (1854; reprint, Grand Rapids, Mich.: Baker, 1980), p. 600.

[10]John Wesley, *The New Testament with Explanatory Notes* (Wakefield, U.K.: William Nicholson & Sons, n.d.), p. 523.

[11]Patrick Fairbairn, *Commentary on the Pastoral Epistles* (1874; reprint, Grand Rapids, Mich.: Zondervan, 1956), p. 128.

[12]C. J. Ellicott, "1 Timothy," in *Ellicott's Commentaries, Critical and Grammatical, on the Epistles of Saint Paul* (1879; reprint, Buffalo, N.Y.: William S. Hein, 1986), 2:53.

ity in creation implies a certain superiority (ver. 13)."[13]

Newport J. D. White: *"The elder should rule.* A more profound statement of this fact is found in I Cor. xi 9."[14]

Burton S. Easton: *"The preeminence of the first-born was axiomatic."*[15]

E. K. Simpson: "Paul reinforces his decision by two arguments drawn from the sacred oracles, to him, as to his Master, a final court of appeal. *One consists in the priority of Adam's creation, consummated by an help-meet.* . . . The independent creation of Adam and the ancillary conformation of Eve typified their prospective offices in the mundane economy, offices not competitive, but concordant and counterpart."[16]

Donald Guthrie: "In 1 Cor. xi. 9, Paul had already made use of the argument that *the priority of man's creation places him in the position of superiority over woman*, the assumption being that the original creation, with the Creator's own imprimatur upon it, must set a precedent for determining the true order of the sexes."[17]

J. N. D. Kelly: "Paul advances two arguments in support of his ban. The first is that Adam was created first, and then Eve. In other words, *what is chronologically prior is taken to be in some sense superior.* He had made the same point in I Cor. xi. 8, pointing out that 'man did not come originally from woman, but woman from man', and deducing from it her dependence on the male."[18]

Pierre Dornier: "Notice the priority of the man over the woman: it was the man who was created first. *Within the framework of Jewish thinking, chronological priority is also at the same time a priority of status. 'First produced' conveys not only the idea of formed first, but of better/superior and favored. The first is not only the first to be born, but the one who receives the greater honor among siblings, the one other brothers and sisters give respect and obedience to.* Similarly, the woman, coming after the man, grants him deference and submission."[19]

Stephen B. Clark: "Man is created first. . . . *He is the 'first-born' and hence would have a natural precedence by birth.*"[20]

George W. Knight III: "So it is not mere chronology ('first . . . then') that

---

[13]Henry Liddon, *Explanatory Analysis of St. Paul's First Epistle to Timothy* (1897; reprint, Minneapolis: Klock & Klock, 1978), p. 19.

[14]Newport J. D. White, "The First and Second Epistles to Timothy," in *The Expositor's Greek Testament*, ed. W. Robertson Nicoll (1897-1910; reprint, Grand Rapids, Mich.: Eerdmans, 1979), 4:109.

[15]Burton S. Easton, *The Pastoral Epistles* (New York: Charles Scribner's Sons, 1947), p. 124.

[16]E. K. Simpson, *The Pastoral Epistles* (London: Tyndale Press, 1954), p. 47.

[17]Donald Guthrie, *The Pastoral Epistles* (Grand Rapids, Mich.: Eerdmans, 1957), p. 77.

[18]J. N. D. Kelly, *A Commentary on the Pastoral Epistles* (London: A&C Black, 1963; reprint, Grand Rapids, Mich.: Baker, 1981), p. 68.

[19]Pierre Dornier, *Les Épitres Pastorales* (Paris: Lecoffre, 1969), pp. 55-56. Translation mine.

[20]Stephen B. Clark, *Man and Woman in Christ* (Ann Arbor, Mich.: Servant, 1980), p. 25.

Paul appeals to here but *what is entailed in this chronology. That drawing such implications from chronological priority is not foreign to the OT is seen from the similar, but different, appeals to the rights of primogeniture."*[21]

Thomas D. Lea and Hayne P. Griffin Jr.: "The chronological priority of Adam becomes the support of Paul's command that the women were to show a spirit of attentiveness to learning and were to avoid an attempt at domineering men. In 1 Cor 11:8 Paul had inferred the dependence of Eve from the chronological priority of Adam. . . . *The designation of Adam as "formed first" reflects the Jewish practice of primogeniture, where the firstborn male inherited a double portion of the inheritance and the responsibility of leadership in the home and in worship (Deut 21:15-17). Paul's point was that Adam's status as the oldest carried with it the leadership role suitable for the firstborn son.* Paul transferred this quality of leadership role in the congregation to the male."[22]

J. M. Bassler: "Two biblical warrants are provided for these injunctions, both derived from Genesis. The first refers to the sequence of creation that is described in Genesis 2 and *rests on the widespread assumption that the first born (here the "first formed") has superior status and rightful authority over younger siblings."*[23]

Summary

Throughout church history many expositors have seen the logic of 1 Timothy 2:13 as rooted in primogeniture or similar logic. Some express the underlying assumption of Paul's reasoning in a most explicit and direct fashion, using terms such as *firstborn, birthright* or *primogeniture* (Luther, Gataker, Easton, Dornier, Clark, Knight and many others).[24] Without using the actual words *firstborn* or *primogeniture,* some are clearly referring to the practice and idea (e.g., White, Dornier).

A number of commentators use language that appears to imply firstborn rights, such as "the male enjoys the higher honor" or "proper rank" (e.g., Chrysostom, Augustine). Some commentators struggle with its logic and thus appeal to the corollary text of 1 Corinthians 11:8-9 (Calvin, Ellicott). Even this appeal may be connected with primogeniture.[25] Those who simply say that "first means superior" (e.g., Wesley, Liddon, Fairbairn, Kelly) may well have a primogeniture

---

[21]George W. Knight III, *The Pastoral Epistles* (Grand Rapids, Mich.: Eerdmans, 1992), p. 143.

[22]Thomas D. Lea and Hayne P. Griffin Jr., *1, 2 Timothy, Titus* (Nashville: Broadman, 1992), p. 101.

[23]J. M. Bassler, *1 Timothy, 2 Timothy, Titus* (Nashville: Abingdon, 1996), p. 60.

[24]See criterion 7.B for citations by today's leading patriarchalists who view the logic of 1 Timothy 2:13 as based on firstborn rights (e.g., Hurley, Piper and Grudem, Blomberg, and Schreiner). Cf. P. C. Spicq, *Les Épitres Pastorales* (Paris: Lecoffre, 1947), p. 70.

[25]See Blomberg's comments on 1 Corinthians 11:8-9 (*1 Corinthians,* NIVAC [Grand Rapids, Mich.: Zondervan, 1994], p. 216) in criterion 7.B.

framework in mind. However, in such cases one cannot be certain. For most of church history verse 14 was viewed as the more substantial of Paul's two arguments in 1 Timothy 2:13-14. Only in more recent discussions have patriarchalists viewed 2:13 as the more compelling argument.

Appendix B

WOMEN AS MORE EASILY DECEIVED THAN MEN

The Traditional Interpretation of 1 Timothy 2:14

Didymus the Blind (313-398): "Being strong [i.e., stronger than the woman who was weak under Satan's deception], *the man is more able than the woman to fight and defend himself against the trickery of the adversary*;[1] he would not (and will not) let himself be drawn into seduction like Eve did."[2]

John Chrysostom (347-407): "For thus they will show submission by their silence. For the sex is *naturally somewhat talkative*: and for this reason he restrains them on all sides."[3]

"The woman [Eve] taught once, and ruined all. On this account therefore he saith, let her not teach. But what is it to other women, that she suffered this? It certainly concerns them; for *the sex is weak and fickle*, and he is speaking of the sex collectively."[4]

---

[1]All italics within this appendix have been added for emphasis.
[2]Didyme L'Aveugle, "Sur La Genèse," ed. Pierre Nautin, in *Sources Chrétiennes* (Paris: Les Éditions du Cerf, 1976), 233:234-35 [§ 100.2]. Translation mine.
[3]John Chrysostom, "Homilies on Timothy (Homilies 8-9)," in *A Select Library of the Nicene and Post-Nicene Fathers of the Christian Church*, 1st series, ed. Phillip Schaff (1886-1890; reprint, Grand Rapids, Mich.: Eerdmans, 1976), 13:435.
[4]Ibid., 13:436.

Augustine (354-430): "And [Satan] first tried his deceit upon the woman, making his assault upon *the weaker part of that human alliance*, that he might gradually gain the whole, and *not supposing that the man would readily give ear to him, or be deceived*, but that he might yield to the error of the woman. . . . For not without significance did the apostle say, 'And Adam was not deceived, but the woman being deceived was in the transgression.' "[5]

Epiphanius (365-403): "*The female sex is easily mistaken, fallible, and poor in intelligence.* It is apparent that through women the devil has vomited this forth. As previously the teaching associated with Quintilla, Maximilla, and Priscilla was utterly ridiculous, so also is this one. . . . Come now, servants of God, let us put on a *manly mind* and disperse the mania of these women. The whole of this deception is female; the disease comes from Eve who was long ago deceived."[6]

Humbert de Romans (1194-1277): "In connection with the preacher's person, we should notice that he must be of male sex. 'I do not permit a woman to teach' (1 Tim. 2:12). There are four reasons for this: first, *lack of understanding, because a man is more likely to have understanding than a woman*."[7]

Bonaventure (1217-1274): "The devil, envious of man, assumed the form of a serpent and addressed the woman. . . . By this temptation, he sought to bring about the fall of *the weaker woman, so that through her he might then overthrow the stronger sex*. . . . But it was by the devil's own cunning that he approached the woman first. It is easier to overcome the weak. A clever enemy always attacks a stronghold at its weakest point."[8]

Thomas Aquinas (1225-1274): "The human group would have lacked the benefit of order had some of its members not been governed by others *who were wiser*. Such is the subjection in which woman is by nature subordinate to man, because *the power of rational discernment is by nature stronger in man*."[9]

"St. Paul says 'that women should keep silence in the Churches', and, 'I per-

---

[5]Augustine, "City of God," in *A Select Library of the Nicene and Post-Nicene Fathers of the Christian Church*, 1st series, ed. Phillip Schaff (1886; reprint, Grand Rapids, Mich.: Eerdmans, 1977), 2:272.

[6]Epiphanius, *Medicine Box 79*, in *Maenads, Martyrs, Matrons, Monastics: A Sourcebook on Women's Religions in the Greco-Roman World*, ed. Ross S. Kraemer (Philadelphia: Fortress, 1988), p. 51.

[7]Humbert de Romans, "Treatise on the Formation of Preachers," in *Early Dominicans: Selected Writings*, ed. Simon Tugwell (New York: Paulist, 1982), p. 223.

[8]Bonaventure, *The Breviloquium*, trans. José de Vinck, in *The Works of Bonaventure* (Paterson, N.J.: St. Anthony Guild, 1963), 2:112-13. From his broader discussion Bonaventure assumes that the greater areas of Eve's "weakness" pertain to her volition, emotions and intellect (pp. 112-17). His thinking appears to accommodate 1 Timothy 2:14 (p. 116).

[9]Thomas Aquinas, *Man Made to God's Image*, trans. Edmund Hill, in *Summa Theologica*, ed. Thomas Gilby and T. C. Gilby (New York: McGraw Hill, 1963-1974), 13:37-39. Although this is not a direct comment on 1 Timothy 2:14, it is found in the context of a discussion on the nature of Eve.

mit no woman to teach or to have authority over men.' [1 Tim. 2:12] But this especially touches the grace of speech. Accordingly that grace [speaking publicly
to the whole church] does not pertain to women . . . because generally speaking
women are not perfected in wisdom so as to be fit to be entrusted with public
teaching."[10]

Erasmus (1466-1536): "Eve was deceived first when, believing the serpent
and beguiled by the enticement of the fruit, she disregarded God's command.
The man *could not* have been taken in either by the serpent's promises or by
the allure of the fruit; only love for his wife drew him into a ruinous compliance."[11]

Martin Luther (1483-1546): "Paul thus has proved that by divine and human
right Adam is the master of the woman. That is, it was not Adam who went
astray. Therefore, there was *greater wisdom in Adam than in the woman.* Where
this occurs, there is the greater authority. . . . He [Adam] persevered in his dominion over the serpent, which did not attack him but rather attacked *the weaker ves-
sel . . .* just as he does today."[12]

John Knox (1514-1572): "And first, where that I affirm the empire of a
woman to be a thing repugnant to nature, I mean not only that God by the order
of his creation has spoiled woman of authority and dominion, but also that man
has seen, proved and pronounced just causes why that it so should be. . . . *For
who can deny but it is repugnant to nature, that the blind shall be appointed to
lead and conduct such as do see? That the weak, the sick, and impotent persons
shall nourish and keep the whole and strong, and finally, that the foolish, mad
and frantic shall govern the discrete, and give counsel to such as be sober of
mind? And such be all women, compared to man in bearing of authority. . . .* I expect such as God by singular privilege, and for certain causes known only to himself, has exempted from the common rank of women, and speaks of women as
nature and experience do this day declare them. *Nature I say, does paint them further to be weak, frail, impatient, feeble and foolish: and experience has declared
them to be inconstant, variable, cruel and lacking the spirit of counsel and regiment.* And these notable faults have men in all ages espied in that kind, for which
not only they have removed women from rule and authority, but also some have

---

[10]St. Thomas Aquinas, *Prophecy and Other Charisms*, trans. Roland Potter, in *Summa Theologica,*
   45:133. For similar statements, though not specifically linked to 1 Timothy 2:14, see Thomas
   Aquinas, *Well Tempered Passion*, trans. Thomas Gilby, in *Summa Theologica*, 44:21.
[11]Erasmus, "Paraphrases on the Epistles to Timothy, Titus, and Philemon," trans. John J. Bateman, in
   Collected Works of Erasmus, ed. R. D. Sider (Toronto: University of Toronto Press, 1993), 44:17.
[12]Martin Luther, "Lectures on 1 Timothy," in *Luther's Works*, ed. Hilton C. Oswald (St. Louis: Concordia, 1973), 28:278-79.

thought that men subject to the counsel or empire of their wives were unworthy of all public office."[13]

John Bunyan (1628-1688): "This therefore I reckon a great fault in the woman, an usurpation, to undertake so mighty an adversary, when she was not the principal that was concerned therein; nay when *her husband who was more able than she*, was at hand, to whom also the law was given as chief. But for this act, I think it is, that they are now commanded silence, and also commanded to learn of their husbands: 1 Co. xiv. 34, 35. A command that is necessary enough for that *simple* and weak sex: Though they see it was by them that sin came into the world, yet how hardly are some of them to this day dissuaded from *attempting unwarrantably to meddle* with potent enemies, about the *great and weighty* matters that concern eternity. 1 Ti. ii. 11-15."[14]

Johann Albrecht Bengel (1687-1752): "In the preceding verse [1 Tim. 2:13], we are taught why the woman ought not to exercise authority, now [1 Tim. 2:14], why she ought not to teach; *more easily deceived*, she more easily deceives; comp. Eccl. vii. 29 [*sic* 7:28]. Deceiving indicates *less strength in the understanding*; and this is the strong ground on which a woman is not allowed to teach."[15]

John Gill (1697-1771): "Now inasmuch as the serpent did not attack Adam, he being the stronger and *more knowing person*, and *less capable of being managed and seduced*; but made his attempt on Eve, in which he succeeded; and since not Adam, but Eve, was deceived, it appears that the man is the more proper person to bear rule and authority, as in civil and domestic, so in ecclesiastic affairs; and it is right for the woman to learn, and the men to teach."[16]

John Wesley (1703-1791): "The preceding verse [1 Tim. 2:13] showed why a woman should not 'usurp authority over the man.' This verse [1 Tim. 2:14] shows why she ought not 'to teach.' *She is more easily deceived*, and more easily deceives."[17]

Patrick Fairbairn (1805-1874): "As already indicated, the case [1 Tim.

[13]John Knox, "The First Blast of the Trumpet Against the Monstrous Regiment of Women," in *The English Scholar's Library of Old and Modern Works,* ed. Edward Arber (1878; reprint, New York: AMS Press, 1967), 1:11-12. Although not a direct comment on 1 Timothy 2:14, this statement is a preamble to a lengthy discussion of 1 Timothy 2:11-15 (cf. pp. 16-30).

[14]John Bunyan, "An Exposition of Genesis," in *The Works of John Bunyan,* ed. G. Offor (1875; reprint, Grand Rapids, Mich.: Baker, 1977), 2:428-29.

[15]Johann Albrecht Bengel, "On the First Epistle to Timothy," in *Gnomon of the New Testament,* trans. James Bryce, ed. Andrew R. Fausset (1759; reprint, Edinburgh: T & T Clark, 1860), 4:254.

[16]John Gill, "I Timothy," in *Gill's Commentary* (1854; reprint, Grand Rapids, Mich.: Baker, 1980), 6:600.

[17]John Wesley, "1 Timothy," in *Wesley's Notes on the Bible,* ed. G. Roger Schoenhals (Grand Rapids, Mich.: Francis Asbury Press, 1987), p. 555.

2:14] is referred to as a grand though mournful example, at the commencement of the world's history, of the evil sure to arise if in the general management of affairs woman should quit her proper position as the handmaid of man, and man should concede to her the ascendancy. *She wants, by the very constitution of nature, the qualities necessary for such a task - in particular, the equability of temper, the practical shrewdness and discernment, the firm, independent, regulative judgment, which are required to carry the leaders of important interests above first impressions and outside appearances, to resist solicitations, and amid subtle entanglements and fierce conflicts to cleave unswervingly to the right.* Her very excellences in other respects—excellences connected with the finer sensibilities and stronger impulses of her emotional and loving nature—tend in a measure to disqualify her here. *With man, on the other hand, in accordance with his original destination, the balance as between the intellectual and the emotional, the susceptible and the governing powers, inclines as a rule in the opposite direction.*"[18]

Henry P. Liddon (1829-1890): "The point is that Eve's *facility in yielding to the deceiver* warrants the Apostolic rule which forbids a woman to teach. . . . The experience of all ages that *woman is more easily led away than man*, is warranted by what is said of the first representative of the sex."[19]

Bernard Weiss: "From this [2:14] it follows that *the woman is more easily susceptible to seduction than the man, and accordingly needs the leadership of man, not vice versa.* From what is said at this place concerning the first woman, the Apostle proceeds to that which is applicable to the woman in general."[20]

Newport J. D. White: "The point in which Adam's superiority over Eve comes out in the narrative of the Fall is *his greater strength of intellect*; therefore men are better fitted for the work of public instruction."[21]

P. C. Spicq: "*A woman will always be more easy to deceive than a man*, that is why the Apostle does not permit women . . . to teach in the church, especially in Ephesus where the faith was being challenged."[22]

Donald Guthrie: "But Paul is concerned primarily with the inadvisability of

---

[18]Patrick Fairbairn, *Commentary on the Pastoral Epistles* (1874; reprint, Grand Rapids, Mich.: Zondervan, 1956), p. 129.

[19]Henry Liddon, *Explanatory Analysis of St. Paul's First Epistle to Timothy* (1897; reprint, Minneapolis: Klock & Klock, 1978), p. 19.

[20]Bernard Weiss, "1 Timothy," in *A Commentary on the New Testament*, trans. G. H. Schodde and E. Wilson (New York: Funk & Wagnalls, 1906), 4:53.

[21]Newport J. D. White, "The First and Second Epistles to Timothy," in *The Expositor's Greek Testament*, ed. W. Robertson Nicoll (London: Hodder & Stoughton, 1897-1910; reprint, Grand Rapids, Mich.: Eerdmans, 1979), 4:109.

[22]P. C. Spicq, *Les Épitres Pastorales* (Paris: Lecoffre, 1947), p. 71. Translation mine.

women teachers, and he may have in mind *the greater aptitude of the weaker sex to be led astray.*"[23]

J. N. D. Kelly: "His point [Paul's in 1 Tim. 2:14] is that since *Eve was so gullible a victim* of the serpent's wiles, she clearly cannot be trusted to teach. If we are to follow Paul's reasoning, we must recall that like other exegetes, Jewish and Christian, he regards Adam and Eve as historical persons, but also as archetypes of the human race. *Their characters and propensities were transmitted to their descendants,* and in their relationship can be seen foreshadowed the permanent relationship between man and woman."[24]

---

[23]Donald Guthrie, *The Pastoral Epistles* (Grand Rapids, Mich.: Eerdmans, 1957), p. 77.

[24]J. N. D. Kelly, *A Commentary on the Pastoral Epistles* (London: A & C Black, 1963; reprint, Grand Rapids, Mich.: Baker, 1981), p. 68.

Appendix C

RESEARCH ON
DETECTING DECEPTION

Many studies have analyzed the factors that make one person more vulnerable to deception than another. In general, gender is not considered a viable component, whereas other factors (such as cross-cultural clues, age, experience, socialization, intelligence or education) play crucial roles. In studies on children, no detectable difference has been found to give one gender any advantage over the other.[1] While an occasional adult study favors male ability to detect deception,[2] by far the majority of research has found either no significant gender difference or a marginal advantage for adult females.[3]

Even in studies of romance (a factor that lessens one's ability to judge between truth and deceit), women are often more accurate than men in detecting de-

---

[1]Bella M. DePaulo and Audrey Jordan, "Age Changes in Deceiving and Detecting Deceit," in *Development of Nonverbal Behavior in Children*, ed. Robert S. Feldman (New York: Springer-Verlaq, 1982). DePaulo and Jordan state, "As in the two Feldman studies (Feldman et al., 1978; Feldman & White, Note 1), there were no significant sex differences in lie detection success" (p. 156).

[2]One of the few studies which found men to be better at discovering the truth is that by Bella M. DePaulo, J. I. Stone, and G.D. Lassiter, "Deceiving and Detecting Deceit," in *The Self and Social Life*, ed. B. R. Schlenker (New York: McGraw-Hill, 1985). Aware that their findings were out of line with most other studies, the authors posited that cultural factors may have played a role in their sampling.

[3]The following studies found women and men to be generally equal in detection of deceit: Stephen J. Dollinger, Mark J. Reader, Joseph P. Marnett, and Barbara Tylenda, "Psychological-Mindedness, Psychological-Construing, and the Judgment of Deception," *The Journal of General Psychology* 108 (1983): 183-91; Mark Edward Comadena, "Examinations of the Deception Attribution Process of Friends and Intimates" (Ph.D. diss., Purdue University, 1983). Several other studies conclude that women are moderately more accurate than men at deception detection: Dilys James Sakai, "Nonverbal Communication in the Detection of Deception Among Women and Men" (Ph.D. diss., University of California, 1981); Pamela Joy Kalbfleisch, "Accuracy in Deception Detection: A Quantitative Review" (Ph.D. diss., Michigan State University, 1985).

ception in such relationships.[4] On the whole, however, deception studies conclude that gender is not a critical factor. Even if a marginal edge were to be given to one sex over the other, it would not favor patriarchal concerns.

Factors Affecting Deception Detection

While gender may be eliminated as a significant factor, current research indicates that other factors do contribute to one's ability to detect deceit. The degree to which one is gullible or "deceivable" relates primarily to a combination of factors such as cultural/economic boundaries, age, experience, socialization, intelligence, education and personality, as well as individual differences.

Crossing cultural/economic boundaries. An understanding of what constitutes deception varies from culture to culture.[5] Consequently, how one views deception within a particular culture will often affect one's ability to detect deception in that setting. A person's ability to detect deception is particularly weak when crossing unfamiliar cultural boundaries.[6] To raise one example, a study by Beverly Ann McLeod on Chinese and Canadian subjects shows how cultural factors can either skew or enhance one's ability to detect the clues for deception.[7] In a similar manner, variations across economic strata adversely affect a person's ability to detect deception.[8] The art of detecting deception often requires an ability to read social aspects within communication. The more that one shares the socio-economic horizon of the person attempting to deceive, the less successful the deception.

Age. Evidence points to age as a significant factor in the detection of deception. Younger children are much less successful at detecting deception than older ones, and this trend continues until adulthood.[9] One reason that children are less effective lie detectors appears to be an incomplete conception of what deception

---

[4]Steven A. McCornack and Malcolm R. Parks, "What Women Know That Men Don't: Sex Differences in Determining the Truth Behind Deceptive Messages," *Journal of Social and Personal Relationships* 7 (1990): 107-18.

[5]J. A. Barnes, *A Pack of Lies: Towards a Sociology of Lying* (Cambridge: Cambridge University Press, 1994), p. 66. Barnes notes, "Societies vary not only in their recognition of the ubiquity of lying and other modes of deceit but also in the way in which they evaluate different kinds of lies."

[6]Paul Ekman, *Telling Lies: Clues to Deceit in the Marketplace, Politics, and Marriage* (New York: W. W. Norton, 1992), p. 262. Cf. Barnes, *Pack of Lies*, p. 106.

[7]Beverly Ann McLeod, "Cultural Influences in Deceptive Communication" (Ph.D. diss., McMaster University, 1988).

[8]Barnes, *Pack of Lies*, p. 75.

[9]DePaulo and Jordan, "Age Changes in Deceiving and Detecting Deceit," pp. 151-80. Cf. Marie E. Vasek, "Lying as a Skill: The Development of Deception in Children," in *Deception: Perspectives on Human and Nonhuman Deceit*, ed. Robert W. Mitchell and Nicholas S. Thompson (New York: SUNY Press, 1986), p. 286.

is.[10] Other factors related to age include the fact that with age one normally acquires more knowledge, experience, critical evaluation skills, and so on (see below).

Experience. As one would expect, a person becomes better at detecting deception the more they experience deception and become familiar with its forms.[11] An interesting example from the animal kingdom that demonstrates this principle is that dogs catch on to tricks played on them by their masters.[12] Within the human domain, childhood games help children become familiar with deception and practice its detection.[13] The process of experience continues through adolescence and into adulthood. The adage "Never cry 'wolf' " reflects the idea of a person's growing awareness of deception based on experience.

Socialization (sheltered or broad exposure). The ability to detect lies may also be a result of one's socialization or upbringing.[14] A sheltered upbringing reduces one's exposure to a large number (and variety) of people and thus can limit one's experience concerning deception. Thus broad exposure during one's upbringing and adult life would seemingly increase one's ability to detect deception.

Intelligence. A person's intelligence plays an important part of deception detection, since there are a number of verbal and non-verbal factors that require mental processing. Evidence for the effect of intelligence can be seen in the detection abilities of people with lower than normal intelligence. On false belief and deception tasks normal children fair better than individuals with autism, mental retardation and Down syndrome.[15] Likewise, learning-disabled students were less likely than non-disabled students to recognize deceptive statements.[16]

Knowledge and formal education. Knowledge is a significant factor in one's

---

[10]Ted Ruffman, David R. Olson, and Tony Ash, "The ABCs of Deception: Do Young Children Understand Deception in the Same Way As Adults?" *Developmental Psychology* 29 (1993): 74-87.

[11]Barnes, *Pack of Lies*, p. 118. Similarly, DePaulo and Jordan highlight the role of knowledge and experience as related to age ("Age Changes in Deceiving and Detecting Deceit," p. 158).

[12]Robert W. Mitchell and Nicholas S. Thompson, "Deception in Play Between Dogs and People," in *Deception: Perspectives on Human and Nonhuman Deceit*, ed. Robert W. Mitchell and Nicholas S. Thompson (New York: SUNY Press, 1986), p. 198.

[13]Vasek, "Lying as a Skill," p. 286.

[14]As Barnes observes, "Common understandings about when to expect lies . . . constitute part of the culture of the community and are learnt in the normal process of socialization" (*Pack of Lies*, p. 112).

[15]Nurit Yirmiya, Daphna Solomonica-Levi, Cory Shulman, and Tammy Pilowsky, "Theory of Mind Abilities in Individuals with Autism, Down Syndrome, and Mental Retardation of Unknown Etiology: The Role of Age and Intelligence," *Journal of Child Psychology and Psychiatry and Allied Disciplines* 37, no. 8 (1996): 1003-14.

[16]Ruth Pearl, Tanis Bryan, Patrick Fallon, and Allen Herzog, "Learning Disabled Students' Detection of Deception," *Learning Disabilities Research and Practice* 6, no. 1 (1991): 12-16.

ability to detect deception.[17] This is true not only of knowledge gained from experience and socialization but also of knowledge gained in formal education. For instance, if one is to effectively deceive another person, the deceiver must possess knowledge that the other person does not.[18] This gap in knowledge is exploited: the person being deceived is led to believe something that is not true.[19] Obviously, well-educated people are not as open to deceit because their knowledge base is stronger. It would be more difficult to deceive a medical doctor in a healthcare scam than the average person who has no medical training.

This knowledge principle can be applied to almost any area of life. Generally, the better educated a person is, the better they will be able to detect deceit, especially if the education is in the field related to the deceit. With the role of knowledge and education, one would expect (as studies have shown)[20] that it is also possible to train people to become better at detecting deceit.

Personality. The ability to detect deception has some correlation with personality. As a complex interaction between nature and nurture, personality is often hard to isolate as a factor on its own in the deception process. However, a few personality differences have been shown to have an effect on deception detection. First, personalities that are effective role-takers, imagining the role of other people, are more effective at detecting deception.[21] Second, those personality characteristics that enable one to decipher conflicting emotional cues also help in detecting deception. When people lie they often send out conflicting signals, called discrepancies.[22] The ability to detect such discrepancies aids one in the detection of deception. People who have a Machiavellian personality have somewhat less success at detecting discrepancies[23] and thus may have less accuracy in deception detection. On the other hand, those people who are good at understanding other people's feelings are often more skilled at detecting discrepancies[24] and

---

[17]See DePaulo and Jordan, who highlight knowledge levels as a distinguishable factor in deception detection ("Age Changes in Deceiving and Detecting Deceit," p. 158).

[18]Vasek points out that "deception requires the recognition that another does not always have access to the same knowledge as does the self; thus the child who knows that another does not know something has the opportunity to inform, not to inform, or to misinform" ("Lying as a Skill," p. 286).

[19]Vasek, "Lying as a Skill," p. 287.

[20]Mark A. deTurck and Gerald R. Miller, "Training Observers to Detect Deception: Effects of Self-Monitoring and Rehearsal," *Human Communication Research* 16, no. 4 (1990): 603-20. Cf. Sid Hall, "The Generalizability of Learning to Detect Deception in Effective and Ineffective Deceivers" (Ph.D. diss., Auburn University, 1989).

[21]DePaulo and Jordan, "Age Changes in Deceiving and Detecting Deceit," p. 156.

[22]Bella M. DePaulo and Robert Rosenthal, "Ambivalence, Discrepancy, and Deception in Nonverbal Communication," in *Skill in Nonverbal Communication: Individual Differences*, ed. Robert Rosenthal (Cambridge, Mass.: Oelgeschlager, Gunn & Hain, 1979), p. 209.

[23]Ibid., p. 229.

[24]Ibid., p. 231.

as a result are often better detectors of deception.

Conclusion

Research indicates that ability to detect deception is not linked to gender in any significant way. Women are not any less accurate at detecting deception than men. (If anything, women have a slight edge over men.) Rather, the ability to detect deception is the result of a combination of factors such as crosscultural differences, age, experience, socialization (sheltered or broad exposure), intelligence, education and personality.

Several of these factors would have influenced the women of Paul's day. In the ancient world the liability for women in age (due to age differential in marriages), experience, social exposure, knowledge and education would have adversely affected their ability to detect deception. In that setting, these factors would have made women (like children) more easily deceived than men. For those familiar with the dynamics of communication, these findings are not entirely surprising. The less any person shares in another's horizon, the more vulnerable they are to being deceived.

Appendix D

WOMAN CREATED
FROM MAN AND *FOR* MAN
An Assessment of
1 Corinthians 11:8-9

Beyond highlighting man's being created *before* woman (1 Tim 2:13), Paul points out that in the Genesis story woman was created *from* man (1 Cor 11:8) and woman was created *for* man (v. 9). Patriarchalists often appeal to these features in the text as support for their understanding of the Timothy text and its prohibitions.

At the outset, a couple of considerations weaken patriarchal agendas in the use of the "from" and "for" arguments. First, Paul does not use these arguments in 1 Timothy 2:13-14 when discussing why women should not be permitted to teach men. At the very least we need to tread softly in our attempts to produce a synthesis between the two passages.

Second, in 1 Corinthians 11:8-9 the "from" and "for" arguments are *not* related to a prohibition against women teaching men. Rather, they support the proposition that "woman is the glory of man" (1 Cor 11:7). This proposition relates to the question of how much of a woman's beauty/glory should be visible in a worship setting—an issue of modesty. A reading of the text will quickly clarify exactly what Paul attempts to argue:

A man ought not to cover his head, since he is the image and glory of God; *but the woman is the glory of man.* For man did not come from woman, but woman from man; neither was man created for woman, but woman for man. (1 Cor 11:7-9, emphasis added)

Since some advocates of patriarchy argue against positions of authority for women using material from 1 Corinthians 11,[1] and since the broader discussion relates to hierarchical ideas, let us say—for the sake of discussion—that Paul is arguing for male headship (and not just addressing the glory issue). Even if the "from" and "for" arguments support male headship, one still has to establish whether these arguments are culturally or transculturally valid.

Woman Created from Man

For several reasons the "from" argument should be viewed as culturally limited. First, Paul himself recognizes the liabilities of his "from man" argument, inasmuch as he later qualifies the point by appealing to the natural birthing process: "as woman came from man, so also man is born of woman" (1 Cor 11:12). For Paul, man and woman are thus interdependent, not independent. Paul thus lets "man born of woman" considerations moderate his "woman from man" comments.

Second, Paul's tipping the scales toward woman coming from man (regardless of man coming from woman) seems to be built on cultural considerations rather than some universal logic. The text literally reads "through" (not "from"); in other words, man comes *through* woman. While the shift is a subtle one, it is important. The idea of man coming "through" woman appears to reflect the ancient view of women as reproductive gardens, contributing nothing more than a fertile environment to the birthing process. Surely his distinction of woman "from" man and man "through" woman is culture-bound: scientific developments since Paul's day have proven such.[2]

Also, one might ask why a single occurrence of woman coming from man would outweigh the multiple occurrences of man coming through woman. The difference between these two events is essentially order: the formation of Eve takes place *before* subsequent generations of man coming from woman. It happens as a creative first.

Once again, we are faced with creative order as a rationale for setting relational priority. As I have already shown, however, the persuasiveness of this kind of reasoning can hardly be viewed as ongoing and transcultural. More important,

---

[1]See, for example, James B. Hurley, *Man and Woman in Biblical Perspective* (Grand Rapids, Mich.: Zondervan, 1981), pp. 209-14.
[2]See criterion 18.C.1.

Paul's tipping the scales in one direction was likely influenced by the pragmatics of dependency considerations within his own social context (cf. 1 Cor 11:11). If so, the cultural reality of women's greater dependence on men probably affected how he weighed the issue. When the two considerations ("woman from man" and "man through woman") are *applied* within his cultural setting, the former has primary strength.

Third, the little phrase "in the Lord" (along with the rest of 1 Corinthians 11:11) suggests the theoretical potential of gender mutuality within the Christian community: "In the Lord, however, woman is not independent of man, nor is man independent of woman." Verse 11 captures the tension between social equality *in theory*, which belongs to the Christian community, and *the reality* of living in the old creation order. It is not that the old creation order has no significance or relevance for the church; rather, the new creation order "in the Lord" (i.e., in the new humanity) carries implications of mutuality and interdependence between genders. Paul certainly felt the tension of new order realities for women, slaves and Gentiles, although within his time frame he carried out to their fullest extent only the implications for Jew-Gentile relations. In other words, 1 Corinthians 11:11 amounts to a "seed idea," setting up the potential for further movement that would be mostly unrealized in Paul's ministry setting.[3]

Patriarchalists often overlook the tension created by the "in the Lord" mutuality of 1 Corinthians 11:11-12. While suggesting that we need to hear the mutuality of verses 11-12, a patriarchalist such as Blomberg argues "verses 8-9 would be meaningless and unnecessary if verses 11-12 canceled them out."[4] In one sense, Blomberg is correct. Paul still makes his point to the Corinthian audience. But the apostle beckons for *actual* moderation—softening of Corinthian social patterns (or at least attitudes)—based on the *theoretical* mutuality found in Christ. Within his own day Paul merely uses mutuality in Christ (11:11) to take the edge off of patriarchy and then carries on without further discussion. However, this outworking does not require that the impact of his words of mutuality fall on deaf ears for every generation to come. In this letter to Corinth Paul does not take his "in Christ" implications to their fullest logical conclusion; but that does not mean (contra Blomberg) that his words do not ultimately lead there. As with Gentiles in Paul's day, and as with slaves later in church history, the fuller implications of gender equality and mutuality in Christ are only starting to be realized.

---

[3]See criterion 2 on seed ideas.

[4]Craig Blomberg, *1 Corinthians*, NIV Application Commentary (Grand Rapids, Mich.: Zondervan, 1994), p. 216.

Woman Created for Man

Paul follows his "from" point with a "for" statement that also goes back to the original creation setting: "neither was man created for woman, but woman for man" (1 Cor 11:9). Patriarchalists appeal to this rationale in support of the subordination of women. While this "for" argument makes a certain amount of sense, and thus contemporary Christians at times appeal to it, the merits of such an argument are heavily rooted in cultural (not transcultural) assumptions. Several considerations place the comment into the cultural realm.

First, how can Paul say, "man was *not* made for woman"? The marks of creation found in human anatomy tell us that man *was* made for woman in various biological ways: penis-vagina compatibility, egg-sperm unification, x-y chromosomal combinations, and so on.[5] Each of these creative features argues for mutuality and makes it clear that man *was* made for woman in some respects. In addition, the Genesis story suggests that the man-woman completeness was similar to the animal kingdom where mutual counterparts were found. So there is much evidence to suggest that man *was* made for woman. Thus, Paul's point is very selective in scope and should be taken as hyperbole.

Second, the part of the creation story that Paul invokes with his "for" statement is probably creation order (Gen 2:7, 22) and the designation of Eve as helper (v. 18). The word *helper* in Hebrew does not *by itself* imply subordination, for it can be used of superiors and equals as well as subordinates.[6] The word *helper* has no inherent meaning of subordination, which would make Paul's point. Nevertheless, the secondary or subordinate status of the woman seems to be drawn from the creation order: man first, then woman.[7] This contextual factor of order, not the word *helper,* leads Paul to this conclusion. In other words, this also is an issue of primogeniture—who came first in the creative order?

Even if the word *helper* were not found in the text of Genesis, it would make little difference. Paul could still say that woman was made "for man" (i.e., to serve man), since primogeniture dictates who serves whom and who has prominence over whom. The "for man" argument is not somehow a *separate* argument from the creative order in Genesis; rather, it is part and parcel of the creative or-

---

[5]See criterion 17.D for a lengthy discussion of mutuality.

[6]See my earlier discussion under criterion 6.C.3.

[7]Egalitarians often err in not seeing the possibility of *helper* being used within a subordinate framework in the Genesis text. On the other hand, patriarchalists err in assuming that the word *helper* inherently conveys subordination. Consequently, Paul's "for" argument cannot be seen as a separate argument from the creation-order package. It is the creation order that provides the subordination idea, not the word *helper.*

der. And if creative-order logic has cultural-component merit (but is not transculturally persuasive), then the "woman for man" argument should not be taken in a binding sense for today.

Third, Paul's mutuality statement in 1 Corinthians 11:11 qualifies and moderates *both* his "from" and his "for" arguments. In other words, not only are Paul's earlier arguments cultural in nature, his mutuality picture of verse 11 provides a healthy tension pulling in another direction. Not only do his "in the Lord" comments take the abrasive edge off of the patriarchy of Paul's day, but resident within them are seed ideas for future development. The unrealized potential of Paul's "in Christ" perspective has already been seen in the case of Gentiles and slaves (Gal 3:28; cf. 1 Cor 12:13; Eph 2:15; Col 3:11).[8] We live in an exciting era where Paul's seed ideas about women may eventually see their fuller realization in the home, the church and society.

One final observation about 1 Corinthians 11 is worth contemplating. Patriarchalists often suggest that women's practice of wearing head coverings is cultural, but the underlying principle of subordination is transcultural. This formula carries more rhetorical punch than substance. A number of concepts and concerns—some explicit and some implicit—within the text of 1 Corinthians appear to shape Paul's exposition:

☐ clear distinctions between genders

☐ modesty in dress (especially within a worship setting where "glory" is to be directed toward God)

☐ ownership of women by men (to whom does a woman's glory/beauty belong?)

☐ subordination of women to men

☐ head coverings for women but not for men (and hair length for men and women)

Even if one views the subordination of women as a cultural component of the biblical text, 1 Corinthians does not necessarily lose its instructive value. The first two concerns *seem to reflect* transcultural values, whereas the last three *appear to be* cultural expressions of gender distinctions and modesty. So the passage still has application for egalitarians, but only along the lines of modesty for worship and maintaining culturally appropriate gender distinctions. Conclusions about what is and what is not cultural within 1 Corinthians 11, however, must be derived from considerations far beyond the chapter itself.

---

[8]Cf. Rom 10:12-13; 1 Cor 7:17-24. Again, see criterion 2 on seed ideas.

Bibliography

Slavery

Barchy, Scott S. *First-Century Slavery and 1 Corinthians 7:21.* SBL Dissertation Series 11. Missoula, Mont. Scholars Press, 1973.

Barclay, J.M.G. "Paul, Philemon and the Dilemma of Christian Slave Ownership," *New Testament Studies* 37 (1991): 161-86.

Bradley, Keith R. *Slavery and Society at Rome.* Cambridge: Cambridge University Press, 1994.

Bradley, Keith R. *Slaves and Masters in the Roman Empire: A Study in Social Control.* New York: Oxford University Press, 1987.

Chirichigno, Gregory C. *Debt-Slavery in Israel and the Ancient Near East.* JSOT Supplement Series 141. Sheffield, U.K.: Sheffield Academic Press, 1993.

Dandamaev, Muhammad A. *Slavery in Babylonia: From Nabopolassar to Alexander the Great.* De Kalb: Northern Illinois University Press, 1984.

Davis, David Brion. *Slavery and Human Progress.* New York: Oxford University Press, 1984.

Drescher, Seymour, and Stanley L. Engerman, eds. *A Historical Guide to World Slavery.* New York: Oxford University Press, 1998.

Epsztein, Léon. *Social Justice in the Ancient Near East and the People of the Bible.* Translated by John Bowden. London: SCM Press, 1986.

Finley, Moses I. *Ancient Slavery and Modern Ideology.* New York: Viking, 1980.

————, ed. *Classical Slavery.* Cambridge: Frank Cass, 1987.

Fisher, Nicholas Ralph Edmund. *Slavery in Classical Greece.* London: Bristol Classical Press, 1993.

Gagarin, M. "The Torture of Slaves in Athenian Law," *Classical Philology* 91 (1996): 1-18.

Garlan, Yvon. *Slavery in Ancient Greece.* Translated by Janet Lloyd. London: Cornell University Press, 1988.

280

  SLAVES, WOMEN & HOMOSEXUALS

Garnsey, Peter. *Ideas of Slavery from Aristotle to Augustine.* Cambridge: Cambridge University Press, 1996.

Garver, E. "Aristotle's Natural Slaves: Incomplete Praxeis and Incomplete Human Beings," *Journal of the History of Philosophy* 32 (1994): 173-95.

Giles, Kevin. "The Biblical Argument for Slavery: Can the Bible Mislead? A Case Study in Hermeneutics," *Evangelical Quarterly* 66 (1994): 3-17.

Harrill, J. Albert. *The Manumission of Slaves in Early Christianity.* Tübingen: J.C.B. Mohr (Paul Siebeck), 1995.

Haas, Guenther. "The Kingdom and Slavery: A Test Case for Social Ethics," *Calvin Theological Journal* 30 (1993): 108-29.

Hanson, Kenneth C. and Scott S. Bartchy. "Slavery." In *The International Standard Bible Encyclopedia*, ed. G. W. Bromiley, 4:539-46. Rev. ed. Grand Rapids, Mich.: Eerdmans, 1988.

Hunt, Peter. *Slaves, Warfare, and Ideology in the Greek Historians.* Cambridge: Cambridge University Press, 1998.

Lewis, Bernard. *Race and Slavery in the Middle East: An Historical Inquiry.* New York: Oxford University Press, 1990.

Matthews, Victor H. "The Anthropology of Slavery in the Covenant Code." In *Theory and Method in Biblical and Cuneiform Law: Revision, Interpolation and Development*, ed. B. M. Levinson, 119-35. JSOT Supplement Series 181. Sheffield, U.K.: Sheffield Academic Press, 1994.

Martin, Dale B. *Slavery as Salvation. The Metaphor of Slavery in Pauline Christianity.* New Haven, Conn.: Yale University Press, 1990.

Meltzer, Milton. *Slavery: From the Rise of Western Civilization to the Renaissance.* New York: Cowles, 1971.

————. *Slavery: A World History.* New York: DaCapo, 1993.

Mendelsohn, Isaac. *Slavery in the Ancient Near East: A Comparative Study of Slavery in Babylonia, Assyria, Syria, and Palestine from the Middle of the Third Millennium to the End of the First Millennium.* New York: Oxford University Press, 1949.

————. "Slavery in the Old Testament." In *Interpreter's Dictionary of the Bible*, ed. G. A. Buttrick, 4:383-91. New York: Abingdon, 1962.

Osiek, Carolyn. "Slavery in the Second Testament World," *Biblical Theology Bulletin* 22 (1992): 174-79.

Rodrigeuz, Junius P., ed. *The Historical Encyclopedia of World Slavery.* Santa Barbara, Calif.: ABC-CLIO, 1997.

Thompson, David L. "Women, Men, Slaves and the Bible: Hermeneutical Inquiries," *Christian Scholar's Review* 25 (1996): 326-49.

Vogt, Joseph. *Ancient Slavery and the Ideal of Man.* Translated by Thomas

Wiedemann. Oxford: Basil Blackwell, 1974.

Watson, Alan. *Roman Slave Law.* Baltimore: Johns Hopkins University Press, 1987.

Wiedemann, Thomas E. J. "The Regularity of Manumission at Rome," *Classical Quarterly* 35 (1985): 162-75.

————. *Greek and Roman Slavery: A Sourcebook.* Baltimore: Johns Hopkins University Press, 1981.

Women's Issues

Multiple Views

Blomberg, Craig L., and James R. Beck, eds. *Two Views on Women in Ministry.* Grand Rapids, Mich.: Zondervan, 2001.

Clouse, Bonnidell, and Robert G. Clouse, eds. *Women in Ministry: Four Views.* Downers Grove, Ill: InterVarsity Press, 1989.

Mickelsen, Alvera, ed. *Women, Authority & the Bible.* Downers Grove, Ill: Inter-Varsity Press, 1986.

Patriarchal View

Barnett, Paul. "Wives and Women's Ministry. 1 Timothy 2:11-15," *Evangelical Quarterly* 61 (July 1989): 225-37.

Blomberg, Craig. *1 Corinthians.* NIV Application Commentary. Grand Rapids, Mich.: Zondervan, 1994.

————. "Not Beyond What is Written. A Review of Aída Spencer's *Beyond the Curse: Women Called to Ministry*," *Criswell Theological Review* 2 (1988): 403-22.

Bowman, Ann L. "Women in Ministry: An Exegetical Study of 1 Timothy 2:11-15," *Bibliotheca Sacra* 149 (1992): 193-213.

Clark, Stephen B. *Man and Woman in Christ: An Examination of the Roles of Men and Women in Light of Scripture and Social Sciences.* Ann Arbor, Mich.: Servant, 1980.

Council on Biblical Manhood and Womanhood (CBMW). An evangelical organization representing patriarchal views.

Crabb, Lawrence J. *Men and Women: Enjoying the Difference.* Grand Rapids, Mich.: Zondervan, 1991.

Davis, John J. "Some Reflections on Galatians 3:28, Sexual Roles, and Biblical Hermeneutics," *JETS* 19 (1976): 201-8.

Dockery, David. "The Role of Women in Worship and Ministry: Some Hermeneutical Questions," *Criswell Theological Review* 1 (1987): 363-86.

Foh, Susan T. *Women and the Word of God.* Phillipsburg, N.J.: Presbyterian &

Reformed, 1979.

Haas, Guenther. "The Effects of the Fall on Creational Social Structures: A Comparison of Anabaptist and Reformed Perspectives," *Calvin Theological Journal* 30 (1995): 108-29.

————. "The Kingdom and Slavery: A Test Case for Social Ethics," *Calvin Theological Journal* 28 (1993): 74-89.

————. "Patriarchy as an Evil that God Tolerated: Analysis and Implications for the Authority of Scripture," *Journal of the Evangelical Theological Society* 38 (1995): 321-36.

Harper, Michael. *Equal and Different: Male and Female in Church and Family.* London: Hodder & Stoughton, 1994.

Hauke, Manfred. *Women in the Priesthood?* San Francisco: Ignatius, 1988.

House, Wayne H. *The Role of Women in Ministry Today.* Grand Rapids, Mich.: Baker, 1995.

Hurley, James B. *Man and Woman in Biblical Perspective.* Grand Rapids, Mich.: Zondervan, 1981.

Johnson, Eric L. "Playing Games and Living Metaphors. The Incarnation and the End of Gender," *JETS* 40 (1997): 271-85.

Kassian, Mary A. *The Feminist Gospel: The Movement to Unite Feminism with the Church.* Wheaton, Ill.: Crossway, 1992.

————. *Women, Creation, and the Fall.* Wheaton, Ill: Crossway, 1990.

Kent, Homer, Jr. *The Pastoral Epistles.* Chicago: Moody, 1958; rev. ed., Chicago: Moody, 1982.

Knight, George W. III. *The Role Relationship of Men and Women: New Testament Teaching.* Chicago: Moody Press, 1985; reprint, Phillipsburg, N.J.: Presbyterian & Reformed, 1989.

Köstenberger, Andreas J. "Gender Passages in the NT: Hermeneutical Fallacies Critiqued," *Westminster Theological Journal* 56 (1994): 269-94.

Köstenberger, Andreas J., Thomas R. Schreiner and H. Scott Baldwin, eds. *Women in the Church. A Fresh Analysis of 1 Timothy 2:9-15.* Grand Rapids, Mich.: Baker, 1995.

Lundy, Daniel G. "The Changing Role of Women in Fellowship Baptist Churches," *Baptist Review of Theology* 3 (1993): 36-52.

————. "A Hermeneutical Framework for the Role of Women," *Baptist Review of Theology* 2 (1992): 55-76.

————. *The Role of Women in the Bible and Today: A Study Guide for Contemporary Christians.* Toronto: Central Baptist Seminary, 1991.

MacArthur, John A. *Different by Design.* Wheaton, Ill: Victor, 1994.

Mabery-Foster, Lucy. *Women and the Church.* Nashville: Word, 1999.

Moo, Douglas. "1 Timothy 2:11-15. Meaning and Significance," *Trinity Journal* 1 (1980): 62-83.

————. "The Interpretation of 1 Timothy 2:11-15. A Rejoinder," *Trinity Journal* 2 (1981): 198-222.

Neuer, Werner. *Man and Woman in Christian Perspective.* Trans. by Gordon Wenham. Wheaton, Ill: Crossway, 1991.

Piper, John, and Wayne Grudem, eds. *Recovering Biblical Manhood and Womanhood: A Response to Evangelical Feminism.* Wheaton, Ill.: Crossway, 1991.

Pride, Mary. *All the Way Home.* Wheaton, Ill: Crossway, 1989.

————. *The Way Home.* Wheaton, Ill: Crossway, 1985.

Ryrie, Charles C. *The Role of Women in the Church.* Chicago: Moody Press, 1978.

Waltke, Bruce K. "The Role of Women in the Bible," *Crux* 31:3 (1995): 29-40.

————. "1 Timothy 2:8-15. Unique or Normative?" *Crux* 28:1 (1992): 22-27.

Egalitarian View

Bilezikian, Gilbert. *Beyond Sex Roles.* 2d ed. Grand Rapids, Mich.: Baker, 1985.

————. "Hermeneutical Bungee-Jumping: Subordination in the Godhead," *JETS* 40 (1997): 57-68.

Christians for Biblical Equality (CBE). An evangelical organization representing egalitarian views.

Bruce, F. F. "Women in the Church: A Biblical Survey." In *A Mind for What Matters.* Grand Rapids, Mich.: Eerdmans, 1990.

Cervin, Richard S. "A Note Regarding the Name 'Junia(s)' in Romans 16.7," *NTS* 40 (1994): 464-70.

Cotter, Wendy. "Women's Authority Roles in Paul's Churches: Countercultural or Conventional?" *NovT* 36 (1994): 350-72.

Douglass, Jane Dempsey, and James F. Kay, eds. *Women, Gender, and Christian Community.* Louisville: Westminster John Knox, 1997.

Evans, Mary J. *Women in the Bible.* Downers Grove, Ill: InterVarsity Press, 1983.

Fee, Gordon. "The Great Watershed—Intentionality and Particularity/Eternality: 1 Timothy 2:8-15 as a Test Case." In *Gospel and Spirit: Issues in New Testament Hermeneutics*, 52-65. Peabody, Mass.: Hendrickson, 1991.

France, R. T. *Women in the Church's Ministry: A Test Case for Biblical Interpretation.* Grand Rapids, Mich.: Eerdmans, 1997.

Grenz, Stanley J., and Denise Muir Kjesbo. *Women in the Church: A Biblical Theology of Women in Ministry.* Downers Grove, Ill: InterVarsity Press, 1995.

Groothuis, Rebecca Merrill. *Women Caught in the Conflict: The Culture War Between Traditionalism and Feminism.* Grand Rapids, Mich.: Baker, 1994.

————. *Good News for Women: A Biblical Picture of Gender Equality.* Grand Rapids, Mich.: Baker, 1997.

Hayter, Mary. *The New Eve in Christ: The Use and Abuse of the Bible in the Debate about Women in the Church.* Grand Rapids, Mich.: Eerdmans, 1987.

Hollyday, Joyce. *Clothed with the Sun: Biblical Women and Social Justice.* Louisville: Westminster John Knox, 1994.

Hull, G. G. *Equal to Serve.* Tarrytown, N.Y.: Revell, 1991.

Keener, Craig S. *Paul, Women, and Wives: Marriage and Women's Ministry in the Letters of Paul.* Peabody, Mass.: Hendrickson, 1992.

Kroeger, Richard C., and Catherine C. Kroeger. *I Suffer Not a Woman: Rethinking 1 Timothy 2:11-15 in Light of Ancient Evidence.* Grand Rapids, Mich.: Baker, 1992.

Longenecker, Richard N. *New Testament Social Ethics for Today.* Grand Rapids, Mich.: Eerdmans, 1984.

Meer, Haye van der. *Women Priests in the Catholic Church? A Theological Investigation.* ET. Philadelphia: Temple University Press, 1973.

Payne, Philip B. "Libertarian Women in Ephesus: A Response to Douglas J. Moo's Article," *Trinity Journal* 2 (1981): 169-97.

Pierce, Ronald W. "Evangelicals and Gender Roles in the 1990s: 1 Tim. 2:8-15: A Test Case," *Journal of the Evangelical Theological Society* 36 (1993): 343-55.

Powell, C. "A Stalemate of Genders? Some Hermeneutical Reflections," *Themelios* 17 (1992): 15-19.

Scanzoni, Letha D., and Nancy A. Hardesty. *All We're Meant to Be: Biblical Feminism for Today.* 3rd rev. ed. Grand Rapids, Mich.: Eerdmans, 1992.

Schmidt, Alvin J. *Veiled and Silenced: How Culture Shaped Sexist Theology.* Macon, Ga.: Mercer University Press, 1989.

Scholer, D. M. *Selected Articles on Hermeneutics and Women in Ministry in the New Testament.* Chicago: North Park College and Theological Seminary, 1989.

Spencer, Aída B. *Beyond the Curse: Women Called to Ministry.* Reprint. Peabody, Mass.: Hendrickson, 1989.

Stendahl, Krister. *The Bible and the Role of Women: A Case Study in Hermeneutics.* Translated by E. T. Sander. Philadelphia: Fortress, 1966.

Swartley, Willard. M. *Slavery, Sabbath, War & Women: Case Issues in Biblical Interpretation.* Waterloo, Canada: Herald, 1983.

Tucker, Ruth A. *Women in the Maze: Questions and Answers on Biblical Equality.* Downers Grove, Ill: InterVarsity Press, 1992.

Van Leeuwen, Mary Stewart. *Gender and Grace.* Downers Grove, Ill: InterVarsity Press, 1989.

—————, ed. *After Eden: Facing the Challenge of Gender Reconciliation.* Grand Rapids, Mich.: Eerdmans, 1993.

Women in the Ancient Near East and the Greco-Roman World

Archer, Léonie J. *Her Price is Beyond Rubies: The Jewish Woman in Graeco-Roman Palestine.* JSOT Supplement Series 60. Sheffield, U.K.: Sheffield Academic Press, 1990.

Bisle, Rachel. *Women and Jewish Law: An Explanation of Women's Issues in Halakhic Sources.* New York: Schocken, 1984.

Blundell, Sue. *Women in Ancient Greece.* Cambridge, Mass.: Harvard University Press, 1995.

Brooten, Bernadette J. *Women Leaders in the Ancient Synagogue.* Chico, Calif.: Scholars Press, 1982.

Brosius, Maria. *Women in Ancient Persia 559—331 BC.* Oxford: Clarendon, 1996.

Clark, Gillian. *Women in Late Antiquity.* Oxford: Clarendon, 1993.

Driver, G. R., and John C. Miles. *The Assyrian Laws.* Oxford: Clarendon, 1935.

Gruber, Mayer I. *Women in the Biblical World: A Study Guide.* ATLA Bibliography Series 38. Lanham, Md.: Scarecrow, 1995.

Henshaw, Richard A. *Female and Male: The Cultic Personal; The Bible and the Rest of the Ancient Near East.* Princeton Theological Monograph Series 31. Allison Park, Penn.: Pickwick, 1994.

Ilan, Tal. *Jewish Women in Greco-Roman Palestine.* Peabody, Mass.: Hendrickson, 1996.

Just, Roger. *Women in Athenian Law and Life.* New York: Routledge, 1989.

Keddie, Nikki R., and Beth Baron, eds. *Women in Middle Eastern History: Shifting Boundaries in Sex and Gender.* New Haven, Conn.: York University Press, 1991.

Lesko, Barbara S., ed. *Women's Earliest Records from Ancient Egypt and Western Asia.* Brown Judaic Studies 166. Atlanta: Scholars Press, 1989.

Levine, Amy-Jill, ed. *"Women Like This": New Perspectives on Jewish Women in the Greco-Roman World.* Early Judaism and Its Literature 1. Atlanta: Scholars Press, 1991.

Matthews, Victor H., Bernard M. Levinson and Tikva Frymer-Kensky. *Gender and Law in the Hebrew Bible and the Ancient Near East.* JSOT Supplement Series 262. Sheffield, U.K.: Sheffield Academic Press, 1998.

MacDonald, Elizabeth Mary. *The Position of Women as Reflected in Semitic Codes of Law.* UTS Oriental Series 1. Toronto: University of Toronto Press, 1931.

Massey, Michael. *Women in Ancient Greece and Rome*. New York: Cambridge University Press, 1988.

Meyers, Carol L. *Discovering Eve: Ancient Israelite Women in Context*. New York: Oxford University Press, 1988.

Perdue, Leo G., Joseph Blenkinsopp, John J. Collins and Carol Myers. *Families in Ancient Israel*. The Family, Religion, and Culture Series. Louisville: Westminster John Knox, 1997.

Tyldesley, Joyce. *Daughters of Isis: Women in Ancient Egypt*. New York: Viking, 1994.

Wolff, Hans Walter. *Anthropology of the Old Testament*. London: SCM Press, 1974.

Other Related Materials

Bellis, Alice Ogden. *Helpmates, Harlots and Heroes: Women's Stories in the Hebrew Bible*. Louisville: Westminster John Knox, 1994.

Dahms, John V. "The Subordination of the Son," *JETS* 37 (1994): 351-64.

Fletcher, Anthony. "The Protestant Idea of Marriage in Early Modern England." In *Religion, Culture and Society in Early Modern Britain*, eds. Anthony Fletcher and Peter Roberts, 161-81. Cambridge: Cambridge University Press, 1994.

Weems, Renita J. *Battered Love: Marriage, Sex, and Violence in the Hebrew Prophets*. Minneapolis: Fortress, 1995.

Witherington III, Ben. *Women in the Earliest Churches*. Cambridge: Cambridge University Press, 1988.

Homosexual Issues
Multiple Views

Balch, David L., ed. *Homosexuality, Science, and the "Plain Sense" of Scripture*. Grand Rapids, Mich.: Eerdmans, 2000.

Batchelor, Edward, Jr., ed. *Homosexuality and Ethics*. New York: Pilgrim, 1980.

Holben, Larry R. *What Christians Think About Homosexuality: Six Representative Viewpoints*. Richland Hills, Tex.: D & F Scott, 1999.

Siker, Jeffrey S., ed. *Homosexuality in the Church: Both Sides of the Debate*. Louisville: Westminster John Knox, 1994.

No Acceptance: Heterosexuality Only View

DeYoung, James B. "The Meaning of 'Nature' in Romans 1 and Its Implications for Biblical Proscriptions of Homosexual Behavior," *Journal of Evangelical Theological Society* 31 (1988): 429-41.

————. "A Critique of Prohomosexual Interpretations of the Old Testament Apocrypha and Pseudepigrapha," *Bibliotheca Sacra* 147 (1990): 437-54.

————. "Contributions of the Septuagint to Biblical Sanctions against Homosexuality," *Journal of Evangelical Theological Society* 34 (1991): 157-77.

————. *Homosexuality: Contemporary Claims Examined in the Light of the Bible and Classical Jewish, Greek, and Roman Literature and Law.* Grand Rapids, Mich.: Kregel, 2000.

Grenz, Stanley J. *Welcoming But Not Affirming: An Evangelical Response to Homosexuality.* Louisville: Westminster John Knox, 1998.

Hays, Richard B. "Relations Natural and Unnatural. A Response to John Boswell's Exegesis of Romans 1," *Journal of Religious Ethics* 14 (1986): 184-215.

Hurtado, Larry W. "The Bible and Same-Sex Erotic Relations," 32:2 *Crux* (1996): 13-19.

Magnuson, Roger L. *Are Gay Rights Right? Making Sense of the Controversy.* Updated ed. Portland, Ore.: Multnomah Press, 1990.

Malick, David E. "The Condemnation of Homosexuality in 1 Corinthians 6:9," *Bibliotheca Sacra* 150 (1993): 479-92.

————. "The Condemnation of Homosexuality in Romans 1:26-27." *Bibliotheca Sacra* 150 (1993): 327-40.

Schmidt, Thomas E. *Straight and Narrow? Compassion and Clarity in the Homosexuality Debate.* Downers Grove, Ill: InterVarsity Press, 1995.

Soards, Marion L. "The Biblical Understanding of Homosexuality," *Presbyterian Outlook* 175 (1993): 8-15.

————. *Scripture and Homosexuality: Biblical Authority and the Church Today.* Louisville: Westminster John Knox, 1995.

Socarides, Charles W. *Homosexuality: A Freedom Too Far.* Phoenix: Adam Margrave, 1995.

Stott, John R. W. *Homosexual Partnerships: Why Same-Sex Relationships Are not a Christian Option.* Downers Grove, Ill.: InterVarsity Press, 1985.

Taylor, J. Glen. "The Bible and Homosexuality," *Themelios* 21 (1995): 4-9.

Ukleja, P. Michael. "The Bible and Homosexuality, Part 1: Homosexuality in the Old Testament," *Bibliotheca Sacra* 140 (1983): 259-66; "Part 2: Homosexuality in the New Testament," *Bibliotheca Sacra* 140 (1983): 350-58.

Wold, Donald J. *Out of Order: Homosexuality in the Bible and the Ancient Near East.* Grand Rapids, Mich.: Baker, 1998.

Wright, David F. "The New Testament and Homosexuality," *Scottish Journal of Theology* 38 (1985): 118-20.

————. "Homosexuality: The Relevance of the Bible," *Evangelical Quarterly*

61 (1989): 291-300.

Yates, John C. "Towards a Theology of Homosexuality." *Evangelical Quarterly* 66 (1995): 71-87.

Restricted Acceptance: Covenant Homosexuality View

Bailey, Derrick Sherwin. *Homosexuality and the Western Christian Tradition.* London: Longmans, 1955; reprint, Hamden, U.K.: Archon, 1975.

Bird, Phyllis A. "Genesis 1—3 as a Source for a Contemporary Theology of Sexuality," *Ex Auditu* 3 (1987): 31-44.

Boswell, John. *Christianity, Social Tolerance, and Homosexuality.* Chicago: University of Chicago Press, 1980.

Brawley, Robert L., ed. *Biblical Ethics & Homosexuality: Listening to Scripture.* Louisville: Westminster John Knox, 1996.

Cleaver, Richard. *Know My Name: A Gay Liberation Theology.* Louisville: Westminster John Knox, 1995.

Countryman, L. William. *Dirt, Greed, and Sex: Sexual Ethics in the New Testament and Their Implications for Today.* Philadelphia: Fortress, 1988.

Edwards, George R. *Gay/Lesbian Liberation: A Biblical Perspective.* New York: Pilgrim, 1984.

Furnish, Victor P. "Homosexuality." In *The Moral Teaching of Paul: Selected Issues*, 52-83. 2d ed. Nashville: Abingdon, 1985.

Goss, Robert. *Jesus Acted Up: A Gay and Lesbian Manifesto.* New York: Harper, 1993.

Hartman, Keith. *Congregations in Conflict: The Battle Over Homosexuality.* New Brunswick, N.J.: Rutgers University Press, 1996.

Horner, Thomas M. *Jonathan Loved David: Homosexuality in Biblical Times.* Philadelphia: Westminster Press, 1978.

McNeill, John J. *The Church and the Homosexual.* 4th ed. Boston: Beacon, 1993.

Mollenkott, Virginia R. *Sensuous Spirituality: Out of Fundamentalism.* New York: Crossroad, 1992.

Nelson, James B. *Between Two Gardens: Reflections on Sexuality and Religious Experience.* New York: Pilgrim, 1983.

————. *Body Theology.* Louisville: Westminster John Knox, 1992.

————. *Embodiment: An Approach to Sexuality and Christian Theology.* Minneapolis: Augsburg, 1978.

Nissinen, Martti. *Homoeroticism in the Biblical World: A Historical Perspective.* Translated by Kirsi Stjerna. Minneapolis: Fortress, 1998.

Pronk, Pim. *Against Nature: Types of Moral Argumentation Regarding Homosexuality.* Translated by John Vriend. Grand Rapids, Mich.: Eerdmans, 1993.

Scanzoni, Letha D., and Virginia R. Mollenkott, *Is the Homosexual My Neighbor? A Positive Christian Response*. Rev. ed. San Francisco: HarperCollins, 1994.

Scroggs, Robin. *The New Testament and Homosexuality: Contextual Background for Contemporary Debate*. Philadelphia: Fortress, 1984.

Seow, Choon-Leong, ed. *Homosexuality and Christian Community*. Louisville: Westminster John Knox, 1996.

Thurston, Thomas. *Homosexuality and Roman Catholic Ethics*. San Francisco: International Scholars Publication, 1996.

Wink, Walter, ed. *Homosexuality and Christian Faith: Questions of Conscience for the Churches*. Minneapolis: Fortress, 1999.

Homosexuality in the Ancient Near East and the Greco-Roman World

DeYoung, James B. *Homosexuality: Contemporary Claims Examined in the Light of the Bible and Classical Jewish, Greek, and Roman Literature and Law*. Grand Rapids, Mich.: Kregel, 2000.

Dover, Kenneth James. *Greek Homosexuality*. Updated ed. Cambridge, Mass.: Harvard University Press, 1989.

Dynes, Wayne R., and Stephen Donaldson, eds. *Homosexuality in the Ancient World*. Studies in Homosexuality 1. New York: Garland, 1992.

Gordon, Cyrus H., and Gary A Rendsburg. *The Bible and the Ancient Near East*. 4th ed. New York: W. W. Norton, 1997.

Malherbe, Abraham J. *Moral Exhortation: A Greco-Roman Sourcebook*. Philadelphia: Westminster Press, 1986.

Martti, Nissinen. *Homoeroticism in the Biblical World: A Historical Perspective*. Philadelphia: Fortress, 1998.

Meeks, Wayne A. *The Moral World of the First Century Christians*. Philadelphia: Westminster Press, 1986.

Verstraete, Beert C. *Homosexuality in Ancient Greek and Roman Civilization: A Critical Bibliography with Supplement*. Toronto: Canadian Gay Archives, 1982.

Wold, Donald J. *Out of Order: Homosexuality in the Bible and the Ancient Near East*. Grand Rapids, Mich.: Baker, 1998.

Other Related Materials

Abelove, Henry, Michèl Aina Barale and David Halperin, eds. *The Lesbian and Gay Studies Reader*. New York: Routledge, 1993.

Bell, Alan P., Martin S. Weinberg and Sue Kiefer Hammersmith. *Sexual Preference: Its Development in Men and Women*. Bloomington: Indiana University

Press, 1981.

Brooten, Bernadette J. *Love Between Women: Early Christian Responses to Female Homoeroticism*. Chicago: University of Chicago Press, 1997.

Cahill, L. S. *Between the Sexes: Foundations for a Christian Ethics of Sexuality*. Philadelphia: Fortress, 1985.

Greenberg, David F. *The Construction of Homosexuality*. Chicago: University of Chicago Press, 1989.

Hanigan, J. P. *Homosexuality: The Test Case for Christian Sexual Ethics*. New York: Paulist, 1988.

Kunin, Seth Daniel. *The Logic of Incest. A Structuralist Analysis of Hebrew Mythology*. JSOT Supplement Series 185. Sheffield, U.K.: Sheffield Academic Press, 1995.

Marcus, Eric. *Is It a Choice?* San Francisco: Harper, 1993.

Nelson, James B. "Homosexuality and the Church: A Bibliographical Essay," *Prism* 6 (1991): 74-83.

Paul, William, James D. Weinrich, John Gonsiorek and Mary E. Hotvedt. *Homosexuality: Social, Psychological, and Biological Issues*. Beverly Hills, Calif.: Sage, 1982.

Ridinger, Robert B., ed. *Homosexual and Society: An Annotated Bibliography*. New York: Greenwood, 1990.

Hermeneutics and Culture

Conzelmann, H., and A. Lindemann. *Interpreting the New Testament: An Introduction to the Principles and Methods of N.T. Exegesis*. Translated by S. S. Schatzmann. Peabody, Mass.: Hendrickson, 1988.

Carson, D. A., and John D. Woodbridge, eds. *Hermeneutics, Authority, and Canon*. Grand Rapids, Mich.: Zondervan, 1986.

————, eds. *Scripture and Truth*. Grand Rapids, Mich.: Zondervan, 1983.

Childs, Brevard S. "Interpreting the Bible Amid Cultural Change," *Theology Today* 54 (1997): 200-211.

————. *Old Testament Theology in a Canonical Context*. Philadelphia: Fortress, 1986.

————. *The New Testament as Canon: An Introduction*. Valley Forge, Penn.: Trinity Press, 1994.

Fee, G., and D. Stuart. *How to Read the Bible for All Its Worth*. 2d. ed. Grand Rapids, Mich.: Zondervan, 1993.

Ferguson, Duncan S. *Biblical Hermeneutics: An Introduction*. Atlanta: John Knox Press, 1986.

Hayes, John, and Carl Holiday. *Biblical Exegesis: A Beginner's Handbook*. Rev.

ed. Atlanta: John Knox Press, 1987.

Hays, Richard B. *The Moral Vision of the New Testament: Community, Cross, New Creation: A Contemporary Introduction to New Testament Ethics.* San Francisco: HarperCollins, 1996.

Hays, Richard B. *New Testament Ethics: The Story Retold.* Winnipeg: CMBC Publications, 1998.

Hayter, Mary. *The New Eve in Christ: The Use and Abuse of the Bible in the Debate about Women in the Church.* Grand Rapids, Mich.: Eerdmans, 1987.

Hesselgrave, David J. *Communicating Christ Cross-Culturally: An Introduction to Missionary Communication.* 2d ed. Grand Rapids, Mich.: Zondervan, 1991.

Hugenberger, Gordon P. "Women in Church Office: Hermeneutics or Exegesis? A Survey of Approaches to 1 Tim. 2:8-15," *Journal of the Evangelical Theological Society* 35 (1992): 341-60.

Johnson, Elliott E. *Expository Hermeneutics: An Introduction.* Grand Rapids, Mich.: Academie, 1990.

Kaiser, Walter C. Jr. *Toward an Exegetical Theology: Biblical Exegesis for Preaching and Teaching.* Grand Rapids, Mich.: Baker, 1981.

Kaiser, Walter C., Jr., and Moisés Silva. *An Introduction to Biblical Hermeneutics: The Search for Meaning.* Grand Rapids, Mich.: Zondervan, 1994.

Keegan, Terrance J. *Interpreting the Bible: A Popular Introduction to Biblical Hermeneutics.* New York: Paulist, 1986.

Klein, William W., Craig L Blomberg and Robert L. Hubbard Jr. *Introduction to Biblical Interpretation.* Vancouver: Word, 1993.

Kuhn, Thomas S. *The Structure of Scientific Revolutions.* 3rd ed. Chicago: University of Chicago Press, 1996.

Larkin, William J., Jr. *Culture and Biblical Hermeneutics.* Grand Rapids, Mich.: Baker, 1988.

Longenecker, Richard N. *New Testament Social Ethics for Today.* Grand Rapids, Mich.: Eerdmans, 1984.

Mayers, Marvin K. *Christianity Confronts Culture: A Strategy For Crosscultural Evangelism.* Grand Rapids, Mich.: Zondervan, 1987.

McCartney, Dan, and Charles Clayton. *Let the Reader Understand: A Guide to Interpreting and Applying the Bible.* Wheaton, Ill: Victor, 1994.

McKim, Donald K. *A Guide to Contemporary Hermeneutics.* Grand Rapids, Mich.: Eerdmans, 1986.

McQuilkin, Robertson, and Bradford Mullen. "The Impact of Postmodern Thinking on Evangelical Hermeneutics," *JETS* 40 (1997): 69-82.

Osborne, Grant R. "Hermeneutics and Women in the Church," *JETS* 20 (1977): 337-82.

Radmacher, E. D., and R. D. Preus. *Hermeneutics, Inerrancy, and the Bible.* Grand Rapids, Mich.: Zondervan, 1994.

Sanders, James A. *Canon and Community: A Guide to Canonical Criticism.* Philadelphia: Fortress, 1984.

——————. *From Sacred Story to Sacred Text: Canon as Paradigm.* Philadelphia: Fortress, 1987.

Scholer, D. M. "Unseasonable Thoughts on the State of Biblical Hermeneutics: Reflections of a New Testament Exegete," *American Baptist Quarterly* 2 (1983): 134-41.

Stein, Robert H. *Playing by the Rules: A Basic Guide to Interpreting the Bible.* Grand Rapids, Mich.: Baker, 1994.

Stott, John R. W., and Robert Coote, eds., *Down to Earth: Studies in Christianity and Culture.* Grand Rapids, Mich.: Eerdmans, 1980.

Stuart, D. *Old Testament Exegesis: A Primer for Students and Pastors.* 2d ed. Philadelphia: Westminster Press, 1984.

Scripture Index